Perl

DEVELOPER'S DICTIONARY

 201 West 103rd Street, Indianapolis, Indiana 46290

Perl Developer's Dictionary

International Standard Book Number: 0-672-32067-3

Library of Congress Catalog Card Number: 00-109554

Printed in the United States of America

First Printing: July 2001

04   03   02   01   4   3   2   1

Trademarks

Warning and Disclaimer

Acquisitions Editor
Shelley Markanday Johnston

Development Editor
Scott Meyers

Managing Editor
Charlotte Clapp

Project Editor
Carol Bowers

Copy Editor
Rhonda Tinch-Mize

Indexer
Johnna VanHoose Dinse

Proofreader
Plan-It Publishing

Technical Editor
Greg Bacon

Team Coordinator
Amy Patton

Interior Designer
Gary Adair

Cover Designer
Alan Clements

Page Layout
Ayanna Lacey

Contents at a Glance

Table of Contents

7   Standard Module Library   537

About the Author

Clinton Pierce is a software engineer, freelance programmer, and instructor. He has programmed almost every kind of software imaginable: financial applications, games, embedded systems, device drivers, OS utilities, and all this under a dozen or so operating systems. He spends his free time preaching the gospels of Unix, Perl, and open-source software to anyone within earshot.

He's currently serving time as a Web architect for Decision Consultants in southeast Michigan. You can visit his Web site at `http://geeksalad.org` or write to him at `clintp@geeksalad.org`.

Dedication

To Heidi, for your patience and understanding. Next time, I promise, a shorter book.

Acknowledgments

Like many Perl books, I'd like to start by thanking Larry Wall for creating such a wonderfully expressive language. In the same breath, I'd like to mildly chastise him for creating a beast so difficult to saddle and tame.

Individually, many people helped out in small ways. Some notables were Greg Bacon, Kevin Meltzer, Abigail, Jarkko Hietaniemi, and Elaine Ashton. Some walk-ons from the far-reaches of the net were Michael Villeneuve, Christian Schneider, Brad Bailey, Andreas Riechert, and Peter Barlow.

Many helpful souls simply provided an honest opinion, moral support, ego stroking, and motivation: Jen, Chris, Bill Crawford, Bill Hiotaky, John, and Gary. Thanks, everyone.

Again, Perl has proved itself a valuable resource as a sounding board and a harsh critic for foolish notions.

From Sams: Shelley Johnston Markanday, Scott Meyers, Patricia Barnes, Rhonda Tinch-Mize, and other behind-the-scenes people were all responsible for helping me put this together without more headaches than necessary.

Tell Us What You Think!

As the reader of this book, *you* are our most important critic and commentator. We value your opinion and want to know what we're doing right, what we could do better, what areas you'd like to see us publish in, and any other words of wisdom you're willing to pass our way.

You can e-mail or write me directly to let me know what you did or didn't like about this book—as well as what we can do to make our books stronger.

Please note that I cannot help you with technical problems related to the topic of this book, and that due to the high volume of mail I receive, I might not be able to reply to every message.

When you write, please be sure to include this book's title and author as well as your name and phone or fax number. I will carefully review your comments and share them with the author and editors who worked on the book.

Email: webdev@samspublishing.com

Mail: Mark Taber
            Associate Publisher
            Sams Publishing
            201 West 103rd Street
            Indianapolis, IN 46290 USA

INTRODUCTION

The world of computer books divides itself into two camps: tutorials and references. Any book that claims to be both should be viewed with suspicion. This book is unashamedly a reference. If you want to learn Perl, I suggest that you pick up a copy of *Teach Yourself Perl in 24 Hours*—when you've got the basics of Perl down, come back to this book.

This isn't to say that you won't learn anything here. There are bits-and-pieces of tutorials throughout this book. If the entire Perl set of jargon and culture were dropped on you at once, without explanation, you'd drown or miss the point entirely.

But again, this book is a reference. It covers the entire Perl language, even some of those parts officially labeled as "experimental" or "incomplete." It's all in here.

What makes this book unique are the examples. *Everything* is demonstrated in here. Reference books without adequate examples are frustrating. Go ahead and flip through this one. There are over 1,000 pieces of code, some large and some small, demonstrating enough Perl so that you're never left stranded. Every example has been tested to verify that it compiles, and it should all work as advertised.

CHAPTER 1
Basic Perl

Getting Started

If you're reading this book, you should already have a passing familiarity with Perl. However, so that everyone starts on equal footing, here is some background.

A Brief History of Perl

Perl is a text processing language invented in 1987 by Larry Wall. It began as a general-purpose text-processing language, designed to fill a niche in text-processing languages in Unix. When it was announced, Larry's own description of Perl read as follows:

> Perl is a interpreted language optimized for scanning arbitrary text files, extracting information from those text files, and printing reports based on that information. It's also a good language for many system management tasks. The language is intended to be practical (easy to use, efficient, complete) rather than beautiful (tiny, elegant, minimal). It combines (in the author's opinion, anyway) some of the best features of C, sed, awk, and sh, so people familiar with those languages should have little difficulty with it. (Language historians will also note some vestiges of csh, Pascal, and even BASIC|PLUS.) Expression syntax corresponds quite closely to C expression syntax. If you have a problem that

would ordinarily use sed or awk or sh, but it exceeds their capabilities or must run a little faster, and you don't want to write the silly thing in C, then Perl may be for you. There are also translators to turn your sed and awk scripts into perl scripts. OK, enough hype.

This sums up the reasons for its creation rather nicely. Subsequent versions of Perl were then released:

- Perl version 1, December 1987

- Perl version 2, June 1988

- Perl version 3, October 1989

- Perl version 4, March 1991

- Perl version 4.036 was released in 1993 and became the most pervasive version of Perl released. Vendors released this version as standard on their operating systems, and Perl's popularity exploded.

- Version 5 of Perl was released in October 1994. It was a complete re-write of the interpreter and introduced object-oriented syntax, modules, lexical variables and embedded documentation (POD).

This book describes version 5.6 of Perl, released in March 2000. The features described within all apply to this version of Perl. Most features are compatible with later releases of Perl 5 (5.005, 5.004, 5.002), but certainly not Perl 4. For the foreseeable future (up to 5.8), the features described herein should continue to work.

For more information on the history of Perl, see `http://history.perl.org`.

The Perl Documentation

No book can honestly make the claim to be a complete reference for Perl. Some reasons for this are as follows:

- The language is constantly changing. Patches and new versions of the interpreter redefine the language regularly.

- The language implementation has bugs. Documented features might not work properly.

- Sometimes features are accidentally created, and noted long after the fact.

- The installation of Perl is customized per platform during installation.

- Some of Perl's behavior relies on underlying operating system characteristics (C Library, Standard I/O library, system calls) that are undefined, but Perl interacts with them anyway.

So there are times when the online documentation will have to be consulted. During installation, at least one version, or perhaps several versions, of the documentation was placed on your system.

The nearly universal method for reading manual pages is to use the `perldoc` program. The `perldoc` program is installed with almost every Perl installation and usually placed in your path. To access the "perlsyn" manual page, from your system's command-line prompt, type the following:

perldoc perlsyn

To access another manual page, say "perlfunc", use the following command:

perldoc perlfunc

The `perldoc` program also can be used to search the Perl FAQ's (also installed with the Perl interpreter) or to look up particular functions in the function reference. To access further instructions on using `perldoc`, see the `perldoc` manual page.

Under Unix, standard `man` pages are installed. Use the `man` command along with the particular section you're interested in seeing, as follows:

man perlpod

Under other operating systems, other kinds of manual pages can be installed. Under MacOS, the `Shuck` utility installed with Perl allows you to search and read the manual pages. Many systems install the manual as HTML somewhere, so look around.

Throughout the book, you will be pointed to extra documentation for many of the entries. There might be other entries within this book, The Perl Docs, man pages, and C API documentation for your particular OS.

External documentation will be referred to in one other format: books. Some topics are simply too deep to cover in a single book. Network programming, the Unix API, algorithms, CGI programming, and regular expressions are topics that deserve entire books (even multiple volumes of books) of their own. Bibliographic information is provided as needed for those subjects.

Maintenance of Perl

There is no specification for the Perl language. Unlike C, Java, or FORTRAN, no external entity has sway over what the Perl language does. The Perl interpreter acts as a reference implementation and a specification in itself. There is only one Perl interpreter. Pre-built Perl versions from ActiveState Tool Corp (for Windows/DOS), MacPerl, and versions from a Unix vendor are all built from the same source code—they're simply pre-compiled and nicely packaged for your convenience.

The source code for the Perl interpreter is Open Source. This means that anyone who desires can examine the source, borrow from it, change it, improve it, or simply read it to learn about Perl. It is licensed under one of two licenses (your choice): the GNU General Public License and the Artistic License. These both allow great freedoms in what can be done with the Perl source. A copy of both licenses is distributed with the Perl source code.

The design and planning of the Perl language comes from two sources. Primarily, it's Larry's language. When he makes a decision about the language, it goes in that direction. He acts as a clearinghouse for ideas and holds veto power over any changes in the language itself. The title normally assigned to Larry is "Language Designer."

The blood-and-guts work for Perl 5 is done by the Perl 5 Porters (p5p) mailing list. The organization is loose, but well-defined. Each release of Perl is assigned a "pumpking." This person controls all changes to the actual source code of the language itself. The pumpking for 5.6 was Gurusamy Sarathy, and the pumpking for 5.8 is Jarkko Hietaniemi.

The rest of the list contributes suggestions, discussions, and occasionally patches to the Perl source code to change and improve the language. In general, good features and patches are included and bad ones are discarded. This is an open mailing list, and those with a strong drive, a lot of patience, and a good grasp of C programming are welcome to contribute patches. Before subscribing (and contributing), you should read the P5P FAQ, which can be obtained by sending a message to `perl5-porters-faq@perl.org`, or through the Web.

Starting with Perl 5.6, the version numbering scheme for Perl changed. The versions for the perl interpreter break down as

```
language version.interpreter version.patchlevel
```

The current version of the language is 5, and the version of the interpreter is now 6. The patchlevel used for writing the examples in this book was 0: Perl Version 5.6.0.

Even-numbered interpreter versions (5.6, 5.8) are production-quality releases. They are intended for consumption by the general public. The odd-numbered versions of the interpreter (5.7) are for testing, patching, and maintenance. These might be highly unstable, and are wholly unsuitable for production use.

The Good, the Bad, and the Ugly

Because of its Unix background, Perl took on many attributes of its surroundings:

- It works well with other tools.

- It binds things together nicely.

- It's a very rapid development environment.

- It can be very forgiving.

- It bundles up the best aspects of Unix into one portable, cross-platform toolkit. Having Perl on an NT system gives your Unix administrators the warm fuzzies, and having it under Unix gives your NT Administrators one familiar landmark.

From Unix, Perl also picked up other attributes that aren't so appealing. It has a steep learning curve. The basics of Perl can be picked up very quickly. It's possible to start writing useful Perl programs quickly, but mastering Perl can take a very long time.

It's a big language, with an enormous toolset. It is very easy to get lost and choose the wrong tools for the job. (Fortunately, they'll probably work despite the poor choice— remember: Perl is forgiving.) Consider that nearly the entire C language can be described in 250 pages of tutorial and reference (K&R second edition), and this reference book alone is 1000 pages.

One of Perl's catchphrases is *TMTOWDI*, which is short for *There's More Than One Way to Do It*. Choosing the wrong tool for the job is okay when you're still learning, but eventually learning good idiomatic Perl programming is essential. Most of the examples in this book use well-known idioms and are very typical Perl programs. There are exceptions, and these are always noted (that is, "this is better done like X") when something is being done for clarity.

Because bits of Perl were picked up from other languages, it can be very eclectic. Other parts of Perl were added as afterthoughts, or re-designed mid-stream. There are many strange corners in Perl that meet at weird angles.

Despite these shortcomings, Perl is an enormously popular language for all kinds of development environments. Currently, Perl is one of the en vogue languages for Web development. With excellent text handling, good module support for CGI programming, an enormous base of developers familiar with Perl, and integrated support into Apache (mod_perl), Perl is well-suited for Web development.

The Web is not Perl's only application, just its most visible. Perl is used by system administrators for every conceivable platform as a glue language: importing data from one tool and exporting to another. It has been used as a general-purpose programming language for projects such as movie CGI (Computer Graphics Imaging), the Human Genome Project, NYSE support, the U.S. Census, and many others. It is included with every copy of the MS Windows Resource Kit and Linux. It's in your back offices, bundled in your vendor's software, and under your client's Web site. In short, it's everywhere.

How Perl Works

Perl programs are written as text files. These are called *scripts* or *programs*; the term you use is up to you. The text files are in the format that your system normally interprets as text (normally, plain 8-bit ASCII).

Perl programs can be contained in a single file or in multiple files. If multiple files are used, one file is considered the *main* portion of your program, and the additional files are called *libraries* or *modules*.

To run a Perl program, the interpreter must be started and presented with the Perl program. The interpreter is generally called perl, and the language itself is Perl (note the case difference). The language is never called PERL or PEARL.

Instructions on running a Perl script are contained in the section "Running Perl from the Command Line." If your OS allows, Perl scripts also can be run as though they were shell scripts (Unix) or batch files (Windows NT). Instructions for running Perl in this manner are contained in the entry on #!.

When the interpreter is running, and it has found your program, a two-step process begins: Compilation and Execution.

In the first compilation step, the entire program is scanned, the tokens are recognized, and the script is turned into an opcode tree. This tree contains the low-level (Perl API) instructions that will be executed by the interpreter.

A second pass is made over the opcode tree to determine whether any optimizations can be made. Opcodes that rely on context are appropriately marked, and opcodes that cannot be reached (void context with no side effects, constants in void context, and so on) are marked for removal.

A third pass is made over the opcode tree. This pass removes unreachable opcodes (marked in the prior pass), notices invalid constructs, and generates warnings, resolving pseudohash references and other optimizations.

After this step, there is sometimes a fourth step in which a code generator is called. These are discussed in the modules section under B::CC, B::C, and B::Bytecode.

Finally, the opcode tree (also called a parse tree) is passed to the interpreter for execution. The opcode tree also can be dumped at this point by the B::Bytecode generator and handed to any Perl interpreter for execution—it's fairly platform independent and certainly not machine dependent. See B::Bytecode for details.

The interpreter acts as a complete virtual machine for the opcode tree—the operating system and the guts of how perl works is abstracted away completely. Behind this is a Perl API that the interpreter then uses to execute the opcode tree. Each Perl process can have multiple interpreters running at once: either as cloned interpreters (ITHREADS, fork() under Win32), or you can have a single interpreter managing multiple parse trees with shared global data (see the Threads entries).

The Perl API also can be programmed directly, without actually writing Perl code or invoking the interpreter. The details of this are far too extensive to cover here. The online manual pages `perlguts`, `perlhack`, and `perlapi` are relevant.

The Look of Perl

As a programming language, Perl can be very elegant, concise, and descriptive; it also can be unreadable, obfuscated, and resemble gibberish. Which opinion you get depends on who you ask, and everyone seems to have an opinion.

Some of the basic rules are

- Statements end at semicolons or at the end of a block. A statement can be one line, or hundreds of lines.

- Statements and expressions can be broken up on separate lines wherever it seems natural (that is, not in the middle of a keyword or quoted string).

- Whitespace (spaces, tabs, newlines) usually isn't significant except in quoted strings or where it's needed to separate two tokens in which there's no clear end to one and beginning to another.

Beyond this, there aren't many other syntax rules.

The look of Perl programs generally reflects the programmer's style. For example, it's entirely possibly to write a Perl program that resembles BASIC-V:

```
L05: REM Yes Virginia, you can program BASIC in Perl too if 0;
L10: print "Hello, ";
L20: goto L10;
```

A Perl program can be written that looks very C-like:

```
for($i=0; $i < length $t; $i++) {
    if (substr($t, $i, length $c) eq $c) {
        return($i);
    }
}
```

Or to write runnable perl program that doesn't look much like a program at all (trust me, it does work):

```
                   '% * % % * % %<>
             * % ~ * % % * % * * % *        *
        * % % * *   % * % *<> * % ~   % % % * %
         * % * % % % % * % % % % % % * % % * %
      % * % % ^ * * % % % % *[] % % * * % * * % %  %
       % * %   % % % % % * * % * * @ *   @ % * % %
     % ^ % * % * % * * % % * %  <> % % % % * % %() %
    % % * * * % % * % % * * % * * * * % * * % % * * *
     %   * * * % % * % % *[]<> % % % % * % * * % % *<>
   % * * % % % * * % * * * \ * %\ * * *   %/ \ # % * *
   % % % *\ * /\ * *// %  %\ <> // % %/ % \// % * %
    * *\ \|| \ \/ / % %// \ \ *\ /<> %// %// % %<>
   * % * %\  \  |   | ||// % || // \// % // * * * %
  %{} % * ----\  \ | /   %||//  /   ---/ / * % % *
   % * *\ ____\  \| |   / / /   /----/ * %
         \ ----\    |  / //   /
            \    \ /      /'
           =~m/(.*)/s;$_=$1;
           s![-\\|_/\s]!!g
            ;%e=('%',0,
            '^',132918,
            '~'=>18054,
            '@'=>19630,
            '*' =>0b01,
            '#'=>13099,
            '[]'=>4278,
            '<>'=>2307,
            '{}'=>9814,
            '()',2076);
            for $a(keys
            %e){$e{$a}=
            sprintf"%b"
            , $e{$a};}
           $y= qq{(}.join(
            '|',map "\Q$_\E"
          ,keys %e).qq{)}};s/$y
        /$e{$1}/gex;print pack"B*",$_;
```

To keep your development environment a sane and happy place, some guidelines have been developed over the years. Some of them are Larry's personal taste; some to which Perl lends itself very well. They are all summarized in the `perlstyle` manual page. Most of them are mundane suggestions to make code readable. Most of them have been followed in this book. Some style rules worth noting are

- Just because you can do something, doesn't mean that you should. If all your programs resemble globes or trees or were written in Haiku, your code maintainers will be miserable.

- Use parentheses (or braces) when necessary to clear up precedence questions. Also use them wherever they make things clearer.

- Perl is a portable language, runnable on many operating systems. Avoid doing OS-dependent things (such as calling the external `ls` program) when there are perfectly good built-ins to accomplish the same thing (`readdir`).

- Variables names should be lowercase, with _ separating words. "BiCapitalization" is hard to read. Function names should be lowercase or mixed case (never all caps). Constants and filehandles should be in all caps. Module and package names should begin with an uppercase letter, and use "BiCapitalization" ("StudlyCaps") to separate words.

- Use the strict and warnings pragmata whenever possible.

- Be consistent!

Perl Culture and Resources

Perl is more than a set of programs for running programs. An entire culture of people, events, and publications are intended to make programming in Perl a little easier.

The online resources for Perl are extensive. There's no official Perl Web site, but you can visit some useful locations for information:

- `http://www.perl.org`—Home of the Perl Mongers (discussed later)

- `http://use.perl.org`—Clearinghouse for the latest news, features, and events related to Perl. Module updates are posted here, as well as references to Perl in other publications.

- `http://cpan.perl.org`, `http://mirror.cpan.org`, `http://search.cpan.org`— Starting points for the *CPAN (Comprehensive Perl Archive Network)*.

If you have questions about Perl or your perl programs, there are online communities where help is available. Of course, before consulting these groups, you should make a first effort at deciphering the relevant documentation.

The oldest of these is the Usenet newsgroup comp.lang.perl.misc created in 1995 (successor to comp.lang.perl). This is a high-traffic newsgroup with lots of questions being asked, and lots of answers dished out. Some of the answers come from professional programmers, instructors, and writers in the Perl Community and some are contributed by complete unknowns (`http://groups.google.com`).

A moderated and low-traffic Usenet newsgroup for the discussion of Perl is comp.lang.perl.moderated.

A newer group for asking questions is the Perl Monks. This is a moderated discussion board on the Web designed around asking code-specific questions and getting answers. The volume is less than comp.lang.perl.misc, but so is the background noise associated with Usenet (`http://www.perlmonks.org`).

A collection of mailing lists about Perl can be found at `http://lists.cpan.org`, and useful Perl Web sites have been bookmarked at `http://bookmark.cpan.org`.

Another resource for programming information is the Comprehensive Perl Archive Network. CPAN is a collection of scripts, modules, source code, and documentation relating to Perl. Many CPAN modules have been demonstrated in the examples in this book, performing everything from Napster access to XML Parsing. If a task needs to be done, and it's likely that someone has done it before, there might already be a solution for you on CPAN. Don't re-invent the wheel (`http://search.cpan.org`). See also the section on the CPAN module in this book.

The primary user group for Perl is the Perl Mongers. The Perl Mongers is a not-for-profit group dedicated to Perl advocacy. It is a chartered organization, holding regional events and meetings across the country with tutorials, guest speakers, and non-specific fellowship (`http://www.pm.org`).

Two major conferences dominate the Perl scene. The first is the Open Source Conference, hosted annually by O'Reilly and Associates in California. This is a typical technology conference with keynote addresses, tutorials, invited talks, Birds Of A Feather sessions, and vendors. The original focus of the conference was solely Perl (it was called The Perl Conference years ago), but it has since expanded to include Python, Apache, and other Open Source products (`http://conferences.oreilly.com`).

The second major conference is the Yet Another Perl Conference (YAPC), hosted by the Yet Another Society (YAS). It is held both in Europe (YAPC::Europe) and on the east cost of North America (YAPC::NA). This conference is a low-cost alternative to the Open Source conference and originated in the Perl Mongers groups. The tutorials, talks and venues have a less polished appearance, but are no less informative (`http://yetanother.org`).

One publication of note is the Perl Journal. The Perl Journal bills itself as a technical resource for the Perl Community and it's just that. Published quarterly, it's filled with articles by Perl experts on every subject imaginable. It's very low on fluff, not crammed with advertising and a good read (`http://www.tpj.com`).

See Also
`perl` in the Perl documentation
`perldoc perl`

Running Perl

`perl`

Usage

`perl [switch(es)] [filename] [args]`

Description

Throughout this book, Perl is presented as a programming language similar to any other. Source files containing Perl programs are presented to a compiler/interpreter and are run.

However, in the greater scheme of things, `perl` is simply a utility among the others available from your operating system. As such, `perl` also can be run from the command prompt and interact that way.

This discussion centers around architectures that actually have a command prompt. Some of them, like the MacOS (prior to OS X), don't have a command prompt by default but can run these examples, nonetheless, by filling out dialog boxes with the appropriate information. The concepts remain the same.

This discussion also assumes that you can find your command prompt. What I mean by this is that most systems have a command line interface buried within them. In Windows 95, this is COMMAND.COM; in Windows NT, it's CMD.EXE; and in Unix, there are a myriad of shells such as the Bourne Shell, Korn Shell, C-Shell, bash, zsh, and others.

The examples in this section should run fine with any of these shells. However, you will want to pay attention to the quirks of your particular shell. Some examples are as follows:

- Windows 95 will not do redirection of errors only (2>).

- Windows NT does not allow nesting of quotation marks (`"\"\""`).

- Shell metacharacters differ slightly under various shells in Unix (`!` is important to bash and C-shells, but means nothing to bourne shells).

Beware of these. To avoid quoting issues, the quote operators `qq{}`, `q{}`, and `qx` are handy.

Your operating system documentation should document the quirks of your individual command prompts.

How to Run Perl at the Command Prompt

First, open a command prompt window (or simply log in). At the command prompt, a good test is to type the following:

```
prompt> perl -v
```

Perl should respond with its version number and copyright information. If it doesn't, you will need to investigate how your shell runs external programs. Usually this involves manipulating some kind of PATH environment variable.

Switches to `perl` are passed using the Unix command-switch character `-`. This is true regardless of your operating system. In general, Perl follows Unix conventions in the way that command-line switches are passed to Perl.

A single switch is a dash followed by a character (the switch itself). For example, a `-v` switch to `perl` is indicated as follows:

```
perl -v
```

Multiple switches can be represented with multiple dashes and switch characters:

```
perl -w -e 1
```

Multiple switches also can be combined with a single dash:

```
perl -we 1
```

Some arguments follow switches immediately:

```
perl -p -i.bak
```

In this example, `-i` is the switch and `.bak` is the switch's argument. In these cases, if you want to "gang up" switches with a single dash, the argument-less switches have to appear first:

```
perl -pi.bak    # Right
perl -i.bakp    # WRONG
```

Some arguments follow switches with a space between them:

```
perl -w -e "print qq{Hello, world}"
```

In this case, if you were to "gang up" the `-w` and `-e` switches, the `-e` switch would have to appear last.

Things that occur after the switches (that don't begin with a `-`) are treated as filename arguments and will be passed to `perl` in the `@ARGV` array for processing. However, if no `-e` is specified, the first of those will be assumed to contain the program you want run (and not be put in `@ARGV`).

```
perl -e '1' foo.txt bar.txt poit.txt
perl myscript.pl foo.txt bar.txt poit.txt
```

In each of these, `foo.txt`, `bar.txt`, and `poit.txt` will be placed in `@ARGV` for processing. In the first, the script is `'1'` (a minimal program in Perl). In the second, the script to be run is contained in `myscript.pl`.

To signal that you're done with switches and want to process files, a special switch of `--` is used. This is especially handy if you're dealing with filenames that have `-`'s on the front.

```
# With a file in this directory named "-K"

perl -e "print qq{@ARGV}" -K        # Error, unrecognized switch.

perl -e "print qq{@ARGV}" -- -K     # OK.
```

See Also

Getopt::Std module documentation

getopts in the C library reference

`#!`

Usage

`#!/.../perl [switch(es)]`

Description

The first line of a perl program typically starts with some variation of

`#!/usr/bin/perl -w`

The reason for this stems from its Unix heritage, but carries over and is useful under other operating systems.

Some Background

Unix does not use file extensions (.txt, .bat, .jpg) to determine which files are executable and which files are not. Most files have a unique signature that determines what kind of file they are; this is called a magic number. Under Unix, the file `/usr/share/magic` (sometimes `/etc/magic`) contains a table of descriptions of these magic numbers.

When a filename with execute permissions is typed, Unix opens the file and uses the magic number to determine how this file should be run. It has a couple of choices. The first choice is it can run the file as a native executable, simply loading and running it (native executables) or using a specialized loader to start the file running (as Linux does with Java).

If the first two bytes are `#!`, this is a signal to the Unix exec system call (which is in charge of setting up and running your program) that this file is to be passed to an interpreter to be run. The next steps are as follows:

1. Take the portion of the #! line leading up to whitespace as an interpreter to be used.

2. Open the interpreter as a native executable.

3. Pass the first argument to the executable as the name of the interpreter.

4. Pass the next arguments, which are the remaining items on the #! line of the script.

5. Pass the name of the script that was invoked.

6. Pass any other arguments that were on the command line with the script name.

The interpreter can now run with its arguments, and those given to the script to be interpreted. Unix systems have many programs that can function as interpreters; some of them are fully-fledged programming languages: awk, sed, tcl, and perl are some examples.

Perl Uses of #!

The #!/.../perl line in Unix is useful only to get the perl interpreter running. Beyond that, anything that happens is Perl's responsibility. The #! line can be used to pass switches to the perl interpreter and to the script itself (with -- and -s) as well as to pass arguments.

The interpreter pathname on the #! line must be correct if you're expecting it to run when called by name. Under Unix, if the pathname in the #! line is not correct, the following error message prints:

```
sh: ./foo.pl: No such file or directory
```

This is a confusing error because the file foo.pl does exist; it's the interpreter in the #! line, which is incorrect. Under Windows, this is not a problem because the file extension, not the #! line, is the hint to the OS on how to run perl.

When the Perl interpreter is invoked, it will rewind the script and scan for a #! line at the beginning (see the -x switch for an exception to this rule). If an interpreter other than perl is on the #! line, it is run instead. For example, when the following is passed to a Perl interpreter (in standard input):

```
#!/bin/sh
```

the interpreter would determine that this is really a Bourne Shell script and invoke /bin/sh and pass the script to it transparently.

Next, the #! line is scanned for switches. If any are found, the interpreter modifies its behavior accordingly (such as -w, turning on warnings, or -s to do argument processing).

The perl script is then run by the interpreter.

Under other operating systems, Perl does look at the #! line's switches and uses them. The primary difference is that the native command interpreter uses a different mechanism to determine how to run the script. For example, under Windows NT with ActiveState's build of Perl, the .pl extension to files is associated with the interpreter. Simply typing the name of the script (ending in .pl) will invoke the interpreter and pass your script to it. This is done through an entry in the registry.

Set user-id **and Set** group-id

An exception to this sequence has to do with set user-id and set group-id scripts under Unix. If the 02000 or 04000 bits are set on a normal executable file (native binaries), when it is run, the process running the program takes on the user-id (or group-id) of the owner (or group) of the program that's being run. In this way, an underprivileged user can run a program that needs some privilege to run. For example, the Unix utilities su, ping, login, newgrp, and chsh normally have set-uid capabilities.

If set-uid scripts are disabled on your OS (which they often are because of security holes) and perl was built with the capability to emulate set-uid programs, perl will

1. Determine whether the script is a set-uid script.

2. Find the set user-id version of itself that was installed with the normal interpreter.

3. Invoke THAT copy of the interpreter to run your script, and tainting will be turned on automatically.

If you invoke the set-uid version of the interpreter directly, it will revert back to your effective user ID automatically.

Example Listing 1.1

```
#!/usr/bin/perl -wT

# -wT do not show up in here.
print "My arguments: ", join(',', @ARGV), "\n";
```

Example Listing 1.2

```
/*

    Short C program to demonstrate interpreter argument
    parsing.  Save as "interp.c" and compile with:

        cc interp.c -o interp

    Then create a file which begins with:

        #!/path/to/interp

    (Using the correct "path to").  Make the file executable
    and try running it with arguments on the #! line and
    try just using arguments with it on the command line.
*/

#include <stdio.h>
main(int argc, char **argv)
{
    int i=0;
    for (i=0;i<argc;i++) {
        printf("Argument: %s\n", argv[i]);
    }
}
```

> **See Also**
> -T and exec in this book

Comments

Usage

```
# your comment here
```

Description

Comments in Perl are introduced with the # character when Perl expects another token in its parsing. The comment continues until the next end-of-line character (or end-of-file) is read by the interpreter.

The # character is not special when it occurs in a context in which Perl is not expecting a new token, such as within a regular expression or a quoted string.

An exception to this is when using the x modifier in a regular expression. In that context, the # character acts as a comment character as it does normally.

```
# Match a reasonable phone number format
#    for the US.  Variations on (313)-248-5167
if ( ($ac,$ex,$ph)=$r=~m/
    (?:    # Match area codes
        \(?
        (\d{3})[-. ]?
        \)?
        [-. ]?
    )?
    (\d+)[-. ]  # Match the exchange
    (\d+)        # Match last 4 digits
    /x ) {
}
```

The # character also is used to force the parser to a certain line number and filename. The format for this is as follows:

```
# line linenum filename
```

`linenum` is the line number that you want to set Perl's internal variable __LINE__ to, and `filename` is the value you want to set for __FILE__. The `filename` is optional, and can be enclosed in quotes (which also will be assigned to __FILE__). The # > must occur at the beginning of the line, followed by whitespace, digits, optionally more whitespace, quote marks, and then the filename (plus any trailing quote marks) ending in a newline. Other forms are ignored. The __LINE__ and __FILE__ values are used primarily in die and warn messages.

Multiline comments in Perl technically do not exist, although they can be emulated by surrounding the code (or text) that you want to be considered a comment with POD.

```
# The section that follows is effectively commented out
=pod

$r=<>;
$r=~s/foo/bar;

=cut
```

Example Listing 1.3

```
# This is a comment
```

Example Listing 1.4

```
# The die() below will always report
# "Died at filefoo line 40."

# line 40 "filefoo"
die;
```

> **See Also**
> POD, __LINE__, and __FILE__ in this book

Basic Data Types

Scalars

Description

The term *scalar* in Perl refers to both a value and a kind of variable used to store that value.

A scalar value is an integer, floating-point number, a string, a reference to a variable, a reference to a scalar value, or a special value such as the undefined value. Scalar values are stored in scalar variables, or as part of one of the aggregate data types arrays or hashes. A reference to a scalar value also can be stored instead of the value itself.

Perl's scalar variables are not typed. You can use the same variable for holding a floating-point number as well as a string; you do not have to declare which you're going to use (since there are no such declarations in Perl anyway) in advance, and you can change your mind later.

```
$r=56.7;   # A float
$r="Hello, planet\n";  # Now a string
$r=undef;  # Special value, undefined
```

Scalar variables are represented by a dollar sign followed by an identifier. Identifiers normally begin with an alphabetic character or underscore, followed by alphanumeric characters or underscores up to 251 characters long.

Scalar variables can belong to a package, and the full package name will consist of identifiers separated by double colons or apostrophes (see packages). Perl has its own private set of special scalar variables that (generally) consist of a dollar sign followed by punctuation, underscores, or numbers.

Scalar variable names are case sensitive in Perl. Also, scalar variables might share the same name as hash variables, array variables, filehandles, or subroutines—each variable type has its own namespace.

Perl's scalars will behave similar to strings and numeric values when required no matter what kind of data is actually stored in the scalar variable. Normally, Perl does the right thing and the expected results are generated. If the scalar variable contains a numeric value and a string is required, as follows:

```
$pi=22/7;
# This is actually a concatenation (.) behind the scenes
print "Pi is about $pi.  Give or take.";
```

Perl will use your system's C library `sprintf()` call with a format specifier of `%g` to do the conversion (see `sprintf` in this book for an explanation of this format specifier). If `gcvt()` or `gconvert()` is available from your system libraries, those are used in preference.

To go the other way, obtain a number when a string is stored in a scalar: Perl will use your systems' C library `atof()` function (or `strtold()` if available and long doubles are supported) to convert from the string format to numeric format, unless the number appears to be an integer; then `atol()` or `atoll()` is used instead.

```
$bignum=" 5.1e+10 ";
print $bignum/2;    # prints the resulting division...
```

In the current implementation of Perl, there is no performance penalty using strings, integers, or floats within scalars and switching between them: Perl remembers the results of the last conversion and will actually store the converted value in addition to the original. If one is modified, the others are destroyed and will be converted again if necessary.

If a string does not convert cleanly to a number, the result of the operation is zero. If warnings are in effect, a warning will be issued when implicitly converting a non-numeric (or empty) scalar to a numeric value.

```
use warnings;

# Results in warning:
```

```
#  Argument "Not A Number!" isn't numeric in addition (+)
$a="Not A Number!";
print $a+0;
```

When storing data in a scalar variable, Perl will allocate the correct amount of storage to hold the value. For simple data (strings), Perl places no limitations on how large the data can be except possibly your system's memory, your operating system's limits, or 4GB on 32-bit systems (size_t in your C libraries) as of this writing. Any value can be stored within a scalar variable, including those containing nulls. If the size of the variable changes, memory will be released (or allocated) as needed; you generally do not need to worry about memory management with Perl, but do use some judgment.

Be aware that some scalar values in Perl are magical (Perl's term, not mine). For example, the $! variable will return a numeric error value in a numeric context, but in a string context, it will return the actual error message:

```
# System's error messages
for $err (0..255) {
    # Force numeric and string context on $!
    $!=$err;
    print $err, " $!\n";
}
```

Also, what appears to be a scalar variable might actually be a tied variable. This means that the normal storage and retrieval mechanisms for the variable have been bypassed for other purposes.

See Also
arrays, hashes, references, undef, and tie in this book

Arrays and Lists

Description

An *array* is an aggregate data type consisting of an ordered group of scalar values. Each scalar value (or empty slot for a scalar value) within the array is called an *element*. An element can hold any kind of scalar value including floating-point numbers, strings, integers, or references.

Array variables are represented by an at sign (@) followed by an identifier. Identifiers normally begin with an alphabetic character or underscore, followed by alphanumeric characters or underscores up to 251 characters long.

Array variables might belong to a package, and the full package name will consist of identifiers separated by double-colons or apostrophes (see packages). Perl has a few private array names, most of which are uppercase (@ARGV, @INC) or contain punctuation (@_, @+).

The size of an array in the current implementation of Perl is limited to 2**31 (2 billion) elements, but you are far more likely to run out of memory first.

A *list* is a collection of scalars in a list (or array) context. Because list values take many forms in Perl, they can be confusing to define. It might be helpful to refer to the section on context while trying to understand lists further.

Literal lists are a series of comma-separated scalars in parentheses used in a list context. Each scalar value within the list is called an *element* (as with arrays). For example, the following is a simple list assignment:

```
($common, $genus)=('bear', 'ursine');
```

The list on the left side of the equal sign determines that this expression is in list context. The elements of one literal list (bear, ursine) will be assigned to the corresponding elements of the other ($common, $genus). An empty list is represented with an empty set of parentheses.

In a list context, array variables also behave similarly to lists. They can be assigned to and from literal lists as follows:

```
@animal=('bear', 'ursine');
```

Functions that take a list of arguments will, in most cases, take an array as well (and the reverse is true). In this respect, arrays and lists are interchangeable syntactically.

An *implied* list is returned by functions. Any function that can return a list can be substituted for a list (or within a list):

```
@columns=split(',', $row);
```

Lists and arrays can both be assigned to also. In order for the assignment to work, the elements on the left side of the assignment must be assignable values. For example, the following will not work:

```
# Will fail because "6" is not an assignable value
($t, 6, $c)=('women', 'rocket', 'animal');
```

If the list on the left side contains an array (or a hash) as an assignable value, the array (or hash) will absorb the remaining values from the right side of the expression. The array will be reduced to fit the values assigned.

```
# @rest gets the third-to-last fields as elements
($first, $second, @rest)=split('', $row);
```

```
# @rest STILL gets the third-to-last fields as elements.
#    $fourth actually winds up with the value undef
($first, $second, @rest, $fourth)=split('', $row);
```

If any variables remain on the left side of the assignment and did not get assigned, they will receive the value undef. The value undef is special on the left side of a list assignment: The value that would normally be assigned to that position will be thrown away.

```
# A prettier form would have been to use a slice (see below)
#
($sec,$min,$hour,undef,undef,undef,$wday)=localtime(time);
print "$hour:$min:$sec ", qw(Sun Mon Tue Wed Thu Fri Sat)[$wday];
```

Lists and arrays are one-dimensional—Perl does not (directly) support multidimensional arrays or lists. Within a list, literal arrays and other lists are flattened to create a one-dimensional list. For example,

```
# The @things that result from this:
@things=('earth','air','fire','water','spirit');
```

```
# Is exactly the same as the @things that result from
@elementals=('earth','air','fire','water');
@things=(@elementals, 'spirit');
```

To achieve multidimensional arrays, you will need to use references.

In scalar context, lists and arrays behave differently. For starters, lists cannot actually exist in scalar context. If (what appears to be) a literal list is used when a scalar is expected, the list is actually a grouping of scalars separated by the comma operator. For example, the following isn't a list assignment at all:

```
$d=('buckle', 'my', 'shoe');
```

The three expressions on the right (buckle, my, and shoe) will all be evaluated in scalar context, left-to-right, by the comma operator. The expressions are simply grouped in parenthesis so that all three of them are evaluated before assignment to $d. The variable $d will wind up with the value shoe.

In a scalar context, array variables will evaluate to the number of elements in the array. This is a property of the array itself, not necessarily of scalar/list context interaction. For more information on context, see the context entry.

```
@a=('buckle', 'my', 'shoe');
print scalar @a;        # yields 3
```

The length of an array also can be obtained by using the form:

```
$#array
```

This returns the subscript of the last element of the *array* (this is the length, minus 1). The length of the array can be changed by altering this value. If the array is empty, this returns -1.

```
$#a--;   # Remove the last element of @a
```

The array in a scalar context is always one less than $#array. If you increase the value of $#array, the array will expand by that many elements. The additional elements will be initialized to undef. To completely initialize an array, you can do either of the following:

```
@array=();   # This works.
$#array=-1;  # So does this.
```

This will not free any memory allocated by the array. To do this, use the undef operator on the array, as follows:

```
undef(@array);
```

Elements in arrays (and lists) can be addressed individually with a subscript. The form for retrieving element n from an array is the following:

```
$array[n]
```

Note that the array name is preceded with a dollar sign instead of the usual at (@) sign because, in this syntax, I'm addressing a single scalar value within the array. Subscripts begin counting at 0 in Perl arrays unless the value of $[has been set. (Altering $[is not advisable.) Using a negative subscript begins counting from the end of the array instead of from element 0.

To address multiple values in an array, use an array slice:

```
@array[m,n,...]
```

The array slice uses an @ in front of the array name (because we're addressing multiple items), and the elements are simply a list (without parenthesis). It is a common mistake to confuse these syntaxes:

```
@rhyme=qw(one two buckle my shoe);
# Generates a warning:
#     Scalar value @rhyme[3] better written as $rhyme[3] at...
print @rhyme[3];

# Generates a warning:
#     Multidimensional syntax $rhyme[0,1] not supported at...
# And doesn't print what you may expect, simply "two"
print $ryhme[0,1];

#
# These are both correct
#
print $rhyme[3];
print @rhyme[0,1];
```

To insert or delete elements from an array, use the functions `splice`, `push`, `pop`, `shift`, and `unshift`, which are documented later in this book.

Retrieving an element from an array that doesn't exist (or hasn't been initialized) will return `undef`. To test whether an element of an array has ever held a value, you can use the exists function. To remove an element from an array (to mark its slot as 'never been used'), you can use the delete function.

A list can be subscripted as well, using brackets as with arrays:

```
# Pick a random letter
print "Letter: ", ('a'..'z')[rand 26];
```

The earlier example using `undef` on the left side of an assignment would look much nicer as a slice:

```
  ($sec,$min,$hour,$wday)=(localtime(time))[0..2,6];
print "$hour:$min:$sec ", qw(Sun Mon Tue Wed Thu Fri Sat)[$wday];
```

A function returning a list can have its return value subscripted (and sliced). To do this, surround the function call with parenthesis and use a subscript on the resulting list:

```
print scalar localtime((stat('/etc/passwd'))[9]);
```

Perl does not have sparse arrays. This means that creating an element with a subscript of 10 (`$a[10]="Howdy"`) would create elements at 9, 8, 7, and so on if they didn't already exist. You should beware of creating a large array of subscripts unless you have the memory to store the entire array. The statement `$a[10000000]=1` allocates nearly 40MB of memory to hold the other elements of the array that are necessary. If you need a sparse array in Perl, a hash should probably be used; or use the `tie` mechanism to create an array with the properties you need.

> **See Also**
> context, hashes, `$[`, packages, `undef`, `exists`, and `delete` in this book

Hashes

Description

A *hash* is an aggregate data type, consisting of scalar values that are stored and retrieved by a key value. Each element of a hash consists of two parts, a key and a value. Both the key and the value are scalars and can contain nearly any kind of data including strings, integers, floating-point numbers or references (see the following note on references). Hashes were historically called associative arrays because keys are associated with values (and other languages call them associative arrays).

Hashes share many commonalties with arrays. To initialize a hash, simply assign a list (or an array) to a hash:

```
%characters=( 'ahab', 'moby dick', 'hawkeye', 'last of the mohicans');
```

The list (or array) should be arranged as a series of key/value pairs. In this case, the keys are ahab and hawkeye, and the values are moby dick and last of the mohicans. If a hash initialization contains an odd number of elements, the last element (a key) will wind up with an undef value. If warnings are enabled, the message "Odd number of elements in hash assignment" will be generated.

It is often more convenient (and readable) to use the comma-arrow operator (=>) for hash initializations. It makes the key/value pairs very distinct:

```
%characters=( 'ahab' => 'moby dick',
        'hawkeye' => 'last of the mohicans',
        'george' => 'of mice and men');
```

Using the comma-arrow operator has the added advantage of making it unnecessary to put the identifier (key) to the left of the => in quote marks (if it's a single bareword, multiword keys will need the quotes):

```
%characters=( ahab => 'moby dick',
        hawkeye => 'last of the mohicans',
        george => 'of mice and men');
```

In this way, use strict subs will not complain about a bare keyword for ahab, hawkeye and george.

Individual elements of a hash can be accessed by using a subscript similar to arrays. In this case, instead of using an element offset, use the key to retrieve (or set) the value:

```
$characters{'ichabod'}="legend of sleepy hollow";
print $characters{ahab};
```

If the key is a single bare identifier, it doesn't have to be enclosed in quotation marks (surrounding whitespace is not important). In the preceding example, Perl understands that ahab is an identifier to be used as a key for the hash %characters. For a keyword that is to be used as an identifier such as the following:

```
print $characters{ pop };
```

the key to be used is the literal word pop. In order for a keyword to be actually interpolated within the braces, it must be made to be something other than a bare identifier. Some methods are

```
print $characters{ +pop };      # Unary plus
print $characters{ pop @ARGV }; # Use the full form
print $characters{ pop() };     # Make it look like a function
```

Hashes will expand automatically to hold any new keys inserted into the hash, and will shrink to fit if keys are removed. To completely remove a hash and release its memory back to Perl (but not to the OS), use the undef function:

```
undef %hash;  # Free up %hash's memory completely.
```

The key in curly braces does not need to be in quotation marks, but it doesn't hurt. Perl assumes that hash keys are simple strings, but will do interpolation within the curly braces. Setting a value for a nonexistent key in a hash creates a new key with that value. Retrieving a value that doesn't exist will return undef.

Using a reference as a hash key is a risky proposal. In the current implementation of Perl, a reference used this way is stringified (turned into a simple string). When this happens to a reference, it can no longer be used as a true reference. String representations of references are unique and make suitable hash keys, but the prospect of a reference becoming unusable can present problems.

```
# Demo of stringification of a hash key
#   strict refs needed so that the string doesn't get seen
#   as a symbolic reference (which are usually a bad idea anyways).
use strict refs;
$r=\"A Scalar Bit of Data\n";
print $$r;     # This works, as expected

# Make the reference a hash key
$h{$r}="Stuff to go with the bit";
# Now pull it out again.
($a)=keys %h;

print $a;      # This still _looks_ like a reference, SCALAR(0x80fe9d8)
print $$a;     # But it's not!  Error: "Can't use string as a reference..."
```

When referring to a single element of a hash, the hash name is preceded with a dollar sign. This is to signify that you're talking about a single scalar value. Perl will use the curly braces as a guide to know that you mean a value from a hash.

To test whether a hash element exists, use the exists function. Do not rely on the hash value being returned as undef as a test for whether a key exists: The value undef is a perfectly valid value to be associated with a hash key. The delete function will remove elements from a hash.

The keys function can be used to retrieve a list of the keys in a hash. The keys will be returned in a pseudo-random order depending on the makeup of the keys and the order in which they were stored. Perl uses a hashing algorithm to store the keys so that they can be stored and retrieved very quickly. A side effect of this is that the order in which they're retrieved cannot be predicted easily. The values function will retrieve the values from the hash as a list.

In a scalar context, a hash variable will return a string representing the ratio of the number of hash buckets used to hash buckets allocated. It doesn't return the number of keys in the hash (use `scalar keys %hash` for that, see `keys`). The number isn't particularly useful unless you're interested in the internals of Perl's hashing algorithm (see the Perl source for more details).

Similar to arrays, several elements at a time can be addressed in a hash with a slice. The syntax for a hash slice is

```
@hash{key1, key2, key3, ...}
```

So to create a mapping of day-of-week-name to number, this snippet would work:

```
@days{qw(Sun Mon Tue Wed Thu Fri Sat)}=(0..6);
print $days{Mon};    # Prints 1
```

Note that the character preceding a hash slice is an at sign (@). This is to signify that you're addressing multiple elements of a hash.

Perl does not support multidimensional hashes directly; there are two ways around this. The first is to use references as hash values and emulate a multidimensional hash—this is the preferred method. It looks very clean and is easy to implement.

The archaic method for a multidimensional hash looks similar to a hash slice:

```
$hash{ key1, key2, key3, ...}
```

What this actually does is join the keys into a single string separated by the value in the variable $; (which is an ASCII RS character by default), creating a single, multipart key. These two lines are functionally equivalent:

```
$dob{ $last, $first } = "4/3/1969";
$dob{ join( $;, $last, $first) } = "4/3/1969";
```

When using this syntax, be very careful that the separator used (in $;) is not also part of the data set. For example, in the previous examples, if the variables $first or $last contained a ASCII RS character, the keys would be garbled.

Also, it's easy to confuse the hash slice and multidimensional hash syntaxes:

```
# Multidimensional hash
$dob{ $last, $first } = "4/3/1969";

# Hash slice -- this is something completely different
@dob{ $last, $first } = "4/3/1969";
```

The preferred way to create a multidimensional hash is to use references and create a Hash of Hashes.

See Also
values, keys, exists and delete in this book

References

Description

References in Perl are scalar values that indirectly point to a real value stored elsewhere. In Perl, there are two kinds of references: *hard references* and *soft references* (also called *symbolic references*, covered elsewhere in this book).

Hard references are created in two ways, either with the \ operator or by creating anonymous storage with {} and []. To create a reference to a variable, place \ in front of the variable name. The \ operator also can be used to create references to a scalar literal as well.

```
$c="Some string";
$ref=\$c;   #  A reference to $c's data

@beatles=qw(george ringo paul john);
$ref2=\@beatles;   # A reference to @beatles' data

%simps=(homer => 'dad', marge => 'mom', bart => 'brat');
$ref3=\%simps;
```

In the preceding example, $ref will contain a reference to the scalar variable $c's data: Likewise, $ref2 will contain a reference to the array @beatles's data, and %ref3 will contain a reference to the hash %simps's data.

In each case, the original values of the scalar, array, or hash can be accessed through the original variable names or through the reference. To access the values in the original structures, simply treat the reference variable as though it were the name of the structure to which you're trying to get. In other words, if $ref2 contains a reference to an array, @$ref2 is the array itself and $$ref2[0] is the first element of that array.

```
print $$c;    # Prints "Some string"

push(@$ref2, "martin");
print $$ref2[3];   # prints "john"

$$ref3{lisa}="brain";
print join(',', keys %$ref3);
```

Accessing a value using a reference is called *dereferencing* the reference. Using the wrong prefix (for example @$ref for a scalar reference) for the particular reference will cause a runtime exception to be thrown.

These represent simple reference expressions. When creating references to references, this can get confusing, so there are a couple of notational conveniences in Perl to help. Given a reference such as $$ref3{maggie}, Perl will do the key or index lookups last, and whichever prefix ($% or @) that is closest to the variable name binds the tightest.

Beyond this, there are two other ways. If you're uncertain about which order the braces, brackets, and prefixes will be evaluated, Perl allows you to surround portions of the expression with braces for clarity much the same as parenthesis in an arithmetic expression. For example, $$ref3{maggie} can be written as ${$ref3}{maggie}; $$ref is the same as ${$ref}, and ${$ref2}[1] is the same as $$ref2[1].

The other clarifying technique involves hash and array elements. Given a reference to a hash or an array, you can access an element using the -> operator. For example,

```
%simps=(homer => 'dad', marge => 'mom', bart => 'brat');
$ref3=\%simps;

# To access 'marge' the old way
print $$ref3{marge};

# To access 'marge' with the -> operator

print $ref3->{marge};
```

The ->[] or ->{} notation gives you a dereference for free, so the extra dollar sign isn't needed. There isn't any confusion about precedence. You cannot create array and hash slices this way, however. They must be done with the original notation.

```
@beatles=qw(george ringo paul john);
$ref2=\@beatles;

# A slice ?
```

```
print $ref2->[0,1];    # WRONG, cannot slice with ->

# A slice?
print @$ref2[0,1];     # CORRECT.
```

Here's a caution on using the \ operator to create references: New Perl programmers often make the mistake of trying to create a reference to a literal list with the \ operator as follows:

```
$lref=\($t, 42, 'pepsi');   # Wrong!  See below for why...
```

This is wrong. The \ operator for creating references only works with variable names. What happens here is that \ is distributive and will apply to each element in the literal list, creating this situation:

```
$lref=(\$t, \42, \'pepsi');   #  Probably not useful.
```

The rules outlined in the context and arrays sections take hold: Lists cannot exist in a scalar context, so the last expression in the parenthesis is returned, and $lref becomes a reference to the literal string pepsi. What the programmer is actually trying to accomplish is to create an anonymous array reference. When references are used without proper dereferencing, Perl takes the reference and stringifies it; that is, a string representation of the reference is returned. This takes the form of a string that indicates the reference type (SCALAR, ARRAY, HASH, CODE, GLOB) and a hexadecimal address.

```
$i="Chips, dips, chains, whips";
$ref=\$i;

print $ref;   # Yields something like "SCALAR(0xc70850)"
```

After a reference has been stringified, it cannot be used as a reference again. There is no way to take the value "SCALAR(0xc70850)" and retrieve the string stored in $i. In general, anything that displays a reference value, alters the reference value itself, or places the reference value in the key of a hash will stringify it, rendering it almost useless.

It is almost useless because representing a reference as a string can be a very valuable debugging tool. Given a reference of arbitrary complexity, and you're not sure what's in it, you can always dereference it and print it until you discover the structure underneath:

```
# $r is a mystery reference to _something_

print $r;    #  printed ARRAY(0x230108)

# So treat it as an array and print again...
print join(',', @$r);  # prints HASH(0x010020),HASH(0x010080)

# Keep going deeper
print join(':', keys %{$r->[0]});  # Prints real hash keys!
```

So in the previous example, $r contains an array reference and the array is full of hash references. This trial-and-error technique is useful if you're just learning references.

This technique also demonstrates one of the primary uses for references, which is creating structures. In Perl, there are only three basic data types: scalars, arrays, and hashes. To create arbitrary structures in Perl, it would be useful to have complex data types such as arrays of arrays (two-dimensional arrays) or hashes of hashes (similar to a two-dimensional array, but better).

To create these structures in Perl, simply remember that any reference is simply a scalar value. To create an array of arrays, simply use one array as the outer array (the rows) and references to the inner arrays as columns as follows:

```
@first=qw(1989, 4.5, 4.7, 4.9, 5.1);
@second=qw(1990, 5.0, 5.1, 5.3, 5.1);

@stats=(\@first, \@second);
```

The array @stats contains two references: one to @first and the second to @second. To access the second row, a third column uses the two-dimensional, array-like syntax:

```
print $stats[1]->[2];  # the value 5.1
```

This works because $stats[1] is simply a reference value. Using the ->[2] notation indicates that it's a reference to an array and that we want to access the third element in that array.

Any arbitrarily complex structure can be constructed this way. For example, a hash of hashes would look very similar to this:

```
%hash1=(hubby => 'fred', wife => 'wilma');
%hash2=(hubby => 'homer', wife => 'marge');

%families=( flintstones => \%hash1,
```

```
        simpsons    => \%hash2);

print $families{simpsons}->{hubby};  # prints "homer"
```

The structure can get as complex as you want. It is now a hash of hashes, and some of the hash elements are arrays:

```
%hash1=(hubby => 'fred', wife => 'wilma',
       kids => [ 'pebbles' ]
       );
%hash2=(hubby => 'homer', wife => 'marge',
       kids => [ qw( bart lisa maggie ) ]
       );

%families=( flintstones => \%hash1,
        simpsons    => \%hash2);

print $families{simpsons}->{kids}->[1];  # prints "lisa"
```

The previous structure demonstrates how anonymous arrays can be used to create these deep structures without having temporary arrays used. In fact, this program can be tightened up quite a bit using just anonymous hashes and arrays:

```
%families=( flintstones => { hubby => 'fred',
        wife => 'wilma', kids => [ 'pebbles' ] },
        simpsons    => { hubby => 'homer',
        wife => 'marge', kids => [ qw( bart lisa maggie ) ] },
       );

print $families{simpsons}->{kids}->[1];  # prints "lisa"
```

An *anonymous* array is a reference to array data, except that there is no actual array. An anonymous array is created by surrounding a list with [ ]; a reference to the list is returned and can be stored so that the following:

```
$ar=[ qw( Opus Milo Binkley Oliver ) ]
```

is (functionally) equivalent to

```
{
    my @arr=qw(Opus Milo Binkley Oliver);
    $ar=\@arr;
}
# $ar still references that array's contents.
```

Anonymous hashes can be constructed similarly using {} instead of [ ]. The hash
occupies storage and can be treated similarly to any other hash using its reference.

```
$ah={ };  # An empty hash.
$ah->{cola}="Coke";
print keys %$ah;
```

Another common use for references is for passing values to and from subroutines. All
values when passed to a subroutine wind up in the array @_. If multiple arrays or
hashes are passed to a subroutine, upon receipt in @_ they become indistinguishable
from each other: the arrays are flattened into a single list (as documented in arrays). So
this syntax will not work:

```
sub pay {
    my(@debts, @income)=@_;
}
@bills=qw(gas electricity mortgage);
@revenue=qw(salary begging couch);
mysub(@bills, @revenue);
```

In the subroutine pay, the array @debts would receive all the values from @_.
References can solve this problem. Instead of passing the actual arrays into the
subroutine, pass a reference to each array and receive them as array references.

```
sub pay {
    my($debts, $income)=@_;
    print "Tell ", join(" ", @$debts), " to bugger off\n";
}
@bills=qw(gas electricity mortgage);
@revenue=qw(salary begging couch);
mysub(\@bills, \@revenue);
```

Passing references to subroutines has two advantages (and possibly one disadvantage).

It makes things possible that might otherwise be very difficult: passing arrays and
hashes to a subroutine. In Perl 4 (where there were no references), passing arrays and
hashes was complex and error-prone.

Passing large amounts of data becomes very efficient. Passing a large array into a
subroutine causes Perl to copy the entire array when the statement my(@array)=@_; is
performed. By passing a reference, the data isn't copied, only a reference is.
Understand that the expense comes during the copy performed by the previous
assignment. By simply using @_ (which contains a special kind of reference called an

alias) instead of real variable names, no copying is ever done, but this gets confusing quickly.

The possible disadvantage is that the subroutine now has access to the caller's data. In Perl this is always the case: @_ is simply an array of aliases back to the caller's data, which can be changed by assigning to elements of @_. However, by handing a subroutine a reference, the subroutine can copy the reference, pass it to other subroutines, and (possibly) alter the data in the original structure. Doing this without explicitly mentioning it in the documentation beforehand is considered bad form.

In Perl, you also can take a reference to a typeglob and a subroutine. To take a reference to a typeglob, use the \ operator as before:

```
$gref=\*FOO;
```

References and typeglobs have some special properties. Consult the typeglobs entry for more details.

Perl also can take a reference to a subroutine. This is done in two different ways. First, the name of the subroutine (with an &) can be used to take a reference, as follows:

```
sub welcome {
    print "Hello, you\n";
}
$sref=\&welcome;
```

The variable $sref winds up with a code reference (printed as CODE when stringified). Note that the subroutine welcome isn't actually run by the reference assignment. The subroutine welcome can then be called by simply treating the reference as a subroutine name:

```
&$sref;   # Actually calling welcome
```

Taking a subroutine reference in this form, & is required in front of the subroutine name. Also, you cannot specify arguments to the subroutine at this time. The following syntax does something completely different:

```
$sref=\&welcome();
```

It actually runs the subroutine welcome, and then takes a reference to the return value (in this case 1, the probable return value of print).

Calling a subroutine with a reference also can use the -> notation. Simply follow the -> with an empty set of parenthesis (if there are no arguments) or a set of parenthesis containing the arguments you want to use:

```perl
$sref->welcome();  # No arguments
$sref->welcome("Whoa");  # With arguments.
```

If a subroutine returns a code reference (as with closures) it is possible to chain the subroutine calls with multiple -> and parenthesis:

```perl
# Assumes that myfunc() will return a
# subroutine reference.

sub myfunc {
    print "Penguin: $_[0]\n";
    return \&anotherfunc;
}
sub anotherfunc {
    print "Boy: $_[0]\n";
}


    $coderef->myfunc("Opus")->("Binkley");
```

You also can create what are called anonymous subroutines. An anonymous subroutine is created by using the sub keyword without a subroutine name. Simply assign the keyword (with the subroutine block attached) to a scalar value:

```perl
my $sref = sub {
    print "Hello, you!\n";
};
&$sref;
```

Now a subroutine is only accessible by the reference value in $sref. This technique is useful for creating callback functions, jump tables, and closures. Closures are covered in the section titled "Closures." A jump table (or a dispatch table) would typically look something similar to the first example at the end of this section. Many modules use callback functions to perform custom operations at certain points of their processing.

```perl
use XML::Parser;

$cdata="";
my $p=new XML::Parser(
    Handlers => {
        Start => sub { push(@stack, $_[1]); },
        Char  => sub { $cdata.=$_[1]; },
        End   => sub { print join('/', @stack), "=$cdata\n";
                pop @stack;
```

```
            $cdata="";},
    }
);
$p->parse($xml);
```

The preceding example uses the XML::Parser module (found in CPAN) to convert
XML data in the variable $xml into a pathname representation of the data. The
interesting things to note about this example is that

> The new() subroutine will receive two arguments in @_: the first is the word
> Handlers. The next is an anonymous hash, which contains code references. This
> technique for passing complicated argument structures to subroutines is very clear
> and concise.

> The parse method will parse the XML and call the subroutines stored at the keys
> Start, Char, and End as each XML element begins, within the element, and as it
> ends.

This kind of callback mechanism is common in modules that require handlers (GUI
modules such as Tk) or maintain state machines that you can hook into.

All data in Perl contains a reference count: This is the number of references made to
the data by variables or is in limbo between statements (sub/return stacks, expression
resolution, and so on). Storage for data isn't released by Perl until there are no
references left. The statement $t="hysteria" creates storage for the string hysteria,
and that storage will have a reference count of 1. If the variable $t is destroyed (goes
out of scope, destroyed with undef), the reference count will be decreased and the
storage for hysteria will be released back to Perl.

A reference to a piece of data increases its reference count. Anonymous hashes and
arrays are simply arrays and hashes with a reference count of 1, despite the fact that
they don't have an associated variable with them. The earlier example for creating
anonymous arrays demonstrates reference counts nicely.

```
my $ar;
{
    my @arr=qw(Opus Milo Binkley Oliver);

    # The array holding the data for
    # Opus, Milo, etc... has a refcount of 1.

    $ar=\@arr;
```

```
    # The array holding the data for Opus, et.al.
    # NOW has a refcount of 2.
}
# The array @arr is destroyed (it is now out of scope).
# But the array holding the data still has a refcount of 1
#   because $ar still holds a reference to it.

$ar="";   # Refcount for the array goes back to 0, and it is freed.
```

It is possible (but not common) to create structures that cannot be properly freed because of circular references. For example, code such as this will cause a memory leak:

```
{
    my($i, $j);
    $i=\$j;
    $j=\$i;
}
```

When the block exits, normally the storage used by $i and $j would be reclaimed. However because the refcount on $i's data is 2 ($i has a reference as the variable, and $j contains a reference to the data), the structure cannot be freed. The same goes for $j; its memory cannot be reclaimed.

To get out of this situation, you must manually break the circular reference yourself before Perl attempts to reclaim the space.

Example Listing 1.5

```
# References demonstration.

# Minimal infix expression evaluator
#   evaluates things like 24+8*5.  Left-to-right,
#   no parenthesis and no precedence.

$expr="24*2+5";

# These each use the reference to @stack passed in to
#   find their own operands and then change the contents of
#   @stack appropriately
# The subs for * and / are functionally equivalent, they don't
#   use a temporary variable and just use the reference in $_[0]
#   directly.  And are much less readable.
```

```
%oper=(
    '+' => sub {    my($stackref)=@_;
            @$stackref=$stackref->[0]+$stackref->[2]; },
    '-' => sub {    my($stackref)=@_;
            @$stackref=$stackref->[0]-$stackref->[2]; },
    '*' => sub {  @{$_[0]}=${$_[0]}[0] * ${$_[0]}[2]; },
    '/' => sub {  @{$_[0]}=${$_[0]}[0] * ${$_[0]}[2]; },
);

foreach(split(/\b/, $expr)) {
    if (/\d+/) {
        push(@stack, $_);          # Push the number
    } else {
        push(@stack, $oper{$_});  # Or push the operator's code
    }

    # If there's two numbers and an operator on the stack,
    #     evaluate them by calling the operator's code
    if (@stack>2) {
        &{$stack[1]}(\@stack);
    }
}
print "Result: $stack[0]\n";
```

> **See Also**
> subroutines, hashes, arrays, closures, and {} in this book

Data Representations

String Literals

Usage

```
"string"
'string'
string
```

Description

String literals are character sequences surrounded by single or double quotes. Within double quotes, interpolation takes place. This means that some variables are expanded into their values and escape sequences are turned into their special values.

Interpolation is covered thoroughly in the quote operators entry. Escape sequences are covered in the section on escape sequences.

A string literal not contained in quote marks is called a *bareword*. Barewords are perfectly valid strings like any others:

```
$r=Hello;
print $r;      # prints "Hello"
```

However, barewords present problems. They can be confused with a function call. Looking at the previous example; it isn't clear whether `Hello` is a bareword (a string literal) or a call to the `Hello()` function with no arguments.

The `strict 'subs'` pragma will disallow barewords within your script; all string literals must be surrounded by quotes.

Filehandles and labels aren't considered barewords because their meaning is enforced by the context in which they appear. However, a bareword in an ambiguous position can cause some confusion:

```
print out;
```

Does this mean to print `$_` to the filehandle `out`, or does it mean to print the literal string "out" to the `STDOUT` filehandle? Perl assumes that the former is meant, which might not be what you want.

See Also
quote operators, escape sequences, and `strict` in this book

Numeric Literals

Usage

```
number
```

Description

Numeric literals in Perl can be written in many different forms. All are treated equally, and which forms you use depend entirely on your taste for clarity. Many of these forms are familiar; some you'll meet for the first time.

```
$a=1521;      # An integer
$a=1_521;     # The same integer.  _ can be used to separate
       #    numbers for clarity...
$a=15_21;     # ...but they don't have to occur where traditionally
       #    found at all.  (The number is still 1521)

$a=3.14159;   # A floating point number
$a=6.626e-34;  # Scientific notation with mantissa and exponent

$a=045;       # An octal number (37 in decimal)
$a=0x25;     # A hex number (also 37 in decimal)
$a=0b100101;    # A binary number (still 37)
```

In general, the unusual forms (hex, binary, octal, and underscored) will only be treated special as a literal within the Perl program itself. Asking Perl to attempt to translate one of these for you probably won't work:

```
$a="045";    # Remember, as octal it's 37 decimal.
$a=$a+1;     # Implicit conversion to numeric
print $a;    # prints...46, not 38!
```

The preceding example doesn't work because for string/numeric conversion, the atof function treats 045 as 45. See the scalars entry for an explanation of implicit numeric conversion.

To convert strings in these formats, you'll need the oct function for hex, octal, or binary. For underscores, remove them with s/// or tr/// and let Perl use the result as a decimal.

See Also
scalars and oct in this book

undef

Usage

```
undef
undef variable
```

Description

The word undef actually has two meanings in Perl. First (and foremost) it refers to the value undef, which is the undefined value. It evaluates to false (in boolean contexts); it isn't zero, the empty string, or null (which has no meaning in Perl).

The value undef is seen in Perl in many places:

- It's the value of an uninitilized scalar variable.

- It's the value of an uninitilized hash or array element.

- It's the return value for many functions in which 0 or " " is a valid return value.

In a strictly non-boolean context, using the undef value can trigger a warning (Use of uninitialized value).

Second, undef is an operator in Perl. Without a variable, undef simply returns the undefined value. So to reset a hash value back to it's uninitialized state, simply assign the result of undef to it:

```
undef $myhash{foo};
```

This doesn't remove the element from the hash (exists can still see it), but assigns it an undefined value.

Given a subroutine name (with &) and typeglob, scalar, hash, or an array variable as an argument, undef will remove the storage associated with that item. This can be used to free memory when a large variable isn't likely to fall out of scope and have its storage reclaimed. Note that removing a typeglob will remove package scalars, arrays, hashes, and subroutines with that name.

The undef value itself shouldn't be used with a relational operator. Perl will issue a warning, and the comparison likely won't compare apples to apples. If you need to test for the undefined value explicitly, use the defined function:

```
if (defined $foo) {
    # Yes, it's there and defined!
}
```

The undef operator also can be used as an assignable value—assigning to undef causes the assigned value to be dropped. This is useful when a function returning a list has values you aren't interested in.

```
(undef, undef, $hour)=localtime;  # Just want the hour!
```

Example Listing 1.6

```
# Beware of this subtle bug, it bites every perl programmer
#    at least once.
# In list (array) context, a simple return should be used to
#    indicate that a function is returning false.  Returning
#    undef explicitly has the effect of returning a 1-element
#    list to the caller, with undef as the element.  And this
#    evaluates to true!

sub myfunc {
    my($arg)=shift;
    if ($arg) {
        # Bad way to fail.
        return undef;
    } else {
        # Good way! False in both scalar and list
        #    contexts
        return;
    }
}
@ret=myfunc();
if (@ret) {
    print "\@ret was empty, false\n";
}
@ret=myfunc(1);
if (@ret) {
    # Whoops, @ret had 1 element in it: undef.
    print "\@ret was NOT empty, true\n";
}
```

> **See Also**
> defined and relational operators in this book

Numeric Conversion

Usage

```
hex expression
hex
oct expresssion
oct
```

Description

The `hex` function converts a string *expression* that is formatted as a `hexadecimal` number into a decimal value. The string might contain the digits `0-9`, `a-f` and `A-F`. In addition, a leading `0x` will be ignored.

The `oct` function converts a string *expression* that is formatted as an `octal`, `hexadecimal`, or `binary` number into a decimal value. If the string begins with `0b`, it will be treated as binary, if `0x`, it will be treated as `hexadecimal`, and anything else as `octal`.

If `oct` and `hex` are not given an argument, `$_` will be used instead.

The reverse of `oct` and `hex` (if you can call it that) is `sprintf` with an appropriate format string.

Example Listing 1.7

```
# Old programming joke

print "Why do programmers confuse Halloween and Christmas?\n";
printf "because %d Oct is %d Dec\n", 31, oct 31;
```

> **See Also**
> `sprintf` in this book

Escape Sequences

Usage

```
\code
```

Description

Escape sequences (also called *backslash sequences*) are used in interpolative contexts (double quotes, qq{}, regular expressions) to represent hard-to-type, but common characters.

The escape sequences all begin with \ and are followed by one or more characters that define the sequence. A literal \ in an interpolative context is represented by \\. Where delimiters are involved, they can be escaped by preceding them with a backslash:

```
$path=~s/\/home\/clintp//g;   # Good, but better written as:
                # $path=~s!/home/clintp!!g;
$name='Patty O\'Hare';        # Good, but better written as:
                # $name=q{Patty O'Hare};
```

The escape sequences are as follows:

Esc Sequence	Meaning
\a	Bell (ASCII 7-BEL)
\b	Backspace (ASCII 8-BS)
\t	Horizontal tab (ASCII 9-HT)
\f	Form Feed (ASCII 12-FF)
\n	Logical newline (usually ASCII 10-LF)
\r	Carriage return (ASCII 13-CR)
\e	Escape (ASCII 27-ESC)
\digits	Arbitrary character (see following)
\ccharacter	Control character (see following)
\x{hex}	Unicode character (see following)
\N{name}	Named Unicode character (see following)

Any ASCII character can be represented by using the octal or hexadecimal code for that character. The format for the codes are: \digits for octal and \xdigits for hexadecimal. So to represent a SYN (ASCII 22) character, you can say:

```
$a="\x16";  # SYN (hex)
$b="\026";  # SYN (oct)
```

Control-character sequences can be specified directly with \c*character*. For example, the control-g character is a BEL, it can be represented as \cg; the control-t character is \ct.

Wide (multibyte) characters can be specified in hex by surrounding the hex code with {} to contain the entire sequence of digits. The utf8 pragma also must be in effect.

```
use utf8;
$indecision="\x{262f}";      # Unicode YIN YANG
```

If the character is a named character and the charnames module has been included, you can specify the name with a \N{*name*} sequence:

```
use charnames ':full';
$storm="And the \N{LIGHTNING} went flash!";
```

Another kind of escape sequence is the translation escapes. These alter the string starting at that point for either a single character or multiple characters.

Esc Sequence	Meaning
\u	Shift the next character to uppercase
\l	Shift the next character to lowercase
\U	Shift the remainder of the string (or until \E is encountered) to uppercase
\L	Shift the remainder of the string (or until \E is encountered) to lowercase
\Q	Escape all characters (as though with quotemeta) until the end of the string or \E is encountered
\E	Terminate \U, \L and \Q sequences

```
$vendor="ibm";
$lang="java";
$buzzadj="VIRTUAL";

print "\U$vendor\E sold us \L\u$buzzadj\E \u$lang.";

# prints "IBM sold us Virtual Java"
```

As shown with \L\u, the translation escapes can be stacked, and they'll be run from left-to-right.

> **See Also**
> regular expression character shorthand in this book

quotemeta

Usage

```
quotemeta string
quotemeta
```

Description

The quotemeta function takes any characters in the string that aren't in the ranges of A-Z, a-z, 0-9, or _, and precedes them with a backslash, and returns a new scalar. If no *string* is specified, $_ is used.

Internally, this is how the \Q escape sequence in double-quoted strings, backticks, and regular expression patterns is implemented. Normally this function is used to clean up data (from files or users) that might have metacharacters to be used in regular expressions or system commands.

If locales are in effect, the character sets that aren't backslashed are those that are true for union of the sets isalpha, isdigit, and _.

Example Listing 1.8

```
# Looks for a filename containing a pattern.
#   Normally if you specify a pattern like
#   "foo*bar" to find files that contain a literal *,
#   the pattern match will fail to run.  Quotemeta fixes this.

use File::Find;

sub matched {
    if ($File::Find::name=~m/$pat/o) {
        print "Found $pat in $File::Find::name\n";
    }
}

print "Pattern to find? ";
chomp($pat=<STDIN>);
```

```
# Backwhack any metacharacters
$pat=quotemeta($pat);

print qq{Looking for "$pat"\n};
find \&matched, ".";
```

Vector Constants

Usage

```
vdigit.digit...
```

Description

Vector strings (also *v-strings* or *version strings*) are used to construct strings when you know the numeric values of each character in each position of the string. The string after $a

```
$a=v67.97.109.101.108;
```

is the same string you would get if you specified it this way:

```
$a=chr(67).chr(97).chr(109).chr(101).chr(108);  #  "Camel"
```

These are handy for specifying version numbers, IP addresses, or sequences of ASCII codes in numeric form:

```
require 5.6.0;        # Make sure the Perl is fairly modern
$myaddr=v192.168.1.2;   # Home machine
$dos_eol=v13.10;     # CR LF
```

If more than one period (.) is specified, the leading v becomes optional, as shown in the preceding require example.

Example Listing 1.9

```
use Socket;
# Re-work of the socket example using a vector string instead
#    of inet_aton()
# Since the address is just a constant, using a vector string
#    like v127.0.0.1 is the same as calling inet_aton("127.0.0.1")
#    -- but easier to read.
$remote_port=sockaddr_in(scalar getservbyname("www", "tcp"),
    v127.0.0.1);
```

Blocks and Subroutines

labels

Usage

```
LABELNAME:
```

Description

Labels are used to mark a statement, block, or loop so that it can be the target of a goto, redo, next, or last.

Labels are simply identifiers that begin with an alphabetic character or underscore, followed by alphanumeric characters or underscores up to 251 characters long. By convention, labels are usually in all uppercase letters.

Labels aren't part of a package, nor are they in a namespace: they're simply attached to the construct with which they appear. Multiple labels with the same name should appear in different scopes, and the scopes are dynamic.

To attach a label to a statement, simply use the *labelname* and a colon before the following statement:

```
RESTART: print "I'm restarting!\n";
```

Now, to jump to that label with a goto statement, just use the label name:

```
goto RESTART;
```

Within loops, labels are used in Perl so that complex loop control can be achieved without resorting to try/catch/throw constructs or flag variables.

```
LINES: while(<FH>) {
    last LINES if /quit/;
}
```

Example Listing 1.10

```
# See if any of a list of patterns is in the input
#   file stream.  A _MUCH_ faster version of this appears
#   in the eval entry.

LINE: while(<>) {
```

```perl
for my $pat (@patterns) {
    if (/$pat/) {
        # The elegance is, we can exit from this
        #  loop and the surounding loop as well.
        last LINE;
    }
}
```

See Also
goto, last, next, and redo in this book

Blocks

Usage

{ }

Description

The *block* is Perl's basic unit for grouping statements in a logical unit. Blocks are declared with a set of brackets enclosing the statements (or a statement) to be grouped.

```perl
{
}
```

This book discusses blocks in three different situations: blocks (this entry), special named blocks (INIT, CHECK, BEGIN, and so on), and blocks in relation to other operators and statements.

To muddy the waters a bit, the Perl source and documentation also consider a file and a string given to eval to be a block. The only purpose this consideration has is during a discussion on lexical scope. All other block semantics do not apply to eval strings and files.

A block is an arbitrary division of code, considered to be a loop that executes exactly once. In addition, blocks have other properties:

- They define the smallest unit of lexical scope in Perl.

- The end of a block can be used as a statement terminator; thus the last statement in a block does not require a semicolon (but it is encouraged).

Bare blocks can be useful for the first preceding property: being a container for lexical scope. Perl has nothing like the static declaration in C, where a variable is initialized once (at compile time) and then never initialized again. It can be done with `INIT` blocks or trickery involving undocumented features and `my`.

Creating a static variable in Perl can be done more easily with

```
use strict;
{
    my $a=56;

    sub mysub {
        #  Now use $a...
    }
}
mysub();
```

The variable `$a` is initialized when the block is first run, presumably before `mysub` is ever called. Because there's no reasonable way to ever run the `$a=56` again, it's effectively a static declaration of `$a`.

This technique also can be used to have a variable that's shared between subroutines:

```
{
    my $common;     # Can be seen in &firstsub and &seconsub
            #  but nowhere else.

    sub firstsub {
        # Code here...
    }
    sub secondsub {
        # Code here...
    }
}

# Can't see $common here!
sub mysub {
    # Can't see $common here either!
}
```

In this case, because `$common` is declared to be lexical in a block along with `firstsub` and `secondsub`, they all share a common lexical scope. Outside of this block, `$common` is invisible. The subroutines (`firstsub` and `secondsub`) are visible outside of the block because subroutine definitions aren't lexically scoped in Perl.

Normally, blocks are attached to statements as follows:

```perl
if ($t>0 and $t==int($t)) {
    print "$t is a positive integer!\n";
}


%square=map { ($_, $_**2) } @numbers ;


do { foo(); bar() } if ($a);
```

Blocks attached to statements must be encased in brackets. Unlike C and Pascal, you cannot substitute a single statement for a block when a block is called for. The places where blocks are attached to statements are covered with the individual statements in this book.

A bare block isn't attached to a statement. It's simply a group of code encased by braces. Bare blocks are subject to loop control with last, redo or next. redo will cause the block to repeat, last will cause the block to exit, and next will not only cause the block to exit but also run any attached continue blocks (see the continue entry).

```perl
{     # Cheap while() loop.
    $task=shift @queue;
    process($task);
    redo if @queue;
}
```

Note that blocks attached to if and unless statements aren't subject to loop control. They aren't considered looping blocks. However, the same effect can be remedied by simply using an inner enclosing block.

```perl
while(<>) {
    chomp;
    if (/target/) {{
        print "Found a match: $!\n";
        last if $not_process;     # Abort the if() early
        process($_);
    }}
}
```

This can be used to implement loop control on any kind of block, even those associated with map, do, sort, and so on.

Bare blocks also can be labeled, and thus the target of a named redo or last. Perl lacks a case or a switch statement (unlike C, shell, Java, and so on), but one can be remedied by using a labeled block, as shown in the examples for this section.

Example Listing 1.11

```
# Implements something like the switch from "The C Programming
#     Language", Kernighan & Ritchie, Section 3.4:
# while((c==getchar() != EOF) {
#   switch(c) {
#     case '0': case '1': case '2': case '3': case '4':
#     case '5': case '6': case '7': case '8': case '9':
#         ndigits[c-'0']++;
#         break;
#     case ' ':
#     case '\n':
#     case '\t':
#         nwhite++;
#     default:
#         nother++;
#         break
#   }
#}    -- but in Perl

# There are _many_ other ways of doing this
#  The perlsyn manual under "Basic BLOCKs and Switch
#  Statements" has half a dozen techniques.
my($nwhite, %ndigits, $nother);
while(<>) {
    for(split//) {
        SWITCH: {
            /\s/   && do { $nwhite++;       last SWITCH; };
            /(\d)/ && do { $ndigits{$1}++; last SWITCH; };
            $nother++;
        }
    }
}
```

Example Listing 1.12

```
# Another switch-like statement
#
# The for() loop seems silly for a single value,
```

```
#    but it a common idiom.  This is because $_ is
#    implicitly set by the for() and localized to the
#    loop.  Convenient for testing with m//.

for($http_response_code) {
    /^2/ and do { $type="OK";             last; };
    /^3/ and do { $type="Redirected";     last; };
    /^4/ and do { $type="Client Error";   last; };
    /^5/ and do { $type="Server Error";   last; };
    die "HTTP fetch returned an unknown code: $_";
}
```

See Also

`perlsyn` module documentation

special named blocks; `last`, `redo`, `continue`, `next`, and `lexical` scope in this book

---

Subroutine Declarations And Definitions

Usage

```
sub block

sub name block
sub name prototype block
sub name : attributes block
sub name prototype : attributes block

sub name
sub name prototype
sub name : attributes
sub name prototype attributes
```

Description

The `sub` keyword is used to introduce subroutines to Perl. It is used in two different instances: to introduce a subroutine definition and a subroutine declaration.

A subroutine definition in its most basic form consists of the `sub` keyword and a *block*; this creates an anonymous subroutine. Simply calling

```
$mysub=sub { print "Hello world" };
&$mysub;
```

returns a code reference and assigns it to `$mysub`. The code reference can then be called by properly de-referencing `$mysub` with `&`. This also can create a closure if there are lexical variables in scope when the anonymous subroutine is created.

Normally the `sub` keyword is used with a *name* and a *block*. This causes Perl to compile the subroutine and place it in the namespace of the current package as *name*. The *name* is an identifier and follows rules similar to those used by variable names and filehandles, and a subroutine can have the same name as a variable or filehandle in the current package. Otherwise, no restrictions are on the name of the subroutine except that you should avoid uppercase-only names because Perl might assign those special meaning in future revisions (as it did with `INIT`, `END`, `BEGIN`, `CHECK`, `DESTROY`, and `AUTOLOAD`).

Once defined, it can then be called from the package using the normal subroutine calling mechanisms:

```
sub hat {
    return (qw(Heidi Jen Chris Bill))[rand 4]
}
hat;

package NotHere;
&main::hat();
```

The `sub` keyword can be followed by a *prototype* or a list of *attributes*. See the prototype and attributes entries for details.

Within the subroutine, any arguments passed to the subroutine are passed in the special variable `@_`. These values are actually aliases to the real values in the caller. See the section on aliases and calling subroutines for details. If you need to modify the arguments in the caller's arena, use the values in `@_` (`$_[0]`, `$_[1]`, and so on) directly. However, unless the caller is expecting this, it's generally considered rude. Making a copy of the arguments is better:

```
sub rude {
    for(@_) { tr/a-z/A-Z/; }
    return(@_);
}
sub nice {
    my @values=@_;
    for(@values) { tr/a-z/A-Z/; }
    return(@values);
}
```

To leave the subroutine, use the `return` function. The subroutine's return value will be whatever arguments are given to `return`. If the end of the subroutine's block is reached, the value of the last expression evaluated will be used as the `return` value.

A subroutine declaration is a promise to Perl that an actual subroutine will be defined sometime in the future. It's intended to give Perl hints to what the subroutine will need and how it will act when it is run. For example, the simple declaration:

```
sub swap ($$);
```

tells Perl that a subroutine named `swap` will be defined later (hopefully before it's needed), and that it has a prototype of `$$`. No actual subroutine has been defined by doing this. Calling `swap` before the definition will still generate an error even with a declaration.

But during compilation, `use strict subs` will know that a subroutine will be defined eventually and not to throw a `bare keyword` error when `swap` is seen without parenthesis or an ampersand.

In general, a declaration has the same form as a definition except that there is no *block*. The actual definition of the subroutine must have the same prototype and attributes if they were present during declaration, or an exception will be thrown during compilation.

Perl's built-in functions can be overridden simply by redefining them in the correct namespace. In general, there are three techniques for overriding a built-in subroutine:

- Using the `use subs` declaration in a package, and then declaring a subroutine with the same name in that package. The redeclaration is limited to that package:

```
use subs qw(ucfirst);
sub ucfirst (;$) {
    # Your equivalent code here
}
```

- Having another package alter your namespace with a typeglob. See the typeglob entry for details. This will only affect the package whose namespace is changed.

- Overriding the function in the pseudopackage `CORE::GLOBAL`. This should be used with caution because it overrides the built-in function everywhere—and this might cause surprises in unsuspecting code such as modules.

```
*CORE::GLOBAL::ucfirst=sub {
    # Your equivalent code goes here
}
```

The list of functions that cannot be overridden is extensive. See the prototypes entry for a technique on determining which can be overridden and which cannot.

Example Listing 1.13

```perl
# Function to find the least and greatest elements in a list
#   (as defined by a sortsub) in O(n) time.

use strict;
sub sortsub { $a <=> $b }  # Arguments just like sort, thanks to local()
sub minmax {
    my $aref=shift;
    my($min, $max);
    for(@$aref) {
        local($a,$b);  # $a and $b are exempt from "strict vars"
        $a=$_; $b=$min;
        $min=$_ if (not defined $min or &sortsub < 0);
        $b=$max;
        $max=$_ if (not defined $max or &sortsub > 0);
    }
    return($min,$max);
}
my @list=(10,23,121,1,2,14,1,2,111,120);   # 1 and 121 for this list.
print join(',', minmax \@list), "\n";
```

> **See Also**
> prototypes, attributes, return, aliases, use strict and calling subroutines in this book

`return`

Usage

```
return
return value
```

Description

The `return` statement causes control to be immediately passed back to the calling subroutine (or the main body of the program) from a called subroutine, eval, or do file. A *value* will be passed back as the return value of the subroutine if one is specified. If no *value* is specified, in a scalar context undef is returned, in a list context an empty list is returned.

Using a `return` in any context other than within a `sub`, `eval` or do file—such as in the main body of the program—will cause an exception to be thrown.

A subroutine that exits without explicitly returning, by "falling off" the bottom, will simply return the value of the last expression in the subroutine evaluated in the appropriate context.

Using a bare `return` instead of `return undef` is the customary way to indicate failure in a Perl function because it evaluates to false in both list and scalar contexts.

Example Listing 1.14

```
# Demonstrates why "return" is used instead of
#    "return undef" for subroutines returning an error.
sub false {
    return;
}
sub not_so_false {
    return undef;
}
my @a=false();
my $a=false();
if (@a) { die "Unlikely to happen"; }
if ($a) { die "Also unlikely to happen"; }

@a=not_so_false();
$a=not_so_false();
if ($a) { die "Should not happen"; }
if (@a) { die "Surprise!"; }  # This actually evaluates to true!
```

Dynamic Scope

Description

Dynamic scope is determined by the context in which the statement appears at that time, rather than its surrounding blocks (which is lexical scoping). In Perl 4, dynamic scoping was the only available scoping.

A new dynamic scope is established with the `local` statement and with the loop control statements that can do automatic assignment to $_L (`while(<>)`, `for`, `foreach`).

Variables declared with local (or $_ with the aforementioned statements) have their
previous values saved and are restored only when the enclosing block is exited. Unlike
lexical scoping, the new value of the variable propagates outward to any subroutines
called within the block. For example,

```perl
sub printit {
    print $t;
}
sub sayhi {
    print $t;    # Prints "Not yet"
    {
        local $t="Hello, World\n";
        &printit;
    }
    print $t;    # Prints "Not yet" again.
}
$t="Not yet.\n";
sayhi;
```

The local declaration creates a dynamic scope for $t. The value of $t when printit
is called is Hello, World. If printit had called any subroutines, the value would have
continued propagating downward.

At the end of the block (within &sayhi), the original value of $t is restored.

Example Listing 1.15

```perl
# Create a local copy of $/ so that we can slurp in
#    the filehandle but not destroy $/ permanently (or
#    explicitly save it off).
open(FH, "/tmp/bigfile.txt") || die;
{
    local $/;  # Create a dynamic scope for $/
          #    and set it to undef
    $t=<FH>;
}
# Old value of $/ is restored!
close FH;
```

> **See Also**
> local and lexical in this book

```
lexical
```

Description

The term `lexical` in Perl refers to a kind of scope that a variable can occupy. It also refers to the scope in which a pragma is active. `lexical` scope is related to a block. A variable that has been declared with `my` is lexical to the block (and any enclosed blocks) and is only visible there.

```
# In the file myprog.pl

my $cell;
sub foo {
    my $var;
    for my $i (@ARGV) {
        my $j;
    }
}
sub bar {

}
```

In the preceding example:

- The variables `$i` and `$j` are only visible to the block attached to the `for` statement.

- The variable `$var` is visible throughout the subroutine `foo` and any enclosed blocks. This includes the `for` block.

- The variable `$cell` is visible throughout the file that contains the code seen here. The variable is visible within the subroutines `foo` and `bar` and within any blocks enclosed in those subroutines.

To determine the visibility of a variable declared with `my`, simply look at the structure of the program. The variable is visible within the block (or compilation unit) it was declared in, and any blocks that physically nest inside it. Contrast this with package variables that are visible everywhere.

Blocks that are attached to control structures (`foreach`, `for`, `while`, `until`, `do`, `if`) consider the control structure to be part of the lexical scope as well.

```
for(my $i=0; $i<10; $i++) {
    print $i;    # This $i is the same $i declared above
}
```

```
# The scope of $user continues down into the else...
if (my $user=$q->param("USERID") eq 'root') {
    print "Welcome $user!\n";
} else {
    die "User $user is not allowed here!";
}
```

A compilation unit is usually a file, but also can be a string. In the case of eval string, the string itself is considered a block (for purposes of lexical scoping) that is lexically within the context of any block (or file) containing the eval statement itself.

Whether a variable is lexical is determined at compile time. A lexical variable does not occupy the symbol table (in which package variables are kept) at all. Instead, each block or compilation unit is assigned a scratchpad and the variables are kept there. Thus it is completely possible—but confusing—to access a package variable and a lexical variable in the same block with the same name.

```
package foo;
$i=50;
{    # This is another lexical scope
    my $i=66;

    print $i;     # Prints 66
    print $foo::$i; # Prints 50

}
```

For details on how Perl decides whether a variable name refers to a package variable or a lexical variable, see the section "Variable Name Resolution."

lexical variables make closures possible. When a closure is created, a reference to the variables needed by the closure subroutine are maintained. When the creating subroutine returns, the lexical variables on the pad are normally destroyed except in the case of a closure.

Pragmas also are lexically scoped. This is done so that the compiler pragmas affect only the code that's intended to be affected by the pragma. For example,

```
use LWP::Simple;
sub fetchit {
    use warnings;
    my $r=get("http://www.geeksalad.org");
    # Process $r...
}
```

The pragma use warnings only affects the subroutine fetchit; it does not affect the get function within the module LWP::Simple. If the get function wasn't safe for warnings (which in this case, it happens to be) this would limit the warnings thrown to just your function and not someone else's that you happened to call. The old way of enabling warnings within a block:

```perl
use LWP::Simple;
sub fetchit {
    $^W=1;    # Warnings on!
    my $r=get("http://www.geeksalad.org");
    # Process $r...
    $^W=0;    # Warnings off!
}
```

would make get susceptible to the warning flag even though it might not be prepared for that. Using a lexically scoped pragma is preferred for this reason.

local

Usage

```perl
local variable
local(variable list)
```

Description

The local operator causes Perl to save a copy of the data represented by the variable. If multiple variables are given, the variable list has to be enclosed in parenthesis.

The variable to be saved can be an array, hash, or scalar. Unlike the my declaration, you also can save off a glob or one of Perl's special global variables (such as $_ or $/). Additionally, individual elements of an array or hash can be localized.

```perl
sub mysub {
    local($_, $t);
    local $SIG{INT}='IGNORE';
    # Rest of sub.
}
```

When the current scope has exited, the original value of the data will be restored. Any subroutines called after the local declaration but before the end of the enclosing scope will see the new value, rather than the saved value. This is called *dynamic scoping*, which is explained further in the section on dynamic scope.

The local declaration can be part of an initialization. If a value isn't assigned, the scalar variables (or variable list) will receive the value undef; hashes and arrays will be empty. The right side of the initialization will be evaluated in a scalar context unless the local declaration is for an array, hash, or the scalar variable is encased in parenthesis.

During an initialization, the right side is evaluated before the localization. This is so that the new variable can be initialized with the old value, as in the following:

```
local @FOO=@FOO;
```

If you're considering using the local declaration, it's generally useful only in the special cases noted previously (globs, individual elements of a hash or array, or a special global variable). The my declaration is probably what you want instead.

Example Listing 1.16

```
# Examples of local.  See body of code.
#    requires the Tk library, used for GUI programming.
# Demonstrates how an external config file could be read in and
#    used by perl to initialize variables, etc..  Of course this is
#    rather simplistic.

use Tk;
use Tk::Dialog;
use strict;
use warnings;

my $wm;
my $config="/etc/configfile";
sub risky {
    # Within this sub, warnings thrown will actually trigger
    #    the gui_warnings subroutine.  But only here
    #    and children of this sub.
    local $SIG{__WARN__}=\&gui_warnings;
    unless(open(CONFIG, $config)) {
        warn "No config file ($config)";
        return;
    }
    {
        # Put perl into slurp-reading mode.  But only
        #    temporarily.
        local $/;
        eval <CONFIG>;  # Potential errors here?
```

```
        }
        if ($@) {
            warn "Config file corrupt: $@";
        }
    }

sub gui_warnings {
    my $d=$wm->Dialog(-text => $_[0], -title => 'Warning!',
        -default_button => 'Ok', -buttons => ['Ok'] );
    $d->Show();
}

$wm=new MainWindow;
$wm->Button(-text => "push me", -command => \&risky)->pack();
MainLoop;
```

> **See Also**
> lexical, dynamic, and my in this book

my

Usage

```
my variable
my(variable list)
```

Description

The my declaration causes the variable (or variables in the variable list) to be lexically scoped for the remainder of the block, file or eval string. The variables listed must be scalar, array, or hash. For more information on lexical scoping, see the lexical entry.

```
my $instance;
my @junk;
```

If multiple variables are specified, the variable list must be contained within parenthesis.

```
sub enable {
    my($socket, $mode);
    # Rest of sub...
}
```

You cannot declare one of Perl's special global variables ($_, %ENV) to be lexical with my. Nor can you declare a package-qualified variable (such as $Foo::narf) to be lexical—package variables (and thus global variables) are in an entirely different namespace. At this time, subroutines cannot be declared lexical with my.

Multiple calls to my on the same subroutine (but different invocations) generate a different variable with that same name. Within a loop, a my declaration causes a new instance of the variable to be created within each loop.

```
my $self=shift;
my @args=@_;
my %envcopy=%ENV;
my($main, @alternates)=@ARGV;
```

The my declaration can be part of an initialization. If a value is not assigned, the scalar variables (or variable list) will receive the value undef; hashes and arrays will be empty. The right side of the initialization will be evaluated in a scalar context unless the my declaration is for an array, hash, or the scalar variable is encased in parenthesis.

Example Listing 1.17

```
# A Napster download bot.  Requires the MP3::Napster module
#   by Lincoln Stein from CPAN.
use strict;
use warnings;
use MP3::Napster;
sub login {    # Each call generates a new napster object
    my($name, $pass, $linespeed, $dir)=@_;
    my $nap=MP3::Napster->new or
        die "Cannot connect: " . MP3::Napster->error;
    $nap->login($name, $pass, $linespeed) or
        die "Cannot login: " . $nap->error;
    $nap->download_dir($dir);
    return $nap;
}
sub search_and_download {
    my($nap,$title)=@_;
    my @results=$nap->search($title);
    warn "Nothing found for $title" unless @results;
    foreach my $song (@results) {
        next unless $song->owner->ping;
        next unless $song->download;
        print "Downloading ", $song->name, " at ",
```

```
                $song->link, "\n";
          last;
        }
    }
}
# Note: downloading copyrighted works that you do not have a license
#    to use may be illegal.  Use your best judgement.
my $conn=login("clintonp", "fishguts", LINK_CABLE, "/tmp");
my @songlist=("Bohemian Rhapsody", "Rhapsody in Blue");
for my $song ( @songlist ) {
    search_and_download($conn,$song);   # Asynchronous!
}
$conn->wait_for_downloads;
$conn->disconnect;
```

See Also
`local` in this book

---

our

Usage

```
our variable
our(variable list)
```

Description

The our declaration causes Perl to recognize the variable as being a valid package variable within the enclosing block, file, or eval string. This is similar in function to the use vars declaration, and is most often used so that package variables can be used in the presence of use strict vars without having to be declared lexical with my or package-qualified.

If multiple variables are to be specified, the variable list must be enclosed in parenthesis. The our declaration also can be used as part of an initialization similar to my and local.

```
use strict;
{
    our $hand;
    sub hold {
        # This is okay.
        print $hand;
```

```
    }
}
print $hand;  # This throws an error at compile time
```

In the previous snippet, the first instance of `print $hand` is allowed by `use strict` because the variable `$hand` has been declared with `our` in the same block (or an outer enclosing block). The second instance will be disallowed because `$hand` is a plain package variable—not allowed under `use strict`.

Declaring a variable with `our` multiple times in the same lexical scope will cause a warning to be issued. However, if the declarations are in different packages (but the same lexical scope), no warning will be emitted.

The `our` declaration is the successor to the `use vars` pragma, and should be used instead of it. The major difference between `our` and `use vars` is that `our` follows lexical scoping rules (similar to `my`), whereas `use vars` affects the entire package that contains the declaration.

The differences between `our` and `my` are that `my` creates a new instance of the variable name each time it's seen at runtime, and `our` simply gives access to a package global variable that already exists.

Example Listing 1.18

```
# An example of a global variable being 'use strict' safe
#  without needing package-qualifiers everywhere.
# Save both examples, and run this one.

use OtherPkg;
use strict;

my $hide="Can't see me!";
our $seek="Here I am!\n";

OtherPkg::testsub();
print $seek;          # No package qualifier needed, just like my()!
```

Example Listing 1.19

```
# Save as OtherPkg.pm

package OtherPkg;
use strict;
```

```
sub testsub {
    print $main::seek;  # I can see it!
                    #    whereas $main::hide is invisible
                    #    from here.
}
1;
```

> **See Also**
> my and lexical in this book

Calling Subroutines

Usage

```
func args
func(args)
&func
&func(args)
```

Description

To call a subroutine in Perl, several syntaxes are allowed and each has its own idiosyncrasies. They have the following similarities:

- The arguments passed to subroutines are passed in the variable @_ (perl will insert them for you). These values are actually aliases to the real values in the caller. See the aliases entry.

- The context that the subroutine call appears in will be known by the subroutine (through the use of wantarray).

- The return value of the subroutine will be evaluated as any other expression— subroutine calls can be used in place of an expression.

Multiple arguments to subroutines are flattened into a single array @_ (except when a prototype says otherwise). This flattening happens to all arguments, regardless of type, thus

```
@boys=qw(greg peter bobby);
@girls=qw(marcia jan cindy);
@parents=qw(mike carol);
@misc=qw(alice sam tiger);
func(@boys, @girls);
```

appears within the subroutine func as a single array, @_, with 6 elements: greg, peter, bobby, marcia, jan, and cindy. To pass multiple arrays (or hashes) into a subroutine, you will have to pass references to those arrays:

```
func(\@boys, \@girls, \@parents, \@misc);
```

The same effect can be achieved using prototypes. See the prototype entry.

The chief differences between each of the function calling methods has to do with the way that the parser examines them and how arguments are ultimately passed to the called function.

syntax	key points
&func	Ignores prototype processing. Passes a caller's arguments along to the called subroutine. Compatible with Perl 4.
&func(*args*)	Ignores prototype processing. The args are passed in @_ as normal. Compatible with Perl 4.
func(*args*)	Not compatible with Perl 4. The args are passed in @_ as normal. Does not need a prior definition or declaration to be valid under strict subs.
func args	Not compatible with Perl 4. The args are passed in @_ as normal. Requires that the subroutine declaration or definition be seen prior to this statement; otherwise, strict subs throws an exception.

Another way to call subroutines is by -> notation, calling subroutines using the -> notation. This is further explained in the entry on calling methods. Subroutine names can always be package qualified to ensure that you're calling the correct subroutine name:

```
use Data::Dumper ();      # Contains a "Dumper" subroutine
sub Dumper {
    print "Surprise!\n";
}
&main::Dumper();        # Call mine for sure.
&Data::Dumper::Dumper();   # Call the module's version of Dumper()
```

Functions in Perl are allowed to call themselves or to call a function farther back in the call stack. This feature is called *recursion*. Perl will allow recursion until no memory remains to make another call. However, Perl will warn you after 100 recursions with: Deep recursion on subroutine.

Example Listing 1.20

```perl
sub func {
    print "Args: @_\n";
}
sub myfunc {
    @things=('thing one', 'thing two');


            # These each print:
    &func;          # Args: One two three
    &func(@things); # Args: thing one thing two
    func;           # Args:
    func @things;       # Args: thing one thing two
    func(@things);      # Args: thing one thing two
}
myfunc("One", "two", "three");
```

Example Listing 1.21

```perl
# Example of recursion: calculation of fibonacci
#    sequences (1, 1, 2, 3, 5, 8, 13, 21, 34...)
#    where f(n)=f(n-1)+f(n-2)
# Also demonstrates memoization, whereby a wrapper
#    function (memo_fib) is used to cache values.
#    This makes the calculations go faster by many
#    orders of magnitude for large fib(n).
{
    my %mem;
    sub memo_fib {
        my($val)=shift;
        return $mem{$val} if (exists $mem{$val});
        $mem{$val}=fib($val);
    }
    sub fib {
        my($val)=@_;
        return 1 if ($val==1 or $val==2);
        return memo_fib($val-1)+memo_fib($val-2);
    }
}
print fib(20);
```

> **See Also**
> aliases, prototypes, want array, context, and calling methods in this book

`exit`

Usage

```
exit expression
```

Description

The `exit` statement causes the running Perl program to `terminate` with expression as its exit value. If the expression is omitted, the exit value of 0 is used.

The exit value from a Perl program is often used by the caller (an operating system shell program, another program, and so on) to determine whether the Perl program performed successfully. Traditionally, an exit status of `0` indicates success and anything else indicates failure. Exit values are limited to 8 bits.

If the Perl program has an `END` block, that block will be run before the program terminates. Also, if there are any objects that have a destructor, those destructors will be called first. It's possible to bypass these mechanisms with the `POSIX:_exit` routine.

Example Listing 1.22

```
if ($success) {
    exit;
}
# Indicate failure
exit 1;
```

> **See Also**
> POSIX module documentation
> die, DESTROY, and END in this book

`if/unless`

Usage

```
if (expression)
    BLOCK
```

```
unless (expression)
    BLOCK

if (expression)
    BLOCK
else
    BLOCK

if (expression)
    BLOCK

elsif (expression)
    BLOCK

statement if expression;
statement unless expression;
```

Description

The if statement is used to express a decision, as well as evaluate an expression. If the expression is true, a block is run. For example, the following statement:

```
if ( $a == 1 ) {
    print "It's one.\n";
}
```

will only run the print statement if $a is equal to 1. The block in Perl must be a normal block, delimited with curly braces, containing zero or more statements to be evaluated. (This differs from C where the conditional statement might be followed by a single statement.)

The definition of truth (true/false) is discussed in the section "Boolean."

Additionally, if a block should be run if a statement is true and an alternate block run if the statement is false, the else clause can be used:

```
if ( $a == 1 ) {
    print "It's one.\n";
} else {
    print "It's Something Else\n";
}
```

The else clause requires a block of its own, just as the if, and must always be attached to an if statement as shown.

If several valid choices all require their own block, the first choice can be stated with an if statement and the alternate choices with an elsif statement:

```perl
if ( $a >= 1_000_000 ) {
    print "It's a big number.\n";
} elsif ($a <= 10 ) {
    print "It's a small number.\n";
} else {
    print "It's something in between.\n";
}
```

The previous snippet demonstrates the elsif clause in conjunction with else for a default block to be run. Multiple elsif clauses with blocks can string together in series.

With if/elseif/else clauses, each conditional expression is evaluated in turn. As soon as one evaluates true, the remaining condition tests and blocks are skipped.

Sometimes it's necessary to perform an action if something isn't true. This form is acceptable:

```perl
if ( not $x == 5) {
    print "Not five\n";
}
```

This is visually awkward with large expressions involving logical or, ands, and multiple expressions. It would be nice to state:

```perl
if ( $x == 5 and $y == 6 or $a > 12 ) {
    1;      # just a placeholder
} else {
    # Your interesting code here.
    print "Say it ain't so!\n"
}
```

This makes for ugly programs. A more ingenious solution is to use the unless statement. The unless statement works the same as an if, except the sense of the truth condition is reversed. The previous block could be stated more easily as

```perl
unless ( $x == 5 and $y == 6 or $a > 12 ) {
    # Your interesting code here.
    print "Say it ain't so!\n"
}
```

The `else` and `elsif` clauses can be attached to an `unless` statement, just the same as `if`. There is no `elsunless` keyword.

The `if` statement also can be used as a modifier to another statement, which will cause the statement to be run only if the conditional expression is true. This form resembles

```
statement if expression;
```

so that the typical statement

```
if (/^quit/) { last ; }
```

can be more concisely be written as

```
last if /^quit/;
```

The `unless` statement also can be expressed as a modifier to another statement.

See Also
Boolean in this book

`for/foreach`

Usage

```
for(list)
    BLOCK
for variable (list)
    BLOCK
for(initialization; test; increment)
    BLOCK

foreach(list)
    BLOCK
foreach variable (list)
    BLOCK
foreach(initialization; test; increment)
BLOCK
```

Description

The `for` statement has two basic forms, the three-part loop and the list-processing loop. The `foreach` statement is a synonym for the `for` statement—they can be used interchangeably.

```perl
for($i=0; $i<10; $i++) {
    print "$i\n";      # Print 0..9
}
```

The three-part loop consists of three expressions separated by semicolons. The three expressions normally correspond to the following:

- `initialization`—This is where variables are set up to begin the loop ($i=0 in the previous loop example).

- `test`—As long as this condition is true (or empty), the loop will continue to run ($i<10 in the loop).

- `increment`—This is used to change the values involved in the test so that the loop progresses ($i++).

The previous `for` loop also can be written in terms of `while`:

```perl
$i=0;
while($i<10) {
    print "$i\n";
} continue {
    $i++;
}
```

The `initialization`, `test`, and `increment` expressions don't have to resemble those shown previously. Absolutely anything can be used for any of those three expressions. For example, increment more than one variable with a loop as follows:

```perl
for ( $i=1, $j=1; $i++, $j*=2; $i<10) {
    # $i goes up by ones
    # $j goes up in squares
}
```

Any of the three components can be left out entirely as long as you provide for the same functionality in some other way:

```perl
# Assumes $i is initialized and incremented...
for( ; $i<10; ) {
```

```
    # ...
}
# Assumes there's some other way out of the loop
for(my $i=0; ; $i++) {
    #... (like last)
}
# An inifite loop
for( ; ; ) {
    # ...
}
```

A variable declared as lexical within the initialization of the for loop has a scope that extends for the remainder of the associated block. See the BLOCK entry.

The list-processing form of for uses a control variable, setting it in turn to each member of list and then executing the body of the loop. If the control variable is omitted, the variable $_ is used. The list processing version of for and the three-part version of for can be distinguished in Perl by the semicolons.

For example, the following code runs the body of the loop 10 times setting $i to 1, 2, 3, and so on in succession:

```
for $i (1..10) {
    print $i;
}
```

The control variable will be localized to the loop (as though you had declared it local), have a dynamic scope, and be visible from any subroutines called from the loop. If you declare the control variable with my in the for statement,

```
for my $name (keys %address) {
    print "Name: $name  Address: $address{$name}";
}
```

the control variable will have a lexical scope limited to the for statement itself and the attached block.

This localization can be used to create a one-element loop simply for the assignment-and-localization effects, for example,

```
for($text) {
    s/^\s+|\s+$//g;  # Remove leading/trailing whitespace
    s/([?.!])\s{3,}(\w)/$1  $2/g;   # Excessive punct. spacing
    s/([,;:])\s{2,}(\w)/$1 $2/g;    # Excessive punct. spacing
}
```

Another example of this is in the BLOCK entry.

The control variable (whether lexical or dynamic) is actually an alias to the values in the list being processed. Thus it's possible to change the list as you iterate over it as shown in the following:

```
# Using list return values in the loop.
while(<>) {                      # Read 'em
    for my $word (split) {       # Split 'em up
        $word=~tr/a-z/A-Z/; # Shift 'em up.
        # more...
    }
}


@vocab=qw(lincoln jefferson washington roosevelt);
foreach (@vocab) {
    $_=ucfirst;
}
print join(',', @vocab);  # gives Lincoln, Jefferson, etc..
```

Of course, the list must actually contain values that can be altered. If you're iterating over a literal list, changing the control variable within the loop will fail:

```
foreach ('amos','joshua','ezekiel','jacob') {
    s/$/ rowed the boat ashore\n/;
    # Modification of a read-only value attempted...
}
```

See the aliases entry for more info.

One shortcoming of the for list is that it's impossible to tell within the loop which position in the list is being evaluated. (Thus, you can't have the list elements and the index at the same time.) In this situation, it might be better to use a three-part for loop or to use a separate counter to keep track of the position:

```
@kids=qw(Kyle Stan Cartman Kenny);
# To have the value and the index
for(local($i, $_)=(0,);
    $i<@kids and $_=$kids[$i]; $i++) {
    print "$i $_\n";
}
# Or, possibly like this
{
    my $i=0;
```

```
    local $_;
    for(@kids) {
        print "$i $_\n";
        $i++;
    }
}
```

Similar to `while`, `until`, and `if`, the `for` and `foreach` constructs can be used as modifiers to another statement. The statement will be run instead of the body of a loop. This form of `for/foreach` resembles

```
statement for list; statement for (init; test; inc);
```

Doing a simple substitution on an array using this form might resemble the following:

```
# Change the well-known abbreviations to the full name
%abbrev=(  FBI => 'Federal Bureau of Investigation',
    CIA => 'Central Intelligence Agency',
    NSA => 'No Such Agency',);
$srch=join('|', keys %abbrev);

s/\b($srch)\b/$abbrev{$1}/ge for @data=<DATA>
```

Whether to use `for` or `foreach` is simply a style choice, and makes no difference to Perl. Typically, use the version that reads best in English. Throughout this book, the `foreach` statement is typically used to iterate over a list, and `for` is used when dealing with the three-part loop. The exception is when space is tight, and then `for` is used.

See Also
while and aliases in this book

---

while, until

Usage

```
while (expression)
    BLOCK
until (expression)
BLOCK
```

Description

The `while` statement executes the given BLOCK as long as the expression is true. The `until` loop works similarly, except that the BLOCK is executed as long as the given expression is false. Remember that in Perl, the BLOCK must contain opening and closing braces.

```
while( $defects < ALLOWABLE ) {
    $line=<BUGREPORT>;
    if ($line=~/status=open/i) {
        $defects++;
    }
}
die "Rotten product!" unless (eof BUGREPORT);
```

There is one special case for the expression in the `while` loop: If the expression is a `<>` operator, unadorned, with just a filehandle (or empty to use ARGV), the following loop:

```
while(defined ($_=<HANDLE>) ) {
}
```

can be more concisely written as follows:

```
while(<HANDLE>) {
}
```

Note that doing other processing in the `while`'s expression will disable this semi-magical feature.

The `$_` assigned to by `while` isn't localized to the loop. In order to have a localized `$_` for the loop, you must explicitly declare one:

```
while (local $_=<FILE>) {
    print;
}
```

But this still leaves `$_` subject to modification to subroutines called by the `while` loop. A lexical variable can be declared as part of the expression, and its scope extends to the end of the block.

```
while(my $line=<FILE>) {
    print;
}
```

Beware that both of these idioms will terminate early if the filehandle FILE happens to read a literal 0 without a newline character (a rather contrived situation, but it can happen).

The while statement also can be used as a modifier to another statement. This will cause the statement to be executed as long as the condition is true.

```
statement while expression;
```

This can be used to concisely write things that might otherwise require a loop:

```
print while <FH>;
$total+=$num while($num=shift @FOO);
```

The until statement also can be used as a statement modifier.

See Also
Boolean in this book

---

goto

Usage

```
goto label
goto expression
goto &subname
```

Description

Although rarely needed, Perl does have a goto statement. The goto statement transfers control of the program to somewhere else. That somewhere else depends on which form of goto is used.

In general, goto cannot be used to transfer control into a structure that requires initialization such as a for loop or a subroutine. You are allowed to use goto to transfer control out of these kinds of structures.

The goto label causes control to be transferred to the given label within the program.

```
L05: REM Yes Virginia, you can program BASIC in Perl too if 0;
L10: print "Hello, ";
L20: goto L10;
```

The goto expression form is similar, except that the label will be whatever the expression evaluates to at runtime. (This should be familiar to FORTRAN programmers.) Thus,

```
# pick one at random
goto (qw(one two three))[rand 3];
{
    one:    print "We're number one!";
        last;
    two:    print "We try harder!";
        last;
    three:  print "Show still pays 3:1!";
        last;
}
```

If the label cannot be resolved at runtime, an exception—Can't find label—will be thrown.

The final form is goto &*subname*, and it causes control to be transferred to the subroutine named as *subname*. The difficulty is that the call stack will no longer contain the current subroutine name. Thus,

```
sub second {
    print "Made it to second base.\n";
    return;
}
sub first {
    print "Made it to first base\n";
    goto &second;
    print "Made it back?\n";    # (Never comes back to here)
}
first();
```

will report that Perl has made it to first, and then to second. Control is never passed back to first because the goto &second replaced the call to first on the stack frame. Examining the call stack with caller within second won't even show first at all.

This is deemed highly magical and is primarily used by AUTOLOAD to load methods without leaving itself on the stack.

The goto statement is rarely, if ever, needed in Perl programming. The loop-control statements of redo, next, and last usually provide all the exception processing needed for goto label, and dispatch tables with hashes of subroutine references are used in favor of the goto *expression*.

See Also
AUTOLOAD in this book

grep

Usage

```
grep expression, list
grep block list
```

Description

The grep function evaluates the expression or the block (in boolean context) for each value in the list. The variable $_ is set to each value in the list as it's being evaluated. In a list context, grep returns those elements for which expression or block evaluated to true. In scalar context, grep returns the number of elements that evaluated to true.

```
if ( grep(/^[A-M]/, @names) > @names/2 ) {
    print "Namelist in \@names is front-heavy";
}
```

The value of $_ is localized to the expression (or block) as though it had been declared with local. Additionally, $_ is actually an alias to the value in list—this means that modifying $_ in the expression (or the block) causes the original list to change. In these ways, grep is very similar to the for statement.

The name grep comes from the Unix utility grep(1), which is used to search files for patterns.

Example Listing 1.23

```
# Get a list of regular files, no dotfiles either.

my $dir="/tmp";
opendir(D, $dir) || die;
my @files=grep { -f "$dir/$_" and !/^\./} readdir D;
closedir(D);
```

See Also
map, aliases, and Boolean in this book

map

Usage

```
map expression, list
map block list
```

Description

The map function evaluates the expression or the block in list context for every element in list. The variable $_ is set to each value in turn.

The return value of map in list context is the accumulated return values of the expression or block. In scalar context, the return value is the number of values returned by the expression or block.

```
# Each element in @wordlist is an array ref containing
#   each of the words for the corresponding line
@wordlists=map { [ split /\s+/ ] } @text;
```

The value of $_ is localized to the *expression (or block)* as though it had been declared with local. Additionally, $_ is actually an alias to the value in list—this means that modifying $_ in the expression (or the block) causes the original list to change. In these ways, map is very similar to the for statement.

```
# Create a hash keyed by day-of-week, value is sequence number
$i=0;
%days=map { ($_, $i++) } qw(Sun Mon Tue Wed Thu Fri Sat);
```

The true value of map comes in the capability to change the nature of the values being processed in the list, as opposed to grep, which must either return the original value or alter it. Also (as shown previously) map is handy for mapping a single value to many values within a list.

Example Listing 1.24

```
# An example of a Schwartzian transform, where a list is sorted
#   by values that are expensive to compute.  In this case, the
#   timestamps are all pre-computed by the outer map, sorted,
#   and the inner map restores the list to normal.
# This trick is familiar to shell programmers where a list to be
#   passed to sort(1) is prepended with the sort key, the list
#   is sorted with that key, and then the key removed with sed(1).
```

```
opendir(D, "/etc") || die;  # a large directory
@files=map { "/etc/$_" } readdir D;
closedir(D);

# The -M (stat) function is somewhat expensive.  To sort this
#   array calling -M for each file within the sort would be _very_
#   slow.
@files=map { $_->[1] }              # Convert back to original values
       sort { $a->[0] <=> $b->[0] } # Sort on the "interesting" half
       map { [ -M $_, $_ ] }        # Convert into value-pairs
       @files;                      # Original list (now read up...)

# Now @files is arranged most recently modified files first...
```

See Also
aliases and grep in this book

---

do (block)

Usage

do BLOCK

Description

The do statement causes Perl to run the statements contained within the BLOCK and return the value of the last expression evaluated.

The do statement is most commonly seen in conjunction with while or until. When while or until are used as a statement modifier, Perl will execute the code in the block once, and then evaluate the conditional statement.

```
do {
    $i++;
} while ($i < 100);
```

Note, do also can be used with a filename, but has a vastly different meaning. See the do file entry for details. Also, see the blocks entry for examples of do without while or until.

Example Listing 1.25

```
# Create a temporary filename
use Fcntl;
use POSIX qw(tmpnam);

# Repeat until we find an unused name
do { $name = tmpnam(); }
    until sysopen(TMPFILE, $name, O_RDWR|O_EXCL|O_CREAT);
```

> **See Also**
> do (file) in this book

do **(file)**

Usage

```
do filename
```

Description

The do function, when given a filename as an argument, will read the given file and
execute the code contained in it similar to a require or use. Historically, it was used to
include library code into Perl scripts, but it now has limited use.

The differences and similarities between do and require/use are as follows:

- The code located in the *filename* with do will be loaded and run in its own lexical
  scope. Lexical variables in the block enclosing the do will not be visible to the
  code read and executed.

- @INC and %INC will be searched and updated as with require and use.

- Multiple invocations of do 'file.pl' will cause file.pl to be read and parsed
  each time. The use and require directives will only compile the file once.

- The do function happens at runtime similar to require, but unlike use.

- If the filename cannot be read, the do function returns undef and sets the reason
  for the failure in $!. If the file can be read, but the perl within won't compile or
  throws an exception, do returns undef and sets $@ to the proper message much
  the same as eval. If all things go right, the file can be read and the perl runs
  without throwing an exception; do returns the value of the last expression
  executed.

Note that do appears twice in this book; the other entry is do (block), which is located with the flow-control constructs.

Example Listing 1.26

```
# Read a configuration file from a hidden directory
#   in your home.  Pull it in and run it.

$config="$ENV{HOME}/.app/config";
if (! do $config ) {
    if ($@) {
        die "Compiling/Running $config: $@";
    }
    if ($!) {
        die "Cannot read $config: $!";
    }
    die "Unknown";
}
```

See Also
require, use, and eval in this book

Loop Control Statements

Usage

```
redo
redo label
next
next label
last
last label
```

Description

The loop control statements allow you to force the next iteration of a loop, exit a loop, or redo the current iteration of the loop. Because of these, you should never need flag variables to exit outer loops from within inner loops or a goto statement.

Each loop control statement affects the innermost block in which it appears. The label is optional. If you want to control a block other than the innermost, you will need to specify which block with the label:

```
OUTER: while( func1() ) {
    foreach( @array ) {
        if ( tragedy() ) {
            last OUTER;  # Bail out altogether
        }
    }
}
```

The loop control statements cannot be used to re-run a block within an eval, do, map, or grep. They also cannot be used to control the blocks attached to an if statement or a subroutine. (See the blocks entry for examples of how to cheat these rules and do it anyway.)

The redo statement restarts the loop block again, without evaluating the conditional. The continue block, if present, is not executed.

The next statement causes the loop block to start again at the next iteration. The conditional is evaluated, of course. The continue block also is executed before the conditional is evaluated.

The last statement will cause the loop block to exit immediately. If there is a continue block, it is not executed.

Example Listing 1.27

```
# Cook up a file to remove comments, look for
#   continuation lines (Unix-style) and early EOF's

while(<FILE>) {
    # Skip blank lines
    next if /^\s*$/;

    # Takes lines that end in \ and appends the next line
    #   to it.
    redo if s/\\$// and $_.=<FILE>;

    # Artificial end of input...
    last if (/\x4/ or /\x1a/);  # Control-d or control-z

    push(@lines, $_);
}
# Process your data in @lines...
```

`continue`

Usage

```
loop statement
    BLOCK
    continue
BLOCK
```

Description

The `continue` block can be attached to the trailing block of the `while`, `until`, `for`, and `foreach` loop statements as well as bare blocks. The code within the `continue` block is run at the end of each loop iteration just before the loop conditional is about to be checked.

The following loop control statements affect whether the `continue` block will be run:

`last` will cause the continue block not to be run.

`redo` will cause the continue block not to be run.

`next` will cause the continue block to be run as normal.

Also, exiting the loop through other flow-control constructs (`goto`, `return`, `exit`, and so on) will cause the `continue` block not to be run.

A lexical (or dynamic) scope declaration in the loop statement extends to the `continue` block as well.

Example Listing 1.28

```
# Process a filehandle, keeping count of all lines
#    even skipped ones.
$lines=0;
while(<>) {
    chomp;
    next if /^\s+#/;   # Skip comments
    next unless length; # Skip blank lines
```

```
    # Your processing here
} continue {
    $lines++;
}
```

See Also
loop control statements in this book

Context

context

Description

Context in Perl refers to the property that many functions and operators recognize how they are being used and can change their operation depending on whether they were called in scalar, list, or void context. This is similar to a natural language in which words can take on different meanings depending on how they're used: "The troll was hairy," or "The teacher assigned a hairy math problem."

Perl has three major types of context: scalar, list, and void context. Context for an expression is supplied by its surroundings. For example, the following expression runs in a list context:

```
@cells=expression
```

The array on the left side of the assignment causes the right side to be evaluated in a list context. All the following assignments provide the right sides with list context:

```
@bands=qw(metallica winger acdc);
@jacksons[0..5]=qw( michael tito latoya jermaine janet );
%s_park=( kids => [ qw( kyle stan eric kenny ) ] );
@s_park{teacher}="garrison";
```

Because it's often seen with arrays, list context is sometimes (mistakenly) called array context.

Assignment with scalars causes scalar context to be given to the right side of the assignment:

```
# All of these right-hand sides are in scalar context
$a = myfunc();
$a[6] = int(22/7);
$a{caution} = ( $c, $d, $e);    # Scalar context too, beware!
```

Assignment isn't the only thing that can cause context. Most functions will cause their arguments to be in one context or another. The print function normally takes a list:

```
print LIST
```

Anything that's used as an argument for print will be set in a list context. Whether a function supplies a list or a scalar context to its arguments can be determined by looking up the function and noticing whether that particular argument is a list or something else. Individual arguments can all have different contexts. For example, join's usage is

```
join string, list;
```

If join is used as follows:

```
join(@delim, @foo);
```

@delim is evaluated in a scalar context and returns the number of elements. That number is used to join the values in @foo together. This isn't a very practical example, but then abusing join like this isn't very practical.

Array variables that occur in scalar context return the number of elements in the array (see arrays). However, there isn't a general rule that says functions and operators which return a list of values will act in any particular way in scalar context. This property of returning the number of elements only applies to array variables (unless otherwise documented).

On the same note, literal lists cannot appear in scalar context. The following resembles a list in scalar context:

```
$h=('apples', 'peaches', 'pumpkin pie');  # Beware!
```

However, it is actually three expressions that will all be evaluated individually, and the rightmost expression will be returned and assigned to $h. The variable $h will wind up with the value pumpkin pie and not 3 as you might expect.

Functions that act one way in scalar context and another way in list context have
been overloaded. An example of this is the `localtime` function. In a scalar context,
`localtime` returns the date formatted as a string:

```
$d=localtime;
print $d;   # prints something like: Wed Jan 10 21:02:54 2001
```

In a list context, the `localtime` function returns a nine element list with all the
components that make up a date (see the `localtime` function).

```
($day, $month, $year)=(localtime)[3,4,5];
```

It's impossible to guess how functions will behave in scalar and list context—you
simply have to look up the function in a reference. The behavior of a function in scalar
and list contexts might have nothing to do with each other.

The other major context in Perl is void context. Void context happens when a
function's return value will not be used. Perl will still run the operation that's in void
context, but will throw away the results. This can be wasteful if the function builds a
large return value and simply throws it away. When it can, Perl will warn of constants
and scalars in a void context:

```
use warnings;

$a=5;
$a;   # at compile time warns: "Useless use of a variable in a void context"
print "Hello, World";
```

Some values (0, 1, and certain barewords) will not generate a void context warning.

If Perl can determine that a value occurs in a void context, there are no side effects,
and it can be optimized away, it will do so. See the void example.

The word context also is used to describe some other kinds of context in Perl: such as
places where Perl expects numbers (*numeric context*), strings (*string context*), or truth
values (*boolean context*). Those are discussed in the section on scalar values and truth.

The `wantarray` function can be used by a user-defined function to determine in what
context it is being called and change its behavior. In this way, you can overload
functions based on context. See `wantarray`.

Example Listing 1.29

```
# Demonstrates some void warnings, and how
#    the interpreter will even remove some code if it's
```

```perl
#    completely useless.

use B::Deparse;
use warnings;
sub simplesub {
    $a;    # Throws a compile warning.
    77;    # Throws a compile warning and _vanishes_.
    $a=('foo', $a);  # Foo does the same.

    # This doesn't vanish or warn: it's the return value.
    0;
}

# This "approximately" prints the source code for
#    simplesub after its been parsed.
print "The sub is now:\n ",
    (B::Deparse->new)->coderef2text(\&simplesub);
```

Example Listing 1.30

```perl
sub mean {
    local $_;
    for my $i (@_) { $_+=$i };
    $_/@_;
}
# A function that will perform differently depending on
#    context.  In void context, it does nothing.
#    In list context, returns a hash-like thing with
#    the statistics name (mean, median, stddev) as a key
#    and the appropriate values.
#    In scalar context, returns a reference to that same hash.
sub statistics {
    # Void context, do nothing
    return unless defined wantarray;

    my @d=sort { $a <=> $b } @_;
    my %stats=( mean => mean(@d) );
    $stats{median}= (@d%2) ?  $d[@d/2] :
            mean($d[@d/2], $d[@d/2 - 1]);
    $stats{stddev}=do {
        my($m, $s)=mean(@d);
        for my $e (@d) { $s+=($m-$e)**2; }
        sqrt($s/(@d-1));
```

```
    };
    unless (wantarray) { return \%stats; }
    %stats;
}
```

> **See Also**
> wantarray and prototypes in this book

Boolean Context

Description

Boolean context isn't really a context similar to scalar, list, and void context. Rather, it's a special case of scalar context in which perl is attempting to determine whether an expression is true or false, for example,

```
if ( $t ) {
    print "true?  false?";
}
```

The variable $t is said to be in a boolean context.

Whether an expression evaluates to true or false is defined in perl as

The null string `""` is false.

The number 0, or the number 0 as a string (`"0"`), is false.

The undefined value (undef) is false.

Everything else is true.

A list of expressions and what they evaluate is as follows.

Expression	True or False?
0	False. The number 0 is false.
10	True. It's a nonzero number and, therefore, true.
9 > 8	True. Relational operators return true/false as you'd expect.

Expression	True or False?
-5+5	False. The expression is evaluated and reduced to 0, and 0 is false.
0.00	False. This is just another representation of 0, as are 0x0, 00, 0b0, and 0e00.
""	False. This is explicitly false.
" "	True. There's a space in the quotes, which means that they're not entirely empty.
"0.00"	True. It's already a string, but not "0" or ""; therefore, it's true.
"00"	True—for the same reason as "0.00".
"0.00" + 0	False. This expression, 0.00+0 is evaluated, the result is 0, and that's false.
(0,5,6,5)	True in scalar context (but not why you think).
(0,5,6,0)	False (in scalar context). This is just a series of scalars separated by the comma operator. The value of the expression is that of the rightmost term—0.

Arrays that appear in boolean context are evaluated as though they were in scalar context—and the value of an array in scalar context is the number of elements in the array:

```
@things=qw(whatchamacallits thingamabobs);
while ( @things ) {
    print "Yup, got some ", shift @things, "\n";
}
```

Lists do not have a boolean context—what appears to be a list is probably just a series of scalar values in parenthesis, separated by a comma operator. References always evaluate to true because the address represented by a valid reference cannot be 0.

Unlike other languages, Perl does not have a special constant value representing the value true (or one for false either).

Example Listing 1.31

```
# Program to reproduce the table seen above (roughly)

use strict;
use warnings;
my @tests=('0', '10', '9>8', '-5+5', '0.00', '""', '" "',
    '"0.00"', '"00"', '"0.00"+0', '(0,5,6,5)', '(0,5,6,0)');

foreach my $trial (@tests) {
    printf("%10s is ", $trial);
    # No warnings void is because the lists are using constants
    #    in a void context.  Unsightly!
    if ( eval qq/ no warnings 'void';
            if ($trial) { 1 } else { 0 }
          / ) {
        print "true\n";
    } else {
        print "false\n";
    }
}
```

See Also
if and while in this book

---

scalar

Usage

```
scalar expression
```

Description

The scalar function causes the given expression to be evaluated in a scalar context. This is used when the expression would have different results in scalar and list context, or when you're interested in the scalar result, and the expression happens to appear in an list context.

For example, the `localtime` function behaves differently in list context and scalar context. To print a nicely formatted timestamp, you need scalar context. The `print` function provides list context to its arguments. So this statement will not work:

```
print "The time is now: ", localtime, "\n";  # True, but garbled.
```

However, using the `scalar` function on `localtime` will have the right effect:

```
print "The time is now: ", scalar(localtime), "\n";  # Right!
```

Scalar context can be coerced through other means, such as string concatenation:

```
print localtime() . "";
```

But this tends to be messy and confusing to ascertain the intention of the original programmer during maintenance.

There is no `list` (or `array`) function in Perl. List context is supplied by a function, and there is generally no need to force list context on an expression.

Example Listing 1.32

```
my($t, $r)=(shift, <STDIN>);
```

See also
Context in this book

---

wantarray

Usage

wantarray

Description

The `wantarray` function determines what context the calling subroutine was called in: scalar, list, or void context. Using this, a function can change its return value based on the context similar to many built-in Perl functions.

In a list context, `wantarray` returns true. In a scalar context, the `wantarray` function returns false—but a defined value, `""`. In a void context it returns `undef`.

Example Listing 1.33

```perl
# sound_alikes uses a wordlist (/usr/dict/words) and the Text::Soundex
#   module to find words that sound like the given word.
# The first pass is _slow_.  Subsequent passes use cached values built
#   when sound_alikes is used in list context to speed things up.
# In void context, it does nothing.  In scalar it returns one sound-
#   alike word.  In list context it returns all of them.

use strict;
use warnings;
use Text::Soundex;
{
    my %word_to_soundex=();
    my %soundex_to_word=();
    sub sound_alikes {
        my($word)=@_;
        my $sound=soundex($word);
        local *DICT;
        return unless (defined wantarray);
        if (keys %soundex_to_word) {
            return unless exists $soundex_to_word{$sound};
            return @{$soundex_to_word{$sound}} if wantarray;
            return ${$soundex_to_word{$sound}}[0];
        }
        open(DICT, "/usr/dict/words") || die;
        while(<DICT>) {
            chomp;
            $word_to_soundex{$_}=soundex($_);
            return $_ if ($word_to_soundex{$_} eq $sound
                and $word ne $_ and not wantarray);
        }
        close(DICT);
        foreach(keys %word_to_soundex) {
            push(@{$soundex_to_word{$word_to_soundex{$_}}},
                $_);
        }
        return sound_alikes($word);
    }
}

my $word;
while(print("Word to find match: "),
```

```
        chomp($word=<STDIN>), $word) {
            print join(',', sound_alikes($word)), "\n";
    }
```

> **See Also**
> context in this book

Plain Old Documentation

Plain Old Documentation

Usage

```
=directive
```

Description

Plain Old Documentation (pod/POD) is Perl's method for embedding documentation in code. POD is a simple markup language, such as roff or HTML. (In fact, POD is easily explained in terms of HTML.)

POD directives begin at an = sign at the beginning of the line followed immediately by a POD directive. The directives are alphanumeric, all begin with a letter, and are outlined later.

Perl programs can have POD anywhere within the program: at the beginning, at the end, or interspersed with code. There might not be any POD, or there might be only POD and no program.

POD is processed by two different entities: the perl parser, and pod translators. The perl parser will ignore all text after a pod directive until the end of the file or the directive =cut is seen. So perl will throw out the POD and keep the program. This is an effective way to "comment-out" a large section of code.

```
=head1 My Program

This code doesn't do much but say "Hi".
The interpreter really doesn't see this.  It's ignored!

=cut

print "Howdy!";
```

POD translators do the opposite: They throw out your program and keep the POD. The POD is then reformatted for display, printing, or any other purpose you can imagine. All the POD markup is simply for the benefit of the translators. The POD translators come with Perl, and are all named starting with "pod".

The POD translators all follow a similar set of rules (some better than others) with regard to directives, markup and paragraph placement. All the following rules are merely guidelines for the translators.

POD translators deal with directives, paragraphs, and markup sequences. Paragraphs are simply text surrounded by a newline character (as though $/ were set to ""). They'll be displayed however their surrounding entity dictates. If there's no surrounding entity, they'll be displayed however seems reasonable for that translator.

Paragraphs that do not appear in column 0 (indented with spaces or tabs) will be considered verbatim and printed as is. None of the formatting codes (italics, bold, code) will work, and a < is treated literally.

The next POD entities are called *directives*. These are used to block off sections of the document and assign them to a purpose. These are similar to HTML's block entities such as <P>, <H1>, or <DIV>.

Some directives are containers for paragraph text (=pod, =item, =for) and some are self contained (=head).

Directive	Meaning
=pod	Marks the beginning of POD. No special formatting of enclosed text will be done.
=cut	Marks the end of POD. Everything afterward is considered program text.
=head1 text	A first-level heading, one that would be translated to <H1> if the document were translated to HTML. This would generally serve as the title for the document. The text which comprises the header must follow on the same line as the =head1 directive.
=head2 text =head3 text ...	Minor-level headings. These would be translated to <H2>, <H3>... by an HTML translator.

Directive	Meaning
=over level =back	The =over directive tells the translator that an itemized list is about to appear and to indent level spaces. Exactly how far over a space is and whether the translator obeys the level hint is up to the translator. The level is optional, and the translator should use reasonable indenting. However, many default translators issue a warning if it's omitted. The =back directive undoes the indenting turned on by =over.
=item type	Inserts an item of *type* into a bulleted list. The type can be a number (for a numbered list), a literal * (for a bulleted list) or text for a list that's itemized by name. Some parsers (pod2html) will take any number and produce a properly numbered list for the current level of indenting (pod2html). In fact, it ignores the number entirely.
=for translator =begin translator	The =for directive marks the paragraph as being for a specific translator. A =for html paragraph should only be parsed by an html POD translator (pod2html). A =for man paragraph should only be parsed by a man POD translator (pod2man). Using an unrecognized translator name will cause the text to be ignored. The special translator name comment is always ignored. The =begin directive is similar to =for, except that the range extends to subsequent paragraphs until the =end directive is seen.
=end translator	Ends the =for or =begin sequences for the particular translator.

Similar to HTML, POD also contains ways of marking off text that's within another block. This can be used for fine-grained formatting of text (bold, italics) or for more complex things such as document links.

Sequence	Meaning
`B<text>`	Marks text as bold. Used for emphasis, options, items in a text `=item`, and program names.
`I<text>`	Marks text in italics. Used for emphasis, script names, book titles and program names.
`C<text>`	Marks text as code. Usually appears in a monospace font.
`C<pathname>`	Indicates a file or directory name.
`C<text>`	Marks the text as having non-breaking spaces (that is, it should not be word-wrapped).
`C<link>`	Indicates a link to another document. The behavior of this varies greatly among translators.
`X<index_entry>`	Indicates an index entry reference should be made for this item. The behavior of this varies greatly among translators.
`Z<>`	A do-nothing directive. Used when a token against the left-edge of the document would cause confusion.
`E<char sequence>`	The character sequence is translated as follows: lt - a literal < gt - a literal > sol - a literal / (required in L<> by some translators) dec - The chr() of decimal number. The corresponding ASCII character will be replaced. entity— (html translators) will replace the entity as `&entity;`.

POD markup sequences can be nested:

```
=pod

Then use the command B<ls -l I<pathname>>.

=cut
```

If the <> delimiters are inconvenient (because of <>'s contained within the text), they can be `<<`*space* and *space*`>>` to provide alternative delimiters:

```
=pod
```

```
C<< while(<STDIN>) { } >>

=cut
```

You can use as many angle-brackets as necessary, as long as the number of opening and closing angle brackets match.

Example Listing 1.34

```
=head1 NAME

DoNothing - a sample program

=head1 SYNOPSIS

    DoNothing -l -n  "Your text here"

=head1 DESCRIPTION

This program does nothing more than demonstrate how a proper POD
document should be written for a program.  Other major headings
might include COPYRIGHT, SEE ALSO or ACKNOWLEDGEMENTS.

I'll have POD interspersed with code in a moment.

See?  This isn't hard at all.

=head1 ARGUMENTS

This program takes the following arguments:

=over 4

=item -l

Prints the name of the I<alphabetic> sponsor

=cut

sub letter {
    print "Sponsored by the letter ", chr(65+rand(26)), "\n";
}
```

```
=item -n

Prints the name of the I<numeric> sponsor

=cut

sub number {
    print "Sponsored by the number ", int(rand(21)), "\n";
}

=back

=head1 AUTHOR

Clinton A. Pierce, E<lt>clintp@geeksalad.orgE<gt>

=head1 BUGS

Undoubtedly.

=cut

#
# Main body of program
#
&letter;
&number
```

Basic Operators and Functions

Operator Precedence

Description

Operators in Perl have a precedence and an associativity. Precedence is the property that some operators in a given expression will evaluate earlier than others, and thus have a higher precedence. For example, in grade school you learned that

```
2+5*6-3
```

evaluates to 29 because * has a higher precedence than + or -. The same kind of rules extend to Perl so that you recognize that:

```
3 | 5 * 2
```

Means 11—3|(5*2)—instead of 14—(3|5)*2.

Operators have an associativity as well. Associativity is the rule for multiple operators of the same precedence to be executed either left first or right first given an expression. So for example, left associativity causes:

```
print 128>>3>>1;    # 128, shifted three, then shifted 1
```

to generate 8 (0b1000) as though it had been evaluated as (128>>3)>>1. But for right associativity, the evaluation happens starting at the right:

```
print ucfirst lc 'BANGLES';
```

This example prints Bangles: lc 'BANGLES' is run first, and then ucfirst is run on the result. That should make sense because for ucfirst to run first would be nearly nonsensical.

The operator precedence in Perl is complicated, but it is generally intuitive for the basic operators. The following table is in precedence order, with the highest precedence operators shown first.

Associativity	Operators
None	Terms and list operators
Left	->
None	++, --
Right	**
Right	unary ops: !, ~, \; unary + and -
Left	binding ops: =~, !~
Left	*, / %, x
Left	+, -, .
Right	named unary ops: my, goto, cos, and so on
None	>, <, <=, >=, lt, gt, ge, le
None	==, !=, <=>, eq, ne, cmp

Associativity	Operators
Left	&
Left	|, ^
Left	&&
Left	||
None	.., ...
Right	?:
Right	=, +=, -=, *=, /=, x=, .=, %=, &=, |=, ^=
Left	,, =>
Right	not
Left	and
Left	or, xor

Just as in algebra, parenthesis can always be used to alter the precedence of portions of an expression.

While on the subject of parenthesis, list operators and named unary operators will accept a parenthesized list as an argument. The items in parenthesis then have the highest precedence of all operators. The rule of thumb is, if it looks like a function, it behaves like a function. So list operators in Perl (such as print) are normally documented as functions—it tends to cut down on confusion; for example,

```
sqrt 5 * 5;   #  Really is sqrt (5 * 5)
sqrt(5) * 5;  #           (sqrt 5) * 5
sqrt +(5)*5;  #           sqrt (5 * 5)
```

Here, a unary + is used to indicate to Perl that the ()'s are simply there for mathematical precedence purposes and that (5) shouldn't be treated as the sole argument to the function sqrt.

A common mistake is

```
print (PI * $rad*2 ), " meters across.";
```

where the programmer expects both items to be printed, and they aren't. This is actually evaluated as follows:

```
(print (PI * $rad*2 )), " meters across.";
```

If warnings are enabled, Perl will inform you that `"meters across"` is actually a constant in a void context—it's being used as the second item in a series of scalars separated with the comma operator.

Unary operators have a higher precedence than most binary and other operators. This means that an expression such as the following:

```
$a=(stat $myfile?$myfile:$otherfile)[7];
```

wouldn't evaluate as you might hope because `stat` is a named unary operator (with high precedence) and absorbs `$myfile` before the ternary operator (lower precedence) has a chance to work. In fact, this gives a warning if warnings are enabled.

Assignment Operators

Usage

```
target = expression
target op= expression
```

Description

The assignment operator takes the value of an expression and stores it in a target location. The target must be a modifiable value (an `lvalue`), which is usually a variable or an `lvalue` subroutine.

The assignment operator returns the value assigned. So, the following expression evaluates to a value of 5:

```
$a=5;
```

This is useful when you need to assign and test a value at the same time:

```
while( $line = <FH> ) {
}
```

It's also useful for stacking assignments. The assignment operator is right associative, so the following assignments begin at the right:

```
$x = $y = $z = 0;
```

For list values, the assignment operator initializes a list (array, hash, and so on) and also returns the list assigned. A list assignment in scalar context returns the number of elements on the right side of the expression:

Basic Operators and Functions

```
$number=(@keys=keys %hash);
while(($key, $value)=each %hash) {
}
if (@words = m/(\w+)/g) {
}
```

For scalar values, the assignment operator can be a little more flexible. In general the following form (where *op* is any binary, two operand, symbolic operator):

```
target = ( target ) op ( expression )
```

can be re-written as follows:

```
target op= expression
```

This is nice shorthand for concise assignment statements. And it seems more natural to read the expression of

```
$i+=2;
```

as "add two to `$i`" rather than "take `$i`, add two to it, and store it back in `$i`."

There are some items to note with this syntax. First, the parenthesis are simply to show that the target and the expression are computed separately:

```
$x *= $y + 1;

# Is the same as:
#    $x = $x * ( $y + 1 );
# And not
#    $x = $x * $y + 1;
```

Second, the target expression is only evaluated once. This makes a difference if the evaluation of target has side effects caused by autoincrement operators, ties, and so on:

```
$a[$t++] += 2;
#  Not the same as:  $a[$t++] = $a[$t++] + 2;
```

The assignment operator in Perl produces a valid `lvalue` as well. This looks something similar to the following:

```
($a=$b)+=3;
```

This has the effect of assigning $b's value to $a and then incrementing $a's value by 3. This is most often seen with the bind operator, where:

```
($lowercase=$original)=~tr/A-Z/a-z/;
```

performs the assignment from $original to $lowercase, and then $lowercase is modified by tr.

Example Listing 1.35

```
# Sometimes it's nice to have here-documents indented to match
#    the indenting of the surrounding code.  This removes the
#    indenting.  Remember, the terminator must _still_ be against
#    the left edge.
($text = <<FIN) =~ s/^\s+//gm
    Fourscore and seven years ago our fathers brought
    forth upon this continent, a new nation, conceived in Liberty,
    and dedicated to the proposition that all men are created equal.
FIN
```

> **See Also**
> subroutine attributes in this book

Arithmetic Operators

Usage

```
operand * operand
operand + operand
operand / operand
operand % operand
operand * operand
operand ** operand
```

Description

I'm sure that you're familiar with most of the operators in this entry. The + (add), -, (subtract), * (multiply), / (divide), and ** (exponentiation) operators all work as you would expect. Note that the precedence of these operators also is what you'd expect from grade-school math.

Similar to most math operations in Perl, if the operands aren't already numeric values, they will be converted to numeric values before the operation takes place. For values that don't convert to numbers directly, 0 will be used instead and a warning issued (if warnings are enabled).

Division is done in floating point, unless the `integer` pragma is in effect for this block. If division by zero is attempted, an error will be thrown. (This can be trapped with `eval`.)

The modulo operator works by first changing the operands into integers and then does integer division. The remainder from the division is then returned.

The exponentiation operator uses the C library's `pow(3)` function, which uses logarithms to calculate the necessary value. If given a first operand that is negative and a second operand that isn't an integer, `nan` (not a number) will be returned.

Example Listing 1.36

```
# Standard leap-year calculation -- guaranteed Y2K compliant.  :)
if (( $year % 4 == 0 and $year % 100 != 0) or ( $year % 400) ==0) {
    print "Yup, it's a leap year.";
}
```

See Also
precedence in this book

Autoincrement and Autodecrement

Usage

```
variable--
--variable
variable++
++variable
```

Description

The autoincrement operator allows you to express the simple statement:

```
$a=$a+1;
```

More concisely as

```
$a++;
```

It simply adds one to the existing value of the scalar variable and stores it back into the scalar variable. The autoincrement also can be expressed as follows:

```
++$a;
```

The primary difference between having the ++'s before the value to be changed (a pre-increment) and after the value (a post-increment) is the value returned by the expression.

A pre-increment of ++$a first notes the value in $a, adds 1 to it, stores the new value in $a, and then returns the new value. A post-increment of $a++ notes the value in $a, adds one to it, stores the new value in $a, and then returns the original value.

```
$a=5;
$c=$a++;    #  $c is 5, post-increment
$b=5;
$d=++$b;    #  $d is 6, pre-increment
```

Autodecrement works similarly, except that 1 is subtracted from the variable.

The autoincrement operator has one additional property: if given a string that matches the regular expression /$[a-zA-Z]*[0-9]*$/, it will increase the string as though the letters were digits, as shown in the example.

The autodecrement operator will work only on numeric values.

Of note is that Perl formally declares its autoincrement and autodecrement operators to work as in C. This means that some of the oddities of C's behavior have been replicated in Perl. One effect is that using an autoincrement or autodecrement on a variable, and then using the variable again in the same expression leaves the value in the other instances undefined (as in "not known," not undef); for example,

```
$a[$i]=$i++;
```

This does not have a defined behavior—the value of $i can either be the old value or the new value of $i. This conforms to the ANSI C (Sec 3.3) standard.

Example Listing 1.37

```
# A utility resembling split(1) in Unix.  It splits large
#   files into sections by lines or by bytes. Arguments are:
```

Basic Operators and Functions

```perl
#    -b specify how many bytes for each file
#    -l specify how many lines for each file
#    -p a prefix to use, not valid with multiple filenames to split
#    the remaining arguments are processed as files to split.
# A couple of places autoincrement is used, one "magical" one mundane.

use strict;
use warnings;
use Getopt::Std;
my(%opts, $lines);
getopts('b:l:p:', \%opts);
{
    my($app, $file);
    sub opt_open {
        if (! @_) { $app="aa"; $file=$ARGV[0]}
            else { $app++;}    # "magical", aa, ab, ac...
        return unless ($opts{p} or $file);
        open(my $fh, ">" .
            ($opts{p}?"$opts{p}$app":"${file}_$app")) || die;
        $lines=0;
        select($fh);
        $/=\$opts{b} if ($opts{b});  # For exact-length reads.
        return $fh;
    }
}
my $handle=opt_open();
while(<>) {
    print;
    $lines++;
    if (eof && @ARGV && not $opts{p}) {
        $handle=opt_open();
    } elsif ( ($opts{b}) or ($opts{l} and $opts{l}<=$lines)) {
        $handle=opt_open(1);
    }
}
```

See Also
math operators and overloading in this book

String Operators

Usage

```
string x count
(list) x count
string . string
```

Description

The x operator is the repetition operator. In scalar context, the string is repeated count times. The following puts 80 -'s in $line:

```
$line="-" x 80;
```

In list context, and when the list is surrounded with parenthesis, the repetition operator returns the list repeated count times, resulting in the following:

```
@text=("\n") x 25;   # Sets @text to 25 empty lines
@deck=(1..13) x 4;   # Creates a list suitable for dealing
```

This also is handy for initializing hash and array slices:

```
open(WORDS, "/usr/dict/words") || die;
chomp(@wl=<WORDS>);
# Create a hash of the words, setting each to 0
@words{@wl}=(0) x @wl;
```

The . operator is used to concatenate strings together. If the operands aren't in their string representation (references and numbers might not be), they will be converted to strings before concatenation:

```
print $obj->salutation . " $name, \n" . $obj->body;
```

For simply combining literals and variables, just use them in a double-quoted string—it's more straightforward and easier to read:

```
# not too grand
print "Dear, " . $name . ",\n\n How are you today?\n\nLove,\n" . $me;
# Better
print "Dear, $name,\n\nHow are you today?\n\nLove,\n$me";
```

> **See Also**
> join, arrays, and hashes in this book

Basic Operators and Functions

Quote Operators

Usage

```
qw()
qx()  / ``
qq()  / ""
q()   / ''
```

Description

Quotes in Perl provide grouping and interpolation function, and are actually considered operators (circumfix operators, if you will). Perl provides the following quotation characters:

Standard	Alternative	Meaning
''	q{}	Grouping of literals with no interpolation
""	qq{}	Grouping of literals with interpolation
``	qx{}	Run the enclosed command with interpolation
	qw{}	Literal word list, no interpolation

Quotes can begin and end on different lines of code in your programs. Thus:

```
$l=q{There once was a man from Nantucket,
    Who kept all his cash in a bucket.
    His daughter named Nan,
    Ran away with a man.
    And as for the bucket, Nantucket.};
```

The entire limerick will be placed in $l, including all the newlines and the leading spaces in front of the last four lines.

Interpolation means that the following items are converted to their real values within quotes:

- Scalar variables: `$height="100ft"; print "The balloon went $height high!";` # prints, The balloon went 100ft high!

- Individual hash and array elements. `$help="Please call $number{emergency} for assistance"; for($i=0; $i<10; $i++) {  print $i+1, ". $topten[$i]\n"; }`

- Entire arrays, if they've been mentioned beforehand. The elements will be joined by the character in $". If not previously mentioned, Perl throws a warning @foo must now be written as \@foo, thinking you're interpolating an array when you really meant an Internet e-mail address such as "me@foo.bar.zz".

- Special characters such as \n, \t, and \b. See the special characters entry for a full list.

Function calls do not interpolate in quotes. However, Perl can be fooled into doing interpolation with this trick:

```
print "The time is now @{[ scalar(localtime) ]}, BEEEP!";
```

The @ introduces an interpolation, and the {}s indicate that a block is going to return an array reference (for @ to de-reference). The []s provide that array reference. The anonymous array contains the result of running the enclosed code. This can be used to run any arbitrary code in an interpolated situation.

Beware of the ' character within double-quoted strings near variables that will be interpolated. The ' is a separator for package names and the following:

```
print "$name's desk is cluttered";
```

will interpret $name's as $name::s—which probably isn't what you'd planned on. Instead, use {} to contain the variable:

```
print "${name}'s desk is cluttered";
```

Within a set of quotes, the quote delimiters (', ", {, and so on) can be included as part of the quoted string by preceding them with a backslash character so that:

```
print 'This is Sri's desk';     # WRONG, unbalanced quotes...print
 'This is Sri\'s desk';   # Right way of handling!
```

The alternative quote marks allow you to pick your own delimiters. This makes it convenient when you have a string that contains the delimiters, but you don't want to go backslash happy:

```
# Acceptable but messy
$html="<INPUT TYPE=TEXT NAME=\"WHO\" VALUE=\"$me, silly\">";

# Easier on the eyes
$html=qq{<INPUT TYPE=TEXT NAME="WHO" VALUE="$me, silly">};
```

In the preceding examples, the qq{}, q{}, qx{}, and qw{} operators are all using {} as the delimiters. You actually can use almost any delimiter that you want (but not whitespace). So each of these is valid:

```
print q.She got up this morning.,
      qq-And went to $mall Mall.  There She met -,
      join(',', qw*Bob Carol Ted Alice and*),
      qx# whoami #, "\n"
```

Use whatever delimiters you think look best. Some things to note are as follows:

- Be consistent.

- The delimiter ' will cause interpolation not to happen, even for those operators that normally perform interpolation. Thus with qq'$foo', $foo will not be expanded to its value.

- Whitespace between the quote operator and the delimiter is allowed, unless you choose # as a delimiter:

  ```
  $opinion=q %The Lions are a poor team this year%;
  #
  # introduces a comment here.
  $reply=q # Don't think so, Jack! #
      ( I respectfully disagree. ); # The real string
  # # Is the quote delimiter here.
  $counter=q#But the statistics never lie...#;
  ```

- Delimiters that don't normally come in pairs (as <>, {}, (), and [] do) need to be matched and not appear within the quoted string itself (unless they're preceded by a backslash, of course).

- Matched-pair delimiters (<>, (), {}, []) can be nested as long as they're balanced (a closer for every opener). Thus these are legal and work as you'd hope:

  ```
  print q(I (meaning me) would really like (no, love) some cake.);
  print q<<script language="javascript">alert("bug!");</script>>;
  ```

- The ' ' and q{} operators do no interpolation. Enclosed backslashes represent backslashes. If a backslash is followed by the delimiter (' or whatever works with q{}) or another backslash, the delimiter or the backslash is inserted literally.

- The " " and qq{} operators do interpolation as noted previously.

- The `` and qx{} operators take the enclosed command and hand it to your command processor for execution. In Unix, this is the Bourne Shell (/bin/sh) or the equivalent. Any shell syntax (redirection, pipes, background tasks, newlines, and so on) will all be passed through to the shell for processing.

- Beware that the qx{} (``) operator performs interpolation, so trying to reference shell variables in the command might require some backslashing or a good choice of delimiters:

```
$list=qx{ls -l $HOME};  # Perl's $HOME -- probably not what you meant
$list=qx{ls -l \$HOME}; # Better!
$list=qx'ls -l $HOME';  # Good too!
```

- Normally STDOUT from the command is returned by the qx{} operator, as shown in the following. If STDERR is required, or both STDOUT and STDERR, shell redirection might be necessary:

```
$clean =qx(/bin/mycmd 2>/dev/null);     # STDOUT only
$output=qx(/bin/mycmd 2>&1);            # Capture STDOUT and STDERR
$errors=qx(/bin/mycmd 2>&1 1>/dev/null); # STDERR Only
```

- Under other operating systems (such as DOS/Windows), the command processor might be different. For example, under Windows NT, CMD.EXE is used as the command processor. Determining what is valid command processor syntax for these systems is left as an exercise for the reader.

- In scalar context, the qx{} (``) operator returns the entire output of the command as a single string. If there are multiple lines of output, they will be properly joined with newline characters. In list context, each line of output from the command is an element in the returned list.

- Before a command is run with qx{}, any filehandles opened for output are flushed before the command is run.

- The qw{} operator simply provides a convenient way to create a list of words ready to use without the trouble of quoting barewords or commas. So,

```
qw(homer marge maggie)
```

is equivalent to the following in all respects.

```
('homer', 'marge', 'maggie');
```

It's simply easier to type and read. Some examples of the qw() operator are

```
use CGI qw(:form -nph);
@days{qw(Sun Mon Tue Wed Thu Fri Sat)}=(0)x7;
use IPC::SysV qw(IPC_CREAT IPC_STAT);
my @chars=qw(Opus Milo Binkley Oliver);

@first=qw(1989, 4.5, 4.7, 4.9, 5.1);
```

- Inserting a comma or a # into the list will cause Perl to issue a warning. Also, you cannot use qw{} for words that have embedded whitespace.

See Also
$", $/, packages, and string literals in this book

Bit Operators

Usage

```
~ operand
operand ^ oeprand
operand | oeprand
operand & operand
operand >> operand
operand << operand
```

Description

The operators listed in this entry all perform operations on the individual bits of a number. Many of them perform similar functions on strings. The operators assume that you have at least 32-bit integers (the smallest that Perl supports). However, on 64-bit architectures, 64 bits will be used.

This also is one of the few cases in which Perl cares whether a variable contains a number that is really a string and vice versa. If you're unsure whether Perl is going to treat a variable as a number (or as a string), you can add 0 to the string (to ensure number-ness), or concatenate a null string to is (to ensure string-ness), or use "it" in double quotes:

```
$t="123.90";   # Definitely a string.
$t+=0;         # Now perl will treat it as a number.
$t="$t";       # Now perl will treat is as a string again
```

With the binary bitwise operators (everything except ~, >>, and <<) if either operand is a number, the other operand is converted to a number (if necessary) before the operation begins.

The ~ operator performs bitwise negation on numbers. All the 1s become 0s and vice versa (1s complement). The reply is directly related to the number of bits available on your architecture. One useful value can be obtained from ~0—the number of bits on your architecture.

```
 ($shift,$v)=(8,~0+1);
until(($v>>=8) == 0) {          # Better be a multiple of 8  :)
    $shift+=8;
}
print "# of bits: $shift\n";    # On my machine, 32.
```

If the ~ operator is used with a string as an operand, a string is returned with every bit complemented. This can be used to flip bits portably because the word size of your architecture isn't involved. Use pack to prepare a string that contains a structure and uses the ~ operator to flip all the bits in the entire structure at once.

The operators &, |, and ^ represent AND, OR, and XOR (exclusive OR), respectively. On numbers, they work as expected, and the values work out to something similar to the following table:

First operand Bin (dec)	Second Operand	Results
000 (0)	000 (0)	AND 000 OR 000 XOR 000
000 (0)	001 (1)	AND 000 OR 001 XOR 001
000 (0)	010 (2)	AND 000 OR 010 XOR 010
000 (0)	011 (3)	AND 000 OR 011 XOR 011
001 (1)	001 (1)	AND 001 OR 001 XOR 000
001 (1)	010 (2)	AND 000 OR 011 XOR 011
001 (1)	011 (3)	AND 001 OR 011 XOR 010
010 (2)	010 (2)	AND 010 OR 010 XOR 000
010 (2)	011 (3)	AND 010 OR 011 XOR 001
011 (3)	011 (3)	AND 011 OR 011 XOR 000

On strings, the operators will perform the operations on each byte of the strings. If one of the strings is shorter than the other, 0 bits will be padded onto the shorter string to make up the difference. This yields something vastly different from numeric OR, AND, or XOR. An example of this is shown in the encryption example at the end of this entry.

The | operator is frequently used to combine flags together for sysopen, fcntl, waitpid, or other stdio calls that take a generic options argument:

```
sysopen(FH, $logfile, O_WRONLY | O_CREAT | O_APPEND)
```

The >> and << operators perform a bit shift on their operands. They return the value of the left operand shifted by the number of bits specified on the right.

```
print 32 >> 2;   # Yields 8: 100000 -> 001000
print 3 << 4;    # Yields 48: 011   -> 110000
```

The >> causes the bits to be shifted to the right (with the least significant bits being dropped as needed) and the << operator causes the bits to be shifted to the left (with 0s being filled in for the now vacant bit positions.

Example Listing 1.38

```
# This uses a bitwise-xor to produce a cypher that's actually
#   unbreakable, providing that:  1. the keystring remains
#   secret  2. the message isn't longer than the keystring
#   3. more than one message is never encoded with the same
#   keystring. 4. Your keystring is fairly random (mine isn't great).
# How does it work?  XORing a bit sequence against another (the key)
#   will result in a third bit sequence.  Taking that third and
#   XORing it against the key again will give the original bit
#   sequence.  Isn't XOR grand?  :)

use strict;
use warnings;
# Some random gibberish.
my $keystring="It is by caffeine alone I set my mind in motion.".
        "It is by the Coca-Cola that the thoughts acquire speed, ".
        "the hands acquire shaking, the shaking becomes a warning.".
        "It is by caffeine alone I set my mind in motion.";
sub encode {
    my($plaintext)=@_;
    my($lp,$lk)=(length $plaintext, length $keystring);
```

```
        # Fix it so that the key is the same length as the string
        my $shift=$keystring x ($lp>$lk ? $lp/$lk : 1);
        $shift=substr($shift, 0, $lp);

        $plaintext ^ $shift;
    }
    # Alias decoding to encoding, they're really the
    #    same operation.
    *main::decode=*main::encode;

    my $encoded=encode("This is a sample"); # $encoded is a mess...
    my $plaintext=decode($encoded);
    print $plaintext;              # Will come back with original.
```

Example Listing 1.39

```
# Generates the previous table that demonstrates AND, OR and XOR

for my $f (0,1,2,3) {
    for my $s (0,1,2,3) {
        next if exists $seen{"$f$s"};
        $seen{"$f$s"}=$seen{"$s$f"}=1;  # Eliminate mirrors
        printf "%03b (%d) op %03b (%d)\t" .
                "AND %03b\tOR %03b\tXOR %03b\n",
            $f, $f, $s, $s, $f&$s, $f|$s, $f^$s;
    }
}
```

Conditional Operator

Usage

expression1?expression2:expression3

Description

The conditional operator evaluates *expression1*. If that is true, *expression2* is evaluated and returned; otherwise *expresssion3* is evaluated and returned. It's similar to the if statement:

```
if (expression1) {
    expression2
```

```
} else {
    expression2
}
```

except that the result of the conditional operator is an expression, and can be used anywhere that an expression is expected; for example,

```
$z=($x > $y) ? $x : $y;   # $z is set to the greater of $x and $y
```

The parenthesis around *expression1* usually aren't necessary because the conditional operator has very low precedence, but they are recommended for clarity. On the subject of clarity, nesting conditional operators deeply can quickly render code quite unreadable (see the example).

The conditional operator also is called the `ternary` (or `trinary`) operator.

Example Listing 1.40

```
# A fairly complex relationship being established as a
#    conditional expression:
$prophet=$jewish?
        $old_testament?
            "elijah":
            "john the baptist"
    :
    $muslim?
        $last?
            "mohammed":
            "abraham"
        :
        $fictional?
            "exidor of venus":
            undef;

# Probably better expressed some other way, perhaps as a
#    hash structure.
```

> **See Also**
> `if` in this book

Relational Operators

Usage

```
operand1 relop operand2
```

Description

The relational operators in Perl are fairly straightforward. Keep in mind that Perl has two sets of them: one for comparing string values and one for comparing numeric values.

Numeric	String	Meaning
>	gt	operand1 is greater than operand2.
<	lt	operand1 is less than operand2.
>=	ge	operand1 is greater than or equal to operand2.
<=	le	operand1 is less than or equal to operand2.
==	eq	operand1 is equal to operand2.
!=	ne	operand1 is not equal to operand2.
<=>	cmp	Comparison of operand1 and operand2 (see the following).

The comparisons (except for the comparison operator) all return "" for false and 1 for true. The operands are both evaluated in a boolean context. The operators are nonassociative, meaning that comparisons such as the following are illegal:

```
$a > $b > $c
```

Additionally, the equality operators (==/eq, !=/ne, <=>/cmp) have lower precedence than the other relational operators so that expressions such as this are valid:

```
$a > $b == $c < $d
```

If a numeric comparison operator is used, warnings are in effect. If one of the operands clearly isn't numeric, a warning will be issued:

```
$c=" ";
$d=3.1415;
if ($c > $d) {  # throws: Argument " " isn't numeric...
    #...
}
```

String comparisons are made in ASCII collating order, and trailing whitespace is significant. If a `locale` directive is in effect, collating order is influenced by the current locale.

The comparison operators (`<=>` and `cmp`) return either s, 0, or 1 depending on whether *operand1* is less than, equal to, or greater than *operand2*, respectively. See the `sort` entry for some potential uses for this.

See Also
sort and if in this book

Logical Operators

Usage

```
operand && operand
operand || operand
! operand
operand and operand
operand or operand
operand xor operand
not operand
```

Description

The operators in this entry are the logical operators in Perl. Most of them are derived directly from C. The operands given to them are evaluated in boolean context and the truth of the expression is determined.

Operator (high precedence)	Operator (low precedence)	Meaning
&&	and	True if both operands are logically true.
||	or	True if either operand is logically true.
(n/a)	xor	True if either operand is true, but not both.
!	not	Reverses the sense of the expression: true becomes false, and false becomes true.

The && (and) and || (or) operators do not return simply true or false; they return the last value evaluated (which will be true or false). This can be used to select from a list of values for the first one that happens to be true:

```
# Sets $value to the first option that's true.
$value = $option1 || $option2 || $option3;
```

The ! and not operators perform logical negation if the operand is true, ! and not return false (""). If the given operand is false, they return true (1).

The logical operators are all short circuit operators. This means that as soon as the truth value of the expression can be determined, the expression will stop evaluating. Thus the logical operators can be used for flow control as well as simply truth determination.

```
open(F, "myfile") || die "Cannot open myfile: $!";
```

The previous idiom is very common in Perl and works because open will return true if it succeeds. For a logical OR to be successful, only one operand must be true. Because logical operators are evaluated left to right, the open is processed first. Further, if open is successful, there's no need to evaluate the die because the expression as a whole is known to be true.

This can be reversed also:

```
open(LOG, ">>/var/logfile") && print(LOG "HELP!") && close(LOG);
```

There are two versions of logical AND and OR: a high precedence and a low precedence version. These exist for two reasons: first, to reduce the line-noise look to Perl—and might be more readable in code than &&. Second, in Perl 5, functions don't require parenthesis and the following statement won't evaluate correctly:

```
open F, "myfile" || die "Cannot open myfile: $!";
```

Because || has a higher precedence than the list operator open, the statement evaluates as follows:

```
open F, ( "myfile" || die "Cannot open myfile: $!");
```

This clearly isn't what was intended. By simply using the low-precedence logical operators, this fault is corrected:

```
open F, "myfile" or die "Cannot open myfile: $!";
```

Example Listing 1.41

```
# Sample of part of a larger program that
#    reads a configuration value from 1. from a
#    command-line option -s 2. a file named
#    .pager in your home directory or 3. uses
#    a default value.

use strict;
use warnings;
use Getopt::Std;

my(%options, %Config);

getopts("s:", \%options);
my $defaultheight=25;
if (open(CONFIG, "$ENV{HOME}/.pager")) {
    while(<CONFIG>) {
        next unless /(\w+)\s+(.*)/;
        $Config{$1}=$2;
    }
    close(CONFIG);
}

my $height= $options{s}      # This doesn't work well
    || $Config{HEIGHT} #   for values of 0...
    || $defaultheight;
```

> **See Also**
> Boolean in this book

```
print
```

Usage

```
print
print list
print filehandle list
```

Description

The `print` function writes a list to the current selected `output` device or filehandle. This is the function through which most normal Perl output is written. The function returns true if the writing was successful and false if not.

The filehandle should be a filehandle as described in the `open` entry in this book. This means that it should be a plain identifier, or a scalar variable that references an `indirect filehandle`. Note that the filehandle is not separated from the list with a comma. Doing so will generate a compile-time error.

If a filehandle is not specified, `print` will use the currently selected default filehandle. This is normally `STDOUT`, but can be changed with the one-argument form of `select`.

If `print` is not given a list to print, the contents of `$_` will be written.

Because `print` takes a list as an argument and will accept an indirect filehandle as a first argument, some ambiguities can arise; for example,

```perl
open($fh, ">/tmp/foo.txt") || die;

print $fh length("Hello, World");   # Prints to filehandle
print $fh + length "Hello, World"; # Performs addition

close($fh);
```

These ambiguities should be resolved with parenthesis:

```perl
print $fh (+length "Hello, World");
```

Also keep in mind that `print` implies a list context on anything printed. Thus,

```perl
print localtime;
```

will display a nearly useless mix of numbers. If you wanted a formatted time to be written, force scalar context:

```perl
print scalar localtime;
```

If the variable `$\` is set, the contents of that variable will be appended at the end of the printed list.

Example Listing 1.42

```perl
# A small, correct CGI program
#
```

```
use CGI qw(:standard);

print header,
start_html('See?  Its easy!'),
h1('Hello, World!'),
hr;
```

> **See Also**
> context, $_, select, open, and $\ in this book

```
printf
```

Usage

```
printf filehandle format, list
printf format, list
```

Description

This function takes a list of elements, formats it according to the format specified, and writes it to filehandle. Upon success, true is returned. If an error occurs, false is returned and $! is set to the error message.

The printf function essentially implements print *filehandle* sprintf *format*, *list*, but more concisely.

If the filehandle is omitted, the currently selected filehandle is used. A filehandle can be an opened identifier or a scalar variable that has a reference to a filehandle-like object. See the print entry for details.

The format is described extensively in the sprintf entry.

Example Listing 1.43

```
  ($name, $balance)=("clinton", 0);
printf "%-10s %5.2f", $name, $balance;
```

Example Listing 1.44

```
# Prints a nicely-formatted 2-column report
#    of the configuration options used to
#    build perl.
use Config;
```

```perl
$pagewidth=79;
$maxkey=0;

foreach( keys %Config) {
    $maxkey=$maxkey>length $_?$maxkey:length $_;
}
$template=sprintf("A%d", $pagewidth-$maxkey-2);

for $param (sort keys %Config) {
    $_=$Config{$param}||"";
    @data=unpack( $template x
        (1+(length $_)/($pagewidth-$maxkey-2)), $_);
    for(@data) {
        printf "%*s  %s\n", $maxkey, $param, $_;
        $param="";
    }
}
```

> **See Also**
> print and sprintf in this book

sprintf

Usage

sprintf *format*, *list*

Description

The sprintf function takes a list of arguments, plugs them into a format, and returns a properly formatted string. This is nearly identical to the standard C library function sprintf. (The native C library sprintf is not used however, so any format specifiers particular to your architecture will not be available.)

The format is a scalar value that contains literal text and format specifiers. Format specifiers each begin with a percent sign, and then a few characters to describe how the field should be rendered. Each specifier then absorbs one item from the list, and formats it properly as part of the string, as the following statement shows:

```perl
$c=sprintf("%s's interest rate is %5.2f", $bank, $rate);
```

Basic Operators and Functions

The first format specifier is `%s` and will use the value in the variable `$bank`, and the second format specifier `%5.2f` will use the value in the variable `$rate`. The remaining text in the format will be returned as is.

There should always be a 1-to-1 correlation between elements in the list and format specifiers in the format. (Exceptions to this are if `*`s appear in the modifiers; or a field specifier of `%n` is used—technically it is used, just not returned.)

The format specifiers currently supported in Perl are as follows:

Specifier	Meaning
`%%`	A literal percent sign.
`%c`	The character (that would be returned by `chr`) represented by the value given.
`%s`	A string.
`%d`	A signed decimal integer.
`%u`	An unsigned decimal integer.
`%e`	A floating point number in scientific notation (for example, -2.45e-09).
`%s`	A string.
`%d`	A signed decimal integer.
`%u`	An unsigned decimal integer.
`%e`	A floating point number in scientific notation (for example, -2.45e+09).
`%E`	Similar to `%e`, except with an uppercase "E."
`%f`	A floating point number in decimal notation (for example, 3.14159). Decimal points are formatted according to the LC_NUMERIC locale, if `use locale` is in effect.
`%g`	A floating point number in `%e` or `%f` notation. The style chosen depends on the size of the exponent and the precision used.
`%G`	Similar to `%g`, except with an uppercase "G" if used.
`%x`	An unsigned integer in hexadecimal format.
`%X`	An unsigned integer in hexadecimal format (Uppercase).

Specifier	Meaning
%o	An unsigned integer in octal format.
%b	An unsigned integer in binary format.
%p	The address of the element in hexadecimal.

There are a few odd format specifiers that nonetheless must be explained. The format specifier %n stores the current count of the returned characters (at that point) into the next element in the list.

```
# returns "Hello, World has 12 characters"
$p=sprintf("%s%n has %d characters", "Hello, World", $t, $t);
```

The format specifiers %i, %D, %U, %O, and %F are equivalent to %d, %ld, %lu, %lo, and %f, respectively and are in Perl for compatibility reasons (mostly so that C programmers don't feel lost).

Within the format specifier, modifiers can be used to alter the appearance of the formatted values.

Modifier	Meaning
0	Zero-fill the number to the left.
-	Left-justify the value in the field (default is right justify).
space	Positive numbers preceded with a space.
+	Positive numbers preceded with a plus sign.
#	Prefix octal numbers with a zero, hexadecimal numbers with 0x.
width	Total width of the field (for example %5d).
.precision	Number of digits after the decimal point for floating point numbers (zero padded); for strings it's the total length of the field (truncated), and the minimum length of the field for integers (zero filled).
l	Field should be treated as a native C long or unsigned long.
h	Field should be treated as a native C short or unsigned short.
*	The next element in the list should be taken as a number either in the position of a width, precision, or both (see examples).

If 64-bit integers are supported by your architecture (and Perl was built with that support), the integer format specifiers can be preceded with ll, L, or q to return a full 64-bit number. Long doubles (if supported by your architecture and Perl was built to support them) can be used by preceding the floating-point specifiers with ll or L.

Example Listing 1.45

```
# Exercise a few of the format specifiers
#

$ay=65;
$pi=3.1415926;
$mole=6.022e23;
$name="Avagadro, Amelio";

print sprintf("%.8s's Number is number of particles contained in %c
mole of a substance and is equal to %g (or roughly %12.0f)\n",
    $name, $ay, $mole, $mole);
print sprintf("Despite efforts to the contrary pi is still closer
to %6.4f than to %d\n",
    $pi, $pi);
print sprintf("Decimal: %d  Hex: %x  Octal: %o  Binary: %b\n",
    $ay, $ay, $ay, $ay);

print sprintf("%*.*f\n", 4, 2, $pi);    # Gives 3.14, same as %4.2f

%acct=( smith => 1523.12, jones => 122.14, lee => 1231.4);
while(my($name, $bal)=each(%acct)) {
    # right-justify names, left justify money.
    # cut off names at 10.
    print sprintf("%10.10s   \$ %7.2f\n", $name, $bal);
}
```

> **See Also**
> printf in this book
> sprintf in the C library reference

Trigonometric Functions

Usage

```
sin angle
sin
cos angle
cos
atan2 y, x
```

Description

These functions provide access to your native math library's trig functions. If you have compiled Perl for long double support, the appropriate functions (atan2l, sinl, and so on) will be used instead.

The sin function returns the sine of angle, where angle is expressed in radians. The value returned will be a number between -1 and 1. The arc sine can be computed with atan2(angle,sqrt(1-angle*angle)).

The cos function returns the cosine of angle, where angle is expressed in radians. The value returned will be a number between -1 and 1.

For sin and cos, if an angle is not supplied, $_ is used.

The atan2 function will return the arc tangent of y and x (opposite and adjacent). The signs of the values are used to determine the quadrant of the result. The result will be a value between PI and -PI.

To calculate a tangent, simply use sin(value)/cos(value).

More trig functions are available in the Math::Trig module or in the POSIX module.

Example Listing 1.46

```perl
# Ring of stars.
#

$high=20;
$wide=40;
my @a=(" "x($wide+1))x($high+1);

for(my $i=0; $i<360; $i+=20) {
    substr( $a[(sin $i/57.2)*($high/2) + ($high/2)],
            (cos $i/57.2)*($wide/2) + ($wide/2), 1)="*";
}
print join("\n", @a);
```

> **See Also**
> `Math::Trig` module documentation

abs

Usage

```
abs value
abs
```

Description

The `abs` function returns the numeric value, without sign. If value is omitted, the value in `$_` is used.

Example Listing 1.47

```
$distance=sqrt( abs(  ( $x - $x2 )**2 +  ( $y-$y2 )**2  ) );
```

Logarithmic and Exponential Functions

Usage

```
log value
log
exp value
exp
```

Description

The `log` function returns the base `e` (natural) `logarithm` of value. If a value is not given, the value in `$_` is used. An exception is raised if value is `0` or negative. The base n logarithm of value is

```
log(value)/log(base)
```

The inverse of the `log` function is the `exp` function, such that y=log(x) is true if x=exp(y). It returns e to the power of value. If a value is not specified, `$_` is used.

To perform exponentiation of a number other than `e` (such as the C math library's `pow` function), use the `**` operator.

Example Listing 1.48

```
# Slide-rule math
#

print "Give me a large number: ";
chomp($num1=<STDIN>);
print "Give me another large number: ";
chomp($num2=<STDIN>);

printf("\nThe log of %9d      %9.4f\n", $num1, $n1l=log($num1));
printf("The log of %9d    + %9.4f\n", $num2, $n2l=log($num2));
print " "x24, "--------------\n";
printf("Their sum                %9.4f\n\n", $n1l+$n2l);
printf("e**%-9.4f is %.2f\n", $n1l+$n2l, exp($n1l+$n2l));
printf "Which is the same as $num1*$num2 = @{[$num1*$num2]}\n";
```

> **See Also**
> log and exp in the C library reference

int

Usage

```
int value
int
```

Description

The int function returns the integer portion of value. If value is omitted, $_ is used instead. The int function performs a simple truncation and not rounding.

The int function shouldn't be used for rounding purposes. For rounding, use the sprintf, printf, or POSIX ceil and floor functions.

Example Listing 1.49

```
$n=5.6;

print int($n), "\n";   # Gives 5
printf("%.0f\n", $n);  # Gives 6
```

See Also
POSIX module documentation

sqrt

Usage

```
sqrt value
sqrt
```

Description

The sqrt function returns the square root of a given value. If value is not given, $_ is used instead. An exception is raised if value is negative.

To extract other roots (cube roots, and so on) use ** operator and the formula (for the Nth root):

```
root=value**(1/N)
```

For roots of negative numbers, use the Math::Complex module.

Example Listing 1.50

```
print "A number?";
chomp($number=<STDIN>);
printf "Square root: %.4f\n", sqrt($number);
printf "Cube root: %.4f\n", $number**(1/3);
```

See Also
sqrt in the C library reference

rand

Usage

```
rand value
rand
```

Description

The rand function returns a positive pseudo-random floating-point number greater than 0 and less than value. If value is not specified, the number returned is between 0 (inclusive) and 1. If you want an integer instead of a floating-point number, use the int function.

Starting in release 5.005, the random-number generator is seeded automatically; so calling srand beforehand is unnecessary.

The quality of the random number varies depending on your system's random number library. For possibly higher-quality random numbers, consult the Math::TrulyRandom module.

Example Listing 1.51

```perl
# Produce a somewhat-random normal distribution.
#  Note: there are other methods of generating normal
#    distributions.  This one is merely simple.

$height=40;
sub rand_normal {
    my($top,$num)=($_[0],0);

    my $clumpiness=10;
    for(1..$clumpiness) { $num+=rand($top); }
    $num/=$clumpiness;
}
for(0..($height*6)) {
    $dist{int rand_normal($height)}++;
}
for $key (sort keys %dist) {
    print "*" x $dist{$key}, "\n";
}
```

> **See also**
> int in this book

srand

Usage

srand *value*
srand

Description

The srand function seeds Perl's random-number generator with a new value. If the value is omitted, Perl will use a suitable source to seed the generator (a kernel device, current time, process ID, and so on).

The random-number generator is the piece of code that Perl's rand function uses to determine which number should be next in a random sequence. Similar to all software random-number generators, the number is based on formulas. To get the formula started, an initial value must be given. The more random the value with which you seed the generator, the better the random number sequence.

In more recent Perls (>5.005), it should not be necessary to call srand; it is called automatically when rand is first called. Also, do not call srand more than once in a program.

For better-than-normal random distributions, see the Math::TrulyRandom module.

See Also
rand in this book

Unary Operators

Usage

- operand
+ operand
\ operand

Description

Unary operators are operators that take exactly one argument. Perl contains two kinds of unary operators: named and symbolic.

The named unary operators are (generally) listed elsewhere in this book and indexed by their name. Some of these are file tests (`-s`, `-T`, `-e`), glob, lc, scalar, eval, goto, chdir, and most of the other one-argument functions that have been listed throughout this book.

The symbolic unary operators also take one argument, and are right-associative. (The ~ operator is unary, but is covered in the bit operators section.)

The + symbol as a unary operator does nothing. It is used to inform Perl that something which looks similar to a function really isn't a function call, or to make identifiers behave differently; for example,

```
rand ($choices * 2) / 5;   # means (rand($choices*2))/5
rand +($choices * 2) /5;   # means rand(($choices*2)/5)
$foo{shift}="FOO";         # means $foo{'shift'}="FOO";
$foo{+shift}="FOO";        # means shift from @_/@ARGV and use that
                #   as a key for %foo.
```

The unary minus, `-`, performs arithmetic negation on numbers. Thus `-6` is the same as `0-6`. On strings it prepends the string literal `-` onto the operand and returns that. This means that `-foo` is the same as `"-foo"`.

The \ operator takes a reference to the operand that follows. (Many more details are in the References entry.) So if the operand is a hash, a reference to that hash's storage is created. One note is that with a list, the \ operator is distributive so that:

```
@arr=\($t, $c, $d);  # Same as @arr=(\$t, \$c, \$d);
```

actually assigns a reference for each of $t, $c, and $d to @arr. Most of the time when this is seen, the programmer meant to use [] to construct an anonymous array.

See Also
bit operators, logical operators, and pack in this book

---

defined

Usage

```
defined
defined expression
```

Description

The `defined` function returns true or false whether the expression has a defined value or not. If no expression is given, the value in `$_` is used.

For details on where the undefined value is seen in Perl, see the `undef` entry.

The defined function can be used to see whether a system call has failed (because `0` may be a valid return value, and is false):

```
while (defined ($name=readdir DIR)) {
    print "$name\n";
}
```

Many functions return `undef` on failure, which allows them to validly return `0` or `""` as a valid value and not have to worry about whether "0 but true" was the exit condition (apologies to `ioctl`):

```
while( defined $obj->size() ) {
    $obj->process()
}
```

The `defined` function also can be used to test whether a function exists. The `exists` function will return true if it's been declared or defined, but `defined` only returns true if the subroutine is really there:

```
if ( exists &WeirdPackage::func ) {
    if ( defined &WeirdPackage::func ) {
        &WeirdPackage::func();  # It's _really_ there.
    } else {
        die "Declaration for func() seen, but no sub!";
    }

}
```

A common mistake is to use the `defined` function to test whether a hash (or an array) element exists. It's perfectly valid for a hash (or an array) to have an element that exists, but isn't defined:

```
%oz=( Lions => undef, Tigers => 1, Bears => 'oh my' );

if (defined $oz{Lions}) {    # WRONG!  It's there, but not defined
    print "It's there!";
}
```

```
if (exists $oz{Lions}) {    # RIGHT!  It's there, but not defined
    print "It's there!";
}
```

To test for the presence of an array element or a hash key, use `exists`.

See Also
`exists` and `undef` in this book

Comma Operators

Usage

```
expression,expression
expression=>expression
```

Description

The `,` operator (comma operator) in scalar context evaluates the two *expressions* left to right and returns the value of the expression on the right. This is actually a flow-control operator allowing you to control the execution order of a series of expressions:

```
$val=func1(), func2(), func3();
```

Each comma represents a sequence point, and the entire expression is guaranteed to evaluate left to right; and side effects of the leftward expression will be complete before the right executes. Because the comma operator has such a low precedence, it's actually quite handy for grouping.

The comma operator in a list context isn't an operator at all—it's simply a separator for the terms of the list and doesn't imply anything about return values or order of execution:

```
@foo=(func1(), func2(), func3());  # NOT a comma operator!
```

The `=>` symbol is simply a synonym for the comma, both in its operator role and in its separating-items-in-a-list role. There is one small added feature, though. The `=>` treats the identifier to its left as though it were a single-quoted string (not-interpolated).

```
# This is slightly more readable...
$t=$mw->Button( -text => 'Hello', -command => sub { 1; })->pack();
```

Basic Operators and Functions

```
# ..than this
$c=$mw->Button( '-text' => 'Ugh', '-command' => sub { 1; })->pack();
```

In the preceding example, the identifier text is actually quoted and not the entire -text. But because unary minus does an implicit concatenation, these are all the same:

```
%h=( -file => 'foo', -'text' => 'narf', '-cmds' => 'poit',
    -'pack',   'hlag', '-carp' => 'bar'   );
```

In hash initializations, the => operator makes it easy to determine which part of the initializing list is the key and which is the value:

```
%beverages=( coke => 'good', pepsi => 'yucky',
    juice => 'yum', tea => 'dirt-water');
```

In this way, the comma operator becomes an "association" operator.

See Also
arrays and hashes in this book

Range Operator

Usage

```
operand .. operand
operand ... operand
start .. end
```

Description

The range operator .. is actually two completely different operators in one. In scalar context, it is a bi-stable flip-flop operator and is explained later.

The most common use for .. is in list context. In list context, .. returns a range of values beginning at start and continuing until end by 1s. So, given the following:

```
print for(0..10);
@top = @popular[-10...-1];  # Slice the last 10 off.
```

this would print the integers 0 through 10, and assign the last 10 elements from @popular to @top.

If the start is greater than the end, the range operator returns an empty list. (You can't use it directly to count backward.)

If the start and end values are alphabetic, the range operator increases values as though an auto-increment were in effect. So that the following expression:

```
for('a'..'z') { }
```

would cycle through each of the 26 letters of the alphabet. The strings can be arbitrarily long of course so the following:

```
for('aaa'..'zzz') { }
```

would loop through 17576 iterations from aaa, aab, and aac to zzx, zzy, and zzz.

In older versions of Perl, the range operator constructed the entire list at once, thus iterations such as follows:

```
for(1..1_000_000) {
    print;
}
```

would produce the entire million element list and then begin the loop. This was a waste of time and memory. This is fixed in Perl 5.6 and a true iteration takes place. Beware that @a=(1..1_000_000) will still construct a terribly large list.

If the end value in the list range operator isn't in the logical progression from the start, as in this example,

```
for('a'..'=') { print "$_\n" }
```

the range operator will stop the progression when the length of the value is longer than the end value. So this loop would progress as though you had said 'a'..'z'. If the start is not numeric, but the end is, a warning will be issued and the start value silently converted to 0.

In scalar context, the .. operator returns a boolean value. The rules for how the .. (scalar) operator work are as follows:

Each .. operator is independent of any other operators in the program.

When the left operand is false, the operator returns false.

When the left operand is true, the operator returns true.

The operator continues returning true until the right operand is true (on the next evaluation).

The right operand will be tested again, and the operator can alternate from true back to false on the same evaluation. Use the ... (3-dots) version of the range operator if you don't want this behavior.

The right operand is not evaluated when the operator is in its false state, and the left operand is not evaluated when the operator is in its true state. A quick demo of the operator might be the following:

```
$a=$b=0;

while (1) {
    if ($seq=$a..$b) {
        print "The operator is true ($seq).\n";
        $b++;
    } else {
        print "The operator is false ($seq).\n";
        $a++;
    }
    last if $a && $b > 1;
}
# Prints: (see below for explanation of "2E0")
# The operator is false ().
# The operator is true (1).
# The operator is true (2E0).
```

If an operand is a numeric literal, the operand is implicitly compared to the variable $. (line input number). This allows you to mimic the behavior of Unix utilities such as sed and awk.

The false value returned by the range operator is the empty string. The true value returned is the sequence number (starting with 1). The final sequence number has the string E0 appended to it—it's still a numeric value (1e0 is just 1), but can be parsed to tell if you've run off the end of the list.

Example Listing 1.52

```
# Very sed-ish way to print the first 10 lines
#   of a filehandle
while( <FH> ) {
    print if (1..10);
}


# From the first blank line to the end of file,
```

# print the lines
while(<OFH>) {
    if (/^$/ .. eof()) {
        print;
    }
}
```

> **See Also**
> $. and arrays in this book

## Case Shifting Functions

### Usage

```
lc string
lc
uc string
uc
lcfirst string
lcfirst
ucfirst string
ucfirst
```

Description

This group of functions takes the string argument, or $_ if no string is specified, and shifts the case of the alphabetic characters in the string.

The uc function shifts the string to uppercase and lc to lowercase. The ucfirst function shifts only the first character of the string to uppercase, and the lcfirst shifts only the first character of the string to lowercase.

The uc, lc, ucfirst, and lcfirst functions are the internal functions that implement the \U, \L, \u, \l escape mechanisms in double-quoted strings, backticks, and regular expression patterns.

Each function respects the use locale pragma, and uses the LC_CTYPE environment variable to figure out how to case-shift if applicable.

Example Listing 1.53

```
# Case shifting.  To see a little about how this works,
#    uncomment the following line.
```
```

```
#use O qw(Terse);

# This is actually noticed by the compiler, and
#     not done at runtime.
print ucfirst("hello, world!\n");

# This is currently done at runtime, as you'd
#     expect.
$author="E.E. Cummings";
print lc($author);
```

> **See Also**
> locale module documentation
>
> tr and quotes in this book

time

Usage

time

Description

The time function returns the number of seconds since the Unix epoch. The epoch is normally 00:00:00 January 1, 1970 UTC, and this might be true even if your OS is not Unix (for example, under MS Windows).

The return value is most often used with the localtime or gmtime function, which will break the number of seconds into a more useful format (month, day, year, and so on). It also is used with stat because the access, modification, and inode creation times of files are expressed as this kind of value.

Example Listing 1.54

```
print "Hit the return key:";
$now=time;
$a=<STDIN>;
print qq{You took }, time-$now, qq{ seconds to do that!};
```

See Also

`POSIX` module documentation

`localtime, gmtime,` and `stat` in this book

---

localtime

Usage

```
localtime expression
```

Description

Returns the `time` as given by expression (which represents a number of seconds since the `epoch`) adjusted for the current `time zone`. If expression is not given, the current time is used.

In a list context, `localtime` returns a nine-element list consisting of members from the `tm` structure from the host architecture's C library function `ctime`:

Member Name	Description	Range
tm_sec	second of the current minute (the extra seconds to allow for leap seconds)	(0-61)
tm_min	minute of the current hour	(0-59)
tm_hour	hour of the day	(0-23)
tm_mday	day of the month	(1-31)
tm_mon	month of the year	(0-11)
tm_year	years since 1900	
tm_wday	day of the week	(0-6, 0=Sunday)
tm_yday	day of the year	(0-365)
tm_isdst	daylight savings in effect flag	(0/1/-1=no information available)

The values of `tm_mon` and `tm_wday`, being 0-based, can be used as offsets into an array containting those names as shown in the following examples.

Note that the year is the number of years since 1900 and not a 2-digit year number. Therefore for the year 2001, the `tm_year` field will be 101.

In a scalar context, it returns a formatted string representing the time and `date`, such as the following:

```
Mon Jun  5 21:15:21 2000
```

This time is reported in the same format on all architectures and is independent of the current `locale`.

Example Listing 1.55

```
# varies slightly based on time zone
$seconds=735513720;   # seconds to Feb 22, 1993 in Unix Epoch
$c=localtime($seconds);
print $c;             # prints "Thu Apr 22 17:22:00 1993"
```

Example Listing 1.56

```
# prints the current year
print "Year is:", (localtime(time))[5]+1900, "\n";
```

Example Listing 1.57

```
# prints the day of the week
@days=qw(Sunday Monday Tuesday Wednesday Thursday
    Friday Saturday);
print $days[ (localtime)[6] ], "\n";
```

See Also

POSIX and Time::Local module documentation

perlfunc in the perl documentation

time and gmtime in this book

ctime(3) in the C library reference

gmtime

Usage

gmtime *expresion*

Description

Returns the time as given by expression (which represents a number of seconds since the epoch) adjusted to the Greenwich time zone; the current time zone. If expression is not given, the current time is used.

In a list context, gmtime returns an eight element list consisting of members from the tm structure from the host architecture's C library function ctime:

Member name	Description	Range
tm_sec	second of the current minute (the extra seconds to allow for leap seconds)	(0-61)
tm_min	minute of the current hour	(0-59)
tm_hour	hour of the day	(0-23)
tm_mday	day of the month	(1-31)
tm_mon	month of the year	(0-11)
tm_year	years since 1900	
tm_wday	day of the week	(0-6, 0=Sunday)
tm_yday	day of the year	(0-365)

The values of tm_mon and tm_wday, being 0-based, can be used as offsets into an array containting those names as shown in the following examples.

Note that the year is the number of years since 1900 and not a two-digit year number. Therefore for the year 2001, the tm_year field will be 101.

In a scalar context, it returns a formatted string representing the time and date, such as the following:

```
Sun Sep 10 18:40:25 2000
```

This time is reported in the same format on all architectures and is independent of the current locale.

Example Listing 1.58

```
$seconds=735513720;   # seconds to Feb 22, 1993 in Unix Epoch
$c=gmtime($seconds);
# prints "Thu Apr 22 21:22:00 1993"
# Note, this differs from the localtime() example because my
# machine is in EDT, a 4 hour difference at this time.
print $c;
```

See Also

POSIX and Time::Local module documentation

perlfunc in the perl documentation

time and localtime in this book

ctime(3) in the C library reference

String Operators

split

Usage

```
split pattern, string, limit
split pattern, string
split pattern
split
```

Description

The split function takes a string and produces a list from it. It does this by separating the string into fields that were separated (delimited) by a pattern. In a list context, the pattern delimited fields are returned (without the delimiters). In a scalar context, the number of fields found is returned. If a string is not specified to split, $_ will be split into fields.

The pattern specified is a regular expression. It can be written as a simple string, but will still be treated as a regular expression. In fact, all the normal regular expression modifiers can be used against the pattern including /x, /e, /i, and so on.

There are a few special pattern rules. If the pattern is omitted or is a literal space
(" "), the pattern /\s+/ is used instead and leading whitespace is ignored. However,
the pattern / / will include null fields if there is leading whitespace.

```
# All of these are equivalent
split;
split " ";
split " ", $_;
split " ", $_, 0;
```

A pattern that can match a null string (for example, /.*/) will split the string into
individual characters. The empty pattern (' ' or //) also is considered to be a null
match and will split the string into characters.

The limit parameter is used to stop the split after a certain number of fields have been
found. Using a limit can speed up split when a very large number of fields are
involved. If limit is not specified (or negative), all the string is split into fields and the
entire list is returned. Also, if limit is 0 or not specified, trailing empty fields are
silently omitted from the return value.

The split function normally returns a list of found fields without the delimiters. If
you want to capture the delimiters as well as the fields, use capturing parenthesis in the
pattern.

The split function will implicitly split into the @_ if used in a scalar context. In a list
context, using ?? to delimit the patterns (instead of the traditional //) also will cause
@_ to receive the values from split implicitly. Using this behavior is dangerous
because it interferes with @_'s use for subroutine arguments.

Example Listing 1.59

```
# Split a text file into a structure of arrays of
# arrays of arrays.  Each level in the array represents:
#     paragraphs, lines and words on those lines.
# "words" meaning whitespace-separated things.
@ARGV=('/tmp/sample.txt');
{
    local $/=""; # Read as paragraphs
    @text=<>;
}
chomp(@text);  # Chuck the trailing \n on paras

# Split the paragraphs into lines
foreach(@text) { $_=[ split(/^/, $_) ]; }
```

```
# Split the lines (within the paragraphs) into words
foreach $para (@text) {
    foreach (@{$para}) {
        $_=[ split(/\s+/, $_) ];
    }
}
```

> **See Also**
> Regular Expressions, join, @_, and sub in this book

index, rindex

Usage

```
index string, substring, offset
index string, substring
rindex string, substring, offset
rindex string, substring
```

Description

The index function searches string for an occurrence of substring (from left-to-right, start to finish, or however you want to look at it). The return value is the character position where substring was found, or -1 if the substring was not found.

If an offset is specified, index begins searching starting with the position within the string.

The rindex function works exactly as index does, except that the search begins from the end of the string and works back to the beginning (right-to-left, if you will).

The offsets start counting at 0, unless $[has been set. If $[has been set, the normal -1 return value for a miss will be $[less 1. If the offset specified is less than $[, the search starts at the beginning of the string.

Example Listing 1.60

```
$lyrics=<<SONG;
I have a little dreidel
I made it out of clay
And when it's dry and ready
Then dreidel I shall play.
```

```
Chorus:
Dreidel, dreidel, dreidel
I made it out of clay,
Dreidel, dreidel, dreidel,
Then dreidel I shall play.
SONG

my $off=-1;
# The lc is because index is case-sensitive
while(($off=index(lc($lyrics), "dreidel", $off)) > 0) {
    print "Found one at $off\n";
    $off++;
}
```

> **See Also**
> regular expressions and pos in this book

substr

Usage

```
substr expression, offset
substr expression, offset, length
substr expression, offset, length, replacement
```

Description

The substr function allows you to extract (or edit) a substring within an expression. The substr function can be used both to extract substrings (when used as an rvalue) or to edit substrings (when used as an lvalue, or with a fourth argument).

To extract a substring, the expression indicates the string to extract from, and the offset (begin counting at 0) is where to begin extracting from.

```
print substr("Homer, Marge, Bart and Maggie", 23);  # prints Maggie
```

If a length is specified, that determines the extent of the extraction. Otherwise, the remaining characters until the end of the string are replaced.

```
print substr("Homer, Marge, Bart and Maggie", 0, 5);  # prints Homer
```

If a replacement string is specified, the original string is modified at that offset for length number of characters to be the replacement string. The expression must be a modifiable scalar, or a runtime exception will be thrown. If the replacement is longer than length, the string is expanded to hold the extra characters (and everything on the right shifts right). If the replacement is shorter, the string is shrunk by the difference, and the characters to the right are shifted left to take up the gap.

```
$simps="Homer, Marge, Bart and Maggie";

# Changes to "Homer, Marge,Santa's Little Helper and Maggie"
substr($simps, 14, 4, "Santa's Little Helper");

# Changes to "Moe, Marge,Santa's Little Helper and Maggie"
substr($simps, 0, 5, "Moe");
```

If offset is negative, substr begins counting from the end (the right) of the expression. If offset is beyond the end of the string, an exception will be raised.

If substr is used with a fourth argument (to replace characters), the substr function returns the characters replaced. The substr function could be used to mimic chop:

```
$char=substr($str, -1, 1, "");  # Same as $char=chop($str);
```

When used as an assignable value, substr replaces length characters starting at offset with the value being assigned. This is most often seen in assignment:

```
$str="Washington";
substr($str, 0, 0)="George ";  # Insert at the beginning.
```

But substr (as an lvalue) doesn't always have to be used in assignment. The next couple of examples all use substr as an lvalue without assignment:

```
# Read 10 characters, and replace at $str starting at 5
read(STDIN, substr($str, 5), 10);

# Shift first three characters to uppercase
substr($str, 0, 3)=~tr/a-z/A-Z/;
```

Example Listing 1.61

```
# A little fanfare, a scrolling message

$|=1;
$mess="News Flash: this isn't that hard";
```

```
for(0..length $mess) {
    printf("%*s\r", length $mess, substr($mess, 0, $_));
    select(undef, undef, undef, 0.25);
}
print "\n";
```

chop

Usage

chop *value*
chop

Description

The chop function removes the last character from a *value* and returns the character removed. If value is an array variable or a list, the last character from each element is removed. If value is a hash variable, the last character from each value is removed (but not the keys).

In Perl 4, chop was typically used to remove the newline character from input records. This is now typically done with chomp, because chop is somewhat indiscriminate at removing any trailing characters, not just newlines. Multiple chops remove multiple characters.

Example Listing 1.62

```
# This is a short and simple example of a JAPH.  A JAPH is
#    a short, obfuscated perl program whose purpose is
#    to print "Just another Perl hacker" in an unusual way.
# A good description (and some wicked examples) of JAPHs is given at:
#    http://ucan.foad.org/~abigail/Perl/Talks/Japhs/

sub TIEHANDLE { $a="rekcah lreP rehtona tsuJ"; bless \$a,shift }
sub GETC { chop ${$_[0]}; }; tie *STDIN,""; print while($_=getc);
```

> **See Also**
> chomp in this book

chomp

Usage

```
chomp value
chomp
```

Description

The chomp function is used to remove trailing newlines from the value specified, or from $_ if no value is specified. The function returns the number of characters removed.

Typically chomp is used right after reading from a file to remove the newlines embedded in text files.

If value is a scalar, the trailing newline is removed. If value is a hash, the newlines are removed from all the hash values (but not the keys!). If value is an array variable, the newlines are removed from each of the elements. If multiple trailing newlines are present, they're all removed.

In actuality, a newline isn't removed: The current value of $/ (input record separator) is removed. And the behavior changes slightly depending on the value of $/. If $/ is " " (paragraph mode), all the newlines are removed from all the strings involved. If $/ is undef (slurp mode) or set to a reference to an integer (fixed length record mode), chomp has no effect.

The chomp function is used in preference to chop (from Perl 4) because chop is rather indiscriminate, whereas chomp removes only newlines.

Example Listing 1.63

```
open(FH, "/tmp/sample.txt") || die "sample.txt: $!";
chomp(@lines=<FH>);
close(FH);
```

> **See Also**
> $/, <, and > in this book

join

Usage

```
join expression, list
```

Description

The join function creates a string from a list by taking the elements of list and joining them together with expression (normally a string). For example, to print the scripts arguments with each one on a new line:

```
print join("\n", @ARGV);
```

The join function also can be used to simplify what would otherwise be a complicated problem, such as editing a particular field in a record. For example, to edit the fifth field in a comma-separated list:

```
@fields=split(/,/, $string);
$field[4]="New Data!";
$string=join(',', $string);
```

Simply using a regular expression, this could have been a messy job. Notice that split rendered the string into a list. The split function is a natural counterpart to join.

Example Listing 1.64

```
# Print a simple list, formatted
#
@mountain=qw(Washington Lincoln Roosevelt Jefferson);
print "Four presidents appear on Mount Rushmore:\n ",
    join(', ', @mountain[0..$#mountain-1]),
    " and $mountain[-1].";
```

> **See Also**
> split in this book

length

Usage

```
length expression
length
```

Description

The length function returns the number of characters in the expression. If expression is not specified, $_ is used instead.

If you're reading this trying to find the length of an array or the number of keys in a hash, please stop. The length function only applies to scalar values and will return interesting (but useless) results on arrays and hashes. To find the number of elements in an array, use the array in a scalar context. To find the number of keys in a hash, use keys hash in a scalar context.

Example Listing 1.65

```perl
# Find the longest word in a wordlist

$max=0;
open(W, "/usr/dict/words") || die "No wordlist: $!";
while(<W>) {
    chomp;
    $max=$_ if (length > length $max);
}
close(W);
print "$max\n";
```

> **See Also**
> arrays and hashes in this book

crypt

Usage

```perl
crypt plaintext, salt
```

Description

The crypt function computes a hash based on the plaintext and salt given to it. The hash produced is a one-way hash, meaning that the original plaintext cannot be discovered using the hash. Using crypt with the same salt and plaintext will always produce the same return value.

The function follows the behavior of the built-in crypt C library call. The actual implementation details might vary from system to system. The most common place to see crypt generated strings is the password field in the Unix password file.

The plaintext is a string that you would like hashed. The crypt function is best suited for small strings, such as those used in passwords. (For large amounts of text, you should consider using a module such as the MD5::Digest module from CPAN.)

The salt is used to further vary the crypt algorithm. The salt must be at least two characters from the set A-Z, a-z, 0-9, ., and /. These should be chosen as randomly as possible to make the crypted string fairly well distributed.

The return value from crypt is a scalar value that the first two characters are the input salt, and the remaining 11 characters are the hash for the text. The characters are all printable ASCII.

Example Listing 1.66

```
# Search the password file to see if a particular
#    string was used as a password.

print "Give me a potential password: ";
chomp($string=<STDIN>);

# This could be /etc/shadow, but you'll need sufficient
#    privilege (i.e. root) to look in there.

open(PASS, "/etc/passwd")
    || die "Can't open the password file: $!";

while(<PASS>) {
    ($id,$pass)=(split(/:/, $_))[0,1];
    if (crypt($string, $pass) eq $pass) {
        print "$id is using $string\n";
    }
}

close(PASS);
```

Character Conversion Functions

chr

Usage

```
chr value
chr
```

```
ord character
ord
```

Description

The chr function returns the character that corresponds to the *value* in the character set (ASCII, Latin-1, Unicode). For example, chr(97) would return a.

The reverse of chr is ord. The ord function converts a *character* back to the corresponding numeric value; for example, ord("a") would return 97. If you want to convert multiple characters to their values, use unpack.

If you do not specify a value (for chr) or character (for ord), the value in $_ will be used.

Example Listing 1.67

```perl
# Prints a nice 4-column ASCII chart

use POSIX qw(isprint);  # Used for isprint

$i=0;
for (0..255) { push(@{$a[$_%4]}, $_); }

ALL:
while(1) {
    for my $col (0..3) {
        $c=shift @{$a[$col]};
        last ALL if (not defined $c);

        # isprint is needed because some unprintables will
        #   mess up the display.
        printf("   %3x %4o %3d  %2s",
            $c, $c, $c, isprint(chr($c))?chr($c):"NP");
    }
    print "\n";
}
```

> **See Also**
> unpack in this book

Hash and Array Operators

`reverse`

Usage

`reverse` *list*

Description

The `reverse` function will take a list and return it reversed. In a list context, the elements of list are returned in reverse order. In a scalar context, the elements of list are concatenated and then reversed character by character. This distinction is important because the following

```
print reverse("hello");
```

might not do what you'd expect. (It will print `"hello"`). What you probably meant was the following:

```
print scalar reverse("hello");
```

Example Listing 1.68

```
# reversing a sorted list, the hard way
#    (it would have been easier to just swap $a and $b
#     in the sort itself)

@by_value_descending=
    reverse sort { $hash{$a} <=> $hash{$b}  }  keys %hash;
```

> **See Also**
> context and sort in this book

`splice`

Usage

```
splice array, start, length, list
splice array, start, length
splice array, start
splice array
```

Description

The `splice` function is used to add or remove elements from an array. It does this by substituting list starting at position start, for length elements; for example,

```
splice(@arr, 0, 5, qw(oats peas beans));
```

This replaces the first five elements of @a with the three elements qw(oats peas beans). The rest of the array is moved around to accommodate and the array as a whole is extended or reduced. In this case the old `$a[5]` is now `$a[3]` (and so on), and the array is now two elements shorter.

If the list is omitted, the elements are simply removed from array. If length is not specified, all the elements from the start to the end of the array are removed. If start is not specified, the entire array is emptied.

Negative start positions will begin counting from the end of the array. For example, to remove the last element (as a `pop` would do):

```
splice(@arr, -1);
```

If you specify a negative starting point that would cause the index to go back beyond the beginning of the array, a runtime exception will occur.

The `splice` function in list context returns the list of removed elements. In a scalar context, it returns the last element removed, or `undef` if nothing was removed.

Example Listing 1.69

```
# Shuffle a deck of "cards",
# hand each "player" 7 cards

@deck=(1..52);
@hands=();

# Fisher-Yates shuffle from the Perl FAQ
for( my $i=@deck; --$i; ) {
    my $j=int rand($i+1);
    next if $i==$j;
    @deck[$i,$j]=@deck[$j,$i];
}

foreach(1..4) {
    push(@hands, [ splice(@deck, 0, 7) ]);
}
```

> **See Also**
> arrays, pop, shift, unshift, and push in this book

pop

Usage

```
pop
pop array
```

Description

The pop function removes the last element—the one with the highest index—from the *array* and returns it. The array is left one element shorter.

When the array is exhausted, pop will return undef and the array will be empty. The pop function will also return undef if an undef element is being removed.

If the array is not specified within a subroutine, the @_ array is popped. Outside of a subroutine (in the main body of the program) the @ARGV array is used by default.

This is equivalent to the commands:

```
$array[$#array--];
```

or

```
splice(@array, -1);
```

Example Listing 1.70

```
@munchies=qw(chips dips pretzels licorice);
$snack1=pop(@munchies);
print $snack1;
```

> **See Also**
> splice, shift, qw, and ARGV in this book

shift

Usage

```
shift
shift array
```

Description

The shift function removes the first element from the array—the one with the lowest index—and returns it. The array is left one element shorter.

When the array is exhausted, shift will return undef and the array will be empty. The shift function also will return undef if an undef element is being removed.

If the array argument is not used within a subroutine, the @_ array is used. Outside of subroutines (in the main body of the program) the @ARGV array is used.

This is equivalent to the command

```
splice(@array, 0, 1);
```

Example Listing 1.71

```
# Using shift to peel off arguments
# From @_
sub foo {
    my $first_arg=shift;
    my $second_arg=shift;
}
```

> **See Also**
> splice, @_, and @ARGV in this book

unshift

Usage

```
unshift array, list
```

Description

The unshift function takes the elements of list and prepends them to the beginning of array—starting at index 0. The number of elements in the array after the unshift is returned.

This is much faster than using splice or simple array assignments for adding to the front of an existing array.

Example Listing 1.72

```
# Snippet from the top of a program which changes
# behavior depending on the name it's saved as.  Either
# running it with a -w switch or calling the script "wonka"
# gets you the same behavior.

use Getopt::Std;

# Add -w into the args
if ($0 =~ /wonka$/) { unshift(@ARGV, "-w"); }

getopts('wv');
if ($opt_w) {
    # Then do w stuff...
}
```

push

Usage

```
push array, list
```

Description

The push function takes the members of list and adds them to the end of array—the end with the highest indexes. The array will be extended to absorb the new values and the new length of the array returned by push.

This function is much faster than either of the following:

```
@a=(@a, @newelements);
splice(@a, @a, 0, @newelements);
```

It also is much easier to read.

The push function can be used with `shift` to create a FIFO stack or with the `pop` function to create a LIFO stack.

Example Listing 1.73

```
# Create a list of all of the .html files under
# DocumentRoot
use File::Find;

@webfiles=();
find( sub {
    if (-f $_ and /\.html\z/) {
        push(@webfiles, $File::Find::name);
    }
},
"/home/httpd");

# Print the list.
print join("\n", @webfiles);
```

> **See Also**
> pop and splice in this book

keys

Usage

keys *hash*

Description

The `keys` function is used to extract the keys from a hash. In a list context, the keys are returned.

The keys are returned from the hash in a seemingly random order. However, the order will be the same between invocations of `keys` (unless the hash has been modified). It is the same order that `each` or `values` on the hash would produce. The `keys` function also will reset the iterator used by the `each` function.

In a scalar context, the number of keys in the hash is returned. For normal hashes this is very fast. For tied hashes or DBM files, the number of keys is determined by walking the entire hash and counting.

The `keys` function also can be used on the left side of an assignment to increase the number of hash buckets allocated for the hash. This can be an efficiency win if the hash will grow to a large size, and the size is known in advance.

```
keys %bighash=100;
```

To use this optimization, you must determine the number of buckets needed. A good technique is to fill the hash with the real data without the optimization. Then print the hash in a scalar context; for example,

```
%hash=(1..1000);        # Keys are odd, values are even.
print scalar keys %hash;  # printed 413/512
```

So the optimum number of buckets for this hash is 512. Do not allocate more buckets than you need; they will remain with the hash until it is destroyed with `undef` or it goes out of lexical scope.

Example Listing 1.74

```
# Dump the environment variables, sorted

for my $var (sort keys %ENV) {
    printf "$var=$ENV{$var}\n";
}
```

See Also

each, hashes, and values in this book

---

each

Usage

each *hash*

Description

The `each` function returns one key/value pair from a hash per invocation. In a list context, `each` returns a two-element list of the key and value. In a scalar context, only the key is returned.

```
while ($key=each %hash) {
    # process key...
}
```

The each function will continue to return key/value pairs until the hash is exhausted when it will return an empty list. If each is performed after the end-of-hash is reached, it will begin again at the beginning. Using each while inserting and deleting keys from a hash is not advised.

The order of the keys returned from a hash with each is a random order. It happens to be the same order as keys hash would return. The iterator used by each to keep track of its position in the hash is shared by the keys and values functions. Thus, using each to traverse part of a hash, and then invoking keys against that same hash will cause each to reset to the beginning. The each position for other hashes are unaffected.

Example Listing 1.75

```
%attributes=( collie => 'smart', greyhound => 'fast',
     daschund => 'long', lhasa => 'hairy',
     chihuahua => 'tiny');
while(($breed, $attrib)=each %attributes) {
    print "The \u$breed breed is known for being $attrib\n";
}
```

> **See Also**
> hashes, keys, and values in this book

delete

Usage

```
delete hashelem
delete hashslice
delete arrayelem
delete arrayslice
```

Description

The delete function removes elements from a hash or array. If hashelem or hashslice are specified, those elements are deleted from the hash. If arrayelem or arrayslice are specified, those elements are removed from the array.

```
delete $hash{key};
delete @hash{ 'key1', 'key2', 'key3' };
delete $arr[13];
delete @arr[1,3,5,7,9];
```

If the array elements removed are at the end of the array, the array is shortened by that number of elements. However, elements deleted from anywhere else in the array do not shorten it—use splice for that.

After the delete, exists on the hash or array elements will return false, as though they had never existed. To remove all the elements from a hash or array, simply initialize it to an empty list—it's far more efficient than delete.

The delete function returns the list of elements deleted.

Example Listing 1.76

```
# Delete an array slice

@ladies=qw(Pat Betty Rosalyn Nancy);
delete @ladies[0,3];
# Now prints 3.  The deletion of Pat doesn't
# shorten the array, but Nancy _did_.
print scalar @ladies;
```

Example Listing 1.77

```
# Delete a hash element

# Strip my environment to minimums
for (keys %ENV) {
    next unless /^(PATH|HOME|LANG|SHELL)$/;
    delete $ENV{$_};
}
```

exists

Usage

```
exists hash_element
exists array_element
exists sub_name
```

Description

The exists function will return true if the specified hash_element or array_element exists, and false otherwise.

```
if (exists $hash{key}) {
    "It's there!\n";
}
```

The `exists` function will return true regardless of the actual value of the element found. For example, this is the wrong way to test for the existence of a hash key:

```
# WRONG
if (defined $hash{key}) {
    # Processing...
}
```

For arrays, the `exists` function returns true if and only if the element being tested has never held a value. Setting an array element to `undef` will still cause `exists` to return true for that element. The only way to make `exists` return false for an array element that's ever been used is to remove it with `delete`.

The `exists` function also can be used to test whether a subroutine exists. The subroutine doesn't necessarily have to be defined, but it does have to at least be declared with `sub`. See the `sub` entry for the distinction between declaring and defining a subroutine. The subroutine name should be passed with a leading `&`.

Example Listing 1.78

```
# Why to use exists, and not defined.

%h=( false => undef,  alsofalse => 0);
$u=undef;
$h{$u}=undef;

# All of these will return false, even though there's
#    an entry in the hash.
if ( $h{alsofalse} ) { print "Got it 1"; }
if ( $h{false} ) { print "Got it 2"; }
if ( $h{$u} ) { print "Got it 3" }

# But these are all true
if ( exists $h{alsofalse} ) { print "Found it!" }
if ( exists $h{false} ) { print "Found it!" }
if ( exists $h{$u} ) { print "Found it!" }
```

Example Listing 1.79

```perl
# Exists on arrays
@f=('apple','orange','pear');

print "First slot" if (exists $f[0]);  # True!
print "Fourth slot" if (exists $f[4]); # False...

# Give the array an element 6, implying a 3,4 and 5
$f[6]="peach";
print "Fifth slot" if (exists $f[5]);  # False...

$f[3]=undef;
print "Third undef" if (exists $f[3]);  # True!

delete $f[3];
print "Third still" if (exists $f[3]);  # False!
```

Example Listing 1.80

```perl
# Include a library which may or may not have what we need.
require WeirdPackage;

# Does this function exist in the package?
if ( exists &WeirdPackage::func ) {
    &WeirdPackage::func(@arguments);
} else {
    die "WeirdPackage does not contain the function func!\n";
}
```

> **See Also**
> arrays, defined, hashes, sub, and delete in this book

values

Usage

values *hash*

Description

The `values` function retrieves the values from a `hash`. In a list context, the values are returned. In a scalar context, `values` returns the number of entries in the hash.

The order in which they're returned is seemingly random. It is the same order used by `keys` and `each`. The `values` function will also reset the iterator used by `each`.

The `values` function in 5.6 actually returns a list of aliases—sort of a pseudo-reference, a similar mechanism used by `for`, `foreach`, and `@_` in subroutine calls.

Example Listing 1.81

```
# Dump the environment's values
print join(',', values %ENV);
```

Example Listing 1.82

```
# Manipulating a hash's values using value's
# aliases.  (5.6+ only)
%hash=( Perl => 'wall', Python => 'rossum', TCL => 'ousterhout');
foreach(values %hash) {
    $_="\u$_";
}

print %hash;
```

> **See Also**
> `each`, `keys`, and `hashes` in this book

sort

Usage

```
sort list
sort subref list
sort block list
```

Description

The `sort` function takes `list` and orders them using a user-defined subroutine, a `block`, or the default sorting order and returns the list of sorted items.

```
@sorted=sort @unsorted;  # Simple sort.
```

The default sorting order is in the standard string comparison order specified by the local `strcmp` C library call. This is normally ASCII order: unprintables, symbols and numbers, uppercase, and then lowercase letters.

If you want to define your own sorting order, you can use a `subref` or a `block`. A `subref` can be a scalar variable that contains the name of the subroutine to use (which should be defined in the same package as the sort call, or fully-qualified) or contains a reference to a subroutine. You also can simply use the name of the subroutine. Note that the `block` or `subref` is not followed by a comma in `sort`'s syntax.

The `block` or subroutine called will have two variables given to it, `$a` and `$b`. These will contain the values of two elements of the list. The subroutine should compare the two values and return `-1`, `0`, or `1` depending on whether `$a` is less than, equal to, or greater than `$b`. The `<=>` and `cmp` operators are handy for these kinds of comparisons. To reverse the sense of the sort, use the `reverse` function on the results or swap the comparisons (that is, use `$b<=>$a` instead of `$a<=>$b`).

The variables `$a` and `$b` are actually aliases to the original list elements, but modifying them in the sort routine is not a good idea. Also, to avoid problems with the sort, your sort routine should be consistent about how it orders any given value of `$a` and `$b`— doing comparisons using different criteria at various times might cause the sort to fail.

The comparison algorithm can be anything you prefer. A simple numeric sort (as opposed to in ASCII order) might resemble the following:

```
@numbers=sort { $a <=> $b } @numbers;
```

If you were sorting the keys to a hash by the values associated with those keys, you wouldn't compare `$a` and `$b` directly—you would use those as an index to the hashes and then compare those values:

```
# Sort a hash by its values
%bills = ( phone => 56.00, electricity => 25.98,
      cable => 36.00, gas => 12.00, car => 205.67,
      internet => 45.99 );
@bills_by_cost=sort { $bills{$a} <=> $bills{$b} } keys %bills;
```

If you want to use variables other than `$a` and `$b`, you can specify a prototype for the subroutine whose reference (or name) is given to `sort`.

```
sub case_insensitively ($$) {
    my($i,$j)=@_;
    return lc($i) cmp lc($j);
}
@out=sort case_insensitively @in;
```

If the sort subroutine is computationally expensive—if data manipulation is necessary to sort the fields—and the data set is large, optimizations such as the Schwartzian Transform or the Orcish Maneuver would prove useful.

The sort function also is special for the use strict pragma. First, the sort subroutine can be specified as just a name in a scalar variable without triggering an exception from use strict 'refs'. Second, the variables $a and $b are exempt from use strict 'vars' checking anywhere in your program.

The use locale pragma will cause sort to use the appropriate ordering algorithm for that locale.

Example Listing 1.83

```perl
# Sort multi-field records by
# Last name, First initial and then
#    date of birth.
@data=( "Smith T 1969", "Smith A 1945",
    "Smith B 1992", "Smythe Y 1967",
    "Smith A 1968");
print join "\n",
    sort  {
        my(@a, @b);
        @a=split(" ", $a);
        @b=split(" ", $b);
        $a[0] cmp $b[0]  # Last name
            ||        #  if equal then..
        $a[1] cmp $b[1]  # First initial
            ||        #  if still equal...
        $a[2] <=> $b[2]  # Date of birth
        } @data;
```

See Also
reverse, strict, and aliases in this book

Pragmas and Directives

use

Usage

```
use module
use module symbols
use module version symbols
no module
no module symbols
use version
```

Description

The use directive takes code in an external file and includes it into the current script at compile time. (Compare this with require, which happens at runtime.) The use directive also calls the import method located in the module, which will (typically) import symbols into the calling package.

The most common form of the use declaration is demonstrated with

```
use CGI;
```

The file CGI.pm will be sought out in the directories listed in @INC and the code from that file read. The code comprising the module must end with a true value signaling a successful module load (it's customary to end modules with a 1; on a line by itself).

Afterward, if the CGI module contains a subroutine called import, it will be run. Thus, the previous statement is equivalent to

```
BEGIN { require CGI; CGI->import(); }
```

The BEGIN causes the require to happen at compile time, and the import is run after the code is brought in.

Some modules allow the import method to accept a list of symbols that will be put into the caller's current package. Exactly what these symbols are depends on the module being imported. Typically it will be either subroutines and variables, or a pseudo-symbol that will represent an entire list; for example,

```
use CGI qw(header);  # Imports just the header() subroutine
use Fcntl ':flock';  # Imports LOCK_NB, LOCK_SH, LOCK_EX, etc..
```

The exact list of what can be imported should be obtained by reading the module's documentation. Modules are actually free to do whatever kinds of initialization they want in an `import` method. Modules typically use the `Exporter` module to handle the actual stuffing of symbols into the caller's package. See the `Exporter` entry.

If you want to `use` a module, but do not want your namespace altered, call use with an empty symbol list. This will prevent the `import` method from being called and the caller's namespace from being altered.

```
use LWP::Simple ();  # Prevent get(), mirror() and others from polluting
            #    the current namespace.


# Have to call get() explicitly, since it wasn't imported.
$content=LWP::Simple::get("http://www.perl.org");
```

If a particular version of a module is needed, a version parameter can be used along with the module name. The `VERSION` method in the module will be called to determine the version. This method is eventually inherited from the `UNIVERSAL` class, which will check the original module's `$VERSION` variable. If the version number is not sufficient, an exception will be thrown.

The version parameter also can be used without a module name. This causes the interpreter to verify that its version is at least version. This is similar to the `require` version syntax but happens at compile time, and `require` at runtime.

The `no` directive does nearly the opposite of `use`. The module specified will have its `unimport` method called (if one exists) and attempt to remove the exported symbols from the caller's package. If symbols are specified, those will be removed explicitly; otherwise, the default list of symbols will be removed. Not all modules define a `no` behavior.

In some cases of `use`, the module can be one of Perl's pragmatic modules. For example,

```
use strict;
```

imports a `strict.pm` from the `@INC` directory list and calls its `import` method. By default, the symbols `refs`, `vars`, and `subs` are used in the case of `strict`. These don't actually import subroutines (or variables) into the current namespace. They simply use that convenient interface to enable certain kinds of stricture—remember that modules can do whatever they want in their import method.

In fact, all the pragmas contain stub modules whose documentation can be browsed and the source code can be examined to see how they work.

Example Listing 1.84

```
# Sets up a function called "message" which sends mail.
#    It uses Net::SMTP if it's there, otherwise it falls
#    back to using the local copy of sendmail.

use 5.005;
use strict;

my $sendmail;
BEGIN {
    $sendmail=0;
    eval "use Net::SMTP";
    if ($@) { $sendmail=1; }
}
sub message {
my($to,$body)=@_;

    if ($sendmail) {
        open(MAIL, "|/usr/lib/sendmail -t") || die;
        print MAIL <<EOM;
From: me
To: $to

$body
EOM
        close(MAIL) || die;
    } else {
        # Change "mailhost" to the ISP's mail host
        my $smtp=Net::SMTP->new('mailhost');
        die "Cannot send message through mailhost";
        $smtp->mail("Me");
        $smtp->to($to);
        $smtp->data();
        $smtp->datasend(<<EOM);
    From: me
    To: $to

$body
EOM
        $smtp->dataend();
        $smtp->quit;
    }
}
```

> **See Also**
> Exporter module documentation, use v5.6.0; Guarantee Perl 5.6, use CGI 2.50 qw(:all); A decent version of CGI.pm, and `require` in this book

require

Usage

```
require module
require expr
require version
```

Description

The `require` directive in its first two forms is used to take Perl code from an external file at runtime and execute it. This differs from `use`, which happens at compile time. It differs from `do` in that `require` raises an exception if the external code cannot be loaded.

If a module name (a bare identifier, or identifiers separated with colons) is specified, Perl will search the directories in `@INC` for the module and include its code into the current running program. Thus, the following forms are acceptable:

```
require Mylib;
require IO::Handle;
```

Perl will first change any double colons to the OS's directory separator and append `.pm` onto the end of the module specified before beginning the search with `@INC`. Thus with the previous example, `Mylib.pm` and `IO/Handle.pm` will be searched for in all the directories specified in `@INC`.

The `require` directive will ensure that any required file is only loaded once. Successive attempts to load the file will do nothing. This is done by editing the `%INC` hash when a module is loaded.

When found, the code in the external file is run. The external code is in its own lexical scope (because it's in another file). As an error check for the loading, the code must return true. Thus it's traditional to end all external modules with a bare:

```
1;
```

This will signify the end of the module.

If a quoted string or a variable is used instead of a module name, the `require` directive performs almost the same except: 1.) double colons are not converted to directory separators in the name, and 2.) A `.pm` is not appended onto the end of the name. Thus:

```
$foo="Mylib";
require $foo;
require "IO::Handle";
```

This will go looking for the files `Mylib` and `IO::Handle` in the current directory. The `%INC` hash is adjusted correctly if these files are loaded, and `@INC` is used to search for the files.

The `require` directive also can be used to specify a minimum version number for the interpreter running the script. The number can be specified in two ways. The first (and deprecated) way is a decimal number such as 5.003 or 5.005. As in the following:

```
require 5.000;     # No perl 4's allowed!
```

The second (and approved) way is to specify a version number string in the form $X.Y.Z$, where X is the language version (currently 5), Y is the interpreter version (currently 6), and Z is the patchlevel. You also can specify the version number as a vector string (`v5.6.1`) in Perl starting with 5.6.0.

Example Listing 1.85

```
# A minimal graphics program.  It tentatively requires Tk
#    in the BEGIN block so that if an error occurs, a nice
#    message can be printed.

use strict;
require 5.6.0;
BEGIN {
    if (! eval "require Tk") {
        die "You must install the Tk package from CPAN";
    }
    Tk->import();
}
my $win=new MainWindow;
```

See Also

`@INC`, `%INC`, `use`, and `do` in this book

```
strict
```

Usage

```
use strict;
use strict stricture type
```

Description

The `strict` pragma enables additional rules in Perl for what is allowed in a Perl program. These rules can help the programmer write Perl that avoids some common mistakes.

The `strict` pragma has three components: `vars`, `refs`, and `subs`. Simply declaring:

```
use strict;
```

enables all three for the remainder of the lexical scope. To enable only certain stricture types, simply list them after the `strict` pragma:

```
use strict qw(vars refs);   # But _not_ subs!
```

To turn off stricture, simply declare `no strict`, or `no strict 'refs'` to turn off only `refs` strictures.

It's advisable for beginners to write programs using `strict` and `warnings`. In the long run, your Perl code will be better and you'll have fewer bugs.

```
strict vars
```

The `strict vars` pragma turns on compile-time checking to make sure that any variable name you've used has been qualified with a package name. So, `$foo` in the current package is no longer a valid package variable name. `$main::foo` is okay, however. Declared with `our` if it is a package variable; declared with `my` if it is intended to be a lexical variable; declared with a `use vars` pragma.

Perl's global special variables (`$_`, `$^T`, `@ARGV`) or package special variables (`$a`, `$b`) are exempt from this stricture.

The purpose of `strict vars` is to prevent you from using variables that you have not declared in some way. If you do so, the error thrown resembles:

```
Global symbol "$x" requires explicit package name
```

The solution is to declare the variable with `my`, `our`, or `use vars`.

strict subs

The `strict subs` pragma causes a compile time exception when barewords are encountered. Barewords are identifiers whose meaning cannot be determined by the parser at compile time. Some examples are as follows:

- Using barewords when you meant a quoted string:

```
$r=foo;   # Did you mean foo() or 'foo' ?
```

- Using functions before they're declared:

```
foo \@junk, 'hello';
sub foo {
    my($aref, $string)=@_;
}
```

Perl does understand barewords in some cases, where the meaning can be determined from the surrounding context. See the `strict subs` example later for examples of this.

strict refs

The `strict refs` pragma is intended to keep you from using symbolic references. Symbolic references can cause all sorts of programming errors, most notably when they're used accidentally. It's also very easy to pollute your symbol table and overwrite other global variables unintentionally. So for these reasons, the use of symbolic references is discouraged.

The `strict refs` exceptions are raised at runtime.

```
use strict 'refs';

$cat="Hoover";

$t="cat";
print $$t;  # ERROR!  Trying to get at $cat through $t is not allowed!

$y=\$cat;
print $$y;  # This is fine though, it's a regular reference.
```

Example Listing 1.86

```
use strict 'vars';

$a="Hello, world!";  # $a is exempt from strict vars, explicitly
```

```
foreach(@ARGV) {
    print;          # exempt too!
}
print $r;           # ERROR!  Won't compile.

my $dog="Max";          # This is kosher
our $house='madness';# This is fine, too.
print $File::Find::name;    # Peachy as well.

local $calls=.25;       # ERROR!  This is not okay.  Won't compile
```

Example Listing 1.87

```
use strict 'subs';

# Bareword, but context implies a filehandle
$r=<FOO>;

use subs qw{foo};
sub walk { 1 };

# Again, barewords but perl's sure these are function calls.
foo @bar, 'hello';
walk %tree;

# key is a bareword here, but => indicates that the thing-on-the-left
#    is to be treated as a quoted-string if it's a plain identifier
%hash=( key => 'data' );

# Same here.  key is still a bareword, but the {}'s indicate that contained
#    identifiers here are string literals
$hash{skeleton}="Soong";
```

Example Listing 1.88

```
# Demonstration of using a symref under stricture.

use strict;

# Create a bunch of functions called sing() in a variety of
#    packages.
```

```
package pink;
sub sing { "Little pink houses for you and me" }
package purple;
sub sing { "I only wanted 2 see U bathing in the purple rain" }
package green;
sub sing { "Now listen while I play, my green tambourine" }
package yellow;
sub sing { "We all live in a yellow submarine" }
package brown;
sub sing { "And don't it make my brown eyes blue" }
*blue=\&brown::sing;  # Two for the price of one

# Now sing a lyric at random...
my $color=(qw(pink purple green yellow brown blue))[rand 6];
print "The lyric for $color is: ";

# Calling a subroutine whose name isn't known until runtime
#   is hard with strict refs in effect.  Without eval with strict refs,
#   nearly impossible.
no strict 'refs';
print &{ $color . "::sing"}();
```

> **See Also**
> use subs, use vars, subroutines, and references in this book

diagnostics

Usage

```
use diagnostics;
```

Description

The diagnostics pragma turns on extended diagnostic messages in addition to Perl's terse warnings and error messages. For example, the snippet:

```
my $foo;
$foo->bar();
```

would normally produce "Can't call method 'bar' on an undefined value" at runtime. However, under the diagnostics pragma, the message would become:

```
Can't call method "bar" on an undefined value at ./foo.pl line 6 (#1)

    (F) You used the syntax of a method call, but the slot filled by the
    object reference or package name contains an undefined value.
    Something like this will reproduce the error:

    $BADREF = undef;
    process $BADREF 1,2,3;
    $BADREF->process(1,2,3);

Uncaught exception from user code:
Can't call method "bar" on an undefined value at ./foo.pl line 6.
```

This diagnostic message is gathered from the `perldiag` manual page. Warning messages from Perl only will appear once per program invocation. Any messages printed by the user invoking `warn` remain unaffected.

Enabling diagnostics automatically turns on warnings (with `-w`) for the entire script. The diagnostics pragma affects both the compilation and the runtime warnings that are generated. (The previous example was a runtime warning.) If there is a `$SIG{__WARN__}` handler, it will be preserved but run after the diagnostics module's handler is run.

In addition to extensive descriptions, passing the `-verbose` flag to the diagnostics module will cause the introduction to the `perldiag` page to print when a message is generated (but only once per invocation).

To turn off the diagnostics at runtime, use the `enable` and `disable` functions that come with the diagnostics module. See Example Listing 1.88 for an example of selectively switching diagnostic modes using the `$^W` variable. You cannot turn off diagnostics by saying `no diagnostics`.

Example Listing 1.89

```
# A somewhat pointless CGI program.  However,
#   It switches diagnostics on and off, and triggers
#   a runtime warning under some circumstances
use diagnostics;
use CGI;

my $q=new CGI;
print $q->header;
{
```

```
    local $^W;
    # Diagnostics won't catch this!  Warnings are off!
    $number=1; # Default
    if ($q->param("FOO")=~/^\d+$/) { #  It's numeric and exists!
        $number=$q->param("FOO");
    }
}

# But they're enabled for this...
#    Given a parameter of FOO=0, nice big diagnostics print
my $quotient=365/$number;
```

> **See Also**
> `perldiag` in the Perl documentation

constant

Usage

```
use constant name => value;
```

Description

The `constant` pragma allows you to declare constant hashes, arrays, and scalars. The constant name will be associated with the value at runtime and cannot be changed; for example,

```
use constant PI => 3.14159;
use constant BOYS => [ qw ( stan kyle kenny cartman ) ];
use constant VILLANS => { superman => 'luthor',
            spiderman => 'goblin',
            batman    => 'penguin' };
```

This allows later references to PI to have the value of 3.14159. The constant value is package scoped so that after:

```
package FOO;
use constant ACCELERATION => 9.8;
```

the constant ACCELERATION can be accessed from different packages as FOO:ACCELERATION.

Some notes on constants declared with use constant are as follows:

- Constants do not interpolate in double-quoted string contexts. So,

  ```
  print "On earth ACCELERATION m/s^2 is the law!";
  ```

  prints just that, without substituting 9.8 for ACCELERATION. You can force interpolation by using @{[ACCELERATION]}.

- Constant lists are returned as lists and not arrays. Thus, if you want to subscript them, you must surround constant lists with parentheses:

  ```
  $first=(BOYS)[0];   # Grab "stan" from the list defined above
  ```

- Constant arrays and hashes place no restrictions on changing the contents of the arrays and hashes at all. You simply can't re-assign to the constant itself.

- Constants must begin with a letter or underscore.

- Constants are created at compile time; proper dereferencing and use of invalid subscripts for arrays and hashes will be checked for at that time.

Example Listing 1.90

```
# Phase of the Moon calculator
#  From today's date, roughly calculates the
#  phase of the moon.
#

use constant LUNARMONTH => 29.530588853;
use Date::Calc qw(Date_to_Days); # For sane date conversions
use strict;

my @phases=(   0 => 'Full Moon',      1 => 'Waning Gibbous',
         7 => 'Last Quarter',    8 => 'Waning Crescent',
        14 => 'New Moon',       15 => 'Waxing Crescent',
        21 => 'First Quarter', 22 => 'Waxing Gibbous',
        28 => 'Full Moon' );

my($m, $d, $y)=(localtime)[4,3,5]; $m++;  $y+=1900;


# Compute the age of the moon in days.
#  Roughly based on a BASIC listing in
#  Sky & Telescope April 1994
```

```
my $jul=Date_to_Days($y,$m,$d) + 1721425 ;
my $v=($jul-2451550.1)/LUNARMONTH;
if (($v-=int($v))<0) { $v+=1; }
my $age=$v*LUNARMONTH;

my $type="";
for(my $day=0; $day<@phases; $day+=2) {
    last if ($phases[$day]>$age);
    $type=$phases[$day+1];
}
print "The moon is $age days old ($type)\n";
```

See Also
subroutines in this book

warnings

Usage

```
use warnings
no warnings
use warnings categories
no warnings categories
use warnings FATAL => categories
```

Description

The warnings pragma (new to Perl 5.6) is used to control warnings lexically. Warning messages emitted by Perl can be turned on and off in a particular lexical scope, and by category.

To turn on warnings for a particular block, simply use the pragma:

```
use warnings;
```

To turn them off again, simply declare no warnings.

Additionally, Perl now has categories of warnings. Each warning emitted by Perl falls into one of the following categories:

all	class	subclass
all	io	pipe, unopened, closed, newline, exec
	syntax	ambiguous, semicolon, precedence, bareword, reserved, digit, parenthesis, deprecated, printf, prototype, qw
	severe	inplace, internal, debugging, malloc
	void, recursion, redefine, numeric, uninitialized, once, misc, regexp, glob, y2k, chmod, umask, untie, substr, taint, signal, closure,overflow, portable, utf8,exiting, pack, unpack	

For example, turn on all warnings except the `"use of uninitialized value"` warning in a block of code using the following:

```
{
    use warnings;
    no warnings 'uninitialized';

    # Rest of your code here...
}
```

Warnings are accumulative. If within a block you turn on consecutive warnings, each of those will be combined with other warnings in effect within the block. Also, turning on a category of warnings will turn on all warnings within that category.

```
no warnings;
{
    use warnings qw( io uninitialized);
    no warnings qw( exec );

    # In effect here is: uninitialized, pipe, unopened,
    #     closed and newline
}
```

If followed with the literal string FATAL, the warnings pragma causes the warnings listed with that pragma to become fatal. Instead of issuing a message to STDERR and continuing, a warning thrown in that category will print the warning message to STDERR and then throw an exception. If the exception isn't caught with eval, the program will terminate.

The warnings pragma interacts with the command-line switches -w, -X, -W and the variable $^W. The rules for which take precedence are as follows:

- Lexical warnings are unaffected by the -w switch and the $^W variable. Lexical warnings, if requested, always take precedence.

- The -W switch overrides the warnings pragma and enables all lexical warnings for every block in the program.

- The -X switch also overrides the warnings pragma (and the value of $^W) and disables warnings in the entire program.

Example Listing 1.91

```
use warnings;   # implies 'all'
no warnings 'redefine';
use warnings FATAL => qw(uninitialized);

$r=1;
# Warns 'useless use of cos in void context'
cos $r;

# The "Subroutine foo redefined" message is skipped!
sub foo { 1; }
sub foo { 1; }

$r=undef;
# Issues "Use of uninitialized value in print"
#    ...and dies!
print $r;

print "Did I make it?";  # No, 'fraid not.
```

See Also
warnings module documentation
$^W and -w in this book

```
warn
```

Usage

```
warn
warn list
```

Description

The warn function causes Perl to print a warning message to STDERR similar to die, except that an exception is not thrown.

If a message isn't supplied in list, the message Warning: Something's wrong will be displayed (in addition to the line number and file). If $@ already contains an error message and list isn't given, ...caught will be appended to $@ when the warning is displayed.

The warn function also triggers the __WARN__ handler if one is installed in %SIG. See the __WARN__ entry for details.

The warn function's operation is not affected by the -w switch, the value of $^W, or the warnings pragma.

Example Listing 1.92

```
warn "I'm gonna count to three..." if ($mom);
```

> **See Also**
> warnings and __WARN__ in this book

```
die
```

Usage

```
die
die list
```

Description

The die function causes Perl to raise an exception and the current script (or eval) to terminate. The die function behaves differently depending on the context in which it was used.

Additionally, if a __DIE__ handler is found in %SIG, that handler is run. See the __DIE__ entry.

In the main portion of your script, raising an exception with die causes the list to be written to the STDERR filehandle, and the exit status of the script set to the current value of $!. If $! is 0, the exit status of the last child process reaped is used (the lower 8 bits of $?, see the wait entry). If that is also 0, 255 is returned from Perl.

If the list does not end in a newline, the following message:

> at *script* line *line* at *script* line *line*, *filehandle* line *inputline*

is printed, where:

> *Script* is the name of the script.
>
> *Line* is the line of the script at which the die occurred.
>
> *Filehandle* is the filehandle that had just been read.
>
> *Inputline* is the line (record) of input just read.

A newline will be appended. If you have a newline at the end of the list, your message will be printed by itself without decoration.

Within an eval, die behaves somewhat differently because die/eval are Perl's general-purpose exception raising and handling mechanisms (see eval for more examples). If the die function is run while Perl is processing an eval statement, eval will terminate returning undef. The list (from the innermost die) will be placed in $@ and not echoed to STDERR.

If the list is empty, and $@ is unset by Perl, the string Died is put into $@. If the list is empty, but $@ is already set, Perl adds the text ...propagated to the error message. Example Listing 1.92 demonstrates this. This is useful when an exception has been raised in an eval and needs to be passed up to a higher level.

Example Listing 1.93

```
# This demo uses eval/die to trap an exception raised in XML::Parser
#    and propagate it upwards.  The message that will get emitted resembles:
#
#    not well-formed at line 7, column 14, byte 114 at /usr/local/lib/perl5...
#                    ..../site_perl/5.6.0/i686-linux/XML/Parser.pm line 185
#       Bad XML in band list after "REO Speedwagon"
```

```perl
#         ...propagated at /tmp/foo.pl line 20.

# The fix is to repair the XML data, of course.
use strict;
use XML::Parser;

sub bandlist {
    my($band, @bands);
    my $parser=new XML::Parser( Handlers => {
        Start => sub { $band=""; },
        Char  => sub { if ( ($_[0]->context)[-1] eq "band") {
                    $band.=$_[1]; } },
        End   => sub { push(@bands, $band) if $band; } });
    eval {
        $parser->parse(*DATA);
    };
    if ($@) {
        # Edit the message from XML::Parser to add the last
        #    band processed to help debug the error
        $@.="\tBad XML in band list ";
        if (@bands) { $@.=qq{after "$bands[-1]"}; }
        $@.="\n";
        die;   # Will add ...propagated for us since no list is specd.
    }
    return @bands;
}
print join(',', bandlist);
__END__
<mp3s>
<song>
<band>REO Speedwagon</band>
<tune>Can't Fight This Feeling</tune>
</song>
<song>
<!-- The ampersand below should be &amp; -->
<band>Simon & Garfunkle</band>
<tune>Homeward Bound</tune>
</song>
<song>
<band>The Who</band>
<tune>Baba O'Reilley</tune>
</song>
<mp3s>
```

See Also

Carp and diagnostics module documentation

eval, wait, warn, $@, $!, and __DIE__ in this book

CHAPTER 2

Advanced Perl

Namespaces and Packages

Packages

Description

Packages are Perl's method of providing multiple namespaces. Package variables are stored separately from lexical variables and from the special global variables. The entire discussion that follows doesn't apply to those.

Variables, filehandles, and subroutines names in Perl are managed by using a namespace called a package. By default, variables in a Perl script are stored in the package named main. Package names are specified by using the name of a package (an *identifier*, such as scalar variables names), followed by a set of double colons. So the variable $i in the package main is referred to as

```
$main::i;   # Package main's $i.
```

The variable type identifier goes before the package name. You can consider $main::i a fully-qualified package variable name and $i as a shorthand version if you choose. Omitting the package name completely (as in $::i) assumes the package main.

If a package name isn't specified, a (non-lexical, non special) variable is considered to be in the current package. The `package` pragma is used to switch between packages. The syntax for `package` is

```
package namespace package
```

If you specify a *namespace*, that becomes the current namespace. (Perl programs start with a current namespace of `main`.) For the rest of the compilation unit, variables will belong to that package, unless they're fully qualified with a package name.

```
$i=4;           # Implicitly, $main::$i
$::j=2;         # Also $main::j
package Cooking;
@eggs=(1..12);   # This is @Cooking::eggs
$::butter=1;     # But this is $main::butter, see preceding note

package main;           # Back to main again.
print "I have @eggs\n";# Nothing!  This refers to @main::eggs
            #     perl throws the error "@eggs better written
            #     as \@eggs" because @eggs is unknown

# This is in the package main, so to get to Cooking:: you have
# to qualify it.
print "I have @Cooking::eggs\n";
```

If you use the `package` pragma without a package name, no default package is used. All variables (other than lexicals and global special) will require a fully-qualified package name in order to be used:

```
package;
$i=4;        # Compilation error:
        #     "Global symbol $i requires explicit package name..."
```

This is similar to `use strict vars`, except that function names also will have to be fully-qualified package names to be compiled.

Package identifiers normally begin with an alphabetic character or underscore, followed by alphanumeric characters or underscores up to 251 characters long. Package identifiers are chained together by double colons and can be as long as you want to indicate namespaces and sub-namespaces.

```
package Astronomy::Stars;
$sun={ color => 'yellow', planets => 9 };
```

```
package Astronomy::Planets;
$earth={ core => 'iron', atmosphere => 'nitrogen' };
```

The `Astronomy::Stars` and `Astronomy::Planets` namespaces aren't necessarily related. They might have nothing to do with a namespace `Astronomy`. The ability to create paths of namespaces is just a convenience for logically organizing your namespaces. (Note: there are no relative package paths.) If a package pathname is specified, it is assumed to be a fully qualified name.

There is one relation between package namespaces with common roots. A package named `Astronomy::Galaxy` exists as a hash entry in the package `Astronomy`. This is a matter of convenience and an implementation detail. Perl doesn't expect any relation between packages other than this.

By convention, namespaces begin with an uppercase letter. Modules normally declare themselves to be in a particular namespace that is the same name as the module. Using an uppercase namespace ensures that a module's name won't overlap with a pragmatic module (such as `strict` or `warnings`).

In older versions of Perl, the package namespace separator wasn't `::`, it was `'` (an apostrophe). So the following two lines refer to the same variable:

```
$Astronomy::Galaxy::m15="Whirlpool Galaxy";
print $Astronomy'Galaxy'm15, qq{ can be seen with a 4" telescope\n};
```

The use of `'` as a package separator is frowned upon because it can be confusing. Notice the following situation:

```
$city=(qw( Detroit Philly Boston ))[rand 3];
print "$city's taxi drivers are rude.\n";
```

A naive programmer would expect that one of the three cities would be replaced for `$city`, except that Perl sees `$city's` as `$city::s`—the variable `$s` in the package `city`. So you won't have a city in the `print` statement. The use of warnings would have tipped you off because `-w` would have generated:

```
Name "main::city" used only once: possible typo at sample.pl line 1. Name
"city::s" used only once: possible typo at sample.pl line 2.
```

This could be corrected by specifying `$city's` as: `${city}'s`.

Packages and the elements that compose a package namespace (hashes, arrays, filehandles) are stored internally as package variables themselves. Each package has a hash that describes the namespace of the package itself. The hash name is

%package::

Where *package* is the package name (or path of package names) whose namespace you're trying to examine. The values in the hash are *typeglobs*, and these can be used to reach the original values stored within the namespace.

Example Listing 2.1 dumps the namespace for the main package using the namespace and typeglobs. The debugger does something similar when the V command is issued.

Portions of the package namespace can be manipulated manually through the use of typeglobs. The typeglob entry contains details of creating aliases for a namespace (or portions of it). See the typeglob entry.

Additionally, the package namespace can be accessed directly through its hash. This allows you to manipulate the symbol table in ways that perl's syntax would not normally allow, and allows you to construct strings that would refer to a variable name and access it indirectly (a *symbolic reference*).

Variable, filehandle, and subroutine names are simple identifiers unless they're fully-qualified package names; in which case, the variable name itself is still a simple identifier.

The variable name $**k3wl** wouldn't normally be allowed in perl syntax. The string **k3wl** isn't a valid identifier—it doesn't begin with an alphanumeric/underscore and contains invalid characters. However, an entry in the symbol table can be made for it:

```
${'**k3wl**'}=99;      # This is now a symbol like $foo would be.
print ${'**k3wl**'};   # Yields 99, like a variable ${**k3wl**} might.
```

In Perl 4, this feature could be used to construct structures similar to hashes of hashes. Thankfully, that nonsense is no longer needed.

Example Listing 2.1

```
# Dump the namespace for the main:: package.
#  Note that namespaces that begin with main:: will
#  be represented as a hash here.
foreach(keys %main::) {
    local *name=$main::{$_};
    if ( defined $name ) {
        print "\$$_ is set to $name\n"
```

```
    }
    if ( @name ) {
        print "\@$_ has ", $#name+1, " elements\n";
    }
    if ( %name ) {
        print "\%$_ has ", scalar keys %name, " keys\n";
    }
    if ( defined &$_)   {
        print "\&$_ is a subroutine\n"
    }
}
```

See Also
lexicals and package in this book

Typeglobs

Description

Typeglobs are a metadata type in Perl. Typeglobs provide access to Perl's internal representation of package variables. This includes scalars, arrays, hashes, subroutines, filehandles, formats, and other typeglobs. Typeglobs are often called "*globs*" for short, but to avoid confusion with the glob function and the glob functionality of the angle-operator, I will refer to them as typeglobs.

Typeglobs are represented by an asterisk followed by an identifier. Identifiers normally begin with an alphabetic character or underscore, followed by alphanumeric characters or underscores up to 251 characters long.

```
*foo="Hello";          # A typeglob in the current package
$p=*File::Find::path;  # A typeglob in the package File::Find
```

Typeglobs represent variables in a package. To qualify a typeglob to a particular package, it should be preceded by the package name. The package name will consist of identifiers separated by double-colons or apostrophes (see packages).

All package variables in Perl are stored internally in a symbol table. The index to the symbol table is the name of the variable (without its type-identifier). Typeglobs are a kind of variable that refers to all variables with that particular name. So *date refers to the $date, @date, %date, the filehandle date, the format date, and the subroutine named date.

Note that a discussion of typeglobs only applies to package variables. Lexical variables (those declared with my) don't use the symbol table and have no typeglobs to represent them. Typeglobs cannot be declared with my, although they can be stored; a reference to a typeglob can be stored in a lexical variable.

Typeglobs represent all the variables of that name at once. Observe the following:

```
$a="Hello, World";  #  $a is not declared with 'my', therefore is a package
                    #  variable
$r=${*a};           #  $r is set to the scalar portion of the typeglob *a
print $r;           #  Yeilds "Hello, World"
```

Using this trick, typeglobs can be used to alias a variable to another variable name. To create an alias for a variable name (or any part of a typeglob), assign a reference to the typeglob.

```
$original="William Shakespeare";
*copy=\$original;
print $copy;   # prints "William Shakespeare"
```

This works because the scalar portion of the typeglob *copy will now refer directly to the data stored in $original. The array, filehandle, and other portions of the *copy typeglob will remain unaffected. Observe the following:

```
# After code above
$original="Bill Shatner";
print $copy;        # Yields "Bill Shatner"
```

The variable $copy is aliased to $original, and changing either changes the data in the other.

This functionality is used by the Exporter module to make functions and variables appear in namespaces in which they weren't originally defined. For example, in a module that's in a separate package, make your function appear in main's namespace as follows:

```
package Mine;
sub myfunc {
    # Do stuff in here....
}
*{'main::myfunc'}=\&myfunc;
```

So, in the main body of the program, after the module had been used, a call to myfunc would actually call Mine::myfunc(). The Exporter module is actually quite a bit more sophisticated than this, but the general idea holds true.

To alias all variable types from one name to another, simply assign their globs to each other:

```
*yours=*mine;
```

After this statement, $yours and $mine will refer to the same scalar value. And similar aliases are set up for @yours/@mine, %yours/%mine, and for the filehandles yours/mine and the subroutines yours/mine.

Individual portions of a typeglob can be accessed using a hash-like syntax:

```
*identifier{reftype}
```

For example, the typeglob *r's scalar value can be accessed with the following:

```
*r{SCALAR}
```

A reference to the scalar portion of the typeglob is returned. The other portions of the typeglob can be accessed with a *reftype* of ARRAY, HASH, CODE, GLOB, IO. Additionally, the values PACKAGE and NAME can be used; these return the package that the typeglob is in and the name of the typeglob, respectively (not as references).

```
$r="Hello World";
%r=qw(one potato two potato);

print *main::r{SCALAR};   # Yields something like SCALAR(0x8090fe4)

print   ${ *r{SCALAR} },          # "Hello World"
    ${ *main::r{HASH} }{one},  # potato
    *r{NAME},                  # r
    *r{PACKAGE};               # main (for package main::)
```

For information on how to deal with the references returned by this notation, see the references entry.

The most common use for typeglobs is for creating filehandles that can be passed to or from a subroutine or private filehandle. There are two ways to do both of these. The first way is to use a lexical variable to hold a IO::Handle object; you can use the object as you would any other.

The second way is by passing a typeglob to (or from) a subroutine. As part of the typeglob, you'll get the filehandle with the corresponding name. By returning (or passing) the typeglob, you can assign the typeglob passed to a local name as follows:

```
# Passing a filehandle with a typeglob
open(FH, "/tmp/sample.txt") || die "sample.txt: $!";
myfunc(*FH);
sub myfunc {
    local(*MYH)=$_[0];
    print <MYH>;
}
```

In order for the filehandle to be local to the subroutine, you must declare the typeglob with `local`. (Remember, you cannot use `my` with filehandles or typeglobs.) To return a filehandle from a subroutine, do the reverse:

```
sub mysub {
    local(*F);
    open(F, "/tmp/sample.txt") || die;
    return *F;
}
*T=mysub();
print <T>;
```

The other common use for typeglobs (as demonstrated) is for altering the symbol table of another package to import subroutine names or variables. For example, constants can be introduced into the caller's namespace with this short module:

```
package myconst;
sub import {
    my($caller)=caller;
    my $package=shift;
    my($const, $value);

    while($const = shift) {
        $value=shift;
        *{$caller . '::' . $const}=
                sub () { $value };
    }
}
1;
```

To use the module, simply specify the constants that you want defined during the use directive:

```
use myconst    pi => 3.14159265358979323846,
        c => 2.99792458e8,
        g => 9.80665,
```

```
    year => 365.2596;

print year;
```

In this sample, four constants have been defined that cannot be changed because they are simply subroutines that return the correct values, imported into the main program's namespace. This is (in large part) how the constant module works from the standard Perl distribution.

See Also
scalars, packages, arrays, and filehandles in this book

Exporter

Usage

```
use Exporter;
@ISA=('Exporter');
```

Description

The Exporter module is actually a class that supplies an import method to modules. It handles the management of which variables and subroutines need to be exported to the caller and allows you to concern yourself with developing a coherent API.

To use the Exporter module, you must perform:

```
use Exporter;
@ISA=qw(Exporter);
```

The @ISA declaration is necessary so that when your module is used, perl won't find a local import method and begin searching the module's ancestors—including Exporter.

The Exporter modules uses three structures to determine which symbols need to be exported: @EXPORT, @EXPORT_OK, and %EXPORT_TAGS. These should be declared as package variables within the module that is exporting symbols, and if use strict is in effect, you'll need to declare them with our or use vars.

The @EXPORT array contains those items that will be placed into the caller's namespace. The variable names need their type identifiers ($@%), and the functions might have a leading ampersand. Thus,

```
@EXPORT=('$foo', '@stuff', '&myfunc');
```

The values must be protected with quotes (or a quote-like operator) so that the variable name itself is exported, not its value. Use @EXPORT with care because anything in here always affects the caller's namespace.

The @EXPORT_OK array contains items that can optionally be imported into the caller's namespace. Items here are not automatically exported when the module is used; they have to be explicitly asked for:

```
package Mymod;
use Exporter;
@ISA=qw(Exporter);
@EXPORT=qw( &walkabout );
@EXPORT_OK=qw( $foo $bar );
```

So in the preceding snippet, the function &walkabout will be placed in the caller's namespace. The variables $foo and $bar will be made available, but the caller has to ask for them by name:

```
use Mymod qw($foo);   # Gets $foo.
```

Finally, the hash %EXPORT_TAGS allows you to specify groups of symbols to export. The %EXPORT_TAGS hash resembles the following:

```
%EXPORT_TAGS = ( tagname => [ symbol list ], tagname => [ symbol list ], );
```

The items in *symbol lists* must also occur in either @EXPORT or @EXPORT_OK. The *tagnames* specify the groups of symbols you want to export. During the use, the caller will specify which symbols to import by preceding the *tagname* with a colon.

When the calling program performs a use, some special tags affect which symbols will be imported. The tag :DEFAULT imports everything in @EXPORT. The tag :*tagname* imports everything from the corresponding *symbol list* in %EXPORT_TAGS. A pattern can be specified to import symbols from @EXPORT and @EXPORT_OK, which match with /*pattern*/.

Preceding the tag name (or symbol name) in a use with ! will cause the symbols in the list not to be exported from the module. Also, performing a use with a bare set of parenthesis will cause the module's import method not to be called at all—thus Exporter can't import any symbols.

```
use Foo ();   # No import(), and thus no Exporter will be run!
```

So using the API described in Example Listing 2.2, this is how the following use statements would work:

```
use City;                # Gets fire and police
use City qw(:advanced);  # Gets garbage, water and sewer (not fire and police)
use City qw(:advanced
        :DEFAULT);   # Gets garbage, water and sewer, fire and police
use City qw(/^@/);       # Gets @schools and @playgrounds
use City qw(!fire        # Gets police only
        :DEFAULT);
```

In general, you should export

> Nothing from OO modules. Strictly speaking, OO modules shouldn't need to export symbols because all the methods will be accessed through a blessed object. All class variables and instance variables should be accessed through a blessed object or class methods.

> As little as possible from other modules. The @EXPORT array should be used sparingly. You're polluting other program's namespaces, remember!

> Classes and groups of symbol names instead of individual symbols. In this way, users don't have to keep referring to the documentation to find every single value and function they want—they can simply import the group of symbols for the task at hand.

Example Listing 2.2

```
# Template for a module that exports symbols back into the
#   caller's package.  Fairly generic, modify to suit your needs.
#   For this example, a module that exports various city services.

package City;
use strict;
our(@ISA, @EXPORT, @EXPORT_OK, %EXPORT_TAGS, $VERSION);
$VERSION=1.01;

use Exporter;
@ISA=qw(Exporter);

# First, define all of the symbols we can export.  Group them
#   appropriately.
%EXPORT_TAGS=(
    basic    => [ qw( police fire ) ],
    advanced => [ qw( garbage water sewer ) ],
    children => [ qw( @schools @playgrounds ) ],
```

```
      senior   => [ qw( busing meals_on_wheels ) ],
      business => [ qw( chamber_of_commerce ) ],
);

# * Force the exporting of the 'basic' list to the caller.
#   This is the only part that should need to be tinkered with.
# * Make sure all of the symbols from %EXPORT_TAGS are
#   in @EXPORT_OK.
# * Create a special import category (:all) that stands for
#   everything.
@EXPORT=@{$EXPORT_TAGS{basic}};
@EXPORT_OK=map @$_, values %EXPORT_TAGS;
$EXPORT_TAGS{all}=\@EXPORT_OK;

# Presumably, here's where you'd begin defining all of
#   the functions, variables, and stuff you've exported...
```

See Also
import and use in this book

Symbolic References

Description

Symbolic references (also called *soft references*) are an alternative to normal references (called *hard references*) documented in the "References" section.

Symbolic references use references to variable names instead of to actual data. There is no operator for creating a symbolic reference (such as \ for hard references). Instead, symbolic references work by simply substituting the name of the variable in which the reference would otherwise go. For example,

```
$teeth="dental";

@$teeth=qw(molars incisors);  # sets @dental
push @$teeth, "canines";      # again uses, @dental.

print $teeth->[0];            # prints "molars" from @dental
print $teeth;                 # prints "dental"
```

For dereferencing a symbolic reference, the syntax is exactly the same as that for hard references (see the "References" section).

The use of symbolic references is discouraged in Perl culture because of the possibility of errors being introduced if the symbol name ($teeth) in the previous examples were wrong. With a symbolic reference, any string can be dereferenced even if it doesn't yet exist as a variable name elsewhere:

```
$foo="Dave";
print $$foo;    # prints $Dave's value, even if that's what you didn't intend
        # and it doesn't exist
```

Curly braces also can be used with symbolic references; in fact, literals can be used within the curlies to cause a symbolic reference to use it as an identifier.

```
# Sets $Dave
${"Dave"}="I'm sorry, I can't do that.";
```

Building package identifiers for manipulating the symbol table takes advantage of symbolic references. To change a variable in a particular package (as demonstrated in the typeglob entry), symbolic references can be used to build the identifier:

```
package Foo;

$var="animal";
${"main::" . $var}="Wombat";  # Sets $main::animal to Wombat
```

Similar to {} in hash keys, identifiers for symbolic references do not have to be enclosed in quotation marks if they are barewords. This makes processing symbolic references that are the same name as a Perl function a problem. Perl has to choose whether you meant the function to be evaluated or taken literally.

```
${a}="Hello";   # Sets $a (might be lexical too)
${"a"}="World";  # Sets $a (certainly a package variable)

# Do you mean $shift or ${shift @ARGV} ?
${shift}="Narf!";        # Perl knows you mean $shift
${shift @ARGV}="Poit";   # This means use the first thing on @ARGV as variable
name
```

To force perl's interpretation of an identifier, simply use it as a function or as part of an expression. See the hashes entry for more examples.

As the preceding example shows, using symbolic references can be dangerous. The possibility of having a program botch its own variables (or one of Perl's special variables) is very real. Because of the possibilities of botching a referent accidentally, the strict pragma allows you to turn off symbolic references entirely. Saying,

```
use strict 'refs';
```

will cause a dereference of anything other than a hard reference to throw an exception at runtime.

Only package variables can be manipulated with symbolic reference. Because symbolic references make use of the symbol table, lexical variables (those declared with my) cannot be used as the target of a symbolic reference. Symbolic references also are a bit slower than hard references.

Example Listing 2.3

```
# Allows a user to print variables directly out
#     of perl's namespace.  For example, try %ENV
#     or @INC for starters.

while(print("\nWhich variable?"),
        chomp($r=<STDIN>), $r) {
    $type=substr($r, 0, 1, "");

    print %{$r} if ($type eq "%");
    print @{$r} if ($type eq "\@");
    print ${$r} if ($type eq "\$");
}
```

> **See Also**
> strict, hashes, packages, and references in this book

Closure

Description

Closure is the term for a subroutine reference that carries with it the variables which were in lexical scope at the time the reference was created. Later, when the subroutine reference is executed, the lexical variables that were around when it was created, are in scope again.

This is normally used to create a subroutine that has state associated with it. The variables created in a closure cannot be modified outside of the closure because they are only in scope within the closure itself.

Example Listing 2.4

```
sub counter {
    my $c=1;
    return sub {
        # $c is lexically scoped above
        # but the scope includes this
        # subroutine
        $c++;
    };

}
my $counter1=counter;  # Create a counter
my $counter2=counter;  # Create a second counter

# counter1 and counter 2 both have independent
# versions of the $c that was in scope when
# they were created.  They will be re-used in those
# anonymous subroutines
print &$counter1, "\n";        # prints 1
print &$counter1, "\n";        # prints 2
print &$counter2, "\n";        # prints 1
print &$counter1, "\n";        # prints 3
```

See Also
perlref in the perl documentation
anonymous subroutines in this book

Advanced Subroutines

caller

Usage

caller
caller stack depth

Description

The `caller` function returns information about Perl's current subroutine call `stack`. In a scalar context, it returns the package name of the calling subroutine (or `main`). In a list context, it returns either three values or ten, depending on whether it was called with a stack depth.

If called from the main body of your program (not from within a subroutine), `caller` will return `undef` in a scalar context, or an empty list in an list context.

If called without a stack depth, caller will return a three-element list consisting of the caller's package, filename, and line.

The *stack depth* refers to the number of subroutine calls (stack frames) to go back to retrieve calling information. A `require` or `use` creates a stack frame, as does an `eval`. The 10 elements returned by `caller` stack depth are as follows:

Element	Meaning
package	The package name of the caller.
filename	The filename of the caller.
line	The line number that the current `sub` was called from.
sub	The subroutine that performed the call, or (eval) if it was called from an `eval`.
hasargs	True if the call had arguments; false if `&foo;` was used and the last subroutine's `@_` was re-used (see calling subroutines).
wantarray	True if the subroutine was called in a list context.
eval	Contains the string that was `eval`'d to call this subroutine. Not effective if `eval {}` was called.
require	True if the stack frame was created as the result of a use/require.
hints	For internal use only
bitmask	For internal use only

Example Listing 2.4

```
# Demonstrate caller() by creating some stack frames
#  with varying information and then dumping them all.
# Output is similar to the following:
```

```
# main ./foo.pl 21 Sub: main::dumper Args: 1 Arr: 1 Eval:  Req:
# main (eval 1)  1 Sub:    main::foo Args: 0 Arr: 0 Eval:  Req:
# main ./foo.pl 24 Sub:       (eval) Args: 0 Arr: 0 Eval: &foo; Req:
# main ./foo.pl 26 Sub:    main::bar Args: 1 Arr: 0 Eval:  Req:

use strict;
use warnings;
sub dumper {
    my $depth=0;
    no warnings 'once';
    while( my($package, $filename, $line, $sub,
     $hasargs, $wantarray, $eval, $require,
     $hints, $bitmask)=caller($depth++)) {
        $eval="" unless defined $eval;
        $require="" unless defined $require;
        $wantarray=0 unless defined $wantarray;
        printf("%6s %8s %2d Sub: %12s Args: %d Arr: %d Eval: %s Req: %s\n",
            $package, $filename, $line, $sub,
            $hasargs, $wantarray, $eval, $require);

    }
}
sub foo {
    my @foo=dumper("Argument", "Fight");
}
sub bar {
    eval "&foo;";
}
bar();
```

> **See Also**
> calling subroutines in this book

Subroutine Attributes

Usage

```
sub : attributes
sub : attributes block
```

Description

During the compilation stage, subroutine attributes inform Perl that the subroutine being compiled has certain attributes. At the moment, three attributes can be defined for subroutines: `locked`, `method` and `lvalue`. Attributes are listed after the prototype (if present), following a colon, immediately preceding the block that defines the subroutine (if present). Multiple attributes can be space separated.

```
sub critical : locked method {
}
```

The `locked` attribute affects subroutines when a multithreaded program is run. More than one thread cannot execute a subroutine with a `locked` attribute at a time. For more information, see the `lock` entry.

The `method` attribute currently only has one effect; it disables the `Ambiguous callresolved as CORE` warning.

The `lvalue` attribute allows a subroutine to return a modifiable scalar value from a subroutine. In this way, a subroutine can appear on the left of an assignment statement. There are some restrictions currently on `lvalue` subs:

- `lvalue` subs cannot return an array or hash (they return a reference instead). `lvalue` subs cannot currently distinguish whether they are being used on the left side of an expression or the right. This means that `a()=a()+1` is not currently possible.

- Do not explicitly `return` a value from an `lvalue` sub; simply have the last expression be the value that you need returned.

Example Listing 2.5

```
# Demo of lvalue subs
{
    my %table;
    sub store : lvalue {
        my($name)=shift;
        $table{$name}="";
        $table{$name};
    }
    sub fetch {
        my($name)=shift;
        return $table{$name};
    }
```

```
    }
    store("Family")=5;
    print fetch("Family");
```

> **See Also**
> lock and sub in this book

Special Compilation Subroutines

Usage

```
sub INIT { }
sub CHECK { }
sub BEGIN { }
sub END   { }
```

Description

These four subroutines are compiled similarly to normal subroutines except that they're executed at various stages of the compile-run cycle that perl scripts go through. They aren't really subroutines, they're just declared that way. During program execution, they cannot be called, except by perl itself. They don't take arguments; they won't return a value.

The BEGIN subroutine is executed as soon as it's recognized by perl. In fact, the file that contains the BEGIN won't be further compiled until the BEGIN has been read, compiled, and executed. This can be used to pull in modules (with use, require, do) and perform other functions that must be done before the remainder of the code can be compiled. You are allowed to have multiple BEGIN's within a single file, and they will be run in the order seen.

Files that are used will have their BEGIN subs run in the order in which they are seen as well. Thus,

```
use Eeyore;    # Contains a BEGIN { } as well..
use Pooh;      # Contains its own BEGIN
BEGIN { }
```

Would run Eeyore's BEGIN, Pooh's BEGIN and then main's BEGIN subroutine. The BEGIN subs will run when perl is run with a -c (compilation) switch because the side effects of the BEGIN might be necessary to complete compilation.

The END subroutine is executed as the perl script is exiting because of a return from the main body of the program, an exit, or an uncaught exception thrown with die. It won't be run if your process is signaled or otherwise terminates abnormally. You might have multiple END subs within a file, and they will be run in the reverse order in which they were seen by Perl. If they were pulled in from a module, they will still be run in reverse order. The END subs aren't run when perl is run with a -c switch.

Within an END subroutine, the variable $? contains the value that the perl interpreter will attempt to return to the calling program (the OS). You are allowed to alter this value within an END subroutine.

The INIT subroutine is run after compilation has completed, but before the program begins executing. Thus, it follows BEGIN blocks, but before the main body of code. Multiple INIT subroutines are run in the order in which they're encountered.

The CHECK subroutines are run after compilation, before the INIT subroutines, before the runtime begins, and in the reverse order that they're found.

These four subroutines (along with AUTOLOAD and DESTROY) actually can be defined without using the keyword sub to introduce them:

```
BEGIN {    }
INIT {    }
CHECK {    }
END {    }
```

To sum up, the order of execution for a perl program is as follows:

1. BEGIN subroutines: as encountered

2. CHECK subroutines: reverse order of encountered

3. INIT subroutines: as encountered

4. The main body of your program

5. END subroutines: reverse order of encountered

So when Example Listings 2.6 and 2.7 are saved and run, they produce this output:

```
Demo Begin #1
Demo Begin #2
In the module code
Begin #1
Begin #2
Check #2
```

```
Check #1
Demo Check #2
Demo Check #1
Demo Init  #1
Demo Init  #2
Init  #1
Init  #2
In the main code
End   #2
End   #1
Demo End   #2
Demo End   #1
```

Example Listing 2.6

```
# Demo.pm, a simple module to show
package Demo;

BEGIN { print "Demo Begin #1\n"; }
END   { print "Demo End   #1\n"; }
INIT  { print "Demo Init  #1\n"; }
CHECK { print "Demo Check #1\n"; }
print "In the module code\n";
BEGIN { print "Demo Begin #2\n"; }
END   { print "Demo End   #2\n"; }
INIT  { print "Demo Init  #2\n"; }
CHECK { print "Demo Check #2\n"; }
1;
```

Example Listing 2.7

```
# Run this, along with Demo.pm to get
#   the results seen above.
use Demo;

BEGIN { print "Begin #1\n"; }
END   { print "End   #1\n"; }
INIT  { print "Init  #1\n"; }
CHECK { print "Check #1\n"; }
print "In the main code\n";
BEGIN { print "Begin #2\n"; }
END   { print "End   #2\n"; }
```

```
INIT  { print "Init  #2\n"; }
CHECK { print "Check #2\n"; }
```

See Also
subroutines in this book

---

prototype

Usage

prototype *function*

Description

The `prototype` function returns the prototype of the given function (see the subroutine prototypes entry). The function can be expressed as a function name (a string) or as a reference to a subroutine.

If the function name begins with `CORE::`, `perl` will attempt to retrieve the prototype for the given `perl` built-in. Only built-ins that can be overridden will return a prototype.

If the function has no prototype, `undef` will be returned.

Example Listing 2.8

```
# Rummage through the perlfunc manual page and get an
#   (incomplete?) list of function and operator names.
# Attempt to look up the prototype for each of those functions

use strict;
use warnings;

my %terms=();
my @pod=`perldoc -u perlfunc`;
for(@pod) {
    while(/C<([a-z][a-z]+)>/g) {
        $terms{$1}++;
    }
}
```

```
for(sort keys %terms) {
    my $proto;

    # eval {} is to trap the exception
    #    "Can't find an opnumber" thrown for non-overridable
    #    functions and operators.
    eval {
        $proto=prototype "CORE::$_";
    };
    next if $@ or not $proto;
    print "$_ $proto\n";
}
```

> **See Also**
> prototypes in this book

Subroutine Prototypes

Usage

```
sub prototype block
sub prototype
```

Description

Subroutine prototypes provide templates for a subroutines arguments, which can be used to force the arguments of a subroutine into a certain context or to be converted into references during the call.

Subroutine prototypes in Perl do not function as prototypes in C or other languages. They cannot be used for compile-time type checking, for controlling the number of arguments, or for casting purposes.

Prototypes affect only the compilation of your perl script. Function calls that use the & character (as with code references or Perl 4 style calls) or method calls are both immune to the affects of a prototype.

The format of a prototype is a set of parenthesis enclosing the characters: $, @, &, %, *, ;, or \. Each character (or pair in some cases) stands for a single argument that is expected.

The meaning of those characters is shown in the following:

Character	Meaning
$	A scalar value is expected. This will cause the first argument of the caller to be evaluated in a scalar context.
@	An array or a list of items is expected in this position. Note that it must be at the end of the prototype list or the following positions become meaningless (unless seen as \@).
%	A hash or (even-numbered) list of items is expected in this position. Note that it must be at the end of the prototype or the following positions become meaningless. If it appears as \%, a hash reference will be passed to the subroutine instead.
\	Takes the character that follows ($%@&) and indicates the type of this position in the function call. It will not be coerced into a particular type; it must really appear as one of these types. For example, \$ indicates that a scalar variable must appear in this position. An array, hash, or constant value will all throw a compile-time exception. A single hash or array element will suffice nicely (they begin with a $). If the type passed is the correct type, a reference to the variable will be passed instead of the variable itself. Thus the prototype \@ will cause an array reference to be passed in @_ instead of the individual elements.
&	A code reference must appear in this position. This can be done with a sub {} or a function reference such as \&func. In the first position of a prototype, the sub declaration is optional, which allows you to construct functions that look like the internal functions map, sort, grep, and so on, which take a block as an argument.
*	In this position, anything that can be used as a filehandle will be accepted: a bareword, expression, typeglob, or a reference to a typeglob. Within the subroutine, the value will appear as a reference (in the case of the typeglob or typeglob reference) or as a scalar value.
;	Within a prototype, it's possible to specify arguments that must be passed as well as optional arguments. The ; character is used to mark the boundary between the mandatory and the optional arguments. This means that the prototype ($\@;@) is expecting a

Character	Meaning
	scalar value, an array (which will be coerced into an array reference). An optional set of array values can be passed after the mandatory arguments.

An empty set of parenthesis will cause perl not to accept arguments for the given subroutine. Beware of the side effects that this can cause. For example, given these two functions and prototypes:

```perl
sub noargs () { print "Args: ", join(',', @_), "\n" }
sub args    { print "Args: ", join(',', @_), "\n" }
```

The following calls will cause different results:

```perl
noargs "Dance!";  # Compile Error: String found where operator expected
noargs("Dance!"); # Compile Error: Too many arguments for main::noargs
noargs + 5;       # prints "Args: \n", yeilds 6, and throws a "void
                  # context" warning.  Return from print + 5 = 6.
args + 5;         # prints "Args: 5"
```

The prototype () has another interesting effect. If a subroutine has an empty prototype, () can be easily determined to have a return value that is only referenced in the subroutine. If it is not called with the & semantics, the subroutine is eligible for inlining as a constant. This means that in this code:

```perl
sub PI () {
    my $t=22/7;
    return $t;
}
print "I'd like a piece of ", PI, "\n";
```

The value of PI can be determined at compile time and will not be called as a function each time it's referenced. This can provide great speed ups at runtime. Perl will do a good deal of introspection to determine whether a function can be inlined or not.

Example Listing 2.9

```perl
# The subroutine here uses prototypes to take a coderef
#   (or just a block) as the first argument and an open
#   filehandle (for read/write) as the second argument.  It
#   sorts the contents of the filehandle and writes it back
# Without the prototype, there's no way for sortfile to look
#   like it were "built-in".
```

```perl
use strict;
use warnings;
sub sortfile (&*) {
    my($sub, $fh)=@_;
    my(@arr)=<$fh>;
    seek $fh, 0, 0 or die "Cannot rewind: $!";
    if (ref $fh) {
        print $fh sort $sub @arr;
    } else {
        eval "print $fh sort \$sub \@arr";
        die if $@;
    }
}

open(FILE, "+</tmp/unsorted.txt") || die;

sortfile { $a cmp $b } FILE;

close(FILE);
```

> **See Also**
> sub in this book

Object-Oriented Perl Programming

Introduction to Perl's OO Concepts

Description

Similar to many modern programming languages (Python, Java, C++, Smalltalk) Perl has support for object-oriented programming. A short introduction in a reference book is far too little space to go into the details of object-oriented programming techniques.

Instead, this is a brief overview of how Perl's object-oriented facilities fit in with the typical terminology used in OO references.

A class in Perl is simply a package (a namespace). This class might (or might not) be part of a module. Most of the examples in this section contain classes that aren't in modules simply for the reader's convenience (the class and its usage are right next to each other). In the real world, classes are typically in modules so that a class is wholly contained within a file by itself.

```
package Hammer;
@ISA=qw( Tool );
sub new {
    my $class=shift;
    my $type=shift;
    my $self={
        type=> $type,
        };
    bless $self, $class;
}
```

Inheritance is handled through the @ISA array associated with each package, and advanced features such as polymorphism and multiple inheritance are possible through the careful construction of the class.

To create an object in Perl, a reference is blessed into a class (remember, a class is just a package). This creates a permanent connection between the reference and the class. Normally, a method named new creates object instances for you.

Methods in perl (accessor, constructor, and so on) are created by simply having a subroutine within a class. Perl doesn't distinguish between instance methods and class methods:

```
# ...Continuation of class "Hammer"...
sub swing {
    print "BANG!";
}
```

The method swing can be invoked on an instance of class Hammer:

```
my $tool=new Hammer("claw");
$tool->swing;
```

Or, it can be called directly from the class:

```
Hammer->swing();
```

Because an object is simply a blessed reference, attributes for the object are typically stored in the reference itself. For example, in the Hammer class, the type hash element stores the kind of Hammer created. The type attribute can be accessed with

```
$tool->{type};    # Bad, breaks encapsulation
```

But this means that the user of the object needs to know the structure. What's better is to create an accessor (or an accessor/mutator) that will hide the actual structure of the object from the user:

```
# ...package Hammer continued...
sub type {
    my $self=shift;
    if (@_) {
        $self->{type}=shift;
    }
    return $self->{type};
}
```

After this, the `type` attribute can be accessed with:

```
print $tool->type();      # Simply fetch it.
$tool->type("ball peen");  # Or change it!
```

Without any loss of encapsulation. In general, Perl doesn't prohibit some OO behavior that other languages wouldn't allow (that is, altering an object's contents without using a mutator method)—Perl relies on the honesty of the programmer.

The Perl documentation contains a couple of tutorials on object-oriented programming in Perl. The appropriate sections are `perltoot` and `perlboot`. The best book on object-oriented perl is *Object Oriented Perl* by Damian Conway (Manning Press), if you prefer your tutorials in book form.

> **See Also**
> `perltoot` and `perlboot` in the `perl` documentation
> `package` in this book

bless

Usage

```
bless reference
bless reference, class
```

Description

The `bless` function is used to create objects in Perl. It takes a reference and associates it with a particular class (package). This is called *blessing* a reference.

`bless` called with only a reference blesses the reference into the current package. If you specify a *class*, the *reference* will be blessed into that class. The reference itself is modified, and the `bless` function returns the reference as well.

The reference to be blessed can be any kind of reference in Perl: scalar, array, hash, typeglob, or subroutine.

After the `bless`, the object will return its classname when queried with `ref` instead of the kind of reference it is:

```
$camera={};
print ref $camera;     # prints HASH

bless $camera;          # Make it an object
print ref $camera;      # Now prints "main" because $camera has been blessed
             # into the current package.
```

After the `bless`, the original reference still can be accessed as though it were still a normal reference. For example, the object $camera can still be accessed with

```
$camera->{film}="Kodak";
```

But it's considered rude to go tinkering with an object without going through its published interface of accessors. Only within the class itself should the actual makeup of the object be a concern.

Example Listing 2.10

```
# An inheritable constructor
#
sub new {
    my $class=shift;
    my $self=[];  # To be different

    bless $self, $class;
}
```

See Also
references, -$gt;, and new in this book

new

Usage

```
new CLASSNAME;
new CLASSNAME arguments;
```

Description

The new function is by convention an object constructor for a module. For example, if the object-oriented module called CGI has established that the new function is the constructor, to create a new instance of CGI:

```
use CGI;
my $query=new CGI;
```

The constructor doesn't necessarily have to be called new for a given module; this is convention only. For example, this module has a constructor called create:

```
package Universe;   # Saved as Universe.pm, of course
sub create {
    my $foo;
    return bless \$foo;
}
```

And to create an instance of Universe, you simply can say

```
use Universe;
my $cosmos=create Universe;
```

It also can be called with a conventional arrow notation ->.

There can be some confusion if the function new (or in the latter case create) exists in the current package. The call $cosmos=create Universe could refer to the function create in the Universe module or to a function called create in the current package.

To clear this up, you can follow the constructor with a pair of colons (::) and this disambiguates the call completely:

```
my $world=new Universe::;
my $all  =Universe::->new;
```

Similar to all function calls, arguments can be passed to the constructor as shown in the following example.

Example Listing 2.11

```perl
use strict;

package Chapter;
my %fields;
@fields{qw(title entries)}=();

sub new {
    my($class, %opts)=@_;
    my $self={};
    for(keys %opts) {
        die "No such property: $_" unless
                exists $fields{$_};
        $self->{$_}=$opts{$_};
    }
    return bless $self, $class;
}

package main;
use Data::Dumper;

my $chapter=new Chapter
        title => 'Pragmas',
        entries => [ qw(strict warnings overload) ];
```

> **See Also**
> - and > in this book

Method Calls

Usage

```perl
object->method
class->method
method object arguments
method CLASS arguments
```

Description

The `->` operator is used in Perl to access object and class methods. Additionally, it's used to access members of hashes and arrays using references. See the references section for details. Perl doesn't distinguish between calling methods on classes and on objects.

By using either the class, or the class into which the object was blessed, Perl will attempt to find and run the method indicated. The method will be passed either to the classname or a reference to the object as the first argument, depending on what was used to call the method. If the method needs to be called with additional arguments, those must be enclosed in parenthesis.

```
print $query->header('text/plain');
```

Because the arrow operator is left associative, you can chain them together to call several functions at once, provided, of course, that the leftmost calls generate classnames or objects to satisfy the rightmost calls:

```
# Assumes that $boss->meeting() produces an object or
# class that can have complete() as a method.
$boss->meet("project")->complete();
```

Methods also can be called with the following form:

```
method object (arguments)
method object arguments
```

This is exactly the same as

```
object->method(arguments)
```

Keep in mind that because there are no operators or parenthesis to give the compiler hints, you will have to be careful with precedence.

The method name called with either syntax can be resolved at runtime. This does not trigger a `strict subs` warning because all method names are resolved at runtime (through inheritance and whatnot; see the following).

When calling a method, `perl` will use the following set of steps to determine which function actually gets called for the syntax:

```
$object->method;
$class->method;
```

1. In the package that $object has been blessed into, or the class represented by $class, look for the subroutine name method. If that's found, run it.

2. If that isn't present, look in the class for a package variable named @ISA. If this is present, recursively search through the list of classes in @ISA for a class that contains a subroutine named method. Call it, if it's found.

3. Look for a subroutine named UNIVERSAL::method and run that.

4. Look for a subroutine named AUTOLOAD in the class to which the object belongs. Run that if it's found (see AUTOLOAD).

5. Recursively search through the @ISA array in the class for packages that contain an AUTOLOAD subroutine, and run those if they're found. See the @ISA entry for notes on how the search is done.

6. If after all this, perl does not find a function to run for the method call, an exception will be thrown.

Example Listing 2.12

```perl
# Defines several classes, all inheriting from Taxonomy and each other.
#   Each class adds attributes to its own base class by defining
#   a method for that attribute (which simply returns 1). A handy method
#   to do this called attrib() creates subroutines on the fly...

use strict;
package Taxonomy;
sub new { my $class=shift; my $self={}; bless $self, $class; }

# Automatically generates named methods in the caller's namespace
sub attrib {
    my($class, @attribs)=@_;
    for(@attribs) {
        no strict 'refs';
        *{$class. "::" . $_}=sub { 1; }
    }
}
# If an attribute for a Phylum, Class...Species is not
#    defined, simply return false
sub AUTOLOAD { return; }

package Animal;     # Kingdom
our @ISA=('Taxonomy');
```

```perl
Animal->SUPER::attrib(qw(multicellular ingestion tissues));

package Chordate;  # Phylum
our @ISA=('Animal');
Chordate->SUPER::attrib(qw(developmental_gillslits nervecord ));

package Mammal;    # Class
our @ISA=('Chordate');
Mammal->SUPER::attrib(qw(warmblooded hair mammaryglands ));

package Primate;   # Order
our @ISA=('Mammal');
Primate->SUPER::attrib(qw(nails collarbone placenta opposabledigit ));

package Hominid;   # Family
our @ISA=('Primate');
Hominid->SUPER::attrib(qw( upright bipedal smallteeth ));

package Man;       # Genus and Species --  Mankind is special :)
our @ISA=('Hominid');

# Normally, this'd be in the main body of the program
#    and the stuff above'd be in a module(s) and use'd.
package main;

# new Man searches from Man, upwards through the @ISA's until
#   it find's Taxononmy's new().  Each method call on $animal
#   will do the same thing.
my $animal=new Man;
if ($animal->bipedal) {
    print "Yup, that we can do.";
}
my $class=new Mammal;
if ($class->photosynthesis) {
    print "Really?  I doubt it.";
}
```

See Also

UNIVERSAL and AUTOLOAD in this book

```
import
```

Usage

```
sub import {}
sub unimport {}
```

Description

The `import` and `unimport` function names are used by the `use` directive to provide a module bootstrap facility for modules. They aren't reserved keywords in Perl otherwise.

When a module is loaded with `use`, the `import` method is called. The first argument is the name of the module. Additional arguments to import are specified as the last argument to the `use` directive (other than an optional version number). Thus,

```
# Cola->import will be called with the arguments;
#   Cola, Coke, Pepsi and Faygo.

use Cola qw(Coke Pepsi Faygo);
```

When the `no` keyword is used, the `unimport` subroutine is called with the same arguments.

Most modules that need to export symbols declare themselves as a subclass of the `Exporter` class. The `Exporter` class has facilities for handling most of your symbol exporting needs. Object-oriented modules rarely (if ever) need to export symbols.

Example Listing 2.13

```
# Example of a module that uses import and unimport to set up
#   a logging environment.  Tries to use Unix::Syslog and failing
#   that uses a logfile in /var/log, /tmp, /temp or /windows/temp.
# Messages are written with logit() which uses the logging channel
#   setup with the import.

package Mylogger;

use strict;
my $syslog=0;
my @prefdir=qw( /var/log /tmp /temp /windows/temp );
```

```perl
sub import {              # Pick a logging method
    # Export logit() to the caller's package
    {
        no strict 'refs';
        my($package)=(caller)[0];
        *{$package . "::logit"}=\&logit;
    }
    my $prog=$0; $prog=~s/.*?([.\w]+)$/$1/;
    eval "use Unix::Syslog qw(:subs :macros)";
    if (! $@) {
        openlog($prog, LOG_NOTICE(), LOG_USER());
        return $syslog=1;
    } else {
        foreach( @prefdir ) {
            return 1 if open(MYLOG, ">$_/errlog_$prog");
        }
    }
    warn "No logging facilities active\n";
}
sub unimport {
    if ($syslog) {
        closelog();
    } else {
        close(MYLOG) if fileno(MYLOG);
    }
}
sub logit {
    if ($syslog) {
        syslog(LOG_NOTICE() | LOG_USER(), "@_");
    } else {
        my $mess="@_";
        chomp $mess;
        print MYLOG "$0 [$$]: $mess\n" if fileno(MYLOG);
    }
}
1;
```

Example Listing 2.14

```perl
# Using the Mylogger module
use Mylogger;

logit("Hey, something bad happened!");
```

> **See Also**
> use and methods in this book

AUTOLOAD

Usage

```
use vars qw($AUTOLOAD);
sub AUTOLOAD { }
```

Description

When a method is called and there is no subroutine by that name in the desired class (or its ancestors), perl will fall back to a subroutine called AUTOLOAD to satisfy the method call. (See methods for a full description of the method search perl uses.)

The AUTOLOAD subroutine will be searched for, and called, in the same order that @ISA is searched to find a parent class that contains a method. If the AUTOLOAD subroutine is found anywhere along that search, it is run and perl stops searching for another AUTOLOAD.

Only one AUTOLOAD can be called by Perl for any method lookup. When an AUTOLOAD is found, perl will stop searching. It is up to the AUTOLOAD subroutine to satisfy the method call.

The AUTOLOAD subroutine will be passed by a variable called $AUTOLOAD. This will contain the fully-qualified package name of the subroutine that perl was looking for when the AUTOLOAD was invoked. The AUTOLOAD subroutine will be passed by the object itself as the first argument (or the class name, if a class method was invoked) followed by any additional arguments given to the called method.

The AUTOLOAD subroutine also will be called when an object is destroyed. The method name passed will end in ::DESTROY, and should probably be ignored. In fact, it's generally safe to skip all uppercase-only method names that are passed to AUTOLOAD.

```
sub AUTOLOAD {
    our $AUTOLOAD=~s/.*:://;            # Remove the package name
    return if ($AUTOLOAD=~/^[A-Z]+$/);  # Skip if all caps.

    # Rest of autoload....
}
```

The AUTOLOAD subroutine is particularly useful in posing as an accessor method for well-known object attributes as shown in the example.

The AUTOLOAD subroutine also can be specified without the keyword sub. The word AUTOLOAD introducing a bare block will do as well.

```
AUTOLOAD { }    # Same as "sub AUTOLOAD { }"
```

Example Listing 2.15

```
# A fairly-standard OO package with an AUTOLOAD subroutine
#    that uses a list of attributes and acts as an accessor
#     method for them.
# Supports simple inheritance by failing up to the SUPER class
#    if a method doesn't exist.

package Employee;
sub new { bless {}, shift }
our @ISA=('Person');

our(%fields, $AUTOLOAD);
for ( qw( hire salary dependants department ) ) { $fields{$_}++;   }
sub AUTOLOAD {
    my($self,$value)=@_;
    my($attribute)=($AUTOLOAD=~m/::(.*?)$/);
    return if ($attribute=~/^[A-Z]+$/);   # Bail if all-caps method

    if ($fields{$attribute}) {
        $self->{$attribute} = $value if $value;
        return $self->{$attribute};
    } else {
        $self->{"SUPER::" . $attribute}(@_);
    }
}
```

See Also
methods and SUPER in this book

SUPER

Usage

SUPER

Description

The SUPER pseudoclass is used by a class (or a method) to force an ancestor to run a method on behalf of a subclass. For example, to have a method determine whether one of its ancestors can run a method named speak, use the following:

```
$self->can("SUPER::speak");
```

The use of the class SUPER will cause perl to begin searching for a method called speak through the class's @ISA array and up through its ancestry. The normal search algorithm (as described in the methods entry) is used, starting in the classes listed in @ISA.

The alternative is to have the subroutine talk to iterate through @ISA itself—or worse, to hard-wire the parent classes—in order to search for the speak method.

Example Listing 2.16

```
# A fictional package.  The method talk() checks to see if one
#   of its ancestors can run speak(), and then actually runs it.

package Singer;
@ISA=qw( Speaker );
#
# Rest of class....
#
sub perform {          # Typical method
    my $self=shift;
    my $words=shift;

    $self->startmusic();
    if ($self->can("SUPER::speak")) {
        $self->SUPER::speak($words);
    } else {
        $self->lipsync();
    }
}
```

> **See Also**
> methods in this book

UNIVERSAL

Usage

```
object->can(method)
UNIVERSAL::can(reference, method)
reference->isa(type)
UNIVERSAL::isa(reference, type)
object->VERSION(minimum)
```

Description

The class UNIVERSAL is the base class for all blessed objects in Perl. The UNIVERSAL class provides three methods: can, isa, and VERSION. Each of these can be called against an object or a class.

The can method determines whether an object supports a method called method. If the method exists, a reference to the subroutine is returned, otherwise undef. Calling can as a function (UNIVERSAL::can) with a reference will return true if the reference is blessed and has a subroutine named method available to it. The subroutine reference will be returned. If reference isn't blessed, or there is no subroutine named method, undef is returned.

Note that can has problems with AUTOLOAD. The can method (and function) has no way to check whether a method will be satisfied through an AUTOLOAD method or not at all. As the first example demonstrates, if you aren't sure, you can check for the presence of an AUTOLOAD method and let it decide what to do.

The isa method will return true if reference is blessed into the package type or inherits from type. One difficulty is if you have only a reference, calling

```
$ref->isa('foo');
```

will result in an error if $ref hasn't been blessed into any class. To determine whether $ref is an object at all, see the first example in the ref entry.

The isa method can be called as a subroutine directly with UNIVERSAL::isa. The subroutine will return true if reference is a reference blessed into type (or a classname) or that inherits from type. It also will return true if reference is a reference of type type (HASH, ARRAY, CODE, and so on; similar to ref).

The VERSION method will return the value of the package variable $VARIABLE from the package into which the object is blessed. If minimum is specified, VERSION will throw an exception if the version returned is not at least minimum.

Example Listing 2.17

```
# Is the method "start" safe to call on the object $ref?

if ($ref->can("start") or $ref->can("AUTOLOAD")) {
    $ref->start;
}
```

Example Listing 2.18

```
# Using a module much like (but not exactly like) the one presented in
#   the "methods" example.

use Taxonomy;
my $manager=new Man;

if ( $manager->isa("Reptile") ) {
    print "I KNEW it!  Cold blooded!";
}
```

> **See Also**
> methods and AUTOLOAD in this book

DESTROY

Usage

```
sub DESTROY { }
```

Description

The DESTROY method is called on an object when the last reference to the object is about to be released. The only argument passed to the DESTROY method is the object itself.

Similar to AUTOLOAD, only one DESTROY method is called per object destruction. The @ISA array is searched (and the ancestors of things named in @ISA) for a DESTROY method if one doesn't exist in the package the object was blessed into. If this fails, the rest of the steps outlined in the methods entry are called: UNIVERSAL is searched for a DESTROY method (there normally isn't one), and then AUTOLOAD methods are called to handle the DESTROY.

In Perl, because memory management is handled by the interpreter, useful DESTROY methods are rarely needed to free memory. Normally, the only need for a DESTROY method is to clean up external references needed by the object (filehandles, sockets, databases, and so on).

The DESTROY subroutine also can be specified without the keyword sub. The word DESTROY introducing a bare block will do as well.

```
DESTROY { }   # Same as "sub DESTROY { }"
```

Example Listing 2.19

```
# Class with an instance that is self-referential.
#    Simply letting the object fall out of scope will not
#    free the memory used by the object, so a destructor
#    is needed to break the circular reference.

package Circular;

sub new {
    my $class=shift;
    my $self={};
    $self->{SELF}=$self;  # Circular reference
    bless $self, $class;
}
sub DESTROY {
    my($self)=shift;
    $self->{SELF}=undef;  # Break the circular reference
}
```

> **See Also**
> methods and AUTOLOAD in this book

Additional Pragmas

`integer`

Usage

```
use integer;
```

Description

The `integer` pragma causes Perl to perform integer arithmetic for the remainder of the block (or file).

Literals will be stored as floating-point numbers, however. So that the following:

```
use integer;
$pi=3.14;
```

will still store `$pi` as `3.14`; however, during arithmetic operations, it will be computed as `3`:

```
print $pi*2;    # Prints 6!
```

Perl reverts to your architecture's native integer arithmetic when `integer` is in effect. The exact behavior of some operations will depend entirely on your system's implementation of them—Perl won't try to give you a portable view of arithmetic.

Using integer arithmetic can have a positive impact on execution speed, especially on machines without special floating-point hardware. However, the extent of this speedup should be tested with `Benchmark` to ascertain just how much of an increase there is.

Example Listing 2.20

```
# Finds prime numbers by successive division of N by
#   (primes < N).  Purposely skips algorithm optimizations.
# Benchmark is used to see which is faster...

use Benchmark;
timethese(50, { float => sub {
        my $n=2;
        NUM:while($n<5000) {
            foreach(@p) {
                if ($n%$_ == 0) { $n++; next NUM; }
            }
```

```
            push(@p, $n++);
        }
    },
int => sub {
    use integer;
    my $n=2;
    NUM:while($n<5000) {
        foreach(@p) {
            if ($n%$_ == 0) { $n++; next NUM; }
        }
        push(@p, $n++);
    }
} } );

# Turns out that integer speeds this up by about 16%
#    on a 300Mhz Intel system the results were consistently around:
# float: 32 clock secs (30.69 usr + 0.16 sys = 30.85 CPU) @ 1.62/s
#    int: 27 clock secs (24.93 usr + 0.11 sys = 25.04 CPU) @ 2.00/s
```

> **See Also**
> Benchmark module documentation

subs, vars

Usage

```
use subs sub list
use vars variable list
```

Description

The subs and vars pragmas are needed only when strict is in effect.

The subs pragma predeclares subroutines in *sub list* so that they can be used without parenthesis before they are declared. Normally, this causes an error under strict:

```
use strict;
foo;            # Won't compile!
sub foo {
    return;
}
```

To correct this, you either can ensure that subroutines are declared before they are referenced without parenthesis, or you can predeclare them with use subs.

The vars pragma is similar. When strict (or strict vars) is in effect, variables must be declared lexically with my, they must be fully-qualified package variables (that is, $main::foo), or they must be declared with our (under 5.6).

The vars pragma exempts the *variable list* from strict vars checking. The variables listed can be used without satisfying any of the previous requirements.

The subs and vars pragmas are file-scoped, and they cannot be turned off with no subs or no vars.

Example Listing 2.21

```perl
# The fairly generic start to a module.
#    ( Everything except the subs stuff is boilerplate)

package Mymodule;
use strict;
use vars qw( @ISA @EXPORT $VERSION );
use subs qw( otherfunc );

use Exporter;
$VERSION = 1.00;
@ISA = qw( Exporter );
@EXPORT = qw( myfunc );

# Note the order in which these are declared and
#    called.  Without the "use subs" above, this won't
#    compile under use strict
sub myfunc {
    otherfunc;
}
sub otherfunc {
    return;
}
1;
```

> **See Also**
> strict in this book

base

Usage

```
use base base classes;
```

Description

The use base pragma establishes an is-a relationship between the calling module and the base classes at compile time.

If the base classes have not yet been loaded, they will be require'd. The @ISA array in the current package will have the base classes added to it.

If one of the base classes has a %FIELDS hash, the %FIELDS hash in the current package will be initialized to it. If multiple base classes has a %FIELDS hash, an error will result because multiple inheritance isn't supported with this interface. See the fields entry for an example with %FIELDS.

Example Listing 2.22

```
# Module to subclass CGI just for kicks

package mycgi;

# This does the:
#     push(@ISA, 'CGI');
#     and the use vars qw{@ISA}
# cheaply.
use base qw(CGI);
sub header {
    my($self)=shift;

    "Content-type: text/html\n\n";
}
1;
```

> **See Also**
> fields in this book

lib

Usage

```
use lib pathlist
no lib pathlist
```

Description

The lib module alters the @INC list at compile time. It is essentially equivalent to the following:

```
BEGIN { unshift(@INC, pathlist) }
```

In addition, if a directory named architecture/auto exists under a directory in the pathlist, it is added as well.

Directories can be removed from @INC with no lib. However, be careful not to remove the default directories, or directories needed by modules you have included—doing so could result in a runtime error.

The original list of directories from @INC is preserved by the lib pragma in the array @lib::ORIG_INC.

Example Listing 2.23

```
# I installed Tk with the option:
#    -PREFIX=~/perl/lib -LIB=~/perl/lib
#    to have a private copy.

use lib '/home/clintp/perl/lib';
use Tk;

my $win=new MainWindow;
```

> **See Also**
> @INC in this book

Tied Variables

`tied`

Usage

```
tied variable
```

Description

The `tied` function determines whether variable is tied to a class and returns the object associated with it. This object was the original return value from `tie` when the variable was tied.

If the variable isn't tied to a class, `undef` is returned.

Example Listing 2.24

```
if ( (ref tied @arr) =~ /MySortArray/) {
    print "The array is sorted automagically...";
}
```

> **See Also**
> `tie` in this book

Scalar Tie

Usage

```
tie variable, class, arguments
```

Description

The `tie` function can be used to alter the behavior of a scalar variable by associating it with a class. The class (a package) will have functions that will mimic the behavior of a scalar variable.

The class that is associated with the variable must already be pulled in to the script with `use` or `require` prior to the `tie` being performed.

The methods required for a class to implement a scalar tie are

```
TIESCALAR
FETCH
STORE
DESTROY
```

However, only the methods actually needed must be declared (in this case, TIESCALAR).

To associate a scalar variable with a class, use the tie function as shown previously. The tie function will call the TIESCALAR method in the class and return a blessed object similar to any other constructor (see new). The object returned by tie isn't necessary to use the variable afterward; it's there for your convenience. Any additional arguments given to tie are passed to the TIESCALAR constructor.

A sample tied scalar class:

```perl
package MemScalar;

# Produce a scalar that "remembers" every value
#    ever assigned.
sub TIESCALAR {
    bless [ undef ], shift;
}
sub FETCH {
    return $_[0]->[-1];
}
sub STORE {
    my($self,$value)=@_;
    push @{$self}, $value;
    return $_[0]->[-1];
}
sub hist {
    return @{$_[0]};
}
1;
```

This example blesses an array reference to be associated with the value. Whenever we assign a new value to the tied variable, we can remember it in the array. The current value is the last element in the anonymous array. Use this class:

```perl
use MemScalar;

my($obj, $var);
```

```
$obj=tie $var, 'MemScalar';

$var=67;
$var++;      # Does a FETCH and a STORE
$var=22/7;

no warnings 'uninitialized';  # First will be undef
print join(',', $obj->hist);
```

Whenever the variable is accessed after the tie, the appropriate method (FETCH, STORE) is run given the anonymous array as the first argument.

The FETCH method is called when the scalar values are retrieved; the only argument is the object. In the case of the example, the last element in the blessed array is returned. You actually can return any value you prefer. For example, this FETCH:

```
sub FETCH { return rand; }
```

Would return a random floating-point number. This probably isn't useful, but gets the point across that almost anything can be returned.

The STORE method is called when the scalar value is assigned to. It will be passed two arguments: the object itself and the value to be stored. In general, the only guideline to STORE methods is that they should return the value assigned the same as a real assignment would expect (but you can break this rule too).

A DESTROY method is called when the scalar value goes out of scope, the program ends, or perl otherwise is planning on reclaiming the memory occupied by the scalar. Most of the time, a DESTROY method isn't required (and no error will result from not having one).

Other methods can be defined for the class, of course. In this case, I've defined a hist method so that I can get to the history of the scalar. In this way, you can extend a scalar variable to have properties that it wouldn't have otherwise.

Example Listing 2.25

```
# The MyTimer class ties a scalar to a subroutine (a closure, actually)
#   which controls different kinds of timers.
# Assigning a non-zero value creates a countdown
#   timer, and SIG{ALRM} will be triggered (unix only)
#   when it reaches 0.  Only 1 timer may be active (for the alarm() to work).
# Assigning a zero value causes the watch to start.
# Fetching the scalar shows the time elapsed, or time left.
```

```
# The nature of the timer can be changed (or reset) by re-assigning to
#    the scalar
use strict;
package MyTimer;

sub TIESCALAR {
    return bless {}, $_[0];
}
sub STORE {
    my($self,$value)=@_;
    eval { alarm $value };
    my $now=time;
    if ($value) {
        $self->{sub}=sub { # Time remaining
            return($now+$value-time);
        }
    } else {
        $self->{sub}=sub { # Elapsed time
            return(time-$now);
        }
    }
}
sub FETCH {
    return $_[0]->{sub}();
}
sub DESTROY {
    eval { alarm(0); };   # alarm unimplemented for Win32
}
1;
```

Example Listing 2.26

```
# How to use the MyTimer class

use MyTimer;
use strict;

my($t,$f);
$f=0;
$SIG{ALRM}=sub { $f=1; };
tie $t, 'MyTimer';
$t=60;             # Wake me in 60 seconds!
```

```
until($f) {
    # Do some task that takes a while....

    print "Time left: $t\n";
}
```

See Also
new, tied, untie, and methods in this book

Tied Arrays

Usage

```
tie array, class, arguments
```

Description

In general, the mechanism for a tied array is the same as that for a tied scalar variable. This entry will describe only those things that differ between a tied scalar and a tied array.

The class in which the array is associated can have any of the following methods called on it:

```
TIEARRAY
FETCH
STORE
DESTROY
STORESIZE
FETCHSIZE
CLEAR
EXTEND
POP
PUSH
SHIFT
UNSHIFT
SPLICE
DELETE
EXISTS
```

The only methods that must be defined are TIEARRAY, FETCH, and STORE. The others will be called as they're needed. Because there are quite a few methods to define, the standard library provides Tie::Array and Tie::StdArray to inherit basic functionality from, and you can override just the methods you need.

Tie::Array provides the methods PUSH, POP, SHIFT, UNSHIFT, SPLICE, and CLEAR as calls to FETCH, STORE, FETCHSIZE, and STORESIZE in your own derived class. The DELETE and EXISTS methods are stubs that will cause an exception to be raised.

The Tie::StdArray class provides all the base functionality by blessing an anonymous array in its TIEARRAY method. Being a complete class, you only need to inherit from it and override those methods that you're interested in overriding. To use these classes:

```
use Tie::Array;
our @ISA=('Tie::StdArray');
```

Or inherit from Tie::Array.

The examples in this section will assume that they're inheriting from Tie::StdArray for brevity.

STORE *self, offset, value*—Requests that *value* be stored at *offset* into the array. Normally, the *value* stored is returned by the method.

FETCH *self, offset*—Requests that the value stored at *offset* be returned.

FETCHSIZE *self*—Requests that you return the number of items in the array. Triggered when the array is used in a scalar context, as in print scalar(@foo).

STORESIZE *self, size*—Requests that the array be grown (or shrunk) to *size* elements. Can be used to presize an array, knowing that large amounts of data will be put into it as if you had said $#foo=999 to pre-extend @foo to 1000 elements.

EXTEND *self, size*—Used to indicate that perl is anticipating that the array will need more elements. It's usually unnecessary to define this.

DELETE *self, offset*—Deletes the element at *offset*. Afterward, that *offset* should return undef as a value and false for exists. The Tie::Array default method will raise an exception. This is called when delete $foo[99] is run. See the delete entry.

EXISTS *self, offset*—Returns true if the element at *offset* has ever held a value, unless that element was removed with delete. The Tie::Array version of this method raises an exception. See the exists entry.

CLEAR *self*—Removes all the elements from the array.

DESTROY *self*—The array variable is falling out of scope, or the program is about to end—perl is garbage-collecting the variable.

PUSH *self*, values—Pushes the *values* indicated onto the end of the array. It should return the number of elements in the array as push does.

POP *self*—Removes the last element from the array and returns it.

UNSHIFT *self*—Removes the first element from the array and returns it.

SHIFT *self*, values—Adds the specified *values* to the beginning of the array. It should return the number of elements now in the array.

SPLICE *self*, offset, length, replacement—Substitutes *replacement* elements starting at position *offset* for *length* elements. Note that there are additional semantics if *length* or *replacement* is omitted. See the splice entry for details.

Example Listing 2.27

```
# An array that is tied to this class will keep its elements in
#    sorted order.  Each time an assignment is made the array internally
#    is re-ordered.  Thus assigning to a particular offset, i.e.
#    $foo[5]=999 is meaningless (it'll be moved).
# Note that for very, very large arrays this class is better implemented
#    with a tree instead of re-sorting the array for each insert.
package MySortArray;
use Tie::Array;
our @ISA=('Tie::Array');
# Push, pop, shift, unshift, etc..
# all inherited from Tie::Array

sub TIEARRAY {
    my($class)=shift;
    bless [ ], $class;
}
sub STORE {
    my($self, $offset, $value)=@_;
    @{$self}=sort { $a <=> $b } @{$self}, $value;
    return $value;
}
sub FETCH {
    my($self, $offset)=@_;
    return $self->[$offset];
}
```

```
sub FETCHSIZE {
    my($self)=shift;
    return scalar @{$self};
}
sub STORESIZE {
    my($self, $size)=@_;
    $#{$self}=$size-1;
}
1;
```

Example Listing 2.28

```
use MySortArray;
my @a;
tie @a, 'MySortArray';

for(0..100) {
    $a[0]=rand;
}
print $a[0];  # Always the lowest number
print $a[-1]; # Always the highest
```

See Also

`Tie::StdArray` and `Tie::Array` module documentation

tied scalars, delete, exists, splice, and arrays in this book

---

Tied Hashes

Usage

```
tie hash, class, arguments
```

Description

In general, the mechanism for a tied array is the same as that for a tied scalar variable. This entry will describe only those differences between a tied scalar and a tied array.

The *class* in which the array is associated can have any of the following methods called on it:

TIEHASH
FETCH

```
STORE
DELETE
EXISTS
CLEAR
FIRSTKEY
NEXTKEY
```

The module `Tie::Hash` can provide the TIEHASH, EXISTS, and CLEAR methods. The sub class `Tie::StdHash` provides the rest of the methods and allows you to have normal hash behavior, enhanced by simply overriding the appropriate methods. The TIEHASH method in `Tie::Hash` will bless an empty hash reference into your class.

The methods available to you are the following:

TIEHASH *self, arguments*—Passes any additional *arguments* to `tie` as arguments to the TIEHASH method. For example, the `dbmopen` call is a thin wrapper for a tied hash and additional arguments hold the permissions of the DBM file to be created and the filename to create.

FETCH *self, key*—Fetches the data for the given *key*.

STORE *self, key, value*—Associates the given *value* with the *key*. The STORE method should return the value stored.

DELETE *self, key*—Removes the *key* from the hash.

EXISTS *self, key*—Returns true if the *key* exists. (Note: the version of EXISTS in `Tie::Hash` simply throws an exception.)

CLEAR *self*—Removes all the keys and values from the hash.

FIRSTKEY *self* NEXTKEY *self, lastkey*—The FIRSTKEY method should return the first key of the hash. The NEXTKEY method should return the key in the hash following *lastkey*. These are used when the `keys` and `each` functions are applied to a hash. Several modules are available from CPAN for doing interesting things with hashes. The `Tie::IxHash` module keeps hash keys in order, `Tie::CPHash` keeps a hash with not case sensitive keys, `Tie::SortHash` for keeping keys in sorted order, and so on.

Example Listing 2.28

```
# Uses tie to connect a hash to a filesystem.  There is no each, keys,
#  or values behavior.  You can only fetch values with known keys.
#  If the key corresponds to a directory, you'll get a structure:
#  { stat => stat info, dir => directory listing, isdir => 1}
```

```perl
#  If the key corresponds to a regular file, you'll get the struct:
#  { stat => stat info, data => file contents }
#  If anything goes wrong, the returned structure will have an err element
#  set to the error message (from $!)
# NOTE: doesn't handle links, devices, etc...

package MyMapFile;
use strict;
use IO::File;
use Errno qw(ENOENT);

sub TIEHASH { bless {}, shift; }
sub FETCH {
    my($self,$key)=@_;
    my $struct={ stat => [ stat($key) ] };
    if (-d _ ) {
        local *D;
        $struct->{isdir}=1;
        if ( opendir(D, $key) ) {
            $struct->{dir}=[ readdir D ];
        } else {
            @{$struct}{qw(dir err)}=([], $!);
        }
    } elsif (-f _) {
        local($/,*FH);
        if (open(FH, $key)) {
            $struct->{data}=<FH>;
        } else {
            @{$struct}{qw( data err )}=(undef, $!);
        }
    } else { $struct->{err} = &Errno::ENOENT; }
    return $struct;
}
sub EXISTS { return (-e $_[1])?1:undef; }
sub STORE { die "STORE is not valid"; }
sub FIRSTKEY { die "FIRSTKEY is not valid"; }
sub NEXTKEY { die "NEXTKEY is not valid"; }
sub CLEAR { die "CLEAR is not valid"; }
sub DELETE { die "DELETE is not valid"; }
1;
```

Example Listing 2.29

```perl
# Simply demonstrates the MyMapFile class

use strict;
use MyMapFile;

my %dir;
tie %dir, 'MyMapFile';
my $a=$dir{'/tmp/bigfile.txt'};

if ($a->{err}) {
    die "$!";
}
if ($a->{isdir}) {
    print "It's a directory with ",
        scalar @{$a->{dir}}, " files\n";
} else {
    print "File with ", length($a->{data}), " bytes\n";
}
```

See Also

AnyDBM_File module documentation

dbmopen in this book

Tied Filehandles

Usage

```perl
tie array, class, arguments
```

Description

In general, the mechanism for a tied filehandle is the same as that for a tied scalar variable. This entry will describe only those things which differ between a tied scalar and a tied filehandle.

The class in which the filehandle is associated can have any of the following methods called on it:

```
TIEHANDLE
PRINT
```

```
PRINTF
WRITE
GETC
READ
READLINE
OPEN
CLOSE
EOF
FILENO
SEEK
TELL
DESTROY
```

At the bare minimum, TIEHANDLE and a few output or input methods need to be defined for most purposes. Defining all of them allows you to simulate a fully-functional filehandle, which is overkill in most cases.

Some uses for tied filehandles are for taking over existing filehandles (such as STDERR or STDOUT) to control formatting or wrapping a complex process such as a database into a filehandle.

In general, you should read the sections in this book that correspond to the calling functions to determine exactly what should be returned under certain conditions. For example, undef is generally returned on error, $! is set to an appropriate error message, and so on.

TIEHANDLE *self, arguments*—The constructor for the filehandle class. The extra arguments from tie are passed directly to TIEHANDLE.

OPEN *self, list*—The OPEN method is called whenever the open function is called with the filehandle as an argument. The arguments to open are passed in the list. Note that the one, two, or three argument forms of open will trigger a call to this method, and a variable number of items in list will result.

CLOSE *self*—This method is called when the close function is called on the filehandle. Note that the filehandle is still valid after the close, as long as you're willing to deal with it.

PRINT *self, data;* PRINTF *self, format, data*—This method is triggered when a print is performed to the filehandle. The data are the arguments to print (excluding the filehandle). The PRINTF method is called when the printf function is used on the filehandle. It's the method's responsibility to combine the data with the format string. (sprintf is handy for that.)

GETC *self*—This is called whenever getc is called on the filehandle. The method should return undef when the filehandle is exhausted.

SEEK *self, offset, whence* TELL *self*—This is similar to the seek and tell functions: SEEK should cause the file pointer to seek to the proper position, and TELL should report the current filehandle position.

READLINE *self*—The READLINE method is called whenever the readline function or the angle-operator <> is used on the filehandle. The method should return undef when the filehandle is exhausted.

READ *self, buffer, length, offset* WRITE *self, buffer, length, offset*— The READ method corresponds to calls to read and sysread, and WRITE is called when the syswrite function is called. Note that the read and sysread functions expect that the buffer argument will be modified as appropriate.

EOF *self*—The EOF method should return true if the filehandle is at EOF.

BINMODE *self*—The BINMODE method indicates that the filehandle should be read and written in binary mode (on those systems that care).

FILENO *self*—The FILENO method returns the appropriate file descriptor associated with the filehandle. Note that the fileno function is often used to test whether a filehandle is still open.

DESTROY *self*—This method should be used to clean up the resources of the filehandle; it is called when Perl is garbage-collecting the filehandle.

Example Listing 2.30

```perl
# Allows you to tie a filehandle so that everything printed to
#  the filehandle is timestamped.  If no file is specified during the
#  tie, then STDERR will be dup'd and used.

package StampLog;
use strict;
use Carp;

sub TIEHANDLE {
    my($class,$file)=shift;
    my $self;
    if ($file) {
        open $self, ">>$file" or croak "Can't open $file: $!";
    } else {
```

```
            open $self, ">&STDERR" or croak "Can't dup STDERR: $!";
    }
    return bless $self, $class;
}
sub PRINT {
    my($self)=shift;
    printf $self "%02d:%02d:%02d ", (localtime)[2,1,0];
    print $self @_;
}
sub PRINTF {
    my($self)=shift;
    $self->PRINT(sprintf $_[0], @_[1..$#_]);
}
1;
```

Example Listing 2.31

```
# An example of using the StampLog class.
use strict;
use StampLog;

tie *LOG, 'StampLog';
print LOG "Bleh!\n";
```

See Also
open, filehandles, and tied scalars in this book

---

untie

Usage

untie variable

Description

The untie function disassociates the variable from the class, thus having the variable revert to its normal behavior.

If the original return value from tie was kept (in most of the examples so far, it has not), untie-ing the variable results in a warning:

untie attempted while X inner references still exist

To avoid this, you must destroy the original object by letting it fall out of scope or setting the object variable to some other value.

Example Listing 2.32

```
# Demonstrates the "untie attempted..." warning.
#    To get rid of it, either not save the return
#    value from tie (as I did in $obj), or let $obj
#    fall out of scope (before calling untie), don't
#    call untie, or set $obj to some innocuous value
#    before the untie.

use warnings;
package ShowErr;
sub TIESCALAR {
    my $self;
    return bless \$self, shift;
}

package main;
my $foo;
$obj=tie $foo, "ShowErr";

untie $foo;   # Throws a warning because $obj is still a reference!
```

> **See Also**
> tie in this book

Miscellaneous

aliases

Usage

```
for(LIST) { $_ }
map { $_ } LIST
grep { $_ } LIST
sub subname { @_ }
sort { $a, $b } LIST
```

Description

Aliases in Perl refer to certain situations in which a variable implicitly becomes a reference to another value. Changing the alias alters the original data to which it refers. In Perl, there are several situations in which this occurs.

In `foreach` (and `for`) loops, the index variable (or `$_` if not specified) becomes a reference to the actual value within the list. This means that changing the value of the index variable changes the value in the original list.

```
@soda=qw( coke pepsi sprite crush faygo );
for $pop (@soda) {
    $pop=ucfirst($pop);
}
print join(',', @soda);  # Prints "Coke,Pepsi,Sprite"
```

Unless the index variable is declared `lexical`—for `my $pop (@soda)`—it is localized to the loop and has a dynamic scope. (See the `local` entry.)

The `map` and `grep` functions both iterate over a given list; within the block (or expression) of the loop, the `$_` variable becomes an alias to the values in the list. Altering `$_` will alter the values in the original list.

```
# Using grep as a substitute for for(){}
# Rather pointless, as the results of grep are thrown
#    away.  But it's not an uncommon thing to see done.
grep s/<(\/)?(\w+)([^>]*)>/<$1\U$2\E$3>/g, @HTML;
```

When calling subroutines, the arguments are passed in the array `@_`. Each element of the array `@_` is an alias to the corresponding argument that was passed in. An example is at the end of this section. If an array is passed in, the alias is to each element of the array, not the array itself (unless a reference is passed).

Finally, the `sort` function uses the variables `$a` and `$b` for the user to specify a sort expression. The variables `$a` and `$b` are actually aliases to the real values in the sorted list. They are package globals, but are exempt from strict `vars` typechecking. Also, `$a` and `$b` shouldn't be declared as `lexicals`, although as of Perl 5.6, if a `sort` subroutine has a prototype of `($$)`, you can declare `$a` and `$b` as lexicals within the routine as shown:

```
sub byvalue ($$) {
    my($a, $b)=@_;  # Do this only with a prototype of ($$)
    return $a<=>$b;
}
```

Although it is possible to modify $a and $b within a sort subroutine, modifying values as they're being sorted doesn't have any practical uses, as far as I know. Don't change the values of $a or $b within a sort.

For any of the functions that create aliases (for, foreach, map, grep, sort, and sub), if you attempt to modify the alias, the values in the list should be writable. Otherwise, perl will complain about the "modification of a read-only variable."

Example Listing 2.33

```
# Demonstration of altering @_ aliases
# See also the program in the references section

# Alters the argument passed, beware!
sub dateformat {    # Changes YYYYMMDD to MMDDYYYY
    (substr($_[0], 4, 4),
     substr($_[0], 0, 2),
     substr($_[0], 2, 2))=$_[0]=~m/(....)(..)(..)/;
}

$date="20010108";
dateformat($date);
print $date;
```

See Also
references, map, grep, sub, sort, and for in this book

---

eval

Usage

```
eval block
eval string
eval
```

Description

The eval function allows perl to evaluate code at runtime, and also allows perl to trap errors that would otherwise be fatal. If given a string, at runtime perl will examine the string, compile it, and execute the code within as though it were a little perl program. As an added bonus, exceptions caught during compilation (bad perl code) or at runtime (die, runtime errors) are trapped. The string being eval'd is considered its own block for lexical scoping purposes, containted within the block holding the eval itself.

Be aware that the string given to eval might be interpolated by perl at compile time, depending on the quotes used to contain the string. Thus the evals in the following code:

```
$a='$foo';
eval "$a=56";
eval '$a=99';
```

do very different things. The double-quoted string for the first eval is interpolated and becomes $foo=56, which is then evaluated. The second eval sets $a to 99.

If eval is given a block, the contents of the block are compiled at compile time and are executed at runtime with the runtime exception trapping (but not with compile time exception handling).

If given no arguments, eval uses $_ to compile and run and acts as though a string were passed.

The return value from eval is the result of the last expression evaluated in the string or block. The expression will be evaluated in scalar, list, or void context depending on the context of the eval itself.

If an exception is trapped by the eval, the eval function itself will return undef and $@ will be set to the error message. See the die entry for details.

The block form of eval is generally quicker to execute. The code is compiled once, at compile time, and then evaluated only when needed. String eval compiles its code each time the eval is run, in addition to actually running the code.

The string form of eval is used for expression evaluation. This can be useful for a variety of things:

- Reading perl code from external sources and running it, such as data structures saved to files with Data::Dumper

- Unrolling loops into code that can be run linearly

- Trapping possible runtime errors

The block form of eval compiles its code at compile time, thus it can't be used to trap syntax errors, compile-time warnings, strict errors, and so on. It can be used only to trap runtime errors.

More importantly, the block form of `eval` is the other half of `perl`'s general-purpose exception handling mechanism. For example, this piece of code:

```
eval {
    setpriority(0,0,10);
};
if ($@=~/implemented/) {
    warn "No setpriority on this architecture";
} else {
    die;
}
```

will trap the `setpriority` if the function is unimplemented on this architecture. This mechanism resembles Java's `try`/`throw`/`catch` statement sequence. The programmer can throw errors within an `eval` with `die`, and the interpreter will throw its own runtime errors—both will be caught by the `eval`. The string `eval` will serve the same purpose, but isn't used as much because normal compile-time errors cannot be caught until runtime.

Example Listing 2.34

```
# Demonstrates how unrolling a loop into a single statement
#    computed at runtime can be a *BIG* speed improvement.
#    For large files (16k lines), search_eval runs 7-8 times
#    faster than search_loop.  $i++ is just dummy-work.
# (Run against the text of Zen and the Art of Motorcycle
#    Maintenance.  The words below are common, but not common
#    enough to be stop words.)

use Benchmark;
use strict;
use warnings;
no warnings 'once';
my($i, @words);
sub search_loop {
    my(@patlist)=@_;
    seek(FH, 0, 0) || warn "seek: $!";
    while(<FH>) {
        for my $pat (@patlist) {
            if (/$pat/i) { $i++; last; }
        }
    }
}
```

```
sub search_eval {
    my(@patlist)=@_;
    seek(FH, 0, 0) || warn "seek: $!";
    # Produces in a while loop:
    #    $i++ if (/Chris/io or /Classic/io or /Phaedrus/io);
    my $code=join ' or ', map { $_=qq{/$_/io} } @patlist;
    $code='while(<FH>) { $i++ if (' . $code . ');}';
    eval $code;
}
open(FH, "/tmp/bigfile.txt") || die "Cannot open bigfile: $!";
@words=("Chautauqua", "Classic", "Romantic", "Ph\x{E6}drus",
    "Chris", "motorcycle");
timethese(10, { eval => sub { search_eval(@words) },
        loop => sub { search_loop(@words) }, } );
```

> **See Also**
> die in this book

ref

Usage

```
ref
ref value
```

Description

The ref function returns true if the value is a reference. If val is not specified, the variable $_ is checked instead.

If the value is an unblessed reference, ref will return the reference type (or undef if it isn't a reference). The following types can be returned: SCALAR, ARRAY, HASH, CODE, GLOB, IO (for an IO::Handle), or LVALUE. Additionally, ref will return REF if the value contains a scalar variable that is a reference to another scalar.

If the value is a reference that has been blessed into a class, ref will return the class name (package name). This is less useful than it sounds. Asking an object what class it belongs to is bad programming practice because a class can inherit from a base class: the name will change, but the functionality remains the same. Use the isa method from the UNIVERSAL class (from which all other classes derive) instead to discover if the object has the properties of whatever class you need. (Note: if a class name is one of the strings previously mentioned (SCALAR, ARRAY, and so on), it is difficult to tell whether a reference is blessed.)

Example Listing 2.35

```
my $t={};
bless $t, "Glue";
print ref $t;      # Prints "Glue";

# Would have been better to discover whether
#    it inherits from class "Glue" with
if (ref $t) {
    if ($t->isa("Glue")) {
        # your code here
    }
}

# To be honest: if you're not sure what's in $t
#    at all, then things begin to get silly.
if ($type = ref $t) {
    eval { $t->isa("UNIVERSAL"); };
    if ( $@=~/unblessed/ ) {
        print "It's a $type, not blessed.\n"
    } else {
        print "It's blessed into class $type";
    }
} else {
    print "Not a reference at all\n";
}
```

Example Listing 2.36

```
# Walk an arbitrarily complex structure looking for
#    a particular array element name, then present the
#    path to that element.
use strict;
{
    my $name;
    my @association;
    sub lookfor {
        my $obj=shift;
        $name=shift if @_;
```

```perl
        local $"="->";  # Array double-quote separator
        if (ref $obj eq 'HASH') {
            for my $item (keys %$obj) {
                push(@association, $item);
                if (ref $obj->{$item}) {
                    lookfor($obj->{$item});
                }
                pop(@association);
            }
        } elsif (ref $obj eq 'ARRAY') {
            for my $item (@$obj) {
                if ($name eq $item) {
                    print "Found $name as @association\n";
                }
                lookfor($item);
            }
        } elsif ( (ref $obj) =~ /SCALAR|REF/ ) {
            lookfor($$obj);
        }
    }
}
my $people={   spouse => [ 'marge' ],
        kids => [ 'bart', 'lisa', 'maggie' ],
        friends => { bar =>      [ 'barney', 'moe', ],
                work =>     [ 'karl', 'lenny', 'grimes', ],
                bowling => [ 'apu', 'otto', 'monty',
                    'wayland', ],
        }
};
lookfor($people, "apu");
```

> **See Also**
> UNIVERSAL module documentation
> references, bless and isa in this book

syscall

Usage

syscall *list*

Description

The `syscall` function allows direct access to the system's API. This isn't used to call shell commands or external programs; it is used to get to system calls that might be unavailable to Perl directly but are available to the C API. The following example accesses the `statfs(2)` system call, which normally isn't available through Perl.

Given the nature of this function, availability varies widely from system to system. Non-Unix systems won't have access to `syscall`. Unix systems are touchy.

The first argument in the list is the system call that you want to access. The list of system calls is in `sys/syscall.h` in the standard include directory for your operating system. A list of constants for these can be generated for use in Perl with the `h2ph` utility.

The other arguments in the list are the normal arguments for the system call. Keep in mind that these are passed directly to the C API for the system, and will be interpreted as C arguments. If an argument is numeric, it is passed as an integer to the C function. If an argument is alphabetic, it is passed as a character pointer. If the function writes to one of the values (through a pointer), you must ensure that the target variable in Perl is large enough to hold the results. You cannot use string literals as arguments to `syscall`.

In the case of a structure, you should build an empty structure with `pack`, and pass that as an argument to `syscall`.

The `syscall` function returns the value returned by the C function. Normally, C functions will return `-1` and set `$!` to an error message if they fail. There are exceptions to this rule: You will need to check your system's manual pages for the return value for system calls.

Example Listing 2.37

```
# Finds the free space on a filesystem.
# Works in Linux kernel 2.2
# You will have to build your own syscall.ph
#    file with "h2ph"
require "sys/syscall.ph";

# For information on statfs, type "man statfs"
$struct_statfs=pack("L7IL2", ());
$path="/tmp";
if (syscall(&SYS_statfs, $path,
        $struct_statfs) == -1) {
```

```
    die "syscall failed";
}
($type, $bsize, $blocks, $free)=unpack("L7IL2", $struct_statfs);
print "$path has ", $free*$bsize, " bytes free\n";
```

See Also

h2ph in the perl documentation

$!, pack, and unpack in this book

sys/syscall.h in the C library reference

__LINE__, __FILE__, __PACKAGE__

Usage

```
__LINE__
__FILE__
__PACKAGE__
```

Description

The tokens __LINE__ and __FILE__ are replaced while perl is tokenizing your code (at compile time) with the current line number and file of your perl script. The __PACKAGE__ token is replaced with the current package name for this file, as declared with the package pragma.

These tokens are replaced at compile time, and will only be replaced where a token is expected. They won't be interpolated into double-quoted strings or into regular expressions.

To reset the value of __LINE__, use the #line pragma. To reset the value of __FILE__, use the #file pragma. These are described in the comments entry. The value of __PACKAGE__ is altered with the package pragma.

Example Listing 2.38

```
if ($should_never_happen) {
    print STDERR "*"x60,
        "\nSomething extraordinary has happened.\n",
        "Alert the programmer at 555-1212 that at\nline ",
        __LINE__-5, " in file ", __FILE__,
        " something Real Bad\nhas gone wrong.  ",
        "Sell your stock.  Move to Guam.\n", "*"x60;
}
```

See Also
__WARN__ and die in this book

__DATA__, __END__

Usage

```
__DATA__
__END__
```

Description

The tokens __DATA__ and __END__ are used to mark the end of the runnable code within a perl script. The information can be used by reading the special filehandle DATA.

In the main portion of your program, either __DATA__ or __END__ will mark the end of code to be compiled. Reading the DATA filehandle will read the contents of the file after that point.

In a module, the __DATA__ token can be used to mark the end of the compiled code and the DATA filehandle can be used (from that package) to read the text after the __DATA__ token. Each package (in different files) can have a DATA filehandle.

Example Listing 2.38

```
# This snippet from a much larger program takes the data at the
#   end and prepares a table based on it.  The data's much more
#   maintainable this way.

our %prognames;
# Fill the tables
while(<DATA>) {
    next unless m/(\w+)\s+([-\w.]+)\s+(.*)/;
    $prognames{$1}={ script => $2, title => $3 };
}

__DATA__
em_pay    nph-em_pay.pl      Employee Pay screen
cm_dep    nph-cm_deptlist.pl Department listing
cm_gen  nph-cm_general.pl Company maintenance
```

Example Listing 2.39

```
# A quine in perl
# A quine is a program that can print its own source code.
#    Most quines are notoriously difficult (and fiendish)
#    to write.  Perl can cheat, though.  :)

seek(DATA, 0, 0);
print <DATA>;
__END__
```

> **See Also**
> default file handles in this book

```
overload
```

Usage

```
use overload oplist
```

Description

The `overload` pragma allows you to overload how a handful of operators will work on their operands. The overloaded operators either can be used with operands that have been blessed into a particular class, or can be used with constants in the `perl` program itself.

Overloading Operators

The *oplist* consists of a list of operators that you want to be overloaded and the corresponding subroutine that will actually perform in place of the operator. These subroutines are called handlers; for example,

```
package Myobj;
use overload    '+' => \&add,
        '-' => "subtract",
        '!' => sub { 0;  };
```

For objects that have been blessed into the class `Myobj`, addition (+) will be performed by the subroutine `add` in the package `Myobj`. Subtraction will be performed as a method call (`->subtract`) in the package `Myobj`. The logical `not` will be performed by the anonymous subroutine shown.

Handlers that are specified as strings (and run as methods) can be inherited from a base class as can all methods. In addition, operators that have been overloaded in base classes will be overloaded in the current class.

The operators that can be overloaded are shown in the following:

Operator type	Operators
assignment	`+=, -=, *=, /=, %=, **=, <<=, >>=, x=, .=`
binary	`&, |, ^`
conversion	`bool, "", 0+`
dereferencing	`${}, @{}, %{}, &{}, *{}`
func	`atan2, cos, sin, exp, abs, log, sqrt`
iterators	`<>`
mutators	`++, --`
numeric comparison	`<, <=, >, >, ==, !=`
special	`nomethod fallback =`
string comparison	`lt, le, gt, ge, eq, ne`
unary	`neg, !, ~`
with assignment	`+, -, *, /, %, **, <<, >>, x, .`
three way comparison	`<=>, cmp`

For unary operators (that take only one operand, such as logical not), the handler will be called whenever the operator is applied to an object that has been blessed into that class.

For binary operators (two argument operators, such as addition) the handler will be invoked when the first operand belongs to the class in which the operator is overloaded, or when the second operand belongs to that class and the first operand hasn't been overloaded at all. For example, if $var is blessed into a class with an overloaded + operator as follows:

```perl
package Foo;
use overload  '+' =>
        sub {
            my($x,$y)=@_;
            $x=ref($x) ? $x->{value} : $x;
            $y=ref($y) ? $y->{value} : $y;
```

```
        $x+$y;
        },
        '!' => sub {
        0;
    };
```

```
my $var1={ stuff => "Huh?", value => 6 };
bless $var1;
```

it wouldn't matter if you write the expression:

```
print $var+7;  # Gives 13
```

or

```
print 7+$var;  # Gives 13 too!
```

If both operands are blessed into classes with overloaded operators, the first operand's overload functions are called.

Notice how the handler for addition was written in the previous example. The handler subroutines are always called with three arguments regardless of what kind of operator is invoked. The first argument is the blessed operand, the second argument is the other operand (whether blessed into the same class or not), and the third argument is a switch to indicate whether they have been switched around.

In the case of addition, the order of the operands normally isn't important. For operations such as division and subtraction, the order might be important, so Perl has to indicate to the handler in what order they originally appeared. For example,

Function	Arguments As Passed to the Handler
7+$var	$var, 7, and 1 (they've been switched)
$var+7	$var, 7, and 0 (they're in the original order)
$var+$var	$var, $var, and 0
! $var	$var, undef (it's a unary operator), and 0

The operators +0, bool, and " " bear some explaining. These are implicit operators that are applied to things as they're being converted from one format to another. The +0 operator is applied when a non-numeric value is being used in a numeric context. The operator will be applied, and then the resulting value used in whatever expression is needed.

The `""` operator is used when something that isn't a string value is being used as a string. For example, printing a reference such as the following:

```
$var=[ qw( go tell it on the mountain ) ];
print "$var";
```

would print something similar to ARRAY(0xbeefed). This is an example of a reference being stringified.

The last implicit operator is bool, and is called when the value is being used in a boolean expression. Usually this involves if, while, for, &&, ||, ?:, or unless, or a block that must return true or false as with grep.

When deciding which operators to overload for a particular class, it's important to note that some operators can be handled through autogeneration. This is when the function of an operator can be used to handle other operations.

For example, the functions of <, >, <=, >=, ==, and != all can be determined with the behavior of <=>. Thus, it's only necessary to overload <=> (but you're welcome to overload the others). And if cmp is overloaded, gt, lt, ge, le, eq, and ne all can be autogenerated.

For a full list of which operators can be autogenerated, see the following table:

This	Can Be Autogenerated from These
$x op= $y	The original operand. Thus $a+=$b can be autogenerated from +
++ --	Can be generated from += and -=
- (unary)	Can be generated from - (subtraction)
!	Can be generated from boolean, string, or numeric conversion
Any comparison	Can be generated from <=> or cmp
abs $x	Can be generated from $x<0 and -$x, or 0-$a

If an overload handler is missing, perl will autogenerate the correct operator. If the operators necessary to autogenerate the correct operator are missing, perl looks for an operator called nomethod. The nomethod operator is a general catch-all operator that will be called if nothing else can be done. (It is very similar to AUTOLOAD for method lookups.)

The `nomethod` handler differs in that it takes a fourth argument, which is the operator that is trying to be emulated. So in the following example, although objects are being used, the class has been overloaded so that everything will call `nomethod`'s handler for computation. It simply cheats, extracts the values from the objects, and uses `eval` to compute the real values.

```perl
package Slowmath;
use overload  'nomethod' =>
        sub {
            my($x,$y,$sw,$op)=@_;
            $x=ref($x) ? $x->{value} : $x;
            $y=ref($y) ? $y->{value} : $y;
            if (defined $y) {
                return
                    $sw?eval "$y $op $x":
                        eval "$x $op $y";
            }
            return eval "$op $x";
            } ;
my $var1={ value => 6 };
my $var2={ value => 5 };
bless $var1;  bless $var2;

print 7+$var1;       # 13, as before
print $var2 / $var1; # 0.83333333333
$fudge=$var1;
```

If an operator overload isn't defined and cannot be autogenerated, an exception is raised.

In addition to the `nomethod` handler, you also can define a key called `fallback`, depending on how you set the key, as follows:

Value for `fallback`	Fallback Sequence
`undef` (the default)	Supplied handlers, autogeneration, nomethod handler, exception raised
`false`	Supplied handlers, nomethod handler, exception raised
`true`	Supplied handlers, autogeneration, nomethod handler, and then perl will revert to the un-overloaded behavior of the operator.

Overloading Constants

It is possible to overload how constants are handled in `perl` scripts as well. The
`overload::constant` function can be used to define a set of handlers. This is usually
done in the package's `import` method, and similar calls to `overload::remove_constant`
should be placed in the `unimport` method. The following constant operators can be
overloaded:

overload::constant key	Explanation
`integer`	Integer constants
`float`	Floating point constants
`binary`	Binary, hex, and octal constants
`q`	Single-quoted strings.
`qr`	Regular expressions

The handlers will be called with three arguments. The first is the constant as it was
found by `perl`. The second is what `perl`'s native interpretation of the constant was.

The third argument is used for q and qr handlers and will be qq, q, s, or tr, depending
on how the string was actually used (its interpolative context). The qq argument means
that the string is part of a double-quoted string, backticks, or a pattern match operator
(`m//` or `s///`). The q argument means that no interpolation is expected.

Example Listing 2.40

```
# Module Realnums
#    Changes numbers embedded in string constants to the
#    full English description of the number.

package Realnums;
use overload;
use Lingua::EN::Numbers qw(American);  # Available from CPAN

sub import {
    overload::constant(
        'q' => \&fixdigits,
    );
}
sub unimport {
    overload::remove_constant('q');
}
```

```perl
sub fixdigits {
    my($orig, $perl, $context)=@_;
    $n=new Lingua::EN::Numbers;
    $orig=~s/([\d+\.,]+)/$n->parse($1) && $n->get_string/e;
    return $orig;
}
1;
```

Example Listing 2.41

```perl
# Short demo for Realnums
#
use Realnums;

$t="He wrote a check for 1,234 dollars";

# Yields: "He wrote a check for One Thousand, Two-Hundred Thirty-Four dollars"
print $t;
```

See Also

overload in the perl documentation

operators in this book

---

vec

Usage

```perl
vec scalar, offset, width
```

Description

The vec function allows you to pack fixed-width unsigned integers into a scalar value. Assigning to vec stores the integers and using vec otherwise retrieves them. It is sometimes helpful to think of vec as allowing you to access an array of small integers.

The width indicates the size of the integers that can be stored; for example, using a width of 4 allows you to store numbers as large as 15 (2 raised to the 4th power, minus 1). The width must be a power of two (1, 2, 4, 8, 16, or 32). Some architectures allow a width of 64.

The offset indicates which element of the array you're accessing. You can use different widths and offsets on the same scalar variable, so you can store bits one way and retrieve them in another.

The bits are stored in the scalar variable in a least significant bit first, packed left to right in the scalar, regardless of the CPU's preference. Values that are larger than 8 bits are stored in big-endian order; that is, most-significant byte first. Retrieving bits beyond the end of the scalar will return 0 in place of the missing bits. Storing bits beyond the end of the scalar will extend the scalar to hold them.

Bitstrings created with vec can be manipulated with the bit operators (|, &, ~, and ^). They also can be used with pack and unpack with the b template.

Example Listing 2.42

```
# Create bit vectors for a fixed number of bits
#   See the select example for another example of vec

$bits=8;

# Store in $bits-bit chunks
for(0..(2**$bits)-1) {
    vec($r, $_, $bits)=$_;
}

# Retrieve a bit at a time
for my $off (0..(2**$bits)-1) {
    for my $bit (0..$bits-1) {
        print vec($r, $off*$bits + $bit, 1);
    }
    print "\n";
}
```

See Also
select in this book

Structure Packing Functions

Pack

Usage

```
pack template, list
unpack template, value
```

Description

The pack and unpack functions are general-purpose functions for converting data to and from other representations into Perl values. They can be used to manipulate C structures, binary data (such as would be found in binary data files), packed network data, or to extract fixed-length fields from records (a torturous task with regular expressions, split or substr).

Most of the terminology used in this section is specific to C programming. To understand what a char, long, short, int, double, and single precision number is, consult any book on C programming. At the systems-programming level (where pack and unpack are generally used), these terms are well-known.

The pack and unpack functions both use a template to describe the data representation they will be using. Within the template, each element of the data is described as a field, and each kind of field has a particular template character. The templates also can contain whitespace (including newlines) and comments that begin with # and continue until the next newline character. An invalid character in a template will throw an exception.

The unpack function takes a scalar value that has data to be extracted and uses the template to extract the data into a list of fields; then the list is returned. The pack function takes a list and uses the template to pack the list into a scalar value, which is returned.

If extra elements are supplied in the list to pack, they are ignored. If extra template characters are in unpack's template and there is no more data, those template characters are ignored.

Template Character	Description
a	String of bytes, null-padded.
A	String of bytes, space-padded During unpack, trailing nulls and spaces are not returned.
b	Bit string, least significant bit first (see vec).
B	Bit string, most significant bit first.
c	Signed char (8-bit).
C	Unsigned char (8-bit).
d	Double-precision, floating-point number.
f	Single-precision, floating-point number.

Template Character	Description
h	Hex string, low 4-bits first.
H	Hex string, high 4-bits first.
i	Signed integer.
I	Unsigned integer.
l	Signed long (32 bits, even on 64-bit systems, see !).
L	Unsigned long (always 32 bits).
n	Short in "network" order (16-bits).
N	Long in "network" order (32-bits).
p	Pointer to a null-terminated string.
P	Pointer to a fixed-length string.
q	Signed integer (64-bit).
Q	Unsigned integer (64-bit).
s	Signed short (16-bit).
S	Unsigned short (16-bit).
u	Unencoded string.
U	Unicode character number.
v	Short in little-endian (vax) order (16-bit).
V	Long in little-endian (vax) order (32-bit).
w	ASN.1 BER compressed integer.
x	Skip forward 1 byte; doesn't cause an element to appear in the output list with unpack.
X	Skip backward 1 byte.
Z	Null padded and terminated bytes. During unpack, everything after the first trailing null is stripped.
@	Null fill.

In addition, each template character can be followed by a modifier to change its behavior. The modifier allowed depends on the particular template character being considered.

Modifier	Allowed With	Action
number	c, C, d, f, i, I, l, L, n, N, p, q, Q, s, S, u, U, v, V, w, x	Repeats *number* many times. So a template of i3 would expect three integers.
*	c, C, d, f, i, I, l, L, n, N, p, q, Q, s, S, u, U, v, V, w, x	Continues packing (or unpacking) until no items are left.
number	a, A, Z	Used for a length to pack the value, null, or space padding as necessary.
number	b, B	Used to determine how many bits to pack or unpack.
*	b, B	(unpack). Uses the remainder of the input field's bits.
!	s, S, l, L, i, I	Use native shorts and longs instead of 16/32-bit representations. On a 64-bit architecture, this is how a 64-bit long would be accessed, for example.
/		(see following text)
%number	any	(unpack). This takes the current field and performs a number-bit checksum. See the following example. If number is omitted, a 16-bit checksum will be produced.

Numeric modifiers and the * modifier only apply to a single field within the template. To repeat a particular portion of a template, you will actually need to construct a template that contains the repeated pattern. For example, to unpack two longs, three 20-character fields, and two ints:

```
@a=unpack("LL" . "a20"x3 . "ii", $string);
```

The modifier / is used to create a template in which the length of a field is encoded within the data. For example, if a series of fields is encoded as

```
$s="07Clinton06Pierce";
```

then the correct unpack template to decode the field would be something similar to the following:

```
@fields=unpack('a2/A*a2/a*', $s);
```

Almost any practical format can be used to encode the lengths in the string, but currently only a*, A*, and Z* can be used to pack and unpack the values. For example, to pack an entire list of records with leading lengths for each line:

```
@stuff=qw( mistletoe holly reindeer santa nativity );
for(@stuff) { $f.=pack('A3/A*', $_) }
print $f;   # prints "9  mistletoe5  holly8  reindeer5  santa8  nativity"
```

When unpacking and packing structures to be used for data interchange with other systems or even with system utilities that are expecting C-like structures (through syscall, select, or other low-level utilities), you need to be aware of the following pitfalls with pack and unpack:

- Native formats for integers (and longs) are importable between machines of different architectures. For example, a number packed with an L format on an Intel architecture machine (little-endian) cannot be unpacked on a SPARC architecture (big-endian). Use the Network formats (n, N) or another format which specifies bit order (v, V).

- When packing structures, be aware that C compilers will byte and word align structures and put padding between elements in a structure so that they align properly. For example, this short C program on an Intel architecture:

```
#include <stdio.h>
main() {
    struct s {
        char c0;
        char c1;
        int i;
    };
    printf("%d\n", sizeof(struct s));
}
```

prints the value 8 because the integers are aligned on 4-byte boundaries. So
when unpacking this structure, use the format ccxxi. (The x's skip over the
unused bytes in the structure.) Compiling short C programs and using sizeof is
a great way to investigate the packing behavior of your system's C compiler.
Similar to many unpack formats, alignment will vary depending on your system's
architecture and operating system. The utmp example contains a fairly complex
example of unpacking a C struct.

- Be aware of the size of the native short, long, and int on your architecture. Perl
  has some idea of what these values are in the Config module. For example, the
  native integer size on your architecture can be determined with:

```
use Config;
print $Config{intsize};   # Prints "4" on Linux 2.2 for 80686
```

Use the C header files to determine what system structures actually resemble.
The manual pages and documentation in books might contain more fields, fewer
fields, or fields with different sizes. While writing this section, I discovered that
the utmp manual page in Linux and the utmp.h header file in C differed enough
to cause great frustration.

Example Listing 2.43

```
# Show the login entries for a Unix system
#    The utmp structure is documented in the utmp man page
#    and is valid for RedHat Linux 6.0 systems (will be
#    similar elsewhere.

$wtmp="/var/log/wtmp";

# The constants and structures came from /usr/include/utmp.h
$utl=32;      #define UT_LINESIZE         32  /* The manpage is wrong :) */
$utn=32;      #define UT_NAMESIZE         32
$uth=256;     #define UT_HOSTSIZE         256
$type=7;      #define USER_PROCESS        7

# The comments in these structures aren't Perl comments
#       they have to be dealt with separately.  They're
#       here for explanatory purposes.
$exit_statusT= "      # struct exit_status {
          s     #      short int e_termination;
          s     #      short int e_exit;
          ";    # };
```

```perl
$timeval_ut_tvT="      # struct timeval {
            L      #      __time_t tv_sec;
            L      #      __time_t tv_usec;
            ";     # }
$utmpT= "               # struct utmp {
    s           #          short ut_type;
    xx          #               ALIGNMENT
    i           #          pid_t ut_pid;
    a$utl       #          char ut_line[UT_LINESIZE];
    a4          #          char ut_id[4];
    a$utn       #          char ut_user[UT_NAMESIZE];
    a$uth       #          char ut_host[UT_HOSTSIZE];
   $exit_statusT    #      struct exit_status ut_exit;
    L           #          long ut_session;
   $timeval_ut_tvT  #      struct timeval ut_tv;
    i           #          int32_t ut_addr_v6[4];
    a20         #          char pad[20];
    ";          #      };

# Remove the "comments", they're for reference only.
$utmpT=~s/(#.*?\n)|(\s)//g;

open(WTMP, $wtmp) || die "$wtmp: $!";

# The 384 was determined by adding up the sizes of the structure
#     elements above.  Can also be done with a c program that prints
#     sizeof(struct utmp)
$/=\384;         # Causes a fixed-length read
while($buff=<WTMP>) {
    @fields=unpack($utmpT, $buff);
    next unless $fields[0] == $type;  # Want user-processes only
    print "$fields[0] $fields[2] $fields[4] ",
          scalar localtime($fields[9]), "\n";
}
close(WTMP);
```

Example Listing 2.44

```perl
# Take the file "mbox" and decode all of the base-64
#   mime-attachments in it.  Relies on the mail user agent
#   using paragraph breaks between important bits (most do).
```

```
$/="";    # Read in paragraph mode
push(@ARGV, "mbox");
while(<>) {
    next unless (/Content-Transfer-Encoding: base64/
        and /filename="(.*?)"/);
    $filename=$1;
    @data=split(/\n/, <>);  # Next paragraph is the data

    # This is *ahem* insecure.  It may overwrite files you
    #    already have.
    open(OUT, ">$filename") || die;
    for(@data) {
        # Converts base-64 to uuencode format
        #    formula from Programming Perl, 2ed.
        tr|A-Za-z0-9+/||cd;
        tr|A-Za-z0-9+/| -_|;
        print OUT unpack("u",
            pack("c", 32+(length $_)*.75) . $_);
    }
    close(OUT);
}
```

Example Listing 2.45

```
# Unpacking fixed-length fields.
#    Unsuitable for split, torurous with substr

@bills=("11/26/00 Detroit Edison          46.35",
        "11/15/00 Consumer's Energy       12.56",
        "12/01/00 Veterinarian            45.00",
        "11/30/00 Car Insurance          123.00");


for(@bills) {
    ($month,$day,$year,$bill,$amount)=unpack("A2xA2xA2xA22A*", $_);

    # Process a bill record
    print "You owe $bill $amount\n";
}
```

See Also
split in this book

```
reset
```

Usage

```
reset
reset prefix
```

Description

The reset function has two distinct uses. The first use is that given a prefix, all the variables in the current package with that prefix will be initialized.

The prefix can either be a string of characters that describe the beginnings of a variable name:

```
use warnings;

@hobbies=qw(painting weaving reading);
$hobbit="Behind the round door";

reset 'hobb';
print $hobbit;  # "Use of uninitialized value..." warning
if (@hobbies) { # Nope, false now.
    # Never be reached
}
```

Or the prefix can be expressed as a range (similar to tr) of single-character prefixes:

```
reset 'a-z';  # Clears all variables starting with a through z
reset 'X-Z';  # Clears variables starting with X, Y or Z
```

Be careful not to indiscriminately reset variables with uppercase letters. You might wind up resetting @INC, %ENV, %SIG, and other variables necessary for perl to run properly.

The reset function doesn't affect lexical variables.

Without an argument, the reset function is used to clear searches that have been performed with the ?? match operator. These searches only will match a particular pattern once. However, reset only will clear one-time-searches within the current package. A demonstration of the 0-argument reset function is in the ?? operator entry.

See Also
?? in this book

CHAPTER 3
Regular Expressions

Regular Expression Basics

Description

Understanding how to use regular expressions is fundamental to any Perl programmer. The essential purpose of a regular expression is to match a pattern, and Perl provides two operators for doing just that: m// (match) and s/// (substitute). (The ins and outs of those operators are covered in their own entries.)

When Perl encounters a regular expression, it's handed to a regular expression engine and compiled into a special kind of state machine (a Nondeterministic Finite Automaton). This state machine is used against your data to determine whether the regular expression matches your data. For example, to use the match operator to test whether the word fudge exists in a scalar value:

```
$r=q{"Oh fudge!" Only that's not what I said.};
if ($r =~ m/fudge/) {
    # ...
}
```

The regular expression engine takes `/fudge/`, compiles a state machine to use against `$r`, and executes the state machine. If it was successful, the pattern matched.

This was a simple example, and could have been accomplished quicker with the `index` function. The regular expression engine comes in handy because the pattern can contain metacharacters. Regular expression metacharacters are used to specify things that might or might not be in the data, look different (uppercase? lowercase?) in the data, or portions of the pattern that you just don't care about.

The simplest metacharacter is the . (dot). Within a regular expression, the dot stands for a "don't care" position. Any character will be matched by a dot:

```
m/m..n/;  # Matches: main, mean, moan, morn, moon, honeymooner,
          # m--n, "m  n", m00n, m..n, m22n etc... (but not "mn")
```

The exception is that a dot won't normally match a newline character. For that to happen, the match must have the `/s` modifier tacked on to the end. See the modifiers entry for details.

Metacharacters stand in for other characters (see "Character Shorthand") or stand in for entire classes of characters (character classes). They also specify quantity (quantifiers), choices (alternators), or positions (anchors).

In general, something that is normally metacharacter can be made "unspecial" by prefixing it with a backslash, which is sometimes called "escaping" the character. So to match a literal `m..n` (with real dots), change the expression to

```
m/m\.\.n/; # Matches only m..n
```

The full list of metacharacters is \, |, ^, $, *, +, ?, ., (,), [, {

Everything else in Perl's regular expressions matches itself. A normal character (nonmetacharacter) can sometimes be turned into a metacharacter by adding a backslash. For example, "d" is just a letter "d". However, preceded by a backslash,

```
/\d/
```

It matches a digit. More of this is covered in the "Character Shorthand" section. The entire set of metacharacters as well as some contrived metacharacters are covered elsewhere in this book.

As you browse the remainder of this section, keep in mind that there are just a few rules associated with regular expression matching. These are summarized as follows:

- The goal is for the match to succeed as a whole. Everything else takes a backseat to that goal.

- The entire pattern must be used to match the given data.

- The match that begins the earliest (the leftmost) will be taken first.

Unless otherwise directed (with ?), quantifiers will always match as much as possible, and still have the expression match.

To sum up: the largest possible first match is normally taken.

For more information on how regular expression engines work, see the book *Mastering Regular Expressions* by Jeffrey Friedl.

See Also

m//, s///, character classes, alternation, quantifiers, character shorthand, line anchors, word anchors, grouping, backreferences and qr in this book

---

Basic Metacharacters and Operators

Match Operator

```
m//
```

Usage

```
m/pattern/modifiers
```

Description

The m// operator is Perl's pattern match operator. The pattern is first interpolated as though it were a double-quoted string—scalar variables are expanded, backslash escapes are translated, and so on. Afterward, the pattern is compiled for the regular expression engine.

Next, the pattern is used to match data against the $_ variable unless the match operator has been bound with the =~ operator.

```
m/(?:\(?\d{3}\)?-)?\d{3}-\d{4}/;      # Match against $_
$t=~m/(?:\(?\d{3}\)?-)?\d{3}-\d{4}/;  # Match against $t
```

In a scalar context, the match operator returns true if it succeeds and false if it fails. With the /g modifier, in scalar context the match will proceed along the target string, returning true each time, until the target string is exhausted.

The modifiers (other than /g and /c) are described in the Match Modifiers entry.

In a list context, the match operator returns a list consisting of all the matched portions of the pattern that were captured with parenthesis (as well as setting $1, $2 and so on as a side-effect of the match). If there are no parenthesis in the match, the list (1) is returned. If the match fails, the empty list is returned.

In a list context with the /g modifier, the list of substrings matched by capturing parenthesis is returned. If no parenthesis are in the pattern, it returns the entire contents of each match.

```
$_=q{I do not like green eggs and ham, I do not like them Sam I Am};

$match=m/\w+/;          # $match=1
$match=m/(\w+)/g;       # $match=1, $1="I"
$match=m/(\w+)/g;       # $match=1, $1="do"
$match=m/(\w+)/g;       # $match=1, $1="not" .. and so on

@match=m/\w*am\b/i;         # @match=(1)
@match=m/(\b\w{4}\b)/i;     # @match=('like');
@match=m/(\w+)\W+(\w+)/i;   # @match=qw(I do);

@match=m/\w*am\b/ig;        # @match=qw( ham Sam Am )
@match=m/(\b\w{4}\b)/ig;    # @match=qw( like eggs like them )
@match=m/(\w+)\W+(\w+)/ig;  # @match=qw( I do not like [...] Sam I am )
```

After a failed match with the /g modifier, the search position is normally reset to the beginning of the string. If the /c modifier also is specified, this won't happen, and the next /g search will continue where the old one failed. This is useful if you're matching against a target string that might be appended to during successive checks of the match.

The delimiters within the match operator can be changed by specifying another character after the initial m. Any character except whitespace can be used, and using the delimiter of ' has the side-effect of not allowing string interpolation to be performed before the regular expression is compiled. Balanced characters (such as (), [], {}, and <>) can be used to contain the expression.

```
m/\/home\/clintp\/bin/;   # Match clintp's /bin
m!/home/clintp/bin!;      # Somewhat more sane
```

```
m/$ENV{HOME}\/bin/;          # Match the user's own /bin
m'$ENV{HOME}/bin';           # Match literal '$ENV{HOME}/bin' -- useless?
m{/home/clintp};
```

If you're content with using // as delimiters for the pattern, the m can be omitted from the match operator:

```
while( <IRCLOG> ) {
    if (/<(?:Abigail|Addi)>/) {  # Look ma, no "m"!

        # See below for explanation of //
        if (grep(//, @users)) {
            print LOG "$_\n";
        }
    }
}
```

If the pattern is omitted completely, the pattern from the last successful regular expression match is used. In the previous sample of code, the expression <(?:Abigail|Addi)> is re-used for the grep's pattern.

Example Listing 3.1

```
# The example from the "backreferences" section
#   re-worked to use the list-context-with-/g return
#   value of the match operator.

open(CONFIG, "config") || die "Can't open config: $!";
{
    local $/;
    %conf=<CONFIG>=~m/([^=]+)=(.*)\n/g;
}
```

See Also
Substitution operator, ??, and match modifiers in this book

Substitution Operator

s///

Usage

s/pattern/replacement/modifiers

Description

The s/// operator is Perl's substitution operator. The *pattern* is first interpolated as though it were a double-quoted string—scalar variables are expanded, backslash escapes are translated, and so on. Afterward, the pattern is compiled for the regular expression engine.

The pattern is then used to match against a target string; by default, the $_ variable is used unless another value is bound using the =~ operator.

```
s/today/yesterday/;          # Change string in $_
$t=~s/yesterday/long ago/;   # Change string in $t
```

If the pattern is successfully matched against the target string, the matched portion is substituted using the replacement.

The substitution operator returns the number of substitutions made. If no substitutions were made, the substitution operator returns false (the empty string). The return value is the same in both scalar and list contexts.

```
$_="It was, like, ya know, like, totally cool!";
$changes=s/It/She/;          # $changes=1, for the match
$changes=s/\slike,//g;       # $changes=2, for both matches
```

The /g modifier causes the substitution operator to repeat the match as often as possible. Unlike the match operator, /g has no other side effects (such as walking along the match in scalar context)—it simply repeats the substitution as often as possible for nonoverlapping regions of the target string.

During the substitution, captured patterns from the pattern portion of the operator are available during the replacement part of the operator as $1, $2, and so on. If the /g modifier is used, the captured patterns are refreshed for each replacement.

```
$_="One fish two fish red fish blue fish";
s/(\w+)\s(\w+)/$2 $1/g;  # Swap words for "fish one fish two..."
```

The /e modifier causes Perl to evaluate the replacement portion of the substitution for each replacement about to happen as though it were being run with eval {}. The replacement expression is syntax checked at compile time and variable substitutions occur at runtime, the same as eval {}.

```
# Make this URL component "safe" by changing non-letters
#   to 2-digit hex codes (RFC 1738)
$text=~s/(\W)/sprintf('%%%02x', ord($1))/ge;
```

Basic Metacharacters and Operators

```
# Perform word substitutions from a list...
%abrv=( 'A.D.' => 'Anno Domini', 'a.m.' => 'ante meridiem',
  'p.m.' => 'post meridiem', 'e.g.' => 'exempli gratia',
  'etc.' => 'et cetera',     'i.e.' => 'id est');
$text=qq{I awoke at 6 a.m. and went home, etc.};
$text=~s/([\w.]+)/exists $abrv{$1}?$abrv{$1}:$1/eg;
```

The delimiters within the substitution operator can be changed by specifying another character after the initial s. Any character except whitespace can be used, and using the delimiter of ' has the side-effect of not allowing string interpolation to be performed before the regular expression is compiled. Balanced characters (such as (), [], {}, and <>) can be used to contain the pattern and replacement. Additionally, a different set of characters can be used to encase the pattern and the replacement:

```
s/\/home\/clintp/\/users\/clintp/g;   # Ugh!
s,/home/clintp,/users/clintp,g;        # Whew!  Better.
s[/home/clintp]
    {/users/clintp}g;                  # This is really clear
```

The match modifiers (other than /e and /g) are covered in the entry on match modifiers.

Example Listing 3.2

```
# This function takes its argument and renders it in
#   Pig-Latin following the traditional rules for Pig Latin
# (Note that there's a substitution within a substitution.)
{
    my $notvowel=qr/[^aeiou_]/i;  # _ is because of \w

    sub igpay_atinlay {
        local $_=shift;

        # Match the word
        s[(\w+)]
            {
            local $_=$1;
            # Now re-arrange the leading consonants
            #   or if none, append "yay"
            s/^($notvowel+)(.*)/$2$1ay/
                or
                s/$/yay/;
            $_;  # Return the result
```

```
        }ge;
      return $_;
   }
}
print igpay_atinlay("Hello world");  # "elloHay orldway"
```

> **See Also**
> match operator, match modifiers, capturing, and backreferences in this book

Character Shorthand

Description

Regular expressions, similar to double-quoted strings, also allow you to specify hard-to-type characters as digraphs (backslash sequences), by name or ASCII/Unicode number.

They differ from double-quoted context in that, within a regular expression, you're trying to match the given character—not trying to emit it. A single digraph might match more than one kind of character.

The simplest character shorthand is for the common unprintables. These are as follows:

Character	Matches
\t	A tab (TAB and HT)
\n	A newline (LF, NL). On systems with multicharacter line termination characters, it matches both characters.
\r	A carriage return (CR)
\a	An alarm character (BEL)
\e	An escape character (ESC)

They also can represent any ASCII character using the octal or hexadecimal code for that character. The format for the codes are: \digits for octal and \xdigits for hexadecimal. So to represent a SYN (ASCII 22) character, you can say

```
/\x16/;  # Match SYN (hex)
/\026/;  # Match SYN (oct)
```

However, beware that using *digits* can cause ambiguity with backreferences (captured pieces of a `regexp`). The sequence \\2 can mean either ASCII 2 (STX), or it can mean the item that was captured from the second set of parenthesis.

Ambiguous references are resolved in this manner: If the number of captured parenthesis is greater than *digit*, *digit* from the capture; otherwise, the value is the corresponding ASCII value (in octal). Within a character class, *digits* will never stand for a backreference. Single digit references such as *digit* always stand for backreference, except for \\0, which means ASCII 0 (NUL).

To avoid this mess, specify octal ASCII codes using three digits (with a leading zero if necessary). Backreferences will never have a leading zero, and there probably won't be more than 100 backreferences in a regular expression.

Wide (multibyte) characters can be specified in hex by surrounding the hex code with {} to contain the entire sequence of digits. The `utf8` pragma also must be in effect.

```
use utf8;
/\x{262f}/;      # Unicode YIN YANG
```

When the character is a named character, you can specify the name with a \\N{*name*} sequence if the `charnames` module has been included.

```
use charnames ':full';
s/\N{CLOUD}/\N{LIGHTNING}/g;  # The weather worsens!
```

Control-character sequences can be specified directly with \\c*character*. For example, the control-g character is a BEL, and it can be represented as \\cg; the control-t character is \\ct.

Example Listing 3.2

```
# Dump the file given on STDIN/command line translating any
#   low-value ASCII characters to their symbolic notation

@names{(0..32)}=qw( NUL SOH STX ETX EOT ENQ ACK BEL BS HT LF VT FF
       CR SO SI DLE DC1 DC2 DC3 DC4 NAK SYN ETB CAN
       EM SUB ESC FS GS RS US SPACE);
$names{127}='DEL';

while(<>) {
   tr/\200-\377/\000-\177/;  # Strip 8th bit too.
   foreach(split(//)) {
       s/([\000-\x1f\x7f])/$names{ord($1)}/e;
```

```
        printf "%4s ", $_;
    }
}
```

> **See Also**
> charnames module documentation
> character classes in this book

Character Classes

Description

Character classes in Perl are used to match a single character with a particular property. For example, if you want to match a single alphabetic uppercase character, it would be nice to have a convenient property to describe this property. In Perl, surround the characters that describe the property with a set of square brackets:

```
m/[ABCDEFGHIJKLMNOPQRSTUVWXYZ]/
```

This expression will match a single, alphabetic, uppercase character (at least for English speakers). This is a character class, and stands in for a single character.

Ranges can be used to simplify the character class:

```
m/[A-Z]/
```

Ranges that seem natural (0-9, A-Z, A-M, a-z, n-z) will work. If you're familiar with ASCII collating sequence, other less natural ranges (such as [!-/]) can be constructed. Ranges can be combined simply by putting them next to each other within the class:

```
m/[A-Za-z]/;    # Upper and lowercase alphabetics
```

Some characters have special meaning within a character class and deserve attention:

The dash (-) character must either be preceded by a backslash, or should appear first within a character class. (Otherwise it might appear to be the beginning of a range.)

A closing bracket (]) within a character class should be preceded by a backslash, or it might be mistaken for the end of the class.

The ^ character will negate the character class. That is, every possible character that doesn't have the property described by the character class will match. So that:

```
m/[^A-Z]/;   # Match anything BUT an uppercase, alphabetic character
```

Remember that negating a character class might include some things you didn't expect. In the preceding example, control characters, whitespace, Unicode characters, 8-bit characters, and everything else imaginable would be matched—just not A-Z.

In general, any other metacharacter (including the special character classes later in this section) can be included within a character class. Some exceptions to this are the characters .+()*|$^ which all have their mundane meanings when they appear within a character class, and backreferences (\1, \2) don't work within character classes. The \b sequence means "backspace" in a character class, and not a word boundary.

The hexadecimal, octal, Unicode, and control sequences for characters also work just fine within character classes:

```
m/[\ca-\cz]/;   # Match all control characters
m/[\x80-\xff]/; # Match high-bit-on characters
use charnames qw(:full);
m/[\N{ARIES}\N{SCORPIUS}\N{PISCES}\N{CANCER}\N{SAGITTARIUS}]/;
```

In Perl regular expressions, common character classes also can be represented by convenient shortcuts. These are listed as follows:

Class	Name	What It Matches
\d	Digits	[0-9]
\D	Nondigits	[^0-9]
\s	Whitespace	[\x20\t\n\r\f]
\S	Non-whitespace	[^\x20\t\n\r\f]
\w	Word character	[a-zA-Z0-9_]
\W	Non-word character	[^a-zA-Z0-9_]

These shortcuts can be used within regular character classes or by themselves within a pattern match:

```
if (/x[\da-f]/i) {  }  # Match something hex-ish
s/(\w+)/reverse $1/e;  # Reverse word-things only
```

The actual meaning of these will change if a locale is in effect. So, when perl encounters a string such as ¡feliz cumpleaños!, the exact meaning of metacharacters such as \w will change. This code

```perl
$a="\xa1feliz cumplea\xf1os!";     # Happy birthday, feliz cumpleaños
while($a=~m/(\w+)/g) {
    print "Word: $1\n";
}
```

will find three words in that text: feliz, cumplea, and os. The \xf1 (n with a tilde) character isn't recognized as a word character. This code:

```perl
use locale;
use POSIX qw(locale_h);
setlocale(LC_CTYPE, "sp.ISO8859-1");  # Spanish, Latin-1 encoding

$a="\xa1feliz cumplea\xf1os!";  # Happy b-day.
while($a=~m/(\w+)/g) {
    print "Word: $1\n";
}
```

works as a Spanish speaker would expect, finding the words feliz and cumpleaños. The locale can be negated by specifying a bytes pragma within the lexical block, causing the character classes to go back to their original meanings.

Perl also defines character classes to match sets of Unicode characters. These are called Unicode properties, and are represented by \p{*property*}. The list of properties is extensive because Unicode's property list is long and perl adds a few custom properties to that list as well. Because the Unicode support in Perl is (currently) in flux, your best bet to find out what is currently implemented is to consult the perlunicode manual page for the version of perl that you're interested in.

The last kind of character class shortcut (other than user-defined ones covered in the section on character classes) is defined by POSIX. Within another character class, the POSIX classes can be used to match even more specific kinds of characters. They all have the following form:

```
[:class:]
```

where class is the character class you're trying to match. To negate the class, write it as follows: [:^*class*:].

Basic Metacharacters and Operators

Class	Meaning
ascii	7-bit ASCII characters (with an ord value <127)
alpha	Matches a letter
lower	Matches a lowercase alpha
upper	Matches an uppercase alpha
digit	Matches a decimal digit
alnum	Matches both alpha and digit characters
space	Matches a whitespace character (just like \s)
punct	Matches a punctuation character
print	Matches alnum, punct, or space
graph	Matches alnum and punct
word	Matches alnum or underscore
xdigit	Match hex digits: digit, a-f, and A-F
cntrl	The ASCII characters with an ord value <32 (control characters)

To use the POSIX character classes, they must be within another character class:

```
for(split(//,$line)) {
    if (/[[:print:]]/) { print; }
}
```

Using a POSIX class on its own:

```
if (/[:print:]/) { }   # WRONG!
```

won't have the intended effect. The previous bit of code would match :, p, r, i, n, and t.

If the locale pragma is in effect, the POSIX classes will work as the corresponding C library functions such as isalpha, isalnum, isascii, and so on.

Example Listing 3.3

```
# Analyze the file on STDIN (or the command line) to get the
#  makeup.  A typical MS-Word doc is about 60-70% high-bit
#  characters and control codes.  This book in XML form was
#  less than 4% control codes, 10.8% punctuation, 18.2% whitespace
```

```perl
#   and 69% alphanumeric characters.

use warnings;
use strict;
my(%chars, $total, %props, $code, %summary);
# Take the file apart, summarize the frequency for
#   each character.
while(<>) {
    $chars{$_}++ for(split(//));
    $total+=length;
}

# Warning: space and cntrl overlap so >100% is possible!
%props=(alpha => "Alphabetic",   digit => "Numeric",
    space => "Whitespace",   punct => "Punctuation",
    cntrl => "Control characters",
    '^ascii' => "8-bit characters");

# Build the code to analyze each kind of character
#   and classify it according to the POSIX classes above.
$code.="\$summary{'$_'}+=\$chars{\$_} if /[[:$_:]]/;\n"
    for(keys %props);
eval "for(keys %chars){ $code }";

foreach my $type (keys %props) {
    no warnings 'uninitialized';
    printf "%-18s %6d %4.1f%%\n", $props{$type}, $summary{$type},
        ($summary{$type}/$total)*100;
}
```

> **See Also**
> bytes, utf8, and POSIX module documentation
>
> perlunicode in the perl documentation
>
> isalpha in the C library reference

Quantifiers

Usage

{min,max}
{min,}

```
{min}
*
+
?
```

Description

Quantifiers are used to specify how many of a preceding item to match. That item can be a single character (/a*/), a group (/(foo)?/), or it can be anything that stands in for a single character such as a character class (/\w+/).

The first quantifier is ?, which means to match the preceding item zero or one times (in other words, the preceding item is optional).

```
/flowers?/;        # "flower" or "flowers" will match
/foo[0-9]?/;        # foo1, foo2 or just foo will match
/\b[A-Z]\w+('s)?\b/;    # Matches things like "Bob's" or "Carol" --
            #   capitalized singular words, possibly possessed

# Match day of week names like 'Mon', 'Thurs' and Friday.
#   (caution: also matches oddities like 'Satur' -- this can be
#    remedied, but makes a lousy example.)
/(Mon|Tues?|Wed(nes)?|Thu(rs)?|Fri|Sat(ur)?|Sun)(day)?/;
```

Any portion of a match quantified by ? will always be successful. Sometimes an item will be found, and sometimes not, but the match will always work.

The quantifier * is similar to ? in that the quantified item is optional, except * specifies that the preceding item can match zero or more times. Specifically, the quantified item should be matched as many times as possible and still have the regular expression match succeed. So,

```
/fo*bar/;
```

matches 'fobar', 'foobar', 'foooobar', and also 'fbar'. The * quantifier will always match positively, but whether a matching item will be found is another question. Because of this, beware of expressions such as the following:

```
/[A-Z]*\w*/
```

You might hope it will match a series of uppercase characters and then a set of word characters, and it will. But it also will match numbers, empty strings, and binary data. Because everything in this expression is optional, the expression will always match.

With * you can absorb unwanted material to make your match less specific:

```
# This matches any of: <body>, <body background="">,
#    <body background="foo.gif">, <body onload="alert()">,
#    or <body onload="alert()" background="foo.gif:>
/<\w+(\s+\w+="[^"]*")*>/;
```

In the preceding example, * was used to make [^"] match empty quote marks, or quote marks with something inside; it was used to make the attribute match (foo="bar") optional, and repeat it as often as necessary.

The + quantifier requires the match not only to succeed at least once, but also as many times as possible and still have the regular expression match be successful. So, it's similar to *, except that at least one match is guaranteed. In the preceding example, the space following the \w+ was specified as \s+; otherwise items such as <bodyonload="alert()"> would match.

```
/fo+bar/;
```

This matches 'fobar', 'foobar', and of course 'fooooobar'. But unlike *, it will not match 'fbar'.

Perl also allows you to match an item a minimal, fixed, or maximum number of times with the {} quantifiers.

Quantifier	Meaning
{min,max}	Matches at least *min* times, but at most *max* times.
{min,}	Matches at least *min* times, but as many as necessary for the match to succeed.
{count}	Matches exactly *count* times.

Keep in mind that with the {min,} and {min,max} searches, the match will absorb only as many characters as necessary and still have the match succeed. Thus with the following:

```
$_="Python";
if (m/\w(\w{1,5})\w\w/) {
    print "Matched ", length($1), "\n";
}
```

The $1 variable winds up with only three characters because the first \w matched P, the last \w's needed "on" to be successful, and that left "yth" for the quantified \w.

Perl's quantifiers are normally *maximal* matching, meaning that they match as many characters as possible but still allow the regular expression as a whole to match. This is also called *greedy* matching.

The **?** quantifier has another meaning in Perl: when affixed to a *****, **+**, or **{}** quantifier, it causes the quantifier to match as few characters as necessary for the match to be successful. This is called *minimal* matching (or *lazy* matching).

Take the following code:

```
$_=q{"You maniacs!" he yelled at the surf. "You blew it up!"};
while (m/(".*")/g) {
    print "$1\n";
}
```

It might surprise you to see that the regular expression grabs the entire string, not just each quote individually. That's because ".*" matches as much as possible between the quote marks, including other quote marks. Changing the expression to:

```
m/".*?"/g
```

solves this problem by asking ***** to match as little as possible for the match to succeed.

Keep in mind that **?** is just a convenient shorthand and might not represent the best possible solution to the problem. The pattern /"[^"]*"/ would have been a more efficient choice because the amount of backtracking by the regular expression engine to be done would have been less. But there is programmer efficiency to consider.

See Also
m operator in this book

Modification Characters

Usage

```
\Q \E \L \l \U \u
```

Description

The modification characters used in string literals (in an interpolated context) are available in regular expressions as well. See the entry on modification characters for a list.

Understand that these "metacharacters" aren't really metacharacters at all. They do their work because regular expression match operators allow interpolation to happen when the pattern is first examined—much in the same way that \L and \U are only effective in double-quoted strings; they're only effective in regular expressions when the pattern is first examined by perl.

```
$foo='\U';
if (m/${foo}blah/) {  } # Won't look for BLAH, but 'Ublah'
if (m/\Ublah/) {  }     # Will look for BLAH
if (m/(a)\U\1/ { }      # Won't look for aA as you might hope
```

Most useful among these in regular expressions is the \Q modifier. The \Q modifier is used to quote any metacharacters that follow. When accepting something that will be used in a pattern match from an untrusted source, it is vitally important that you not put the pattern into the regular expression directly. Take this small sample:

```
# A CGI form is a _VERY_ untrustworthy source of info.

use CGI qw(:form :standard);
print header();
$pat=param("SEARCH");
# ...sometime later...
if (/$pat/) {
}
```

The trouble with this is that handing $pat to the regular expression engine opens up your system to running code that's determined solely by the user. If the user is malicious, he can:

- Specify a regular expression that will never terminate (endless backtracking).

- Specify a regular expression that will use indeterminate amounts of memory.

- Specify a regular expression that can run perl code with a (?{}) pattern.

The third one is probably the most malicious, so it is disabled unless a use re 'eval' pragma is in effect or the pattern is compiled with a qr operator.

The \Q modifier will cause perl to treat the contents of the pattern literally until an \E is encountered.

Example Listing 3.4

```
# A re-working of the inline sample above a little
#   more safe.*  A form parameter "SEARCH" is used to
```

```
#    check the GECOS (often "name") field.
# *[Of course, software is only completely "safe" when
#    it's not being used. --cap]

use CGI qw(:form :standard);

print header(-type => 'text/plain');
$pat=param("SEARCH");

push(@ARGV, "/etc/passwd");
while(<>) {
    ($name)=(split(/:/, $_))[4];
    if ($name=~/\Q$pat\E/) {
        print "Yup, ${pat}'s in there somewhere!\n";
    }
}
```

> **See Also**
> Modification characters in this book

Anchors, Grouping, and Backreferences

Grouping

Usage

```
(pattern)
(?:pattern)
(?=pattern)
(?!pattern)
(?<=pattern)
(?<!pattern)
(?#text)
internal modifiers: i, m, s, x
```

Description

Parenthesis in regular expressions are used for grouping subpatterns within the larger pattern. This can be done to provide

- Limited action to quantifiers: `/\bba(na)+na\b/ # "But I don't know when to stop"`
- Limited scope to alternation: `/my favorite stooge is (Moe|Curly|Larry)\./`
- Limited range for modifiers: `/The dog made a ((?i)spot)\./`
- Introduction for assertions: `/Jimmy (?=Buffet|the Greek)/`
- Capturing for backreferences: `/\b([a-z]+)\s+\1\b/`

The ability to capture subpatterns for backreferences is covered in the entry on backreferences. Some of the examples in this section assume prior knowledge of backreferences.

Simple parenthesis (*pattern*) and the (?:*pattern*) form allow you to group a subpattern of a regular expression. Once grouped, quantifiers can be applied against just that portion of the regular expression:

```
m/\w+:              # Match the first field (it's required)
  (?:[^:]*:){3}    # Match (and discard) the next three fields
  ([^:]*)          # Match (and capture) the next field
/x;
```

Also, alternation can be limited so that when an alternation symbol is seen, exactly what's being alternated against can be determined:

```
m/oats|peas|beans$/;  # oats, peas or beans (but beans at the end)
m/(oats|peas|beans)$/;# Any of oats, peas or beans only at the end
```

Internal modifiers can have their scope limited (in fact, internal modifiers can only be specified with parenthesis). So in the following:

```
m/Tony\s(?i:the)\sTiger/;
```

the phrase will be matched only if the capitalization is just as it appears; however the word `the` will not be matched case sensitively. (This could have been accomplished with `[Tt]he` as well.)

The difference between `()` and `(?:)` is that the (?:*pattern*s form of parenthesis doesn't capture the subpattern matched and that (*pattern*) does—it provides grouping without the capturing side effect. This makes a difference if you're using backreferences. See the backreferences entry.

The constructs (?=*pattern*), (?!*pattern*), (?<=*pattern*), and (?<!*pattern*) are all
used to "look around" the current match to see what either precedes or follows it.
They are zero-width assertions, meaning that the subpattern contained within is only
used to look ahead or look behind the current point of the match to see whether
something is true or not.

Pattern	Name
(?=*pattern*)	Positive lookahead. Is only true if *pattern* is seen after the current point of the match. So /Abraham\s(?=Simpson|Lincoln)/ matches only if Abraham is followed by Lincoln or Simpson. The benefit is that the last name is not absorbed by the match. See the later examples.
(?!*pattern*)	Negative lookahead. True only if *pattern* is not seen after the current point of the match. So if /^(?:\d{1,3}\.){3}\d{1,3}$/ matches an IP address (and some bad ones too, such as 999.888.777.666), /^(?!(?:0+\.){3}0+)(?:\d{1,3}\.){3}\d{1,3}$/x matches those same IP addresses, but disallows 0.0.0.0.
(?<=*pattern*)	Positive lookbehind. This asserts that *pattern* was seen before the current point in the match. /(?<=bar)foo/ matches only if foo was directly preceded by bar. There is a restriction on this subpattern: it must be fixed-width, so /(?<=bar.*)foo/ isn't allowed.
(?<!*pattern*)	Negative lookbehind. True only if *pattern* was not seen before the current point in the match. /(?<!bar)foo/ is true only if foo was not directly preceded by bar. Like positive lookbehind, the subpattern must be fixed-width.

The (?#*text*) construct is used to place comments in the body of a regular expression.
For example, if the expression is long and convoluted, you might say:

```
/\D\d{5}(-\d{4})?($# ZIP+4 optional)\D/
```

Because perl needs the) to know when to terminate the comment, you cannot
include a literal) in the comment itself.

A cleaner way to include comments within a regular expression is to use the /x
modifier to the expression.

The internal modifiers are modifiers (such as /i, /s, /x) that are applied to only a portion of the regular expression. They are specified with the non-capturing parenthesis mechanism by inserting the modifier after the ? but before the next token or by using them within parenthesis with a lone ?:

```
(?modifiers:pattern) (?modifiers)
```

To add a modifier to a portion of the expression, use the following modifier value:

```
if (/Linus Torvalds wrote L(?i:inux)/) { }
```

This match is case sensitive except the letter-sequence inux, which can be uppercase, lowercase or a mix. A modifier can be removed by preceding it with a dash:

```
(?modifiers_to_add - modifiers_to_remove:pattern)
```

For example,

```
if (/(?-i:Linus) wrote Linux/i) { }
```

The preceding match is not case sensitive, except the portion matching Linus.

Alternation

Usage

```
pat|pat
```

Description

The | metacharacter is used to make the regular expression engine choose between two potential matches; this is called *alternation*. The | should be placed between potential choices within the pattern:

```
/cat|dogfish/
```

Would match either cat or dogfish. The alternation extends outward from the | to the end of the innermost enclosing parenthesis or to another alternation symbol.

```
/(cat|dog)fish/;      # Either "catfish" or "dogfish"
/(cat|dog|sword)fish/;  # catfish, dogfish or swordfish
```

The alternation extends outward to include any anchors or zero-width assertions that are within the enclosed scope:

```
s/^\s+|\s+$//g;  # Remove leading/trailing whitespace
```

An empty alternative can be specified, which allows you to choose between a few choices or nothing at all:

```
/(cat|dog|sword|)fish/;   # catfish, dogfish or swordfish or just fish
```

Perl's regexp engine will process the alternations left-to-right and select the first one that matches. Thus, if you have an alternation that is the prefix of a following alternation, or an empty alternation, it should be placed at the end:

```
/paper|paperbacks|paperweight/;   # The last two will never match
/(paperbacks|paperweight|paper)/; # Better!
/paper(backs|weight)?/;           # Even better still!

/(|bugle|bugs|bugaboo)/;          # The empty choice will always match
```

Alternation isn't always the best choice for determining whether a list of things will match. Because of the way that Perl's regex engine works, a list of alternations such as the following:

```
/than|that|thaw|them|then|they|thin|this|thud|thug|thus/
```

will run much slower than if the match is re-written as follows:

```
/th(?:an|at|aw|em|en|ey|in|is|ud|ug|us)/
```

The regex engine can't scan through the alternations and notice the obvious: the program is trying to match four-letter words that begin with th—it's not that smart (yet). By giving it a hint, that a literal th will need to match before the alternations need to be searched, the speedup time is tremendous. In this case, it is nearly 25 times faster for a large volume of text.

So avoid alternation for simple cases similar to:

```
m/\b\w(a|e|i|o|u)\w\b/;   # 3 letter words, vowel in the middle
```

when a character class ([aeiou]) or another construct would work better.

See Also
character classes in this book

Capturing and Backreferences

Usage

```
()
\1  \2  \3  \n
$1  $2  $3  $n
```

Description

The parenthesis in regular expressions, in addition to grouping and other functions mentioned in the grouping entry, also have a side effect—patterns matched within parenthesis are stored, and can be used later in the expression or later in the program outside of the expression. This storage of matched patterns is called *capturing*, and referring to the captured values are *backreferences*.

Each set of capturing parenthesis encountered takes the portion of the target string matched by the pattern and stores it in a register. The registers are numbered 1, 2, 3, and so on up to the number of parenthesis in the entire pattern match.

During the match, any captured values are available by referring to the proper register with \register. This allows you to refer to something previously matched later in the pattern:

```
/(\w+)\s\1/;   # Look for repeated words, separated by a space.
```

In the preceding example, (\w+) captures word characters into the first capture register, and \1 looks for whatever word was stored there after the whitespace character.

After the match has completed (or during the substitution-phase with the s/// operator), the captured value will appear in the variables named $1, $2, $3, and so on up to the number of parenthesis captured in the match.

```
if ( s/(\w+)\s\1/$1/ ) {  # Remove repeated words, separated by a space.
   print "Removed duplicate word $1\n";
}
```

In this example, the backreference \1 is used to find the repeated word as shown previously. During the substitution, $1 is used to put back just one instance of the repeated word. After the match, $1 is still set to the captured value during the match.

Some notes about the variables $1, $2, and so on are as follows:

- They're dynamically scoped. So, given the following code:

```
$_="She loves you yeah yeah yeah";
{
    if ( s/(\w+)\s\1/$1/ ) {
        $match=1;
    }
}
print "Removed a $1" if $match;
```

Because the match occurred within a block of its own (the bare block), $1's value isn't valid outside of that block. Treat them as though they had been declared with local.

- They're only set if the match succeeds. If the match fails, the values in them are indeterminate. A very common programming mistake is to assume that the match succeeded and then proceed using $1 and company without whatever values they happen to have:

```
@addr=(q{From: Bill Murray <bmurray@ttsd.k12.or.us>},
       q{From: Clinton Pierce <clintp@geeksalad.org>},
       q{From: Chris Doyle him@bootlegtoys.com},
       q{From: Shelley.Robertson@samspublishing.com},);
for(@addr) {
    m/From: (\w+ \w+) <?([\w@.])+>?/;
    print "You got mail from $1\n";
}
```

In this example, because the last bit of data isn't as well-formed as the others, the match actually fails, but the program goes blindly on using $1.

- You cannot use $1, $2, $3, and so on in the left-hand portion of the substitution operator. Notice this attempt:

```
s/(\w+)\s$1/$1/;   # WRONG
```

The $1 is scanned as a regular variable name when the regular expression is first parsed. It will have the old value of $1 (if any) from a previous match.

- Multiple sets of parenthesis will cause the capture registers to be used in the order encountered. If the parenthesis nest, each opening (assigns the next register.

```
$name="James T. Kirk";
if ($name=~m/^((\w+)\s(\w+.?)?\s(\w+))$/) {
    print "First: $2\n";  # First name
    print "Middle: $3\n"; # Middle name/initial
    print "Last: $4\n";   # Last name
    print "Whole: $1\n"   # Whole name

}
```

Example Listing 3.5

```
# Read a file in the format
#       key=value
#       key2=value2
#   and assign the data to %conf appropriately
# ** This is done with a clever code trick in the
#    match operator entry.  See TIMTOWDI in action!

open(CONFIG, "config") || die "Can't open config: $!";
while(<CONFIG>) {
   if (m/^([^=]+)=(.*)$/) {  # Look for FOO=BAR
       $conf{$1}=$2;
   }
}
```

> **See Also**
> local, dynamic scope, match operator, Regular Expression Special Variables, and Character
> shorthand in this book

Line Anchors

Usage

\A ^ \z \Z $

Description

Anchors are used within regular expression patterns to describe a location. Sometimes
the location is relative to something else (\b) or the location can be absolute (\A).
Because they don't match an actual character but make an assertion about the state of
the match, they also are called *zero-width* assertions.

Anchors, Grouping, and Backreferences

The first anchor (appropriately) is ^, which causes the match to happen at the beginning of the string. So,

```
if (m/^whales/) { }
```

will only be true if whales occurs at the beginning of $_. If whales occurs anywhere else in $_, the match won't succeed.

Next is the $ metacharacter that only matches at the end of a string:

```
if (m/Stimpy$/) { }
```

This pattern will only match if Stimpy occurs at the end of the string. These two metacharacters can be combined for interesting effects:

```
if (/^$/) {  }    # Matches empty lines
# Here, the middle "doesn't matter", but the beginning and
#    endings that must match are well-defined.
if (/^In the beginning.*Amen$/) {}
if (m/^/) { }     # Will always match
```

When you think you understand $ and ^, read on.

The first few anchors describe the beginning and ending of a string. These are complicated by the fact that "end of a string" can often mean "end of a logical line" or "end of the storage unit," depending on who you ask. The /m modifier on a regular expression match (or substitution) can change which meaning you want. The same goes for "beginning of a string."

From now on in this entry, I'll refer to a logical line and a string. A *string* is the entire storage unit. A *logical line* begins at the beginning of the string and extends to a newline character. It also begins after a newline character and extends to the next newline character in the (or the end of a) string. Take, for example, the string of characters in $t the following:

```
$t=q{That whim on the way
And again I took the day off
To roam the river's edge};
```

The string contains two newline characters: one following the word way and one following off. Three logical lines are in the one string.

The ^ metacharacter will match at the beginning of the string, unless /m is used as a modifier on the match. In that case, ^ can match at the beginning of any logical line in the string.

The $ metacharacter will match at the end of the string, unless /m is used as a modifier on the match. If that is the case, $ can match at the end of any logical line in the string.

So observe the following matches against $t from the preceding:

```
if ($t=~/way$/) { }  # False!  Without /m way isn't at the EOL
if ($t=~/way$/m) { } # True!  With /m way is at the End Of Line
if ($t=~/^That/) { } # Always true!
 if ($t=~/^And/) { }  # False!  Without /m, And isn't at the beginning
if ($t=~/^And/m) { } # True!  With /m, And is at the beginning of line

while($t=~/(\w+)$/g) {  # Prints only "edge", because
   print "$1";    #  without /m, there is only one "end of line"
}

while($t=~/(\w+)$/gm) { # Prints way, off and edge
   print "$1";      #   because each represents an "end of line"
}                   #    with /m
```

The \A metacharacter matches the beginning of the string always, and without regard to the /m modifier being used on the match. So in the sample string $t, the expression $t=~/\A\w+/m will only match the word That. The \z metacharacter similarly will always match at the end of the string, regardless of whether /m is in effect.

The \Z metacharacter is similar to \z with a bit of a difference: \z anchors at the end of the string behind (to the right of) the newline character if any. The \Z metacharacter anchors at the end of the string just in front of the newline character, if there is one, and at the end of the string if there isn't.

> **See Also**
> multi match and word anchors in this book

Word Anchors

Usage

```
\b \B
```

Description

The word anchors \b and \B are zero-width assertions that deal with the boundary between nonword characters (\W) and word characters (\w). The beginning and ending of a string are considered nonword characters.

The \b character matches the boundary between \w and \W characters. So, \bFOO matches FOO but only if the character preceding FOO is not a \w. The \B character matches between \W and \W characters; thus \BFOO will find FOO, but only if it's preceded by a word character.

```
$t=q{There was a young lady from Hyde
Who ate a green apple and died.
While her lover lamented
The apple fermented
And made cider inside her inside.};

$t=~m/\bher\b/;    # Matches "her" but not "There"
$t=~m/\Bher\B/;    # Matches the "her" in "There"
$t=~m/\bide\b/;    # Matches nothing!  Not cider nor inside
$t=~m/\bThere/;       # Matches There, because ^ is a word-boundary
```

Within a character class, \b stands for backspace and not a word boundary.

A common mistake is to assume that \b matches what people consider to be word boundaries (because _ is a word character). So, clintp@geeksalad.org is three words, U.S.A is also three, but War_And_Peace is only one word.

> **See Also**
> line anchors in this book

Multimatch Anchor

Usage

\G

Description

Similar to the line anchors, the *multimatch* anchor is used to match positions within a string as opposed to actually matching characters. It is in that class of metacharacters called zero-width assertions.

The \G metacharacter matches the position right after the previous regular expression match. For example, given the following code:

```
$_="One fish, two fish, red fish, blue fish";
m/\b\w{3}\b/g;   # Matches "One"
m/\G\W+(\w+)/;   # $1 is fish
m/\b\w{3}\b/g;   # Picks up "two"
m/\G\W+(\w+)/;   # $1 is fish (number two)
```

\G is useful for incrementally bumping along within a string with regular expressions. The location marked by \G can be reset by calling the pos function with an argument:

```
pos($_)=0;       # Reset \G to the beginning
```

The advantage of \G to look-ahead or look-behind assertions is that you get to write smaller (and simpler!) regular expressions. The /g modifier will cause the match to go back to the position where the last /g left off. The \G assertion allows you to look ahead without destroying your last position.

Example Listing 3.6

```
# Take apart the given paragraph looking for
#   phrases joined with the conjunctions "nor" and "or".
# Note that "now or later" and "later Or no" are both
#   picked up.  With a single regular expression and no \G
#   this would be much more complicated.

# C.J. lyrics and music by Bob Dorough (c)1973
$t=q{Conjunction Junction, what's your function?
Hookin' up two cars to one when you say
Something like this choice: Either now or later,
Or no choice.  Neither now nor ever.  (Hey that's clever)
Eat this or that, grow thin or fat.};

# The expression here picks up a word at a time, remembering
#   where we left off with /g
while( $t=~m/(\w+)/g ) {
    $left=$1;

    # Matching with \G here doesn't ruin our position in
    #   the match above...because we didn't use /g.
    if ($t=~/\G\W+(n?or)\W+(\w+)/i) {
        print "$left $1 $2\n";
    }
}
```

> **See Also**
> line anchors in this book

Match Modifiers

Usage

```
m//cgimosx
qr//imosx
s///egimosx
```

Description

This section describes the modifiers used with regular expression matches, substitutions, and compilations. Some modifiers are particular to an operator:

Modifier	Particular To
/g	Match and Substitution Operators
/gc	Match Operators
/e	Substitution Operators

These modifiers are discussed along with the particular operators to which they apply elsewhere in this book.

The /i operator causes the regular expression to not match case sensitively. During the match, no distinction is made between upper and lowercase letters, including those within character classes:

```
m/Scrabble/i;    # Matches scrabble or scrabble or sCrAbBlE or...
```

The `locale` pragma causes a wider range of alphabetic characters to be recognized, and sensitivity of upper- and lowercase characters will expand appropriately.

The /m modifier causes the meaning of the ^ and $ anchors to change. With the /m modifier, ^ and s will match at the beginning and end of logical lines (possibly multiple logical lines) within a target string. Some examples of this are in the "Anchors" section.

The /s modifier causes the nature of the . (dot) metacharacter to change. Normally, dot matches any single character except a newline character (\n). With /s in place, the newline is a potential match for .:

```
$text=q{You are my sunshine, my only sunshine.
    You make me happy, when skies are grey.};
m/You.*/;  # Matches from "You are" to "sunshine."
m/You.*/s; # Matches from "You are" to "grey."
```

The /o modifier causes perl to only compile a regular expression once. Normally, a regular expression containing variables is recompiled each time perl encounters the expression.

```
$pat='\w+\W\w+';
while(<>) {
    if (/$pat/o) {
        $a++;
    }
}
```

In this example, the pattern in $pat is only changed outside of the loop. Perl doesn't realize this, so each pass through the loop, the pattern /$pat/ has to be recompiled by the regex engine. Giving perl the hint with /o that the pattern won't change allows the regex engine to skip the recompilation.

This optimization only makes sense when the pattern contains a value that could potentially change ($pat shown previously). Also, if the /o optimization is used and you do change the variables that make up the pattern, subsequent pattern matches won't reflect those changes.

The /x modifier allows you to specify comments within a regular expression. Specifically, comments are as follows:

- All whitespace in a regular expression becomes insignificant, except within a character class.

- Comments extend from the # character to the end of the line, or the end of the expression.

- Literal #s in the expression must be escaped with a \ or represented as a hex or octal constant.

```
# The FAQ answer to "how to print a number with commas"
$_="1234567890";
1 while             # Repeat ad nauseam...
    s/^            #     start at the beginning, and
        (-?\d+) #     absorb all of the digits (maybe a -)
        (\d{3}) #     except for the last three.
    /$1,$2/x;      #     Put a comma before those three
```

> **See Also**
> match operator and substitution operator in this book

Miscellaneous Regular Expression Operators

Binding Operators

Usage

```
expression =~ op
expression !~ op
```

Description

The binding operators bind an expression to a pattern match or translation operator. Normally the m//, s///, and tr/// operators work on the variable $_. If you need to work on a variable other than $_, use the binding operator from before as follows:

```
$line=~s/^\s*//;
```

This causes the substitution operator to work on $line instead of $_. The return value for the operator on the right is returned by the bind operator.

The !~ operator works exactly the same as the =~ operator except that the return value is logically inverted. So, $f !~ /pat/ is the same as saying not $f =~ /path/.

Because =~ has a higher precedence than assignment, this allows you to do curious (and useful) things with the return value from =~. To return a list from a pattern match on $_, you would normally capture that as follows:

```
($first, $second)=m/(\w+)\W+(\w+)/;
```

With the bind operator, it's no different except that you can name your variable:

```
($first, $second)=$sentence=~m/(\w+)\W+(\w+)/;
```

Coupling this with the fact that the assignment operator yields an assignable value, you can assign, bind, and alter a variable at the same time:

```
# Okay, here's an assignment, bind and change.
$orig="Won't see this trick in Teach Yourself Perl!";
($lower=$orig)=~s/!$/ in 24 hours!/;
```

```
# $lower is now "Won't see this [...] Yourself Perl in 24 Hours!"

# Watch this:
$changes=($upper=$lower)=~s/(\w\w+)/ucfirst $1/ge;
```

That last statement is kind of difficult and bears some explanation. The highest precedence operator in this expression is =~, but in order for the bind to happen, the ($upper=$lower) must be taken care of. So, $lower's value is assigned to $upper. The bind then takes $upper and performs the substitution. The substitution operator returns the number of substitutions made. This value passes back through the bind and is assigned to $changes. So $changes is 11 and $upper is "Won't See This Trick...".

A special note, if the thing to the right of the bind operator is an expression instead of a pattern match, substitution, or translation operator, a pattern match is performed using the expression.

```
$pattern="Buick";
if ($shorts =~ $pattern) {
    print "There's a Buick in your shorts\n";
}
```

Using the bind operator as an implicit pattern match is slower than explicitly calling m// because perl must re-compile the pattern for each pass through the expression.

> **See Also**
> substitution operator, pattern match operator, and translation operator in this book

??

Usage

`?pattern?modifiers`

Description

The ?? operator works the same as the m// operator, with one small difference. The operator only attempts to match the pattern until it is successful and thereafter the operator no longer tries to match the pattern.

Each instance of the ?? operator maintains its own state. Once latched, the ?? can be reset by using the reset function. This resets all the ?? operators in the current package.

Example Listing 3.7

```
# Prints a summary of a given mailbox file.
# Unix mailbox format is extremely common and uses a paragraph
#   beginning with "From " to describe the start of a message header.
#   The body of the message follows in subsequent paragraphs.

use strict;
use warnings;
my($from, $subject, $to)=("","","");
open(MBOX, "mbox") || die;
$/="";            # Paragraph mode.
while(<MBOX>) {
    $from=$1     if (?^From: (.*)?m);
    $to=$1       if (?^To: (.*)?m);
    $subject=$1  if (?^Subject: (.*)?m);
} continue {
    if (/^From/ or eof MBOX) {
        print "From: $from\nTo: $to\nSubject: $subject\n\n"
            if $from;
        # The 0-argument reset function resets all of the ??
        #   latches above for use in the next message.
        reset;
        $from=$subject=$to="";
    }
}
```

> **See Also**
> reset, match operator, and match modifiers in this book

pos

Usage

```
pos
pos target string
```

Description

The pos function returns the position in the target string where the last m//g left off. If no target string is specified, the target string $_ is used. The position returned is the one after the last match, so

```
$t="I am the very model of a modern major general with mojo";
$t=~m/mo\w+/g;
print pos($t);
```

prints 19, which is the offset of the substring " of a modern...".

The pos function also can be assigned; doing so causes the position of the next match to begin at that point:

```
$t="I am the very model of a modern major general with mojo";
$t=~m/mo\w+/g;      # Now we're at 19, just as before.
pos($t)=38;        # Skip forward to the word "general"
$t=~m/(mo\w+)/g;# Grab the next "mo" word...
print $1;     # It's "mojo"!
```

Example Listing 3.8

```
# Sample from a text-processing system, where tags of the form
#   <#command> are substituted for variables, and other files can
#   be included, and so on.
# pos() is used to return to the original matchpoint to re-insert
#   the new and improved text.

use strict;

# Just some sample data to play with.
our $r="Hello, world";
my $data='bar<#var r/>Foo<#include "/etc/passwd"/>';

while($data=~/(<#(.*?)\/?>)/sg) {
   my($whole, $inside)=($1,$2);

   if ($inside=~/var\s+(\w+)/) {     # Grab a variable from main::
       no strict 'refs';
       substr($data, pos($data)-length($whole),
           length($whole))=${'main::' . $1}
     }
   if ($inside=~/include\s+"(.*)"\s*/) { # Include another file..
       open(NEWFH, $1) ||
```

```
            die "Cannot open included file: $1";
        {
            local $/;
            my $t=<NEWFH>;
            $t=eval "qq\\$t\\";
            die "Inlcuded file $1 had eval error: $@"
                if $@;
            substr($data, pos($data)-length($whole),
                length($whole))=$t;
        }
    }
    # ...and many more
}
print $data;  # Gives "barHello, worldFoo[contents of /etc/passwd]"
```

> **See Also**
> match operator in this book

Translation Operator

Usage

```
tr/searchlist/replacement/modifiers
y/searchlist/replacement/modifiers
```

Description

The tr/// operator is the translation (or transliteration) operator. Each character in searchlist is examined and replaced with the corresponding character from replacement. The tr/// operator returns the number of characters replaced or deleted. Similar to the match and substitution operators, the translation operator will use the $_ variable unless another variable is bound to it with =~:

```
tr/aeiou/AEIOU/;     # Change $_ vowels to uppercase
$t=~tr/AEIOU/aeiou/; # Change $t vowels to lowercase
```

The y/// operator is simply a synonym for the tr/// operator, and they are alike in every other respect.

The `tr///` operator doesn't use regular expressions. The searchlist can be expressed as the following:

- A sequence of characters, as in `tr/aeiou/AEIOU/`

- A range of characters, similar to those used in character classes:

```
tr/a-zA-Z/n-za-mN-ZA-M/;   # ROT-13 encoding
```

Special characters are allowed, such as backslash escape sequences (covered in the "Character Shorthand" section). Special characters that represent classes (`\w\d\s`) aren't allowed. (`tr///` doesn't use regular expressions!)

No variable interpolation occurs within the `tr///` operator. If a character is repeated more than once in the searchlist, only the first instance counts.

The replacement list specifies the character into which searchlist will be translated. If the replacement list is shorter than the searchlist, the last character in the replacement list is repeated. If the replacement list is empty, the searchlist is used as the replacement list (that is, the characters aren't changed, merely counted). If the replacement list is too long, the extra characters are ignored.

The modifiers are as follows:

Modifier	Meaning
/c	Compliments the search list. In other words, similar to using a ^ in a character class; all the characters not represented in the searchlist will be used. `$consonants=$word=~tr/aeiouAEIOU//c;   # Count consonants`
/d	Deletes characters that are found, but doesn't appear in the replacement list. This bends the aforementioned rules about empty or too-short replacement lists. `$text=~tr/.!?;://d;   # Remove punctuation`

/s	Takes repeated strings of characters and squashes them into a single instance of the character. For example,
	
	`$a="Pardon me, boy.  Is that the Chattanooga Choo-Choo?"`
	
	`$a=~tr/a-z A-Z//s;   # Pardon me, boy. Is that the`
	`Chatanoga Cho-Cho?`

> **See Also**
> character shorthand and character classes in this book

`study`

Usage

```
study
study expression
```

Description

The `study` function is a potential optimization for `perl`'s regular expression engine. It prepares an expression (or `$_` if none is specified) for pattern matching with `m//` or `s///`. It does this by prescanning the expression and building a list of uncommon characters seen in the expression, so that the match operators jump right to them as anchors.

Calling the `study` function for a second expression undoes any optimizations by the previously studied expression.

Whether `study` will save any time on your regular expression matches depends on several factors:

- The `study` process itself takes time.

- The kinds of data that makes up the expression being studied.

- Whether your search expression uses many constant strings (`study` might help) or few constant strings (`study` might not help).

As always, with any optimization, use the `Benchmark` module and determine whether there really is a cost savings to using `study`. Constructing a case in which `study` is actually useful is difficult. Do not use it indiscriminately.

> **See Also**
> `qr` in this book

Quote Regular Expression Operator

Usage

```
qr/pattern/
```

Description

The qr operator takes a regular expression and precompiles it for later matching. The compiled expression then can be used as a part of other regular expressions. For example,

```
$r=qr/\d{3}-\d{2}-\d{4} $name/i;
if (/$r/) {
    # Matched digits-digits-digits and whatever was in $name...
}
```

Similar to the match operator, the delimiters can be changed to any character other than whitespace. Also, using single quotes as delimiters prevents interpolation.

Example Listing 3.9

```
# A short demo of the qr// operator.  The fast subroutine
#   runs nearly 4 times faster than the slow subroutine
#   because the qr// operator pre-compiles all of the regular
#   expressions for &fast.
# Remember, if you're not sure something is faster: Benchmark it.

use Benchmark;
sub slow {
    seek(BIG, 0, 0);
    @pats=qw(the a an);
    while(<BIG>) {
        for (@pats) {
            if (/\b$_\b/i) {
                $count{$_}++;
            }
        }
    }
}
sub fast {
    seek(BIG, 0, 0);
    # Pre-compile all of the patterns with
     #   qr//
```

Miscellaneous Regular Expression Operators

```
    @pats=map { qr/\b$_\b/i } qw(the a an);
    while(<BIG>) {
        for (@pats) {
            if (/$_/) {
                $count{$_}++;
            }
        }
    }
}

open(BIG, "bigfile.txt") || die;
timethese(10, {
    slow => \&slow,
    fast => \&fast, });
```

See Also
match modifiers in this book

CHAPTER 4

Special Variables and Command-Line Options

Perl Command-Line Arguments

$ARGV

Usage

@ARGV
$ARGV

Description

The variables @ARGV and $ARGV are related to argument passing from the operating system to the perl script.

The array @ARGV contains the arguments passed in from the OS that weren't originally intended for the perl interpreter itself. So,

```
perl -w myscript.pl file1 file2 file2
```

would put file1, file2, and file3 into the array @ARGV. This differs from the argv pointer in C because the executable program name isn't the first element in @ARGV. To get that name, see $0. The number of arguments passed will be in $#ARGV.

The variable $ARGV contains the argument that's currently being processed by the <> operator on the ARGV filehandle. See the <>, ARGV, and -n/-p entries for more details on <> processing.

Example Listing 4.1

```
# Does a line-count for the files given as
#    arguments.  Prints the number of lines
#    and the file that's being processed.

exit unless @ARGV;
print "Processing ", 0+@ARGV ," files.\n";
while(<>) {
    # See the eof() entry to see how eof
    #     works with <>
    if (eof) {
        print "$. $ARGV\n";
        $.=0;
    }
}
```

> **See Also**
> ARGV, -n, -p, and $0 in this book

-a, -F

Usage

```
perl -na
perl -pa
perl -Fpattern -na
perl -Fpattern -pa
```

Description

The -a switch to perl causes the interpreter to split each line as it's read into the array @F. This is done only if the -n or -p switch also is specified. The split that's done is on whitespace so that the command

```
perl -ane "print qq{$F[4]\n};"
```

actually translates into something such as the following:

```
LINE: while(<>) {
    @F=split(/\s+/);
    print "$F[4]\n";
}
```

To change the `split` delimiter, use the `-F` switch followed immediately by the new pattern to split on. The pattern can be encased in slashes (`//`) or quotation marks (`""`). You should be wary of complex patterns and escape and quote them appropriately for your command interpreter.

This switch finds its roots back in the Unix `awk` utility, where each line would be split into an array-like structure automagically as it was read.

Example Listing 4.2

```
# Print a dump of visitors to the website
#     assumes a standard NCSA-format log file

perl -MData::Dumper -ane '/GET/ && $h{$F[0]}++;END{print Dumper \%h}'
 /var/log/httpd/access_log
```

> **See Also**
> `split`, `-n`, `-p`, and `-F` in this book

-c

Usage

```
perl -c
```

Description

The `-c` switch to `perl` causes `perl` to compile your program, but not actually run it. This is useful for checking syntax before you actually run code. As a side effect of compilation, the `$^C` variable is set to `1`.

The `-c` switch also causes any `BEGIN` and `CHECK` blocks that are in your script to be run as well as running any `use` directives.

Example Listing 4.3

```
# Syntax check and emit any compile-time warnings

perl -wc /tmp/foo.pl
```

> **See Also**
> BEGIN and CHECK in this book

-e

Usage

```
perl -e code
```

Description

The -e switch to perl causes perl to execute the code specified. The code following the -e is built up as part of a perl program, and can contain as many statements as you wish (given the line-length limits of your command interpreter).

Multiple -e switches can be specified with code for each. They will be concatenated together to form a code block to be run. (Each -e is at the same scope as the others.) Remember that perl requires a semicolon to separate statements, even those assembled with -e. The first -e switch is considered the first line, the second is the second line, and so on. If a code block has embedded newlines in it, they increase the line count accordingly.

The -e switch also alters perl's argument processing somewhat. If the -e switch (or multiple -es) is specified, the first nonswitch argument to perl is no longer treated as the name of the script to be run—it's a normal file for @ARGV processing.

Example Listing 4.3

```
# Reverse file(s) by paragraphs
perl -00 -e 'print reverse <>' /tmp/sample.txt
```

Example Listing 4.4

```
# Check to see if a module "FOO" is installed
perl -MFOO -e 1
```

-i

Usage

```
perl -i
perl -iextension
```

Description

The -i switch to perl allows perl to modify files "in place" while processing them with the <> operator.

The "in place" editing is done by renaming the input file, opening it, opening the output file with the original name, and then selecting the output filehandle (ARGVOUT) as the default filehandle. When the processing is done, the input file is removed.

If the extension is specified, the input file is renamed to its original name with the extension appended before processing begins. When processing has finished, the input file is left behind, thus creating a backup copy. If the extension contains a * character, the filename is substituted for the * character, which is used as the new filename during the renaming.

If no files are specified to perl for <> processing, the -i switch has no effect.

Example Listing 4.5

```
#!perl -piorig_*

# Insert html boilerplate on the first line
#    Run using filenames to change as arguments
# (This is a standalone script: it could be a 1-liner but a very
# long one.  The #! must be the first line in the script.)

print qq{<!DOCTYPE HTML PUBLIC "-//W3C//DTD HTML 4.01 Transitional//EN"
            "http://www.w3.org/TR/html4/loose.dtd">
} if $. == 1;
close ARGV if eof;
```

Example Listing 4.6

```
# Simply substitute lollipop for bubblegum in all files named .txt

perl -pi.bak -e 's/bubblegum/lollipop/g' /tmp/*.txt
```

Example Listing 4.7

```
# Slightly verbose 1-liner to highlight spelling mistakes in
#    a text file with **'s.  Uses the unix spell(1) utility.

perl -pi.badspell -e 'BEGIN {chomp(@_=`spell @ARGV`); $re=join("|", @_);
 $re=qr{($re)} }' \
    -e 's/$re/**$1**/g;' /tmp/sample.txt
```

-l

Usage

```
perl -l
perl -ldigits
```

Description

The -l switch to perl has two purposes. The first is that it automatically removes the record separator character from each line when used with -n or -p (as if a chomp had been done). The second is that it also sets the output record separator ($\) to the ascii value of *digits*. If *digits* is omitted, the current value of $/ is used instead. The *digits* parameter is expected to be in octal.

This switch is meant to make processing with <> easier by eliminating the need to chomp each record and then print them again with a \n character.

If you need to change the output record separator ($\) but not the input record separator ($/), the command-line switches are processed in order for you to specify -l before -0 (as documented in the -0 switch).

Example Listing 4.8

```
# Reverse the fields on each line.  Without -l, chomp and
#    \n would have been needed.

perl -lane 'print join(" ", reverse @F)' /tmp/sample.txt
```

> **See Also**
> $/, -a, and $\ in this book

-M

Usage

```
perl -Mmodule
perl -Mmodule=args
perl -mmodule
```

Description

The -M (-m) switch to perl is used to load a module on the command line, similar to the use directive in the body of the script.

Depending on how you specify the module name, the module will change the behavior of how it's used. A leading - in front of the module name causes a no instead of a use. If the module name is followed by a =, the = can be followed by a comma-separated list of symbols to import. The module name otherwise is passed to perl literally for parsing, and can contain your own import directives.

The -m switch implies that no default imports should take effect. However, following -mModule with a = negates that effect.

Example	Equivalent Use Directive
perl -MModule	use Module;
perl -M-Module	no Module;
perl -mModule	use Module ();
perl -M'Module qw(:all)'	use Module qw(:all);
perl -MModule=a,b	use Module qw(a b);

The -M and -m switches cannot be used in the #! line of a perl program; they're only effective when perl is run from the command prompt.

Example Listing 4.9

```
# See if Foomod is installed

perl -MFoomod -e 1
```

Example Listing 4.10

```
# Fetch and display a web page
perl -MLWP::Simple -e "getprint(q{http://www.amazon.com});"
```

Example Listing 4.11

```
# Show perl opcode tree for code.pl

perl -MO=Terse /tmp/code.pl
```

> **See Also**
> modules in this book

-n, -p

Usage

```
perl -n
perl -p
```

Description

The -n switch wraps the following code around your script:

```
LINE:
while(<>) {
    # Your script here
}
```

and the -p switch wraps the following code around your script:

```
LINE:
while(<>) {
    # Your script here
} continue {
    print or die "-p destination: $!\n";
}
```

Quite literally, these blocks of code are wrapped around your script before compilation. What is the major difference between the two? The -p switch prints the value of $_ as each line is processed, and -n doesn't.

These two switches are particularly useful in constructing one-liners that act as file filters. For example, change FOO to BAR in a file:

```
perl -pe 's/FOO/BAR/' textfile.txt
```

This would be translated into the following:

```
LINE:
while(<>) {
    s/FOO/BAR/;
} continue {
    print or die "-p destination: $!\n";
}
```

The normal semantics of <> will cause each file on the command line to be opened and then processed by the `while` loop. The value of `$_` is printed automatically in the `continue` block at the bottom of the loop.

If an error occurs while opening a file, a warning is printed, the file is skipped, and `perl` moves on to the next argument to be processed.

The label `LINE` can be addressed within your script (with `goto`, `next`, `last`, `redo`) as it would for any other script.

Example Listing 4.12

```
find /tmp/trashcan -type f | perl -nle "unlink or warn qq{$!}"
```

See Also
`while` in this book

`-s`

Usage

```
perl -s
```

Description

The `-s` switch allows your programs to process command-line switches in a simple way. If your script was invoked using the interpreter name, Perl's switches are processed, and then filenames. Any remaining switches are considered switches to your program (but not the interpreter).

A variable will be created for each switch, with that switch as the name of the variable. For example, the switch `-name` would create a variable called `$name` and set it to a true value. If the switch is written as `-name=value`, the switch will be set to *value* (instead of true). The variables created are global variables and if `use strict` is in effect, they

will cause an exception, and they cannot be declared as lexical. You must use vars
qw($name), declare them with our, or use the full package name such as $main::name.

Unlike Perl's switches, you cannot combine switches that are intended for -s
processing. For example, -name and -display cannot be combined into -namedisplay.

The Getopt::Std and Getopts::Long modules (both standard) are the preferred way to
process command-line switches.

Example Listing 4.13

```
#  Creates $display within myscript.pl
#        and sets it to true
#  @ARGV contains file1, file2 and file3
#
perl -s myscript.pl -display file1 file2 file3
```

Example Listing 4.14

```
# Does not create $display
#   @ARGV contains -display and file1-3
perl -s myscript.pl -- -display file1 file2 file3
```

Example Listing 4.15

```
#  Creates $display within myscript.pl
#    and sets it to "HLAG".  $speed is
#    set to "max"
#  @ARGV contains file1, file2 and file3
#
perl -s myscript.pl -display=HLAG -speed=max file1 file2 file3
```

> **See Also**
> Getopt::Long and Getopt::Std module documentation

-u

Usage

```
perl -u
```

Description

The -u switch to perl causes perl to compile your script and then immediately dump core. Under Unix, a core file is produced, and under Windows, the program simply dies with an "abnormal program termination" error.

This (and the dump function) was originally intended to allow you to produce an executable program by taking the resulting memory core file and running it through an "undump" program to produce an executable. In theory, a native executable perl program would be faster because each invocation no longer requires the time to parse the script to produce the op tree.

The undump program is not currently distributed.

This mechanism has been replaced by the B module's capability to generate C code from Perl code and then compile the C into a standard executable. The C backend is an experimental feature.

See Also

B::C module documentation

dump in this book

-D

Usage

```
perl -Dflags
```

Description

The -D switch allows you to access perl's debugging information. This is probably more useful for inspecting the workings of perl's internals than in debugging your programs (see the debugger for that). If you're considering tinkering around in Perl's internals or writing XS programs, this is a good technique to learn.

The *flags* specified are one or more alpha or numeric flags from the following table. You can specify either kind of flag: alpha or numeric (but not a mix).

Numeric	Alpha	Meaning
1	p	Show perl parsing your program.
2	s	Take stack snapshots (most useful with the next entry).

Numeric	Alpha	Meaning
4	l	Context and label stack processing.
8	t	Trace execution through the call tree.
16	o	Show method and overloading resolution steps.
32	c	Show the automatic string and numeric conversions.
64	P	Show preprocessor commands.
128	m	Show when memory is allocated and deallocated.
256	f	Format processing.
512	r	Regular expression parsing, both compilation and execution.
1024	x	Dump the syntax tree after compilation.
2048	u	Show runtime tainting checks.
4096	L	When `perl` is compiled with `-DLEAKTEST`, debug memory leaks.
8192	H	Dump hashes the `values()` function and returns information about the hash structure.
16384	X	Scratchpad allocation (entering, leaving functions, and so on).
32768	D	Cleanup.
65536	S	Thread synchronization.

In order to use this particular option, you must have the `perl` executable compiled for debugging. By default, Perl doesn't come this way in any prebuilt distribution (RedHat, ActiveState), and the default build options don't build Perl this way. There is a runtime penalty for a debugging version of Perl. If you try to use these without a debugging version of Perl, this error is thrown:

```
Recompile perl with -DDEBUGGING to use -D switch
```

The instructions for building Perl are in the INSTALL file in the Perl source distribution.

Example Listing 4.15

```
perl -D14 -e 'sub foo { my $t=$_[0]; print $t; } foo(q{Hello, World});'
```

> **See Also**
> debugger in this book

-I

Usage

```
perl -Ipathname
```

Description

The -I option adds pathnames to the @INC array, which is the search path for modules and header files for the C preprocessor. This is nearly the same thing as the use lib directive during compilation.

The pathname will be added to the beginning of the @INC array. Perl also will search the platform-specific directories *pathname/architecture/*auto and *pathname/architecture* for modules automatically.

Example Listing 4.16

```
# Use an uninstalled module, assumes you're in the
#  same directory as the "Makefile.PL" script and that
#   "make" has already been run.
# Type this as a 1-liner at a command prompt

perl -Iblib/lib -Iblib/arch -MDate::Calc=:all  -e 'print join("/",
Easter_Sunday("2001"))'
```

> **See Also**
> use lib in this book

-P

Usage

```
perl -P
```

Description

The -P switch causes the perl interpreter to present your script to the C preprocessor. This is usually cc -E, cpp or whatever is defined in your perl configuration under $Config{cpp} (see the Config module).

The commands accepted by the C preprocessor are dependant on the C compiler installed on your system, of course. If you're using this switch, you should be aware of two things. First, that a # followed by if, else, define, and so on might be interpreted as C preprocessor directives and not comments.

Second, by doing this, your perl script needs to be run on a system with a C preprocessor installed. Moving the script to a system without a C development environment might cause the script to no longer compile. Thus, -P is a portability hazard.

Example Listing 4.17

```
#!/usr/bin/perl -P

#define INDIANA

#ifdef INDIANA
#define PI 3.2
#else
#define PI 3.14159
#endif

print 5*PI;
```

> **See Also**
> Config module documentation

-S

Usage

```
perl -S
```

Description

The -S switch to perl causes the perl interpreter to search the PATH environment variable to find the script to execute. For example, when executing from the following command line:

```
perl -S foo.pl
```

the directories in PATH will be searched for foo.pl. If the machine is a Windows/DOS system, .bat and .cmd will be appended to the scriptname and those variants will be searched for in PATH as well.

This switch is most often used on systems to emulate #! behavior, which works on most systems anyway.

Example Listing 4.18

```
# For Unix, but works similarly elsewhere

PATH=/bin:/usr/bin:/usr/local/bin:.:/home/clintp/bin

# The following paths will be searched for test.pl
#    in this order:
#    /bin/test.pl
#    /usr/bin/test.pl
#    /usr/local/bin/test.pl
#    ./test.pl
#    /home/clintp/bin/test.pl
#    ./test.pl

perl -S test.pl
```

> **See Also**
> Findbin module documentation

-T

Usage

```
perl -T
```

Description

The `-T` switch to `perl` turns on `perl`'s data tainting mechanism. In short, this causes `perl` to distrust any data retrieved from outside sources and not allow it to be used in risky situations.

The `-T` switch must be specified on the command line when the interpreter is invoked, or in the `#!` line if the script is invoked directly by name. This is because `-T` must be seen before any processing takes place. For example, if the script `foo.pl` contained the line `#!/usr/bin/perl -T`, and it were invoked with

```
perl foo.pl
```

Perl would respond with

```
Too late for "-T" option at foo.pl line 1.
```

The solution is, of course, to invoke it with `perl -T foo.pl` or directly by name with `./foo.pl` (if it's executable).

Every scalar value in Perl (scalar variables, hash elements, array elements) has a taint flag associated with it. Values can become tainted by

- Reading them from a filehandle

- Obtaining them from the filesystem (`readdir`, `readlink`)

- Obtaining them from the operating system (`getpw*`)

- Inheriting them from the environment (`PATH`, `IFS`, and so on)

- Locale modifiers (`use locale`)

- Command-line arguments (`@ARGV`, variables created with the `-s` flag)

Within an aggregate data type (hashes or arrays), taint is associated with individual elements, not the entire variable. So it is possible to have an array with tainted and untainted elements.

Once tainted, a scalar value's "taint" can be spread to other scalar values by using them together in expressions. In this example:

```
$a=$ARGV[0];    # $a is tainted
$b=$a+1;        # $b is now tainted
$c=$b . "Hello";# $c is tainted as well
$r=0;           # $r is not tainted
$r=$c, $r;      # $r is tainted
```

A tainted scalar value cannot be used in any command that modifies files, alters directories, or causes perl to run external code or processes. If any of these is attempted, perl will throw an exception similar to:

```
Insecure dependency while running with -T switch at foo.pl line 10
```

This exception can be caught with eval. This is the canonical way to test whether a value is tainted. The following example works because the entire join/kill expression would become tainted if any of the arguments are tainted. The kill function cannot be used in the context of a tainted expression and would throw an exception. If the arguments weren't tainted, kill 0 is a no-op.

```
# Returns true if any of the arguments are tainted.
#    from the perlsec manpage distributed with Perl
sub is_tainted {
        return ! eval {
        join('',@_), kill 0;
        1;
        };
    }
```

The rule stating that a tainted value cannot be used to run external code has an exception: When exec or system is used with a list argument, the values passed aren't checked for taintedness. It's assumed that the programmer knows what he is doing at the time.

When a scalar value is tainted, it cannot be untainted. The only mechanism that can be used to obtain an untainted value from a scalar is to match the tainted scalar with a regular expression with capturing parenthesis, and then use the matched portions of the expression from $1, $2, and so on. For example,

```
print "Relative pathname?";
chomp($path=<STDIN>);
if ( $path=~m!^(\w+[/\w]*)$! ) {
    $safe_path=$1;
} else {
    print "The path specified was not relative or ";
    print "contained invalid characters.";
    exit;
}
```

In the previous example, the regular expression accepts only relative pathnames (those not starting with /) and then a reasonable subset of characters in the rest of the pathname (word characters and slashes). The $1 variable contains the match and is unaffected by the taint from $path.

Some tips on untainting with regular expressions are as follows:

- Use anchors (^, $, or \z) so that nonsense can't be inserted before or after your expression.

- It is far safer to specify what you want than what you don't want.

- Don't blindly untaint data; it is tainted for a reason, so to do things such as the following:

```
($data)=$data=~/(.*)/;     # Bad!  Bad programmer!
```

defeats the whole purpose of using the taint switch.

The requirement that environment variables are considered tainted can cause issues with system, exec, and backticks; namely that because $ENV{PATH} is considered tainted, perl in taint mode won't let you use those commands and will return the error:

```
Insecure $ENV{PATH} while running with -T switch at foo.pl line 6.
```

Other environment variables are involved with execution of shell commands, and might need to be reset to reasonable values before you can use system, exec, or backticks. The current list of environment variables that will be checked for taintedness are PATH, BASH_ENV, CDPATH, and IFS.

Example Listing 4.19

```
#!/usr/bin/perl -T


# Allow users to download only zip/tgz/gz files.
#    target of an HTML form which contains something like:
#    <FORM><INPUT TYPE=TEXT NAME=PATHNAME>
#        <INPUT TYPE=SUBMIT NAME=FETCH></FORM>
# This is a fairly secure program, and runs under -T

use CGI qw(:all);
$path=param('PATHNAME');
```

```
unless ( $path=~m@^(\w+\.(zip|tgz|gz))$@ ) {
    print header;
    print "Path $path is not acceptable";
    exit;
}
unless (open(P, "/home/clintp/tmp/$1")) {
    print header;
    print "Error /home/clintp/tmp/$1: $!";
    exit;
}
print header('application/octet-stream');
binmode P;
binmode STDOUT;
print <P>;
close P;
```

See Also
exec, system, #!, and eval in this book

-U

Usage

```
perl -U
```

Description

The -U switch allows perl to perform unsafe operations. Only two functions are
currently considered unsafe:

- Removing a directory with unlink as root

- Running set-uid programs (Unix) with taint checks emitting only warnings

See Also
-w and -T in this book

-v

Usage

```
perl -v
perl -V
perl -V:parameter
```

Description

The -v and -V switches to perl cause the interpreter to print version information and then exit.

The -v switch prints the current version of the perl executable and a short copyright notice. On my system at the time of writing, this results in

```
This is perl, v5.6.0 built for i686-linux

Copyright 1987-2000, Larry Wall
```

Perl can be copied only under the terms of either the Artistic License or the GNU General Public License, which can be found in the Perl 5.0 source kit.

Complete documentation for Perl, including FAQ lists, should be found on this system using 'man perl' or 'perldoc perl'. If you have access to the Internet, point your browser at http://www.perl.com/, the Perl home page.

The -V switch causes perl to dump out a variety of configuration information. This information is what would be needed by the Perl developers to completely debug any problems with the interpreter. Included in the information is the following:

- The version of perl being run.

- A description of the perl compilation options selected when Perl was built.

- The compiler and compiler options that were in effect when Perl was built.

- The list of libraries perl was linked with.

- Extra compilation options selected (such as DEBUGGING).

- The contents of @INC, the installed path for Perl and its modules.

The -V: switch causes perl to use parameter as a pattern and dump any configuration options that match the pattern. Those options (and their values) are dumped and then perl exits.

Example Listing 4.20

```
perl -V
```

Example Listing 4.21

```
# Dump out options relating to the C Preprocessor

perl -V:cpp.*
```

> **See Also**
> Config module documentation

-w, -W, -X

Usage

```
perl -w
perl -W
perl -X
```

Description

These three switches all have to do with controlling the warnings mechanism of perl. For specific details on warnings and an explanation of lexical warnings versus $^W warnings, see the warnings entry.

The -w switch sets the $^W variable to true, enabling warnings. Lexical warnings are unaffected by the -w switch.

The -W switch enables warnings. If warnings are enabled with this mechanism, they cannot be turned off, regardless of whether the perl script uses the no warnings pragma or sets the $^W to false. This applies to modules and files included with require or do as well.

The -X switch does the opposite of -W; it turns off warnings and they cannot be re-enabled with use warnings or setting $^W to true.

Example Listing 4.22

```
# Check test.pl for compilation errors and compile-time warnings

perl -wc test.pl
```

> **See Also**
> warnings in this book

-x

Usage

```
perl -x
perl -xdirectory
```

Description

The -x switch to perl causes perl to read the script file and discard text until a line is found that:

begins with #!

contains the word perl

This is treated as the first line of the script. The script is then run as though all the data leading to the #! line wasn't there.

This option is particularly useful for running perl scripts that are embedded inside other scripts, or are inside of mail messages or text files.

If the script contains trailing garbage, __END__ or __DATA__ must be used to terminate the script compilation. The DATA filehandle can be used to read the information following the __END__ and __DATA__ tokens, and can even be rewound—with seek—to read the information at the front of the script.

If a directory is specified, the perl interpreter will switch into that directory before beginning to execute the script.

Example Listing 4.23

```
From: heidi@christmas.com
To: jen@aol.com
```

```
Subject: Working example

Here's the working example, save this entire message to a file named
"testprog.txt" and then run it by typing:

perl -x testprog.txt

And that should do it.

#!perl

print "Hello world!\n";
```

> **See Also**
> seek and DATA in this book

-0

Usage

`perl -0digits`

Description

The -0 switch to perl sets the input record separator ($/) to the character specified by the octal value of digits. For example, specifying

`perl -0174`

would mean that the pipe symbol would separate input records.

Some special values for -0 are as follows:

- Specifying -0 uses the null character (ASCII 0) as the input record separator.

- Specifying -00 puts perl into paragraph mode. This is similar to setting $/="" within the body of the code.

- Specifying -0777 causes perl to read the entire file as a single record (slurp). This is used because no character has that octal value.

If you specify an invalid octal digit (for example, 8), perl will attempt to use that as another switch (and will likely give an "Unrecognized switch" error).

Example Listing 4.24

```
# print sample.txt with </p> markers around paragraphs

perl -00pe "print qq{</P>}" /tmp/sample.txt
```

See Also
$/ in this book

Switch-Related Special Variables

Usage

```
$^C
$^D
$^I
$^W
```

Description

These global special variables all relate to command-line options that can be given to Perl. If the English module has been used, they can be addressed by alternate names:

Variable	English Name
$^C	$COMPILING
$^D	$DEBUGGING
$^I	$INPLACE_EDIT
$^W	$WARNING

The $^C flag is set to true if the -c switch was given at the command prompt. It's primarily used by the backend code generators (see -M) to generate code at compile time, which normally would have been deferred until runtime.

The $^D flag is used to determine whether the debugging flags are in effect (and if so, which ones).

The $^I flag is a read-write flag that allows you to determine whether in-place editing is in effect. If not, you can set this flag to true to alter the behavior of the <> operator. See Example Listing 4.25 and the -I switch.

The $^W flag is used to turn warnings on and off, and indicate the state of the -w switch from the perl command line. If true, warnings are enabled. This can be used to turn global warnings on and off, although lexical warnings are unaffected by this variable.

Example Listing 4.25

```
# Take files passed on the command line and strip all
#   of the high bits and remove the unprintables.

# Save a backup copy whether or not they asked for one!
$^I=".bak" unless ($^I);
while(<>) {
    # Strip the 8th bit
    tr [\200-\377] [\000-\177];
    # Now remove "unprintable" things
    tr [\000-\010\016-\037] [ ];
}
```

Example Listing 4.26

```
$_="Watch this!";

$^W=0;
print FOO;  # Does nothing, really.

$^W=1;
print FOO;  # warns: Filehandle main::FOO never opened
```

> **See Also**
> warnings, -w, -i, -D, and -c in this book

Perl Special Variables

%ENV

Usage

$ENV{var}

Description

The hash named %ENV contains a mapping to your system's environment variables. The keys to the hash are the environment variable names, and the values are the associated values of the environment variables. The keys are, of course, case sensitive.

The actual environment variables available to you vary drastically depending on your OS, your command interpreter, and your environment in general. Under Unix a typical (but small) environment might include PATH, SHELL, HOME, LOGNAME, and TERM. Under Windows NT 4, you might see PATH, OS, PROMPT, TEMP, and windir.

Setting environment variables involves assigning to %ENV. Under most operating systems (Unix, Windows, and so on), setting an environment variable only affects the current process and children created with fork, system, backticks, and qx.

Each value in %ENV at the start of your program is considered tainted by default unless the taint flag has been cleared (see -T).

Example Listing 4.27

```
# Run an external Java program and then come back to Perl

# Set CLASSPATH because Java can't find it's classes
#   without a white cane and a dog.
$ENV{CLASSPATH}="/usr/local/java";
$ENV{JDK_HOME}="/usr/local/javadevel";
system("java myapp");
```

> **See Also**
> -T (tainting) in this book
> setenv in the C library reference

@ISA

Usage

```
@ISA=base classes;
```

Description

The @ISA array is used by perl to create a relationship between base classes and subclasses. The name is said "is-a", as in, "a spider is a bug."

Each class that inherits from a base class uses `@ISA` to specify what its base classes are. The `@ISA` array must be a package variable—it cannot be declared with `my`. A typical module with inheritance might start:

```
package Sitcom;
use strict;
our @ISA=qw( Comedy TVShow );
```

During a search for a method, `perl` will search the current package and then begin searching through the `@ISA` arrays of the current package and the `@ISA` arrays of the ancestors. Having multiple base classes in the `@ISA` array is an example of multiple inheritance. The search is left-to-right in the `@ISA` arrays and depth first.

Example Listing 4.28

```
# A series of classes exhibiting multiple inheritance.

use strict;
# Typical toy car
#
package Toy;
sub new { bless {}, shift }
sub cost { "cheap" }

package Model;
our @ISA=qw(Toy);
sub weight { "light" }
sub brand { "Mattel" }
sub decals { 1 }

# Typical real car
#
package Automobile;
sub new { bless {}, shift }
sub cost { "expensive" }
sub weight { "heavy" }
sub wheels { 1 }

package Car;
our @ISA=qw(Automobile);
sub brand { "Ford" }

# Now this inherits from both trees
#
```

```
package ModelCar;
our @ISA=qw(Model Car);


# Now use the classes.
#
package main;
my $hotwheels=new ModelCar;   # new comes from Toy, right most first
print $hotwheels->cost;       # "cheap", still right most first
print $hotwheels->wheels;     # 1 (true), going through left branch (Car)
```

> **See Also**
> methods in this book

@_

Usage

@_

Description

The array @_ is used in two different places in perl. It is predominantly used as the place where arguments are received in subroutines. When arguments are passed to a subroutine, aliases appear in @_ to the original arguments in the caller. See the subroutine section for details.

The @_ also is used as the implicit target for a split (if no assignment is being made). For example,

```
split(/:/, @FOO);
```

would split into @_ because the result of the split wasn't assigned to any variable. This use is discouraged and will throw the warning at compile time: Use of implicit split to @_ is deprecated.

Example Listing 4.29

```
sub mysub {
    print "@_";
}
mysub("Call", "Me", "Ishmael");
```

> **See Also**
> subroutines, aliases and split in this book

Include Array and Hash

Usage

```
@INC
%INC
```

Description

These variables are tied to Perl's mechanisms for finding and including other files into the current running script.

The @INC variable contains a list of directories that will be searched for modules when a use, require, or do file are performed. It is initially set to all the following: Any pathnames indicated with -I command-line switches to perl. Pathnames in the PERL5LIB environment variable. This is a colon-separated list of pathnames. If PERL5LIB isn't found, PERLLIB is searched for and used instead.

Pathnames were baked into the perl interpreter when it was built. These can be permanently changed only by recompiling the interpreter.

A typical list of files in @INC for an Intel/Linux system is as follows:

```
/usr/local/lib/perl5/5.6.0/i686-linux
/usr/local/lib/perl5/5.6.0
/usr/local/lib/perl5/site_perl/5.6.0/i686-linux
/usr/local/lib/perl5/site_perl/5.6.0
/usr/local/lib/perl5/site_perl
.
```

Pathnames added to @INC with PERL5LIB, -I and the use lib directive will have the architecture-dependant subdirectories added as well. So that adding /home/clintp/perl also will add (on an Intel/Linux system) /home/clintp/perl/5.6.0 and /home/clintp/perl/5.6.0/i686-linux if they exist at the time.

Remember that use directives are processed at compile time; thus it's typically a mistake to alter @INC at runtime. If you must include a directory for a use module statement to work, do it with use lib or perform the alteration to @INC in a BEGIN block.

After a module (or file) has been pulled into the current script, it is also added to %INC. The hash %INC is used to keep track of which files have been included into the current perl script so that you (or perl) can determine whether a module is already included so as not to include it again.

The key to the hash is the name of the file you specified to use, do file or require. The values are the full pathname of the file actually read and included.

Example Listing 4.30

```
# Determine the startup cost for including a well-connected
#    module like IO::Socket.

BEGIN { # Store this away before the use below is run
    %OLDINC=%INC;
}
use IO::Socket;

foreach(keys %INC) {
    next if exists $OLDINC{$_};
    $total+=-s $INC{$_};
    printf("%6d %20s\n\t\t%s\n", -s _,
        $_, $INC{$_});
}
printf("%6d total\n", $total);  # Almost 200K bytes!
```

> **See Also**
> use, require, and do in this book

$@

Usage

$@

Description

The variable $@ contains the error message given by the last eval statement. If a syntax error is raised or an exception is thrown with die, the message will be placed in $@.

This can be used to test whether an eval statement was successful. A true value of some sort is guaranteed to be in $@ if there was a runtime exception, or a compilation error. If no error occurred, $@ is guaranteed to be empty.

Only die messages will appear in $@; warnings won't.

Example Listing 4.31

```
$answer=eval {
    $a/$b;    # Trap "divide by zero";
};
if ($@) {
    warn $@;
} else {
    print "Answer: $answer\n";
}
```

> **See Also**
> eval and die in this book

$^T

Usage

$^T

Description

This variable holds the time (in seconds since 1970) that the perl script started. It is the offset that the -M, -A, and -C file tests use to report the file modification times.

Example Listing 4.32

```
# A demonstration of signal catching
#    This is nearly as safe as signal catching gets.
# Hit this program with a HUP signal, and it will
#    tell you how long it's been running and when it started.

$r=0;   # Do not make lexical with my()
$SIG{HUP} = sub {
    $r=1;
};
```

```
while(1) {
    select(undef, undef, undef, 0.5);
    if ($r) {
        print "I have been running since ",
            scalar(localtime($^T)),
            " for an elapsed time of ",
            time-$^T/60, " minues\n";
        $r=0;
    }
}
```

See Also
-T and file tests in this book

$,

Usage

$,

Description

The variable $, is used by the print statement when print is given a list of items. Normally, print displays comma-separated items in print's list together with no separation. So, when the following is done:

```
print "My","Dog","Has","Fleas";
```

it prints

```
MyDogHasFleas
```

By setting $, each item in print's *list* will be separated by the contents of $,.

Example Listing 4.33

```
$,=" ";
# Displays
#     My Dog Has Fleas
# contrast this without $,
print "My","Dog","Has","Fleas";
```

> **See Also**
> print in this book

Deprecated Global Special Variables

Usage

```
$*
$#
$[
```

Description

The variables in this section are all deprecated. This means that their use is discouraged, and that you shouldn't use them in any new code being produced. They remain in the language for backward-compatibility purposes.

The variable $* is a flag variable that causes the regexp engine to assume that m (the capability to match embedded \ns with anchors ^$) is set on pattern matches, unless s is specified.

The variable $# represents the output format for numbers. If set to a printf-like format, all numbers displayed will be in this format; for example,

```
$#="%06.2f";
$pi=22/7;
print $pi;  # Would print 003.14
```

Setting $[to any positive integer causes that integer to be the base for array offsets. Setting it to 1 causes array elements to start numbering from 1 (as in FORTRAN) instead of 0 (as in Perl and C). This also affects the offsets into strings used by index, rindex and substr.

The $[variable is now treated as though it were lexically scoped, and cannot affect offsets in other files. This was done so that modules and external routines can safely assume that offsets start at 0—the way they were meant to be.

> **See Also**
> arrays, substr, index, and regular expressions in this book

$.

Usage

$.

Description

The variable $. represents the current record number for which the last filehandle was read. Normally, the record number is an input line. (See $/ for how to change that.)

To reset $., close the filehandle. However, reading the filehandle ARGV (with <>) doesn't reset $..

The $. value, if localized, will remember which filehandle was last read from within that block.

Example Listing 4.33

```
# N-File comparison
# Assumes the first file in the list is the "master" and
#    eliminates others as they don't compare equally.

use IO::File;
@files=qw( /tmp/logfile /tmp/logfile2 /tmp/logfile3 );

foreach(@files) {
    push(@fhs, { val => "", line => 0, name => $_,
            fh => new IO::File $_ });
}
while(@fhs>1) {
    for my $file (@fhs) {
        $file->{val}=$file->{fh}->getline();
        $file->{line}=$.;
    }

COMPARE:
    my $ov=undef;
    for ( 0..$#fhs ) {
        if ( defined $ov and $ov ne $fhs[$_]->{val} ) {
            print "Differed at ",
                $fhs[$_]->{line}, " in ",
                $fhs[$_]->{name}, "\n";
```

```
        splice(@fhs, $_, 1);
        goto COMPARE;
    } else {
        $ov=$fhs[$_]->{val};
    }
}
}
}
```

Example Listing 4.34

```
# Perl Command-line program to
#    count the number of lines in file
# Obfuscated, but fun.  Courtesy of Abigail.
# If you're stumped as to how it works, contact
#    the book's author, clintp@geeksalad.org
perl -wlpe '}{$_=$.' /tmp/output
```

See Also
$/ in this book

$^E

Usage

$^E

Description

The variable $^E—$EXTENDED_OS_ERROR when use English is in effect—is used to hold additional information about operating system error messages.

Under Unix operating systems, $^E contains the same information as $!. Under OS/2, Microsoft Windows, and MacPerl, it contains additional information.

Example Listing 4.35

```
# Program to dump the extended error messages.  Contrast the
# default messages with the extended ones.  For example, under
# Windows, message 27 (File Too Large, EFBIG) has the extended
# message "The drive cannot find the sector requested".
```

```
for (0..255) {
    $^E=$_;
    $!=$_;
    print "$_ \t $^E \t $!\n";
}
```

> **See Also**
> $! in this book

Error Special Variables

Usage

```
$!
%!
```

Description

These variables are set when a system call (to the OS, not a perl function call) encounters an error.

The $! variable in a numeric context yields the error number of the last failed system call. In a string context, it gives the actual message; for example,

```
unless( open("F", "C:/Windows/Bill_Loves_Janet_Reno") ) {
    print "Error number: ", $!+0, "\n";
    print "Error message: $!\n";
}
```

Would yield something similar to 2 and No such file or directory, in numeric and string contexts, respectively.

The $! variable mimics the errno value in C's stdio library. It shouldn't be checked unless the system call actually fails. The value of $!, if the system call succeeds, is indeterminate.

The value in $! can be changed if you have a function of your own and want to use it as part of your own API. For example, an internal security error in your module could return false, and set $! to 1 (Operation not permitted). The full list of values and messages can be obtained by using the following example.

The hash %! is keyed on an error string determined by your vendor. If the corresponding element is true, the error is currently thrown. The %! only works if you've already performed a use Errno in your program.

```
use Errno;

unless( open(AUDIO, ">/dev/audio") ) {
    if ($!{ENOENT}) {
        die "Your /dev/audio file doesn't exist, can't play this song.";
    }
    die "Error: $!";
}
```

Some common error strings for Unix and Windows are

Numeric	String	Message
13	ENOPERM	Permission denied
2	ENOENT	No such file or directory
5	EIO	I/O Error
26	ETXTBUSY	Text file busy

But you should check your vendor-specific C header files to be sure. These values were meant to be set by the system and checked by the programmer, not necessarily set by the programmer.

Example Listing 4.36

```
# Small program to dump the error number, symbolic names
#   and messages.  Some of these may not exist on your
#   platform, however.
use Errno;

for $err (0..124) {
    $!=$err;
    %h=reverse %!; delete $h{0};
    printf("%3d %12s %s\n", $err, values %h, $!);
}
```

See Also
Errno module documentation

errno in the C library reference

I/O Record Separators

Usage

```
$/
$\
```

Description

This section describes the special global variables used in perl's IO (excluding $|, $,, $., and $^F). Each of these control input and output, and relate to perl's notion of a line.

When a *line of input* is discussed in Perl documentation, it normally means reading a filehandle until the next input-record separator is encountered. This unit is considered a line of input.

An input record separator is normally \n. What this means exactly depends on your architecture. Under Unix, this is an ASCII 10 (LF), under DOS, this is an ASCII 13,10 (CRLF), and under Mac OS, it's ASCII 13 (CR). The variable $/ contains the current input record separator that perl will use. On these architectures, this is the default setting.

However, there are occasions that it's useful to change the value of $/. For example, given the text of this telegram:

```
HELP STRANDED IN STRANGE COUNTRY STOP ENEMIES
EVERYWHERE STOP AM FUGITIVE FROM LOCAL POLICE STOP
NO BEER STOP WIRE BEER MONEY STOP LOVE HOMER
```

Each sentence is terminated by the word STOP. To read this text one sentence at a time, if it's open on the filehandle TELEGRAM:

```
$/=" STOP";
while(defined ($sentence=<TELEGRAM>)) {
    chomp $sentence;
    print "$sentence. ";
}
```

Each sentence read will still have the newlines that were embedded in the sentence (after the words ENEMIES, HOMER, and before NO BEER).

Setting $/ also affects the behavior of chomp, as in the preceding example, it will remove the trailing STOP from each sentence.

The variable $/ can be set to any string (but not to a regular expression). Some values stored in $/ are special. Setting $/ to the empty string ("") causes perl to begin reading filehandles in paragraph mode. This means that input records are separated by one or more blank lines. *Blank* means no spaces, tabs or other special characters—just the newline. In other words, each read will read in one visual paragraph. The following example reads by paragraphs.

Another special value for $/ is undef. If $/ is undefined, the next read on a filehandle will read the filehandle until end of file. This is useful for simply slurping in the rest of the file instead of dealing with it a line at a time:

```
open(MP3, "music/mp3/Also_Sprach_Zarathustra.mp3") || die;
{
    local $/;    # Sets $/ to undef, and it's local
    $data=<MP3>;
}
```

It's useful to declare a block and set $/ to undef locally so that when exiting, the block $/ will return to it's normal value and other filehandle reads won't be affected. You don't have to remember to set it back when you're done.

If you're processing arguments to the perl script (from @ARGV) using the <> mechanism, setting $/ to undef causes each read from <> to read the entire next file from the argument list:

```
{
    local $/;
    while( <>) {
        # $_ contains an entire file from @ARGV
    }
}
```

Finally, $/ can be set to a reference to an integer, a reference to a string containing an integer, or a reference to a scalar containing an integer.

```
$/=\512;   # Read no more than 512 bytes
```

This will cause reads to read a fixed number of bytes at a time. The pack entry contains an example of reading a fixed-length record from a file. If $/ is in fixed-length record mode, chomp has no effect.

The output record separator ($\) is much easier to understand than $/. The output record separator is written to the filehandle after every print statement. Normally, $\ is empty and nothing is written after a print, so

```
print "Pardon me Boy, ";
print "is that the Chattanooga Choo Choo?";
```

would appear on one line. However, by setting $\ to \n, you can get the output to appear on two different lines:

```
$\="\n";
print "Pardon me Roy, ";           # A \n will be printed here!
print "is that the cat who chewed your new shoes?";      # And here!
```

The variable $\ applies only to print, and not to printf or any other output statements.

Example Listing 4.37

```
# Take a windows .ini file which has the structure:
#   [windows]
#   load=
#   NullPort=None
#
#   [Desktop]
#   Wallpaper=(None)
#   WallpaperStyle=0
#
#   [intl]
#   iCountry=1
#   ICurrDigits=2
#
# And make it perl-friendly by creating a structure like:
# $inifile= { 'windows' => { load => '',
#                            NullPort => 'None' },
#             'Desktop' => { Wallpaper => '(None)',
#                            WallpaperStyle => 0 },
#             'intl'    => { iCountry => 1,
#                            iCurrDigits => 2 }
#
open(INI, "win.ini") || die "No win.ini?";
my $inifile={};
{
    # Make $/ local to the block so other reads
    #   don't go haywire.
    local $/="";   # ini files usually have paragraphs!
                   # if they didn't we could use [ as a record-separator
                   # and made due.
```

```
    while(<INI>) {
        next unless ( s/\[([^]]+)\]// );
        my $header=$1;
        $inifile->{$header}={};
        while( m/(\w+)=(.*)/g ) {
            $inifile->{$header}->{$1}=$2;
        }
    }
}
close(INI);
```

> **See Also**
> -0, -1, print, pack, chomp, <, and > in this book

$^O

Usage

$^O

Description

The variable $^O contains the operating system name that Perl was compiled for. For example, this might contain: linux, MSWin32, os2, VMS, cygwin, netbsd, os390, solaris, aix, or any of dozens of other operating systems.

This value also can be obtained from the Config module's $Config{osname} value, at the cost of dragging in 1,000 lines of the Config module.

Example Listing 4.38

```
if ($^O =~ /Win32/) {
    @files=`dir`;
} else {
    @files=`ls -l`;
}
```

> **See Also**
> Config module documentation

$|

Usage

```
$|=val;
```

Description

The $| variable accesses the autoflush flag on the currently selected filehandle. After writing to a filehandle with print, printf, or write, if the autoflush flag on the filehandle is set to true, perl will flush the output instead of buffering it.

The $| variable doesn't set the flag for a particular filehandle, only the selected one. If you have a filehandle and need to turn on autoflushing, select it first:

```
open(LOGF, ">>/tmp/logfile") || die;
select(LOGF);
$|=1;
select(STDOUT);  # Back to STDOUT...
```

To select another filehandle, turn on its autoflushing flag, and then re-select the current filehandle. This idiom works nicely:

```
select((select(LOGF), $|=1)[0]);
```

See the select entry for details.

A common misconception is that this removes stdio buffering of the filehandle. It doesn't. It merely causes the filehandle to be flushed after every write by perl. If the filehandle has output pending at the time that $| is set, it will be flushed immediately.

A cleaner approach than selecting filehandles and setting the $| variable is to use the IO::Handle module to access the filehandle's properties directly. This way the ugliness with select is avoided, but the same effect is achieved.

```
use IO::Handle;
LOGHANDLE->autoflush(1);
```

This is done at the cost of speed because of retrieving a module (IO::Handle), which in turn might retrieve other modules (Symbol, SelectSaver) and additional C code (IO's XS code).

Example Listing 4.39

```perl
# This function returns a subroutine reference (a closure).
#    Call the returned subroutine to print busy-please-wait
#    dots across the screen.  If you pass an number to the
#    dots function, the returned subroutine will limit the dot-width
#    to that number.
sub dots {
    my $max=shift || 10;
    my($dotc,$w)=(1,0);

    # If STDOUT is not buffered, the dots will come out
    # all at once, in a big messy clump.
    select((select(STDOUT), $|++)[0]);
    return sub {
        if ($dotc) {
            print STDOUT ".";
            $dotc=0  if (++$w>=$max);
        } else {
            print STDOUT "\b \b";
            $dotc=1 if --$w==0;
        }
    }
}


# This creates a dots subroutine instance.
$counter=dots(15);

# This while loop does nothing.  In here, where you're doing
#    something that takes a long time, call &$counter occasionally
#    to give the user something to look at.
while() {
    select(undef, undef, undef, .25);  # 1/4 sec. delay
    &$counter;
}
```

See Also
select and filehandles in this book

Process Special Variables

Usage

```
$$
$(
$)
$<
$>
$?
$^F
```

Description

These special variables all describe (and sometimes modify) various properties of the current running process. As a result, some don't translate directly into operating systems other than Unix. These will be noted.

In addition, most of the variables listed here have an alternate name that can be provided from the English module. These are listed as follows:

Variable	English Name
$$	$PID or $PROCESS_ID
$(	$GID or $REAL_GROUP_ID
$)	$EGID or $EFFECTIVE_GROUP_ID
$<	$UID or $REAL_USER_ID
$>	$EUID or $EFFECTIVE_USER_ID
$?	$CHILD_ERROR
$^F	$SYSTEM_FD_MAX

The variable $$ is the process ID of the current running perl process. Under Unix this can be used to uniquely identify a process at any given point in time. Each process ID is unique for the life of that process. The process ID can be used for a variety of purposes. To see examples using $$, see the fork, getpgrp and kill entries.

The parent process ID can be obtained with getppid.

The $(and $) variables contain the real and effective group IDs of the current process. The $< and $> variables contain the real and effective user IDs of the current process. These are both numeric values, not alphabetic. For example, the user ID for the superuser will (typically) be reported as 0 and not root.

The real user ID is the user number with which you've logged in. This reflects the entry in the password file in effect at the time you logged in. It normally doesn't change. It can be changed if the current process is the superuser and your system supports the setreuid() system call.

An effective user ID is the identity assigned to your process if it's run as a set-UID program. This is done in Unix by assuming the owner of a file if the 04000 bits are set in the file permissions. A set-uid program resembles

```
-rwsr-sr-x   1 root      mail       76432 Feb  7  2000 /usr/bin/procmail
```

In this case, when procmail is run, it will assume the user ID of root and the group ID of mail.

The real and effective group IDs work similarly with respect to set-gid programs. There is one difference: under some kinds of Unix, you are allowed to be in multiple groups at once. The variable $(will contain a space-separated list of groups. To set $(, you must set it to a numeric group ID number (only one). To set $(, you must set it to a list of space-separated group IDs. (Multiples are allowed.)

The $? variable contains the exit code for the last pipe, wait, waitpid, system, or backtick commands. The 16-bit word returned has the exit status, plus any flags that indicate whether the process dropped core or was sent a signal. Typically under Unix, an exit status of 0 indicates success and others indicate failures. To extract the various parts, see Example Listing 4.40.

Lastly, the $^F variable controls the number of the highest system file descriptor. This is used by perl to flag file descriptors (the part underneath filehandles, see fileno) as to whether or not they should remain open when perl exec's a new program. When a filehandle is opened, $^F is examined, and if the file descriptor is flagged to whether it should be closed during the exec. Typically $^F is set to 2, which causes STDIN, STDOUT and STDERR to remain open during the exec.

Example Listing 4.40

```perl
# Run an external command, get its exit status,
#    the signal that killed it and whether or
#    not it dropped core
$output=`some_external_program`;
```

```perl
print "Whole 16-bits: $?\n";
print "Exit status: ", $?>>8, "\n";
print "Signal?       ", $? & 127, "\n";
print "Core?         ", $? & 128, "\n";
```

Example Listing 4.41

```perl
# Demonstrates $^F.  Opens a file descriptor when $^F is
#    set very high, then execs *itself* with the file descriptor
#    as an argument.
# When the unless block is run, the filedescriptor is
#    re-attached to a filehandle, and the data is read back.

# Normally, this is a coordinated effort between two distinct
#    processes.

# No arguments, just open the file descriptor
unless ( @ARGV ) {
    local $^F=256;            # 3 should be high enough, but better safe.
    open(LOGFILE, "+>/tmp/log") || die;
    print LOGFILE "Hello, world!";

    # Run myself, passing the file descriptor as an argument.
    exec "$0 " . fileno(LOGFILE);
} else {

    # The file descriptor (probably 3) is already open, attach
    #    it to a filehandle and read it back
    open(MYCOPY, "+>>&$ARGV[0]") || die "Cannot dup the fd: $!";
    seek(MYCOPY, 0, 0);
    $text=<MYCOPY>;
    close(MYCOPY);
    print "Text was: $text\n";
}
```

Example Listing 4.42

```perl
# Are we running in some kind of set-uid environment?
#
if ($> != $<) {
    print STDERR "You cannot run this program with different\n";
    print STDERR "real and effective user id's!";
    exit(99);
}
```

`$"`

Usage

`$"`

Description

The `$"` variable represents the character that will be used to separate array (or slice) elements when they're interpolated in a double-quoted string (or in qq{} and <<).

Normally this is set to space.

Example Listing 4.43

```
@kids=qw(stan cartman kyle kenny);
{
    local $"=", ";
    print "Third grade: @kids\n";

    # Kind of like doing:
    # print "Third grade: ", join(", ", @kids), "\n";
    # but a bit easier to read.
}
```

Regular Expression Special Variables

Usage

```
@+
@-
$+
$^R
```

```
$&
$'
$`
```

Description

The variables listed in this section all have to do with the regular expression operators and language used in perl. These variables are set when a regular expression match takes place. For details on regular expressions in general and the regular expression operators, see the section on regular expressions.

Each variable is localized to the block in which the last pattern match was done. For example, these two matches are performed in different blocks, so $& for each is preserved.

```
$song1="Can you tell me how to get,";
$song2="how to get to Sesame Street?";
if ($song1=~m/\w{4}/) {
    # Provides a block which lets $& be
    # localized for each match as though:
    # local $&;
    if ($song2=~/[A-Z]\w+/) {
        print qq{Name was: "$&"\n};   # Sesame
    }
}
# $& is still preserved from above.
print qq{Four letter word: "$&"\n};  # prints tell
```

In addition, most of the variables listed here have an alternate name that can be provided from the English module. These are listed in the following table:

Variable	English Name
@+	@LAST_MATCH_END
@-	@LAST_MATCH_START
$+	@LAST_PAREN_MATCH
$^R	$LAST_REGEXP_CODE_RESULT
$&	$MATCH
$'	$POSTMATCH
$`	$PREMATCH

During a regular expression match, parenthesis capture the results of the match stored within them. The variable $+ contains the match for the last set of parenthesis. This is most useful if you have a series of alternations, and are only interested in the set of parenthesis that matched regardless of how many alternations there are.

```
if ( m!\d{1,2}[-/]\d{1,2}[-/](\d{4})   |  # Matches 2/22/1993 or 04/03/1969
     \u\w\w+\s\d{1,2},\s(\d{4})    |  # Matches December 7, 1941
     \d{4}[-/.]\d{1,2}[-/.]\d{1,2} |  # Matches 1944.06.06
     !x ) {
     $year=$+;    # Could be $1, $2 or $3!  This will do the Right Thing
}
```

The @- and @+ variables hold the positions of the beginnings and endings of the entire regular expression match, and the positions for each of the parenthetical matches. So, the expression

```
$_="Previous: 36.00   Payment: 11.05 (thank you!)  Balance: 24.95";
if (m/\d+.\d+$/) {
    print "Begins: $-[0]\n";
    print " Ends: $+[0]\n";
    print " Match: ", substr $_, $-[0], $+[0]-$-[0];
}
```

offset 0 in @+ and @- hold the starting and ending positions for the entire match. In this case, 56 and 61 for 24.95.

The other elements of @+ and @- hold the values for matches in parenthesis. Additionally, the variable $#+ will hold the total number of groups that were last matched. In the first example, $+[1] is used to find the position of the first match so that pos can be used to reposition the search at the character starting after the first match.

The variables $', $&, and $` are set during a regular expression match. The variable $& is set to the portion of the pattern actually matched by the regular expression. For example, after the statements:

```
$_="I think that I shall never see";
m/s\w+/;
```

the variable $& will be set to shall. The variable $' is set to the portion of the original string after the regular expression match; the variable $` is set to the portion of the string preceding the match. All three variables are scoped to the block that contained the regular expression match.

Additionally, the variables $&, $', $`, @-, @+, and $+ (similar to $1-$*n*) should only be used if the match actually succeeds. If the match doesn't succeed, they're not guaranteed to hold any particular value and might cause bugs in your programs if you're not vigilant.

The variable $^R is used with (?{}) constructs in regular expressions. The pattern (?{*code*}) is used to run code within the body of a regular expression. As each code block runs, the return value of each block is stored in $^R. If the regular expression has to backtrack, the value if $^R is restored to the last block which successfully matched; so,

```
$_="a poem as lovely as a tree";
# Extract words, shifted to uppercase
#   there are easier ways to do this...
while(m/(\w+)(?{ "\u$1" })/g) { push @w, $^R }
```

Keep in mind that the (?{}) construct is still labeled as experimental and that the interface to it (including $^R) might change in future revisions of Perl.

Example Listing 4.44

```
$t=<<'TEXT';
In the beginning God created the heaven and the earth.
And the earth was without form, and void; and darkness
was upon the face of the deep.
And the Spirit of God moved upon the face of the waters.
TEXT

# Given a string in $t find the longest repeated substring
my $long="";
$t=~s/\n//g;  # Book formatting.  :)
while($t=~m/(..*).*(\1)/omg) {
    $long=$1 if ((length $1) > (length $long));

    # Reposition the start of the search to the character after
    # the first character of the first match of the pair.
    pos $t=$+[1];
}
print "Longest: $long\n";  # prints " upon the face of the "
```

<table>
<tr><td>

See Also
regular expressions in this book

</td></tr>
</table>

`$;`

Usage

`$;`

Description

The variable `$;` is used in `perl`'s emulation of multidimensional arrays. By default, this value is set to ASCII `0x1c` (FS).

If a hash index is separated with commas, the keys of the hash index are concatenated to create a new hash key. In this way, *n*-dimensional arrays can be emulated. For example,

`$grid{$x,$y}`

would be roughly equivalent to

`$grid{join($;, $x, $y)}`

However, be cautious not to indicate a hash slice:

`@grid{$x,$y};`

This means something completely different. See the hashes entry for an explanation of the difference between a hash slice and a multidimensional hash created with `$;`.

Note that using binary values for keys might interfere with ASCII `0x1c` being used as the key-separator character.

The preferred method for creating multidimensional arrays and hashes is to use references. This is covered in the references, hashes, and arrays sections. The use of `$;` is discouraged.

Example Listing 4.45

```
# Find most common word-start characters
#    Yes, it's cheesy but there aren't many uses for $;

open(W, '/usr/dict/words') || die "words: $!";
while(<W>) {

    # This could have been done more easily with
    #    $wl{lc(substr($_, 0, 2))}++ if length>1;
```

```
      last unless ($f,$s)=m/(\w)(\w)/;
      $wl{"\l$f","\l$s"}++;
}
for ( (sort { $wl{$b} <=> $wl{$a} } keys %wl)[0..5] ) {
    print "$_ occurrences: $wl{$_}\n";
}
```

See Also
references, hashes, and arrays in this book

$_

Usage

$_

Description

In perl the variable $_ is heavily used; for many operators, functions, pattern matches, and loops $_ is the default variable used when no argument is specified. With the English module, it is also known as $ARG.

The following example shows several places where $_ is the implied argument for the operation. In general, $_ is used.

- For pattern matching operations unless another value is bound to the operation with =~

- The iterator for the map and grep functions

- The default iterator in for and foreach loops, unless another variable is indicated

- Where the input record goes if a <> or glob is used (by itself) in the test portion of a while loop

Also, many functions (print, split) and operators (sin, cos) will use $_ if no other value is supplied. See the documentation for that particular function to verify whether or not this is the case.

Example Listing 4.46

```
while(<INPUT>) {
    chomp;
    s/foo/bar/;
    print;
}


# Is functionally identical to the following,
#   using $x instead of the implicit $_

while(defined($x=<INPUT>)) {
    chomp $x;
    $x=~s/foo/bar/;
    print $x;
}
```

> **See Also**
> for, foreach, map, grep, =~, <, >, and glob in this book

Version Special Variables

Usage

```
$]
$^V
```

Description

The variables $] and $^V both contain version information for the current perl interpreter.

The variable $] represents the current major revision of Perl (4 prior to 1994, and 5 since then), plus the patch number. So, perl version 4, patchlevel 36 would be represented as 4.036.

For Perl 5.6, this versioning system was abandoned. Instead, $^V contains a version number represented as a vector. So that v5.6.0 represents a revision 5, version 6, subversion 0 of the perl interpreter. This string is also represented as chr(5).chr(6).chr(0) and can be compared as a literal (see the following examples).

These can be used to check whether the perl interpreter is at least the expected version before attempting something that might not work under older versions.

Example Listing 4.47

```
# Use $^V to determine if a feature is supported in a
#   core piece of perl before we try to use it.

use Data::Dumper;
if ($^V and $^V ge v5.6.0) {
    $Data::Dumper::Maxdepth=10;
} else {
    warn "Data::Dumper maxdepth is not supported.\n";
}
```

See Also

use, require, and vectors in this book

$0

Usage

$0

Description

The variable $0 contains the name of the of the file of the perl script being executed. For example, under Linux if a script is executed in /usr/local/bin/myscript.pl, running it with the following:

/usr/local/bin/myscript.pl

would put /usr/local/bin/myscript.pl into $0. Beware though that the actual pathname put into $0 will vary depending on your shell, the location of the script, the method you used to start the script (by name, or as an argument to perl, or on STDIN) and how your system's C library will report the pathname to Perl. It could show up as any of the following:

```
/usr/local/bin/myscript.pl
./myscript.pl
myscript.pl
-
```

depending on these circumstances.

Changing $0's contents might change the system's name for the current process. This can be used so that ps(1) (under Unix) or the Task Manager (under Windows NT) will report a name for the process different from the script name. This behavior isn't portable, and not guaranteed to work everywhere.

Example Listing 4.48

```
# Start a daemon, using the method from fork()
use POSIX qw(setsid);
chdir("/") || warn;
open(STDIN, "/dev/null") || die "STDIN: $!";
open(STDOUT, ">/dev/null") || die "STDIN: $!";
open(STDERR, ">/tmp/logfile") || die "STDIN: $!";
die "$!" if (POSIX::setsid()==-1);
$pid=fork();
die "Cannot fork: $!" if (! defined $pid);
exit if $pid;

#   Have the daemon rename itself.
#   so it shows up this way in ps(1)
$0="perldaemon 1.0";
```

> **See Also**
> argv in the C library reference

CHAPTER 5

Files and Directories

This section of the book describes the built-in functions used to query the filesystem and make modifications to the filesystem.

Perl and File Systems

Description

Most of the functions and concepts in this section derive directly from the Unix notions of how filesystems work; however, Perl maps these functions to your operating system's equivalent concepts wherever possible. For example, unlink is a Unix API function for deleting files, but a similar function will exist under VMS, MacOS, and Microsoft Windows. Perl will take care of the translations for you.

Where functions don't map cleanly from the Unix paradigm to your OS, it will be noted in the individual entry.

Primer on Unix Filesystems

Before you begin, even if you're not a Unix user, you should take just a moment to learn a bit about Unix filesystems, at least to understand the odd terminology you'll soon see. This is a somewhat generic description, and certainly doesn't describe all the features you'll see on every Unix filesystem.

A Unix filesystem is simply a portion of the disk (a partition, or a logical volume) that has been formatted such that there is a hierarchy of directories and files in that area. Under Unix, the various filesystems on the disk are mounted on branches of each other so that a continuous tree of file hierarchies with a single root node is created. Contrast this with MS Windows where each filesystem constitutes another root node: The concept of drives doesn't exist in Unix—everything is part of a single hierarchy of files.

Within each filesystem, there are two organizational structures: i-nodes and blocks. The i-nodes consist of two parts: a portion devoted to storing information about a file, and a portion that contains pointers to blocks of data on the disk (the file's contents).

Files are created by obtaining a new i-node from the filesystem, and then associating blocks of data with it. Retrieving file data by having to know the file's i-node number would not be fun. So in order to organize these in a human-readable form, a special kind of file, a *directory*, is created. Directories simply contain lists of filenames and their associated i-node numbers. To create a new file, the steps are: 1. Obtain an i-node from the filesystem, 2. Create an appropriate directory entry to refer to that i-node. The entire Unix (and Perl) API hides these troublesome details from you behind nice interfaces such as open and unlink. It's that simple. (Of course, this has been grossly oversimplified.)

Reading and Manipulating Directories

The first thing in managing a filesystem is to be able to navigate around it, so Perl gives you tools to open, read, and close directories. Actually it gives you two sets of tools. The opendir, readdir, and closedir functions provide a rather low-level directory reading tool—no filtering is done on the files retrieved, they're not sorted, and you have to be able to tell directories from files. (But that's easy.)

The other interface is glob; glob provides a simplistic way to retrieve only the directory information in which you're interested. The tradeoff is that it isn't quite as flexible and it's a little slower.

After reading directories, it would be useful to be able to manipulate them. The unlink function removes files; rename, link and symlink will create them for you (along with open and other commands described elsewhere). The mkdir function creates a new directory entry for you and rmdir removes directory entries.

The link function takes an existing file (remember, files are just i-nodes) and creates a second directory entry in the filesystem referring to that file. The second directory entry can be in the same directory (with a different name) or in another directory. For link, both files must be in the same filesystem. The symlink function does something similar; it creates a special file (called a *symbolic link*), and in it is the real name of the file that it refers to. The referred file might be on the same filesystem, a different one, or might not exist at all.

In the case of a regular link (sometimes called a *hard link*), the link and the linked file are indistinguishable. In the case of symlinks, the other operating system commands (open, unlink, rename, and so on) are designed to recognize symbolic links and possibly treat them differently.

The link and symlink functions are available only under Unix-like operating systems.

Tinkering with I-Nodes

The file i-node contains the metadata about the file. Of course, a true i-node only exists under Unix, but other operating systems have ways of storing metadata for files, just in different mechanisms. Perl (normally) translates all the Unix mumbo jumbo into the appropriate concepts for your system when possible.

For example, the stat function retrieves all the i-node meta-information. You can find out how large the file is, how many disk blocks it occupies, and the permissions associated with the file. Some information is specific to operating systems: The file's mode (permissions) might only make sense under Unix. And other information is a careful translation: The device under Unix refers to a mounted device number; in MS-Windows the device is the drive letter (more or less). The lstat function does a stat but for symbolic links—under other OS's, lstat just reverts to being stat.

Some of the information on an i-node is read-only, such as the size of the file that changes when you write to it. Other bits can be changed indirectly. For example, the timestamps on the file can be changed with utime; the permissions can be changed with chmod (Unix); and the ownership of the file with chown (Unix).

What's Standard I/O?

For purposes of this explanation, consider Disk I/O. Typically there are two things you need to do to disk files: read and write. At a very low-level in the operating system, there are routines to read and write disk files, and the C language contains routines to access the operating system's reading and writing routines directly.

When a C program opens a file, it is given a file descriptor by the operating system. This file descriptor is nothing more than a pointer to a table that indicates to the operating system which file you're talking about. When you want to read the file, you call the read stdio function and give it the file descriptor, a buffer, and how much data you want read. The operating system uses the file descriptor to determine which file you're interested in, requests the data from the filesystem (which involves hardware interaction), and then puts the requested data in the buffer.

This happens every time a C program performs a read system call. A similar set of steps occurs with writing, except that the write(2) system call is performed and data goes out, not in.

Operating system kernels are designed to be small, fast, and as a result tend to be very stupid. If a C program makes a series of 1-byte read calls on a particular file in sequence, the kernel is going to spin the disk, read the disk block, copy the data from the kernel back to the user's buffer, and return. This is very wasteful of resources. A sensible alternative would be to read the data in large chunks, for instance, 4K or 8K at a time, and then simply return the next byte in the chunk when it's requested. Reading 8K from a disk all at once is almost always faster than reading 8K in smaller chunks spread out over time.

However, this is very hard to do in your programs. Consider a program that reads and writes a disk file. If the program reads a block and performs a write on the same block, the read and write routines need to be smart enough to recognize that these reads and writes are on the same block and do the updates properly.

Other things to consider are interrupts. What do you do when your read doesn't read all the data it should have because it was interrupted? The read system call doesn't have to return all the data requested, even though more might be available. So your programs that use read have to contend with the possibility that read might return short reads.

The ANSI C standard canonized a set of library routines to do all this for you. Collectively, these are known as the *Standard I/O library* (also *stdio*, or *STDIO*).

If your C program needs to read, wants to take advantage of buffering, and needs to be fairly immune to interrupts, call fread instead of calling read. The same kinds of arguments are needed: a filehandle, which is similar to a file descriptor, only better, a buffer, and a description of how much data you want read. The results are the same. The difference is that the data is read (or written) much more efficiently and the fread is guaranteed to return whole chunks of data instead of possibly returning only a partial chunk.

How does Standard I/O Relate to Perl?

By default, most Perl programs use the Standard I/O library for their reading or writing. In fact, most of the I/O routines have further layers between the Standard I/O library and your program. This is for efficiency and convenience. The <>, `readline`, `print`, `getc`, `seek`, `tell`, `eof`, and `read` functions all use the standard I/O library.

In case your program needs access to I/O but not through the Standard I/O library, Perl provides direct-access counterparts to those: `sysread`, `syswrite`, and `sysseek`.

In C there's a distinction between file handles (`FILE *`, obtained with `fopen`) and file descriptors (`int`, obtained with `open`); one is used for standard I/O, and the other is used with the low-level access routines. Perl makes no such distinctions. A filehandle is a filehandle, and can be used for both standard I/O routines and direct access routines. Try not to let the fact that there is both a `sysopen` and an `open` in Perl confuse you; they both open a filehandle, but simply go about it in different manners.

The most important thing to remember about standard I/O and non-standard I/O is not to mix calls to them. If you're reading a file with `read` (stdio) and suddenly decide to start using `syswrite` (not stdio) on the file, the standard I/O library has no idea that the file is being written to—this is a recipe for data corruption. Find a set of routines and stick to them.

Filehandles

Default File Handles

Usage

```
STDIN
STDOUT
STDERR
DATA
ARGV
ARGVOUT
```

Description

When the `perl` interpreter runs a script, normally these five (or sometimes six) filehandles are available for use.

The STDIN, STDOUT, and STDERR filehandles correspond to the stdin, stdout, and stderr filehandles from the C Standard I/O library. The STDIN, STDOUT, and STDERR filehandles are *inherited* from the parent process (under Unix). Whether they're inherited by perl's children is up to the $^F variable and whether the close-on-exec flag has been cleared with fcntl.

To simplify, the STDIN filehandle is normally connected to the input device (the *keyboard*). Thus, reading STDIN reads from the keyboard. STDOUT is the default output filehandle and is normally connected to the output device (the *screen*). So writing to STDOUT writes to the screen. The STDERR filehandle is normally connected to the same output device as STDOUT, except that it isn't buffered—anything written to STDERR appears immediately on the output, whereas STDOUT's writing might be deferred.

In actuality, of course, the three filehandles are normally all connected to a terminal or console device that provides a convenient API to video memory, keyboard interrupts, modems, DTE/DCE devices, and so on. The screen and keyboard are simply nice abstractions.

Under non-Unix operating systems, each filehandle points to a reasonable facsimile of this description.

Because the filehandles are inherited from the parent process, it's possible to have the parent reconnect them elsewhere before the Perl program starts. Normally, this is done at the command line with redirection and piping. For example, to have STDOUT go into a file, instead of to the screen, simply start the perl program and have the command interpreter redirect standard output:

```
perl myscript.pl > /tmp/outputfile
```

This syntax works under Unix shells, NT's CMD.EXE, Win9X's command.com, and possibly under other command interpreters. To redirect the error output (standard error), use a slightly different syntax:

```
perl myscript.pl 2>/tmp/errors
```

This works under NT's CMD.EXE and under most Unix shells. Most command interpreters allow for some kind of piping. A *pipe* is when two processes are connected so that the standard output of one becomes the standard input of another. In Unix (and Windows) shell syntax, piping one command to another would resemble the following:

```
ls | myscript.pl
```

Within myscript.pl, the filehandle STDIN would be connected to ls's standard output.

To determine whether a particular filehandle is connected to another program, a file, or your terminal, you can use the -t file test operator on the filehandle:

```
if (-t STDIN) {
    # Input is from a terminal, or a terminal-like thing
} else {
    # Input is from a pipe, or from redirection
}
```

It also is possible to re-open STDOUT, STDIN, or STDERR against anything you want by using the open or sysopen functions. Remember that reopening those filehandles will lose what they were originally connected to; for example, if STDIN is connected to a pipe, re-opening it will disconnect it from the pipe, and there's no way to restore that connection. You always can save a copy of the filehandles before re-opening them; see the open entry for details.

The DATA filehandle relates to the __DATA__ or __END__ tokens in a perl source file. If a DATA filehandle is read, anything after the __DATA__ token in the source file is read. The DATA filehandle is *per-package*, meaning that if multiple files (say modules) each have a __DATA__ token, the DATA filehandle in each of those refers to its own __DATA__. The DATA filehandle in the main package reads from the __END__ token in the main package if one is present; otherwise it reads from the __DATA__ token. For more information, see the __END__ and __DATA__ entries.

The seek and tell functions can work on the DATA filehandle. When DATA is first read, the information after the __DATA__ identifier is returned. However, seeking backward in __DATA__ allows you to access the source code of the script, or module, itself.

The ARGV filehandle is the implicit filehandle used for argument processing with <>. For example, the statement while(<>) {} is the equivalent of while(<ARGV>) {}. For more information on the ARGV filehandle, see the <> entry.

The ARGVOUT filehandle is used during processing with the -i switch on the command line (or the #! line). The -i switch allows you to process files in-place on the disk. While files are being processed, the ARGV filehandle is open for input to the current file. The ARGVOUT filehandle is open for output to what will become the replacement file for the file being processed. Perl selects ARGVOUT as the default filehandle during -i processing, but STDOUT is still available; you just need to write to it explicitly.

```
perl -pi -e '$|=1;' -e 's/foo/bar/; print STDOUT "."' *.txt
```

More information on -i processing can be found in the command-line options section.

Example Listing 5.1

```
# Show the states of the 3 default filehandles.
#    Try redirecting, piping and playing around with how
#    this script is run.

# /dev/tty is particular to unix.  It's always supposed
#    to be connected to your terminal.
open(TTYOUT, ">/dev/tty") || die "Can't open a terminal";
select(TTYOUT);

for my $i (STDIN, STDOUT, STDERR) {
    print "The filehandle $i is ";
    unless (defined fileno $i) {
        print "closed\n";
        next;
    }
    print "not " unless (-t $i);
    print "a terminal\n";
}
```

Example Listing 5.2

```
# Fun with the DATA filehandle
# This _must_ be run as a perl script from a file,
#    it won't work if you feed it to the interpreter
#    on standard input

$start=tell(DATA);
@lines=<DATA>;
$end=tell(DATA);
seek(DATA, 0, 0) or warn "Cannot seek: $!";

print "This program is $end bytes long.\n";
print "The textual data starts at byte $start and goes:\n";
for(@lines) { print "\t$_"; }
print "The entire source reads:\n";
while(<DATA>) { print "\t$_"; }


__END__
```

```
Come live with me and be my love,
And we will all the pleasures prove,
That valleys, groves, hills, and fields,
Woods, or steepy mountain yields.
```

> **See Also**
>
> open, file test operators, fcntl, $|, __DATA__, __END__, and command line options in this book

Testing and Manipulating Filehandles

fcntl

Usage

```
fcntl filehandle, command, value
```

Description

The fcntl function is used to adjust the properties of a filehandle that is already open; for example, to make the filehandle non-blocking or to make a filehandle that is open for reading now available for reading and writing without having to re-open it.

Upon success, the fcntl function returns a non-zero number or the special string 0 but true. If the fcntl function fails, undef is returned and $! is set to the error message. The 0 but true string is true for boolean operations, and 0 in a numeric context. This particular string won't throw a warning when used in numeric context.

If fcntl is used on an architecture where fcntl isn't available, an exception will be thrown and can be caught with eval.

The fcntl function requires constants that are available from the Fcntl module. Most documentation on the fcntl commands and values will refer to these constants. The filehandle must refer to a currently-open filehandle.

The actual allowable values for command are documented in your system's documentation and vary from system to system. Depending on the command, a value might be required to set attributes. This is passed as the third argument. When not needed, the value is ignored, but must be present. Some common commands are as follows:

Command	Meaning
F_DUPD	Duplicates the file descriptor. The fcntl function will return the newly opened file descriptor. To obtain a filehandle so that you can read or write the file, use open with a &.
F_GETFD	Gets the file descriptor flags.
F_SETFD	Sets the file descriptor flags. Currently the only flag used is FD_CLOEXEC.
F_GETFL	Gets the file status flags. Then the flags can be compared with the masks in the next table to determine which flags are set (and can be set).
F_SETFL	Sets the file status flags.
F_GETLK	Gets the flock structure for the filehandle.
F_SETLK	Sets the flock structure for the filehandle (non-blocking).
F_SETLW	Sets the flock structure for the filehandle (blocking).

Status Flag	Description
O_ACCMODE	Mask to extract the I/O modes from the F_GETFL value
O_RDONLY	Read-only mask
O_WRONLY	Write-only mask
O_RDWR	Read/write mask
O_NONBLOCK	Nonblocking I/O
O_APPEND	Appends on each write
O_SYNC	Waits for writes to complete

The most common command is F_GETFL, which is used to get the file status flags. These have information on the mode in which the filehandle was opened (read-only, read/write, and so on) and attributes of the filehandle (blocking/nonblocking, append mode). To set the attributes, use the F_SETFL command, changing the flags appropriately.

The F_GETFD and F_SETFD commands are used to set or clear the close on exec flag for a file (FD_CLOEXEC).

Example Listing 5.3

```
# (Part 1 of two)
# Open a log file and exec a second program passing
#    the file descriptor

use Fcntl;

open(LOG, ">/tmp/logfile") || die;
$flags=fcntl(LOG, F_GETFD, 0)
    or die "Cannot get flags: $!";

# Clear the close-on-exec flag
$flags=fcntl(LOG, F_SETFD, $flags & ~FD_CLOEXEC)
    or die "Cannot set flags: $!";

# Now run part 2
exec("part2", fileno(LOG));
```

Example Listing 5.4

```
# (Part 2 of two, expected to be named part2)
# Write to the already-opened file descriptor passed
#    in as the first argument.  The open is merely to
#    give us a filehandle from the descriptor.

open(NEWDESC, ">&$ARGV[0]") || die "Cannot dup the fd: $!";
print NEWDESC "Log THIS!\n";
close(NEWDESC);
```

Example Listing 5.5

```
# Sets O_SYNC on a file descriptor.  Handy to have
#    a log that's always written to and flushed immediately.

use Fcntl;
open(LOG, ">/tmp/logfile") || die;
$flags=fcntl(LOG, F_GETFL, 0)
    or die "Cannot get flags: $!";
fcntl(LOG, F_GETFL, $flags | O_SYNC) or die "Cannot set O_SYNC: $!";
print LOG "Error message\n";
```

See Also
Fcntl module documentation
fileno, eval and open in this book
fcntl in the C library reference

---

truncate

Usage

```
truncate filehandle, length
truncate filename, length
```

Description

The truncate function takes the file specified by the opened filehandle and shortens it to the length given. If a filename is specified, it is opened and truncated to the proper length. If the truncate function was successful, a true value is returned; otherwise undef is returned.

The filehandle must be an open filehandle, represented either as an identifier or as a scalar variable that refers to an IO::Handle like object. See the open entry for details.

Some systems don't implement truncate, and on those platforms truncate will cause an exception that can be trapped with eval.

A special case of truncate, truncating a file to 0 bytes, can be emulated with sysopen using the O_TRUNC flag:

```
use Fcntl;
sysopen(SHORTEN_ME, "file_to_empty", O_WRONLY | O_TRUNC) ||
    die "Cannot truncate file_to_empty: $!";
```

If the file was previously less than length bytes before the truncate function was called, the results are system dependant.

Example Listing 5.6

```
# Reduce a file to its last 10 lines as if trimming
#    a log file.  Should be surrounded by a locking
#    mechanism (such as described in the bind or flock
```

```
#    entries) to prevent concurrent access.

use Fcntl qw(:seek);

open(LOG, "+</tmp/log.txt") || die "Cannot open log.txt: $!";
while(<LOG>) {
    shift @LINES if ( push(@LINES, $_) > 10);
}

# Rewind in the file, re-write the lines and truncate there.
seek(LOG, 0, SEEK_SET);
print LOG @LINES;
$where=tell LOG;

truncate LOG, $where or warn "Cannot truncate to $where: $!";
close(LOG);
```

See Also

open, sysopen and eval in this book

ftruncate in the C library reference

---

select

Usage

```
select
select filehandle
select readfds, writefds, errfds, timeout
```

Description

The select function in Perl has two distinct and completely unrelated functions. The first function for select is the selection of a default filehandle (or returning the default filehandle); the second is polling file descriptors to see which ones are ready for reading, writing, or have errors pending.

In Perl, there is the concept of a currently selected (default) filehandle. Normally functions such as print use this filehandle when none are specified. For example, print "Hello World" will send the output of this statement to the currently selected filehandle. By default, this is STDOUT.

The `select` function, with no arguments, returns a filehandle that represents the currently selected filehandle. This is usually done to save the filehandle before changing it to something else. With one argument, it sets the default filehandle to the indicated filehandle, and returns the filehandle that was previously selected.

```
$fd=select;
select OUTFILE;
print "Hello World!";  # Now goes to OUTFILE, instead of STDOUT
```

In conjunction with $|, this can be used to select a current filehandle, turn on autoflushing, and then re-select the old filehandle with this idiom:

```
# select a different filehandle, turn on autoflushing,
#   re-select the prior filehandle.
select((select(OUTHANDLE), $|=1)[0]);
```

But this is somewhat obfuscated, and a simpler, more straighforward way of accomplishing the same is with the following:

```
use IO::Handle;
OUTHANDLE->autoflush(1);
```

IO::Handle is a big module and the earlier idiom has worked for a decade, so you're likely to see either in actual code.

The second form of select allows you to multiplex I/O. The basic logic behind the four-argument `select` is that select is called with 3-bit vectors that indicate what file descriptors you would like to read from, write to, and which have errors pending (*readfds*, *writefds*, *errfds*). You also pass in a *timeout*, which indicates how long the system should wait for information on these descriptors.

The `select` function in a scalar context returns a count of how many file descriptors are ready for processing (combined for reading, writing, and errors). In a list context, a two-element list is returned with the first element being the number of descriptors ready and the second element being the number of seconds left in the timeout that were not needed. (It might not work everywhere: On systems where it doesn't, the original value of timeout is returned.)

The bit vectors that were passed in as arguments are modified, and those bits corresponding to I/O streams that are ready will be turned on in the vectors; those not ready will be turned off. This is how you later determine which of the file descriptors are ready.

For example, if you have three file descriptors that might have data to be read, you must first construct a bit-vector. This is nothing more than a packed series of bits, one for each file descriptor on the system. The appropriate bit for a file descriptor that you're interested in must be turned on as follows:

```
$in_bitvector;
vec($in_bitvector, fileno(INFILE), 1)=1;
vec($in_bitvector, fileno(OTHERINFILE), 1)=1;
vec($in_bitvector, fileno(OTHERINFILE2), 1)=1;
```

Now to check whether any of those vectors can be read, simply call `select`:

```
($readable, $timeleft)=select($in_bitvector, undef, undef, 4);
```

The timeout is expressed as a number of seconds. Fractional timeouts are indicated as a decimal number of seconds (1.5 would represent a second-and-a-half timeout). Any bit-vectors you're not interested in can be replaced with `undef`. In the previous case, we weren't interested in seeing whether any file descriptors could be written or had errors.

To extract which file descriptors are ready to be read from the bit vector, use `vec` again against `$in_bitvector` (which has been modified with `select`):

```
if ($readable) {  # Something is readable
    if (vec($in_bitvector, fileno(INFILE), 1)) {
        unless (sysread(INFILE, $data, 0)) {
            die "Error: $!";
        }
    }
    if (vec($in_bitvector, fileno(OTHERINFILE), 1)) {
        unless (sysread(OTHERINFILE, $data, 0)) {
            die "Error: $!";
        }
    }
    if (vec($in_bitvector, fileno(OTHERINFILE2), 1)) {
        unless (sysread(OTHERINFILE2, $data, 0)) {
            die "Error: $!";
        }
    }
}
```

The bit-masking can be a bit confusing (Perl is simply mimicking the underlying C library calls), and a simpler interface for I/O multiplexing can be found in the `IO::Select` standard module.

It is important to note that you shouldn't use the Standard I/O–based reading (<>, readline, read), writing (print), and positioning (seek) routines with select. Buffering can cause file descriptors that appear to be ready (from select's viewpoint) to actually block when you try to use them. Use sysread, syswrite, and syssek instead.

As an interesting side-effect, a four-argument select can be used as a higher resolution sleep function. Called with three undef bit vectors, select will sleep for timeout seconds. And because timeout can be a fractional number, it's possible to sleep for less than a second, or other fractional values.

Example Listing 5.7

```
# Capture a bunch of output into a log file
#    without having to recode print statements
#    or rely on shell redirection.

open(CAPTURE, ">/tmp/logfile") || die;
# preserve old default filehandle
$old=select(CAPTURE);

# Run code here with "print" statements

select($old);
close(CAPTURE);
```

Example Listing 5.8

```
# A non-forking echoing network server
#    I/O is multiplexed and each response is handled
#    individually.  Anything sent is echo'd back.

use Fcntl qw(O_NONBLOCK F_GETFL F_SETFL);
use POSIX qw(:errno_h);
use Socket;
use IO::Handle;

socket(SOCK, AF_INET, SOCK_STREAM, getprotobyname('tcp')) || die "$!";
bind(SOCK, sockaddr_in(1100, INADDR_ANY)) || die "$!";
listen(SOCK, SOMAXCONN) || die "Listen failed: $!";
fcntl(SOCK, F_SETFL, fcntl(SOCK, F_GETFL, 0) | O_NONBLOCK) or
    die "Cannot set non-blocking";
```

```perl
while(1) {
    my $ns=IO::Handle->new();
    my ($address, $bits);
    $bits='';
    $address=accept($ns, SOCK);
    if (defined $address) {
        $ns->autoflush(1);
        $SOCKS{$ns}=$ns;
    } elsif ($! != EAGAIN) {  # Just nothing there to process if EAGAIN
        die "Error with accept: $!";
    }
    # Now process any I/O
    for(keys %SOCKS){ vec($bits, fileno($SOCKS{$_}), 1)=1; }
    $nf=select($bits, undef, $ebits=$bits, 0);
    while(($key, $fd)=each %SOCKS) {
        next unless vec $bits, fileno($fd), 1 or
            vec $ebits, fileno($fd), 1;
        $num=sysread($fd, $data, 1);
        $num or delete $SOCKS{$key} and next;
        print $fd $data;
    }
}
```

Example Listing 5.9

```perl
# Looks cool, but not entirely accurate.
sub fast_timer {
    my($duration, $resolution)=@_;
    $|=1;  # Turn on auto-flushing
    while($duration>$resolution) {
        $duration-=$resolution;
        select(undef, undef, undef, $resolution);
        printf("%5.2f\r", $duration);
    }
}
fast_timer(5,0.1);
```

> **See Also**
>
> IO::Select module documentation
>
> open and vec in this book
>
> select in the C library reference

ioctl

Usage

```
ioctl filehandle, command, value
```

Description

The `ioctl` function retrieves or alters the underlying properties of a filehandle that is connected to a `device` (similar to `fcntl`, but for device files).

It is available only under Unix, and because of its nature, it should be considered very unportable even between Unix systems. It is a catch-all function in Unix to adjust properties of `devices`. It does everything from ejecting CD-ROMs to controlling terminal behavior.

The constants needed for `ioctl` are in the `ioctl.ph` file that can be retrieved into your script with

```
require "ioctl.ph";
```

If the file doesn't exist, you will have to create one with the `h2ph` utility shipped with Perl, or by hacking your own by reading your systems' `sys/ioctl.h` C header file.

The `ioctl` function returns a number upon success or the string `0` `but` `true`. The string `0` `but` `true` is explained in the `fcntl` entry. Upon failure, `undef` is returned, and `$!` is set to the error message.

The commands are system-specific, as well as the values associated with those commands. The `ioctl` manual page for your system will have general documentation, and the `device` manual pages will have specific information for those devices.

Example Listing 5.10

```
# Read the number of characters pending at the
#    terminal using FIONREAD.  The terminal
#    setup could have been done with ioctl() but
#    Term::ReadKey is much more sane.
# Works under Linux kernel 2.2, after running
#    cd /usr/include; h2ph -r -l .    as root.

use Term::ReadKey;
require 'sys/ioctl.ph';
```

```
open(TTY, "/dev/tty") || die;
ReadMode 'raw';           # So that a return isn't necessary

# During this sleep, type some characters.
#   No need to hit return.
sleep 3;

$bytes=pack("L", 0);      # FIONREAD expects a long
ioctl(TTY, FIONREAD(), $bytes) or die "ioctl: $!\n";
$bytes=unpack("L", $bytes);

ReadMode 'restore';       # Put the terminal back
print "Bytes waiting: $bytes\n";
```

> **See Also**
> `Term::ReadKey` module documentation
>
> `fcntl` in this book
>
> `ioctl` in the C library reference

binmode

Usage

```
binmode filehandle
binmode filehandle, disciplines
```

Description

On operating systems in which file I/O distinguishes between text and binary files, Perl opens files in text mode by default. Using disciplines with the open function allows you to change the type of filehandle that is opened. The binmode function takes an existing filehandle and causes Perl to start treating the filehandle as binary.

Whether to use binmode depends on the operating system and the kinds of data you're dealing with. Common operating systems that distinguish between text and binary mode are VMS and MS-DOS based systems (including MS-Windows). If you're dealing only with text files, binmode is unnecessary.

If you're dealing with binary files, the operating system will do automatic translation of some byte sequences that are being read or written. For example, writing \n on an MS-DOS system will always cause a carriage-return/linefeed character sequence to be written to a text stream. This is expected because \n represents a logical end-of-line. However, if you want to write a literal carriage return to a file by itself, and if the stream is in text-mode, MS-DOS will translate that to carriage-return/linefeed automagically.

This can cause problems when dealing with data that shouldn't be treated as text, such as images, database files, and executable object code. In those situations, you should use binmode on those filehandles.

The binmode function does nothing on operating systems that don't distinguish between binary and text files (such as Unix).

The second form of binmode is new in 5.6 and allows you to assign a discipline to an already open filehandle. For a full discussion of disciplines, see the discipline entry in this book. This form also is useful on systems that don't distinguish between text and binary files.

Example Listing 5.11

```
# A CGI script that puts up an appropriate image
#    (in files named month1.jpg, month2.jpg, etc...) for each
#    day of the month.  Called with:
#            <IMG SRC="/cgi-bin/scriptname.pl">

use CGI qw(:standard);
print header("image/jpeg");

($mday)=(localtime)[3];
open( CNT, "/home/httpd/counter/month$days.jpg") || die;

# Both input and output must be in binary!
binmode(STDOUT);
binmode(CNT);
print STDOUT <CNT>;
close(CNT);
```

> **See Also**
> disciplines and open in this book

eof

Usage

```
eof filehandle
eof
eof()
```

Description

The eof (*end of file*) function tests a filehandle to see whether any data is left to be read, or whether it is open. If the filehandle is exhausted, or not open, eof will return true. Otherwise it returns false.

The filehandle can be an identifier, or it can be an indirect filehandle as explained in the open entry.

It is common to mistake eof for a character in a data stream (^Z in DOS, or ^D in Unix). The eof function reports on the state of the filehandle, and true end of file has nothing to do with whether those characters have been read (or are about to be).

Calling the eof function with empty parenthesis—eof()—will test the ARGV pseudo-filehandle. This filehandle is used by the <> operator (when empty) to read the contents of the arguments passed to the script, or STDIN.

An eof function all by itself—with no parentheses, and no filehandle—will test the status of the last file read. While reading <>, this means the file currently being processed.

The eof function doesn't work well with programs that are using terminal I/O, socket I/O, or anything reading on a stream. It works by reading a byte from the input stream and pushing it back, which is unsuitable for interactive use.

Example Listing 5.12

```
# Print the files given on the command line
#    with formfeed characters between them

while(<>) {
    if (eof) {
        print "\n\cL";
    }
    print;
}
```

> **See Also**
> open, <, and > in this book

`fileno`

Usage

```
fileno filehandle
```

Description

The `fileno` function returns the file descriptor represented by the given filehandle. Internally the C library (which Perl is built on) represents files as a simple number, a positive integer with a range of 0 to `INT_MAX` on your system, although the practical limit is the number of open files allowed by your process and the OS. If the filehandle is closed, `fileno` returns `undef`.

A *filehandle* is a structure in Perl (and in C) that contains a standard I/O structure (called a `FILE *`), and the I/O libraries in C use this as a high-level interface to the underlying filesystem. In actuality, open files are merely referred to as an integer offset in an open file table in the OS. The Standard I/O library keeps a lot of meta-information on the file separate and above your OS's information.

For example, `STDIN` is a filehandle. The file descriptor usually associated with `STDIN` is 0; `STDOUT` is 1, and `STDERR` is 3. The next file opened will normally receive the next available file descriptor (in the normal case, 4). But this isn't guaranteed.

The file descriptor is needed by some I/O functions (notably, `select`) in order to function properly.

Example Listing 5.13

```
print fileno(STDIN), "\n";    # Expect 0
print fileno(STDOUT), "\n";   # Expect 1
print fileno(STDERR), "\n";   # Expect 2

open(FOO, ">&=STDOUT") || die "$!";  # dup STDOUT
print fileno(FOO), "\n";      # Expect 1 as well.
```

> **See Also**
> `select` and `open` in this book
> `fileno` in the C library reference

`flock`

Usage

```
flock filehandle, lock_type
```

Description

The `flock` function provides advisory locking under POSIX operating environments (for example, Unix or NT). The `flock` function is used to set, upgrade, and release a lock. Upon success, `flock` returns true; otherwise it returns `undef` and sets `$!` to the error message.

If a lock cannot be set because of another lock that has the resource, the `flock` function will block, or wait, until the lock can be set. This behavior can be changed by bitwise oring the flag `LOCK_NB` with `lock_type` when requesting the lock.

The *filehandle* is an open filehandle or a filehandle-like object. See the `open` entry for details. The `lock_type` is a mask of flags that determine what kind of lock you're trying to set or unset. The constants for the `lock_type` flags are available in the `Fcntl` module, and are in the import group `:flock`.

Advisory file locking is exactly as it sounds: A `flock` doesn't prevent others from modifying the file; it only prevents others from obtaining a lock. In order to protect your data from concurrent access (and corruption), each process that accesses the data must take out a lock on the same resource.

Three kinds of locks can be obtained with `lock_type`. The first is `LOCK_SH`, which is a shared lock: More than one program can obtain a shared lock at a time. While a shared lock is in effect, an exclusive lock cannot be obtained. Normally, a shared lock is used when read access to a file is desired, and the file must be opened for reading.

A `LOCK_EX` is an exclusive lock. In order for a `LOCK_EX` to be set, no other locks can be present. The exclusive lock is typically used when writing to a file is desired, and normally the file has to be open for writing.

To release the lock on the file, specify a `lock_type` of `LOCK_UN` or close the filehandle. Locks aren't inherited from parent to child in Unix, so if a fork is done after a lock is obtained, only the parent will retain the lock. On some systems, locks are retained across `exec` if the `close-on-exec` flag for the file is false (see `fcntl`).

The `flock` function can be implemented at the system level with the I/O library calls to `fcntl(3)` or `flock(3)` (most of the time it's `fcntl`), but Perl's `flock` imitates the `flock` behavior from your system's documentation.

Care should be taken to avoid *deadlocks*, which are two processes waiting on each other's locks. This usually can be solved by always obtaining multiple locks in the same order each time, and releasing them in the reverse order in which they were obtained.

Another danger to be aware of is race conditions. For example, because the `flock` function requires an open filehandle, the following statements:

```
# DANGER: Bad code, explained below.
use Fcntl qw(:flock);
open(FH, ">/tmp/file") or die;
flock(FH, LOCK_EX) or warn "Cannot lock: $!";
```

generate a condition in which you've modified the file (truncating it with `open >`) before a lock on the file was obtained. This is wrong. To avoid this, obtain a lock on a second file (a *semaphore* file) whose contents can be trashed, and use this as a general-purpose locking mechanism. Example Listing 5.14 shows a good set of general-purpose lock functions.

Example Listing 5.14

```
# General-purpose locking functions.  Ready to cut-and-paste
#   read_lock and write_lock will be non-blocking if
#   passed a true argument.  It is up to the caller
#   to check for errors.
{
    use Fcntl qw(:flock);
    use IO::Handle;
    my $semaphore_file="/tmp/sem";
    my $sem=IO::Handle->new();

    sub make_lock {
        unless ( defined fileno($sem)) {
            open($sem, ">$semaphore_file")
                or die "Cannot create lockfile: $!";
        }
```

```
    }
    sub read_lock {
        make_lock();
        my $st=flock($sem, LOCK_SH | (@_?LOCK_NB:0) );
        return $st if (! $st );
        1;
    }
    sub write_lock {
        make_lock();
        my $st=flock($sem, LOCK_EX | (@_?LOCK_NB:0) );
        return $st if (! $st);
        1;
    }
    sub un_lock {
        close($sem);
    }
}
```

Example Listing 5.15

```
# Exerciser for the locking functions above (you must include them).
#    Updating a counter in a file.

# Try this without the locks sometime, to see how data gets
#     mangled from concurrent access.
#   Make more evil by forking more than once.

use Fcntl qw(:DEFAULT :seek);
use IO::Handle;

sysopen(SCORE, "/tmp/score", O_CREAT | O_RDWR | O_TRUNC) || die;
SCORE->autoflush(1);

$pid=fork;
foreach(1..1000) {
    write_lock;
    seek SCORE, 0, SEEK_SET;
    $r=<SCORE>;
    sysseek SCORE, 0, SEEK_SET;
    $r++;
    print SCORE "$r\n";
    un_lock;
}
```

```
exit unless $pid;
wait;
seek SCORE, 0, SEEK_SET;
print <SCORE>;
close(SCORE);
```

See Also
Fcntl module documentation

open, sysopen, and fcntl in this book

flock and fcntl in the C library reference

Reading and Writing Filehandles

open

Usage
```
open filehandle
open filehandle, pathname
open filehandle, command
open filehandle, mode, list
```

Description

The open function associates a filehandle with a file, file descriptor, pipe, or other filehandle. Upon success, the open function returns true. If the open function were used to create a pipe to another process (under Unix), the process ID of the child is the return value.

Upon failure, the $! variable will contain the error message. (It is only valid if the open function actually returns false.) It is a common programming mistake to forget to check the return value of open. File opens can fail for a variety of reasons including insufficient permission, if the file does not exist, or if your system has run out of open files.

```
open(MYFILE, ">myfile");    # WRONG
print MYFILE "Hello, world";
```

The common form of open is the two argument form. Most of the time, the filehandle is simply an identifier (by convention, uppercase). This identifier can be used wherever Perl expects to find a filehandle.

```
# Simple identifier
open(SAMP, "/tmp/sample.txt") || die "Cannot open sample.txt: $!";
```

The filehandle also can be an expression whose value will be associated with the opened filehandle. The expression can be a simple `scalar` value, or it can be a reference to an object that is interpreted as filehandle (such as an `IO::Handle` object). These are called *indirect filehandles*.

Indirect filehandles can be used anywhere a normal filehandle is expected.

```
# Indirect filehandle
$password="Password";
open $password, "/etc/passwd" or die "Cannot open /etc/passwd: $!";

$first=<$password>
```

It is often useful to have automatically generated filehandles. One way of doing this is to use a scalar variable for an indirect filehandle whose value is undef at the time the open is performed. The open function will define the variable for you, and set it to an open filehandle reference—if the open succeeds.

The other method is to use the `Symbol` module's `gensym` function to create a unique reference for you (an anonymous `GLOB`) that can be used as a filehandle. In either case, when the scalar variable falls out of scope, the filehandle will be closed for you.

```
sub process {
    my $handle;
    if (open($handle, ">/tmp/proc.pod")) {
        print $handle $$;
        return;
    } else {
        warn "Cannot write to PID file: $!";
    }
}  # $handle is automagically closed for you here.
```

A finite number of open files are available to your process. Opening too many will cause future opens to fail (with `EMFILE`) until some open files have been closed. Calling open on a filehandle that is already open will cause the filehandle to be closed and then re-opened (it does not however reset $.).

If open is called with only one argument, there is assumed to be a `scalar` package variable (not a `lexical`) with the same name as the filehandle present in the current scope. The variable should contain the pathname (pipeline, and so on) and any mode information you need to open the filehandle:

```
$FILE=">+/tmp/sample.txt";
open FILE or die "Cannot open $FILE: $!";
```

When open is called with two arguments, the first argument is the filehandle. The second argument indicates the pathname or command that is to be opened and the modes that should be used.

If the second argument is a pathname, it consists of a mode followed by the pathname of the file to be opened. The mode will be explained shortly. The pathname should be in the format that your operating system expects. For example, Windows and Unix should use forward slashes as pathname separators, and MacOS should use colons. If you indicate a relative pathname, it should be relative to the current working directory of the Perl process—this can be found out with the Cwd module.

The pathname shouldn't contain environment variables, tildes, or other OS shell metacharacters. They won't be passed to a shell in the case of a normal open. So,

```
open(MAIL, "~/mbox") || die "Opening mbox: $!";  # WRONG
```

probably won't work the way you would expect. This will attempt to open the literal filename mbox in the subdirectory ~.

If the pathname comes from an environment in which the data is not trustworthy (users, CGI forms, network clients, and so on), the pathname could contain characters that might cause unexpected and unsafe behavior. For example, if you're expecting a simple filename to be opened as follows:

```
chomp($file=<STDIN>);  # Get the filename
open(LOGFILE, ">$file") || die;
```

this could be subverted if the user types > at the beginning of the filename (not to mention .. or / within the filename). This particular shortcoming can be avoided if you use the three-argument form of open, explained in the following. You also might think of using taint-mode Perl.

The mode argument indicates how the file (or pipeline) should be opened. It can be opened generally for reading, writing, or both.

The mode in which the file is opened can be indicated to open in one of two ways. In the two-argument form of open, the mode is appended to the front (or the back) of the pathname or command to be opened; for example, to open a file for writing:

```
open(OUTFILE, ">/tmp/output") || die "output: $!";
```

The > character indicates that /tmp/output is opened for write access, and that it should be created if it doesn't exist. If the file does exist, the contents of the file should be *clobbered* (erased). The default mode, if not specified, is <, which is an input mode.

To be completely unambiguous, the mode can be specified as a separate argument to open (the three argument form of open). If, for example, you want to create a file that begins with a > character, the three-argument form can be used to indicate this as follows:

```
# Because open(F, ">>outfile") is not our intent
#
open(F, ">", ">outfile") || die "Cannot create >outfile: $!";
```

The modes that are available are

Mode	Read	Write	Append	Create if Doesn't Exist	Erase if Exists
<pathname	Yes	No	No	No	No
>pathname	No	Yes	No	Yes	Yes
>>pathname	No	Yes	Yes	Yes	No
+>pathname	Yes	Yes	No	Yes	Yes
+<pathname	Yes	Yes	No	No	No
+>>pathname	Yes	Yes	Yes	Yes	No
|command	No	Yes			
command|	Yes	No			

Append indicates that when the file is opened, the file pointer will be placed at the end of the file, and all subsequent writes will occur at the end. The create option indicates that if the file doesn't exist and the user has sufficient permission, the file will be created. The file will be created with the permissions of 0666 (Unix) modified by the umask. The erase option will clear the contents of the file when it is opened.

The + in a mode indicates that you want to read and write to the filehandle. With the seek function, you can move the current file pointer around in the file to read and write to different parts of the file (if this is allowed).

Also allowed in the mode (three-argument form only) are I/O disciplines. These are essentially filters that process the data as they're being read. In Perl 5.6, only two disciplines are enabled: `:raw` and `:crlf`. These correspond to binary and text modes for operating systems that distinguish between the two (MS-Windows, DOS and VMS). For operating systems that don't care about binary, these have no effect. The disciplines are indicated as follows:

```
open(IMAGE, "<:raw", "picture.jpg") || die "Cannot open picture: $!";
```

More disciplines are planned: most to enhance Unicode and alternate character set handling.

Some kinds of filenames cause the `open` function to behave in special ways.

Using `-` as a filename indicates that `STDIN` or `STDOUT` should be used. This allows you to connect another filehandle `STDIN` or `STDOUT`.

```
open(IN, "-") or die "Cannot dup STDIN: $!";
```

A filename that is a simple identifier preceded by an ampersand is treated as a filehandle. This filehandle will be duplicated onto the new filehandle specified with `open`:

```
open(OUTF, ">outfile") || die "Cannot open outfile: $!";
open(OUTF2, ">&OUTF") || die "Cannot dup filehandle: $!";
# OUTF and OUTF2 now are both opened for output to outfile.
```

Unix filehandles are assigned numbers (file descriptors) in the kernel. Some of these are well-known, and others can be created in a shell with a specific number. To duplicate an already open file descriptor by number, you can use a number with `&` instead of an identifier:

```
open(ERRCOPY, ">&2") || die;  # Dup's standard err (STDERR), normally fd 2
```

The most useful reason to `dup` filehandles is to save them before re-opening them to another target (for example, to redirect `STDOUT` and `STDERR` to hide an external command's output). An example of this is given later.

Also unique to Unix is the `close-on-exec` attribute for filehandles. Normally in Perl, the three standard filehandles—`STDOUT`, `STDIN` and `STDERR`—remain open after an `exec` is performed. All other filehandles are closed. To have a filehandle remain open for an exec'd process, you should either use the `$^F` special variable to raise the number of file descriptors that will be passed through the `exec`, or use the `fcntl` function to clear the `close-on-exec` attribute for the filehandle after it has been opened.

In addition to opening associating filehandles with files and file descriptors, the `open` function also is used to connect a filehandle with an external process's input or output. This is called *opening a pipe*.

To run an external command and read its output, simply put a pipe symbol (|) behind the *command* in the `open` function:

```
open(DIR, "ls -l|") || warn "Cannot start command: $!";
@DIRECTORY=<DIR>;
close(DIR) || warn "ls -l failed with status $?: $!";
```

This causes `ls -l` to be run as an external command. Any output from the command can then be read as it's produced using the filehandle `DIR`. The filehandle is read-only, and you cannot use `seek` to reposition it.

To write to an external command, put the pipe symbol before the command in the `open` function:

```
open(PRINTER, "| lpr") || warn "Cannot start lpr: $!";
print PRINTER @data;
close(PRINTER) || warn "Printing failed: $?: $!";
```

This creates an output handle to the `lpr` process that, presumably, will take the information sent to it and queue it for printing.

It is important when opening a pipe to check both the `open` and `close` functions for successful completion. The `open` function will fail only if the initial `fork` to create the new process fails. If the external command itself fails and returns an error status, the calling program won't know until the `close` is performed. At this point, the exit status is returned to the caller.

The command used is subject to processing by your shell if it contains shell metacharacters (other than the |). For example, to capture both the STDERR and STDOUT of a command, you can use normal shell redirection syntax:

```
open(CMD, "command 2>&1 |") || warn "command failed: $!";
```

The command syntax allowed is for `/bin/sh`, or its equivalent under Unix. Under other operating systems, it's the default command interpreter. For example, under Windows NT, it's `CMD.EXE`.

If you want to avoid this command interpretation, you can use the three-argument form of `open` with a list.

```
open(CMD, "|-", "pod2html", "myprog.pm") || warn "pod2html failed: $!";
```

This will prevent metacharacters from being interpreted by a shell. This is similar to the mechanism used by the system function.

The - (as you've just seen) is special when used with pipes also. In its simplest form, it causes the perl process to fork: One process will be designated as the parent (the one for which open returns true) and the other the child. Two processes can then communicate through the pipe.

Whether the parent reads or writes is determined by the position of the pipe. Opening the pipe -| makes the parent process the reader, and the child the writer. Opening the pipe |- makes the parent process the writer, and the child the reader.

The open function won't allow you to open a pipe both to and from a command at the same time. To achieve this functionality, you should investigate the IPC::Open2 and IPC::Open3 modules.

Example Listing 5.16

```perl
# Open up all of the logfiles in /var/log/httpd
#     build a hash of open filehandles.
#
use Symbol;

foreach( glob "/var/log/httpd/*.log" ) {
    $logfh{$_}=gensym();
    open( $logfh{$_}, $_ ) || warn "Couldn't open $_: $!";
}
```

Example Listing 5.17

```perl
# Run an external command, while transparently
#   hiding its output and errors in a file
# Uses POSIX to generate a unique, safe, temporary
#   filename.

use POSIX;

# Save off STDOUT and STDERR
open(OUTCOPY, ">&STDOUT") or warn;
open(ERRCOPY, ">&STDERR") or warn;

$tmp=POSIX::tmpnam();
open(STDOUT, ">$tmp" ) || die "Cannot open $tmp: $!";
```

```perl
open(STDERR, ">&STDOUT") or warn;

system("lsof");   # Gets redirected to our tempfile.
close(STDOUT);
close(STDERR);

open(STDOUT, ">&OUTCOPY");
open(STDERR, ">&ERRCOPY");
```

Example Listing 5.18

```perl
# Having a process fork, and then talk to itself
#    via a filehandle
#
unless (defined ($pid=open(CHILD, "-|"))) {
    die "Cannot fork: $!";
}
if ($pid) {
    print <CHILD>;
} else {
    # Stdout of the child is now connected to
    #       CHILD in the parent process.
    print "Here's the results!\n";
}
```

See Also

IPC::Open2, IO::Handle, and IPC::Open3 module documentation

perlopentut in the perl documentation

close, filehandles, exec, seek, pipe, binmode, $?, $!, $., system, fork, umask, $^F, and fcntl in this book

open in the C library reference

---

sysopen

Usage

```perl
sysopen filehandle, pathname, mode, mask
sysopen filehandle, pathname, mode
```

Description

The sysopen function provides the same basic services as the open function; however, finer control over how the operating system opens the file is provided because sysopen is simply a front end to the native OS's open system call. See the open entry for a general description of Perl's file I/O.

A regular identifier can be used for a *filehandle*, or a scalar variable that contains a reference to an IO::Handle object as described in open. The filehandle sysopen'd is completely compatible with all the normal I/O functions.

The *pathname* describes the file that you want opened. Unlike open, the pathname cannot contain pipes, use disciplines, or use any of the & syntax for duplicating an open filehandle, and the pathname cannot contain leading and trailing whitespace or a - (unless you mean them literally). The sysopen function is limited to opening files in the filesystem.

The *mode* describes how you want the file opened. The constants are available from the Fcntl module, and will differ from one operating system to another. Some of the more common modes are described as follows:

Flag	Meaning
O_RDONLY	Opens the file for read-only access
O_WRONLY	Opens the file for write-only access
O_RDWR	Opens the file for reading and writing
O_CREAT	Creates the file if it doesn't exist
O_EXCL	Fails if the file already exists (normally coupled with O_CREAT)
O_APPEND	Writing should append to the end of the file
O_TRUNC	Truncates the file (set the file length to 0, use with O_WRONLY or O_RDWR)
O_NONBLOCK	If the pathname is a named pipe, or device file then reads and writes will not block
O_TEXT	Opens in text mode (on systems that distinguish text/binary)
O_BINARY	Opens in binary mode (on systems that distinguish text/binary)
O_LARGEFILE	Enables files >2GB. Default in 5.6.
O_SYNC	Writes to the physical I/O device after every logical write.

For a full list of modes, check your system's open manual page. To combine various modes together for a single open, simply bitwise-or them together:

```
sysopen(LOGFILE, "/tmp/proclog", O_WRONLY | O_CREAT | O_SYNC, 0644)
    or warn "Logfile cannot be opened: $!";
```

The *mask* is the set of permission bits that you want on the file created (if the O_CREAT flag is specified) under Unix. The mask is modified by your current umask. If no mask is specified (and O_CREAT is), the mask 0666 will be used.

Example Listing 5.19

```
# Open a file for writing and append, but it must have
#    previously existed
use Fcntl;
sysopen(FH, $logfile, O_WRONLY | O_APPEND) ||
    die "Cannot append to $logfile: $!";
```

> **See Also**
> umask, open, and Fcntl in this book
> open in the C library reference

disciplines

Usage

```
open filehandle, discipline, pathname

use open IN => discipline
use open OUT => discipline
```

Description

Disciplines are a new feature to 5.6, and their stated intent is to allow filtering of input and output streams transparent to the perl program (for example, to allow Unicode I/O for a program that isn't Unicode aware, or to handle binary and text translations for operating systems that differentiate).

As of this writing, discipline support in Perl 5.6 is somewhat incomplete.

A discipline can be established on a filehandle when it is opened:

```
open LOG, ":crlf", "/var/spool/logfile" or die "logfile: $!";
```

The input or output filehandles can be tagged with a discipline within a lexical scope using the use open pragma. Within the lexical scope, input and output filehandles are affected by any use open pragmas. This affects the implicit filehandles used by backticks, qx, and pipes. It doesn't affect filehandles opened with sysopen or opened with open and a specific set of disciplines.

Example Listing 5.20

```
use open OUT => ":raw";

open(FH, ">/tmp/mixed") || die;
print FH "How's it hanging?\r";
close(FH);
```

> **See Also**
> open module documentation
> open in this book

`<>`

Usage

```
<>
<filehandle>
<globpattern>
```

Description

The angle bracket operator (<>) actually has three distinct uses in Perl. Depending on what's inside the angle brackets, it can be used for processing @ARGV files, reading filehandles, and globbing files.

The most common use for the angle operator is when it's used as a line input operator (synonymous with the readline function). In this form, the angle operator contains a filehandle to be read:

```
$c=<FH>;   # Same as $c=readline(FH);
```

The filehandle can either be an identifier that has been opened as a filehandle, or it can be a plain scalar variable that represents an open filehandle object, such as an indirect filehandle or an IO::Handle object (described in the open entry).

It is important to note that any old scalar value isn't an acceptable substitute in angle brackets (unlike almost everywhere else in Perl in which a scalar value and a scalar variable are nearly interchangeable). For example, `<$foo>` represents an indirect filehandle being read with the line input operator; `<$hash{foo}>` represents a glob being performed with (see the following).

In a scalar context, the line input operator returns one line of input, which includes the trailing input record separator—usually a newline character, a carriage-return linefeed, or something similar; it's specified in `$/`.

In a list context, the file is read and assigned to the list. Each element of the list (or array) will receive one line of input. When the end of file is reached, the operator will return `undef`.

The return value from the angle operator is normally assigned to a variable explicitly. There is a special case, however. When the angle operator is the only operator within a `while` condition, the results of the read are assigned to `$_` automatically; for example,

```
while(<FH>) {
    print;
}
```

The line input operator will assign to `$_` automatically and then execute the loop until the filehandle `FH` is exhausted. (angle bracket operator)>)> (angle bracket)> (angle bracket) operator>This is functionally the same as stating the following:

```
while(defined ($_=<FH>)) {
    print;
}
```

but much more terse and to the point. And because `for(;;)` is just a convenient synonym for `while()`, the loop `for(;<FH>;)` does about the same thing. The longer `while` form is generally more useful when you want to explicitly assign to a variable other than `$_` in a `while` loop. If you want to assign to a variable and localize it to the `while` loop, you can declare the variable with `local` or `my` within the loop:

```
while(local $_ = <FH> ) {
    # dynamically scoped $_ in here
}

while(my $line=<FH>) {
    # lexically scoped $line in here
}
```

It's a common mistake to simply use the line input operator as a statement by itself:

```
print "Hello, World\n";
<FH>;                    # Wrong!
print "The value is: $_";
```

Because the filehandle will be read and then the value discarded, $_ is unaffected by this piece of code. The <>/$_ magic only works by itself in a while loop.

Be careful of context with the line-input operator. Using the operator in a list context will cause the entire file to be read in, which could consume a lot of memory:

```
@lines=<FH>;  # Nice feature, but can use a lot of memory.
```

The other accidental consequence is using it in a context that wasn't intended; for example,

```
($c)=<FH>;  # keep only first line, discard the rest
```

This is probably a waste. The remaining portion of the file is read and discarded, and only the first line is assigned to $c.

The second use for the angle brackets is a special case of the line-input operator. When no filehandle is specified, the angle operator opens and reads files that are specified in the @ARGV array (script arguments). If the array is empty, standard input is used. In this way, a perl program can be called as a filter on a pipeline:

```
program | myscript.pl > outfile
```

or on the command line with files to process as arguments:

```
myscript.pl file1 file2 file3
```

without having to do anything special in the script other than to read <>. So the following loop:

```
while(<>) {
    # Process lines...
}
```

will essentially:

If @ARGV is used, shift the first value from @ARGV into the special variable $ARGV. If @ARGV is empty, assign - to $ARGV (which will cause STDIN to be read).

Read a line from the file specified in $ARGV and continue to read until no lines are left. Each line is assigned to $_. When the file is exhausted, loop up and get another file from @ARGV.

This allows for some useful tricks. Anything that open can deal with can be put into the @ARGV array (because it'll just be passed implicitly to open anyway). You can push - into @ARGV to process STDIN, pipes to process input from other processes, or regular files. For example, as a shortcut for the following:

```
if (open(FH, "myfile")) {
    while(<FH>) {
        print;   # print the file's contents
    }
    close(FH);
} else {
    warn "Cannot open myfile: $!";
}
```

you could simply say

```
@ARGV="myfile";
while(<>) { print; }
```

When end of file is encountered while reading, <> will return undef and eof returns true. If you attempt to read <>, STDIN will be processed from that point on.

The last (and somewhat looked-down-upon) use for the angle brackets is for file globbing. File globbing is taking a pattern (something similar to a regular expression, but not quite) and letting Perl return all the filenames that match the pattern.

To do file globbing, inside of the angles, you need to place a pattern to be expanded. Anything other than a simple scalar variable or an identifier (representing an open filehandle) will trigger the globbing behavior.

The globbing operator in a scalar context returns one globbed name at a time. In a list context, it returns the entire list of files matching the glob. If no files are found, it returns undef. Within the angles, some interpolation is done; however putting a simple scalar variable in the angles won't cause it to be interpolated—instead it'll be treated the same as an indirect filehandle.

For example, to return a list of files that have the extension .c, the syntax is as follows:

```
@cfiles=<*.c>;
```

The more acceptable way to perform a glob is to use the `glob` named operator, which, in turn, is simply a wrapper for the module `File::Glob` as explained in the `glob` entry.

The globbing operator, when performing a `glob`, will behave similar to the line input operator performing a file read inside a `while` loop. That is,

```
while(<*.txt>) {
    $size+=(stat)[7];
}
```

will cause `$_` to be assigned to each file returned by the `glob` one at a time. It is important to note that a glob's position in the list can be reset only by finishing the `glob` read. For example, if the `glob` in scalar context has returned 5 of 20 matching files so far, the remaining 15 must somehow be returned before the `glob` can be used again to read the list.

Full details on the patterns used by the file `glob` operator are found in the `File::Glob` module's documentation. The globbing angle operator (and the `glob` function) are just front ends for the `File::Glob` module's `glob` function.

Example Listing 5.21

```
# Process some command-line arguments (-d,-e arg or -t)
#    and any files that are in the bunch.  Or STDIN if no
#    files specified

use Getopt::Std;

getopts('de:t',\%opts);
while(<>) {
    print $_;
}
```

Example Listing 5.22

```
# Copy all important files into a temporary
#    backup directory
```

```
use File::Copy;
warn "backup directory cannot be created: $!"
    unless mkdir "/tmp/backup";
die "backup is not a directory" unless (-d "/tmp/backup");
while(<*.c *.pl *.pm *.html *.txt>) {
    ($targ=$_)=~s#^#/tmp/backup/#;
    copy($_, $targ);
}
```

> **See Also**
> File::Glob module documentation
> glob, readlline, $/, eof, $_, and @ARGV in this book

getc

Usage

```
getc
getc filehandle
```

Description

The getc function reads one byte from the filehandle and returns it. If the filehandle isn't specified, one byte will be retrieved from STDIN. If the filehandle is exhausted or an error occurs, getc will return undef.

The getc function works by reading one byte from the C Standard I/O library buffers. Because of the buffering, it's not well-suited for trying to grab one character from an interactive source (such as a socket or a keyboard). If the buffer is empty, the terminal driver must fill it, which might mean waiting for a carriage return to be pressed.

A good solution for single-key responses from a user is the Term::ReadKey module from CPAN or using the Termios structure in the standard POSIX module. These can be used to put the terminal into cbreak mode, where input can be processed one character at a time.

Example Listing 5.23

```
# Retrieve 1 key of input from the user

use Term::ReadKey;

ReadMode('cbreak');
$|=1;                    # Auto-flush output

print "Press any key to continue: ";
$key=getc;

ReadMode('normal');
```

> **See Also**
>
> Term::ReadKey and POSIX module documentation
>
> readline in this book
>
> getc in the C library reference

read

Usage

```
read filehandle, scalar, length, offset
read filehandle, scalar, length
```

Description

The read function reads length bytes from the specified filehandle into the variable at scalar. If an offset is specified, the read begins placing its data at offset bytes from the start of scalar. Upon success, read returns the number of bytes read (or 0 at eof). If read fails, it returns undef and sets $! to the error message.

If offset is negative, read places the data starting at offset bytes from the end of the scalar. If offset isn't specified, the data is placed at the beginning of the variable. The scalar variable is stretched or shrunk to fit the data.

The filehandle must be an open filehandle, represented either as an identifier or as a scalar variable that refers to an IO::Handle like object. See the open entry for details.

The read function is the opposite of the print function in Perl—read is the general-purpose standard I/O reading function, whereas readline and <> read data a line at a time. The write function, oddly, has nothing at all to do with the read function, so beware.

Because the read function is a standard I/O function, do not use syswrite, sysread, or sysseek on the same filehandle as read.

Example Listing 5.24

```
# Display a file as though typed by a painfully
#    slow typist.

open(TXT, "/tmp/sample.txt") || die;
$|=1;
while(read(TXT, $let, 1+rand(2))) {
    print $let;
    select(undef, undef, undef, rand(10)/10);
}
close(TXT);
```

> **See Also**
> print and open in this book
> fread in the C library reference

readline

Usage

```
readline filehandle
```

Description

The readline function is the internal mechanism by which the <> line input operator works—but it's available for you to use as well. (However, it doesn't duplicate the globbing or @ARGV processing properties of <>.)

In summary, the readline function reads the next line of input from filehandle and returns it in a scalar context. In a list context, it reads the remainder of the filehandle and returns that. When the filehandle is exhausted, it returns undef. For more details, see the <> entry.

The filehandle for `readline` can be an identifier that has been opened as a filehandle or an indirect filehandle as with `<>`. However, you also can use a `typeglob`, a reference to a `typeglob`, or an `IO::Handle` object with `readline`.

Example Listing 5.25

```
# Demonstrate the possible variations of
#    reading a line from a file.  Read the first 9 lines
#    using a different method for each.

use IO::Handle;
use Fcntl qw(:seek);

my $handle=new IO::Handle;
open(FOO, "/tmp/sample.txt") or die "Sample: $!";
open($handle,  "/tmp/sample.txt") or die "Sample: $!";
$indirect="FOO";

# All of these do essentially the same thing
for (    q{ readline FOO },
    q{ readline "FOO" },
    q{ readline *FOO },
    q{ readline \*FOO },
    q{ <FOO> },
    q{ <$handle> },
    q{ readline($handle) },
    q{ readline $indirect },
    q{ ndirect } ) {

    # Keep the two filehandle positions in sync
    tell(FOO) > tell($handle)?seek($handle,tell(FOO), SEEK_SET):
        seek(FOO, tell($handle), SEEK_SET);

    print "$_:", scalar eval;
}
```

> **See Also**
> `IO::Handle` module documentation
> `< >`, and `open` in this book

sysread

Usage

```
sysread filehandle, scalar, size, offset
sysread filehandle, scalar, size
```

Description

The sysread function attempts to read size bytes from filehandle into the scalar variable. Upon success, the number of bytes successfully read is returned (it might be less than the size you requested); at the end of file, 0 is returned. If an error occurs, undef is returned and $! is set to the error message.

The filehandle doesn't have to be opened with sysopen and can be any open identifier or reference to an IO::Handle object.

The scalar variable will shrink and grow to hold the data read by sysread. If offset is specified, the read data will be put starting at that position from the beginning of scalar. If the offset is outside of the size of the scalar, an exception will be raised.

The sysread function bypasses the standard I/O libraries for your system and uses a low-level read function. This means that mixing calls with read, readline, <>, print, seek, tell, eof, printf, write, or any other standard I/O function isn't advisable. Buffering issues, as well as interrupted reads, must be handled by you.

Example Listing 5.26

```
# Read a single key from the keyboard
#  Unix-only.  Win32 solution will involve the
#  Win32::Console module

use Term::ReadKey;
$|=1;
print "Press a key: ";
ReadMode 'raw';           # So that a return isn't necessary
unless ( defined (sysread(STDIN, $key, 1))) {
    die "sysread error: $!";
}
ReadMode 'restore';       # Put the terminal back
print "\nYou typed: $key\n";
```

> **See Also**
> syswrite and sysseek in this book

syswrite

Usage

```
syswrite filehandle, scalar, size, offset
syswrite filehandle, scalar, size
syswrite filehandle, scalar
```

Description

The syswrite function writes size bytes to the filehandle from the scalar variable. If an offset is specified, the bytes are taken starting at that offset. A successful syswrite will return the actual number of bytes written (which might be less than size). If an error occurs, undef is returned and $! is set to the error message.

If offset is beyond the end of the scalar, an error will occur. If offset is specified as a negative number, syswrite begins using data at offset bytes from the end of the scalar. If offset isn't specified, the offset is assumed to be 0. If size isn't specified, the entire scalar value will be written.

The filehandle doesn't have to be opened with sysopen and can be any open identifier or reference to an IO::Handle object.

The syswrite function bypasses the standard I/O libraries for your system and uses a low-level write function. This means that mixing calls with read, readline, <>, print, seek, tell, eof, printf, write, or any other standard I/O function isn't advisable. Buffering issues, as well as interrupted writes, must be handled by you.

Example Listing 5.27

```
# Create a file with a hole in it. (A "sparse" file.)
#    The actual space used will be 5 bytes, the size
#    reported will be almost 1MB.

use Fcntl qw(:seek);

open(OUT, ">/tmp/output") || die "output: $!";

sysseek(OUT, 1024000, SEEK_SET);
unless (syswrite(OUT, "Hello")) {
    die "Could not write: $!";
}
```

See Also
sysread and sysseek in this book

close

Usage

```
close filehandle
close
```

Description

The close function closes the filehandle specified. If a filehandle isn't specified, the currently selected filehandle is closed (see select, 1-argument form).

```
close(LOGFILE);
```

The close function returns true if the close succeeds, or false otherwise. For regular files, close can fail if the filesystem is full.

The filehandle specified might be an indirect filehandle in addition to being a simple identifier. See open for information on creating an indirect filehandle.

```
my $foo;
open($foo, "/tmp/sample.txt") || die "Cannot open sample: $!";
#
close $foo;
```

The close function operates on a filehandle associated with a file, pipe, or socket. In each case, the proper kind of close is done.

For a pipe, the close will reap the child process created by the open. The close function also will return false if the child process returns a nonzero exit status, or the fork/exec used to create the pipe failed. In addition, the variable $! will be set to the error (if the pipe itself failed), and $? will be set to the return value for wait on the process. See the wait entry for details.

If you reap the child yourself (through an explicit wait or in a $SIG{CHLD} handler), the close function also will report failure.

Example Listing 5.28

```
# Thorough checking of a pipe for success or
#    failure.

open(LPR, "|lpr -Plp2")
    || die "Cannot fork: $!";
print LPR @output;
if (! close(LPR)) {
    print "Printing failed.\n";
    if ( $! ) {
        print "Pipe failed: $!\n";
    } else {
        print "Exit status: ", $? >> 8, "\n";
    }
}
```

> **See Also**
> open, wait, select, socket, Signal Handlers, $?, and $! in this book

seek

Usage

```
seek filehandle, offset, whence
```

Description

The seek function positions the file pointer for the filehandle. Positions within the file are byte offsets counted from the first position in the file, which is 0. If positioning the file pointer is successful, seek returns true. Otherwise it returns false and sets $! to the error message.

The filehandle can be a normal identifier that refers to an open file, or it can be a scalar variable that refers to a file handle as described in the open entry in this book.

The offset is specified as a number of bytes from whence, where whence is one of the following:

Symbolic Name	Value	Meaning
SEEK_SET	0	From the beginning of the file
SEEK_CUR	1	From the current position
SEEK_END	2	From the end of the file

If you want to use the symbolic names instead of the numeric values, use the Fcntl module to retrieve them. For positioning with SEEK_CUR and SEEK_END, the offset can be a negative number.

The seek behavior on most systems has some peculiarities:

The seek function is a standard I/O function and shouldn't be used with sysread, syswrite, or anything else that bypasses standard I/O for files. The sysseek function should be used then.

When seeking and reading or writing files, it might be necessary to seek again after performing the read or write because the C library might reposition the file pointer.

The seek function used as follows:

```
seek(FH, 0, SEEK_CUR);
```

will have the effect of clearing any end-of-file errors on the filehandle. This is the same effect achieved with the following:

```
use IO::Handle;
FH->clearerr();
```

For text files on systems that distinguish between the two, the file's current position might not be accurately placed using seek. Writing out lines of text of N bytes might actually result in $N+1$ bytes being written. In those cases, use tell to accurately determine your position.

Example Listing 5.29

```
use Fcntl qw(:seek);

# Manipulate a file with known contents
#    from something like this:
#        Wed Oct 25 20:46:46 2000

open(FM, "+>/tmp/date") || die "/tmp/date: $!";
print FM scalar localtime;
```

```
# To this:
#        Wed/Oct/25 20:46:46 2000

seek(FM, 3, SEEK_SET);  # 3 from the start
print FM "/";
seek(FM, 3, SEEK_CUR);  # Forward another 3
print FM "/";

seek(FM, -4, SEEK_END); # 4 from the end
$year=<FM>;
seek(FM, -13, SEEK_CUR);# Backup 13 from there.
read(FM, $time, 8);

seek(FM, 11, SEEK_SET); # Re-write the year/time
print FM "$year $time";

# Go back to the beginning
seek(FM, 0, SEEK_SET);
$line=<FM>;              # Read it all back.
print $line;

close(FM);
```

> **See Also**
> Fcntl and IO::Handle module documentation
> tell and sysseek in this book
> seek in the C library reference

sysseek

Usage

sysseek filehandle, offset, whence

Description

The sysseek function sets the filehandle's current read/write position. The whence argument describes where the position should be made from (SEEK_SET, SEEK_CUR, or SEEK_END), and the offset describes relative to that position where the pointer should be placed.

Upon success, sysseek returns the current I/O pointer offset (after the sysseek). If the position is 0, the string 0 but true is returned. This string has some special properties, explained in the fcntl entry. On failure, sysseek returns undef and sets $! to the error message.

There is no systell. Simply use the return value from:

```
sysseek(filehandle, 0, SEEK_CUR)
```

The sysseek function is the nonstandard I/O version of the seek function. For a description of how SEEK_SET, SEEK_CUR, and SEEK_END work, see the seek entry. Do not use sysseek on filehandles that are being operated on with standard I/O functions such as print, read, <>, and seek.

Example Listing 5.30

```
# Manipulate the file's contents

use Fcntl qw(:seek);

open(FH, ">/tmp/test") || die;
if( syswrite(FH, " "x100) ) {
    sysseek(FH, 0, SEEK_SET);
    while(sysseek(FH, 2, SEEK_CUR+2) < -s FH) {
        syswrite(FH, "+");
    }
}
close(FH);
```

See Also
sysread, syswrite, and seek in this book

```
tell
```

Usage

```
tell filehandle
tell
```

Description

The `tell` function returns the current position of the file pointer associated with filehandle. This position is measured in bytes starting from the beginning of the file (`offset 0`). In the event of an error, `tell` returns `-1` and sets `$!` to the error message.

If filehandle isn't specified, the `tell` function uses the last filehandle read. The filehandle might be specified as an identifier or as a `scalar` variable indicating an indirect filehandle—see the `open` entry for details.

The `tell` function doesn't give meaningful results on stream or socket filehandles. Also, because `tell` uses the standard I/O library, it might not give meaningful results for filehandles that are being read and written using `sysread`, `syswrite`, and `sysseek`.

Example Listing 5.31

```
# Build an index of /etc/passwd so that lookups
#   can jump directly to the correct entry.
# Password entries resemble:
#   clintp:x:500:500:Clinton A. Pierce:/home/clintp:/bin/bash

use Fcntl qw(:seek);

open(FM, "/etc/passwd") || die "password: $!";
$pos=0;
while(<FM>) {
    $index{ (split(/:/, $_, 0))[0] }=$pos;
    $pos=tell;
}
do {
    print "Name? ";
    chomp($n=<STDIN>);
    if (exists $index{$n}) {
        seek(FM, $index{$n}, SEEK_SET);
        print scalar(<FM>);
    }
} while($n);
close(FM);
```

> **See Also**
> Fcntl module documentation
>
> seek, open, and sysseek in this book
>
> tell in the C library reference

stat

Usage

stat expression

Description

The stat function returns a 13-element list giving information about a file's entry in the filesystem. expression can represent an open filehandle, a pathname to the file in the filesystem, the special filename _, or whether omitted to $_, which should contain a pathname.

If stat fails, an empty list will be returned. In a scalar context, stat will return true or false depending on whether the file exists.

The entries returned by stat vary by filesystem. Under Unix operating systems, the list mirrors the stat structure described in C header file sys/stat.h. Under other operating systems, the same fields are used for the closest equivalent concepts for that OS. The number of fields remains the same, but their meanings will change.

element	Unix description	Windows description
0 dev	device	drive number
1 ino	i-node number	0
2 mode	mode (permissions and type)	unused
3 nlink	number of hard links	0, NTFS might have links
4 uid	user ID of owner	0
5 gid	group ID of owner	0
6 rdev	device type (if inode device)	drive number (again)
7 size	total size, in bytes	size of file, in bytes
8 atime	time of last access	time of last access
9 mtime	time of last modification	time of last modification
10 ctime	time of last inode change	time of creation
11 blksize	blocksize for filesystem I/O	0
12 blocks	number of blocks allocated	0

The `stat` function also can be used on `directory` entries, or any entry in a filesystem. The meaning of these fields will vary slightly depending on the kind of filesystem entry being examined.

The times represented in the stat structure are the number of seconds since the Unix epoch (Jan 1, 1970). These can be converted using the `localtime` or `gmtime` routines.

Using the special filename _ won't cause a system-level `stat` to occur. Instead, the results of the last `stat` will be re-used. If a file was queried with any of the file test operators, this also causes a `stat` to occur internally and that information will be the one re-used by _.

The mode entry under Unix contains several pieces of information including the `permissions` of the file and the file type. The permissions are contained in the least-significant, four-octal digits. To retrieve just the permissions, use the & operator to extract those bits:

```
$mode=(stat("."))[2]; # current directory permissions
printf "%04o", $mode & 07777;
```

Under Unix, permissions are normally represented in octal and can be printed that way with the `printf` (or `sprintf`) `%o` format.

Example Listing 5.32

```
($dev,$ino,$mode,$nlink,$uid,$gid,$rdev,$size,
        $atime,$mtime,$ctime,$blksize,$blocks)
        = stat("stat.txt");
print scalar(localtime($mtime)), "\n";  # Last changed on...
print "Size: $size\n";
```

> **See Also**
> perlfunc in the perl documentation
> lstat, time, localtime, gmtime, &, printf, sprintf, and file test operators in this book
> stat in the C library reference

`lstat`

Usage

```
lstat pathname
lstat
```

Description

The lstat function retrieves information on a file in much the same way that the stat function does. In fact, the return values are identical.

The difference is that if the last portion of pathname (or $_ if pathname isn't specified) is a symbolic link, the link itself is examined instead of the file it refers to.

On systems in which symbolic links aren't used, or if pathname refers to a regular file, lstat reverts to just doing a stat.

Example Listing 5.33

```
# Note differences between a symlink's mtime
#   and a file's

$local="local_sample.txt";
symlink "/tmp/sample.txt", $local
        or die "Cannot create symlink: $!";

print "The symbolic link for $local was last modified on ",
    localtime((lstat($local))[9])."", "\nThe actual file ",
    "was last changed on ", localtime((stat($local))[9])."", "\n"
```

> **See Also**
> readlink, stat, and symlink in this book

Modifying the Filesystem

rmdir

Usage

```
rmdir pathname
rmdir
```

Description

The rmdir function removes the directory specified by pathname. If the removal is successful, rmdir returns true. Otherwise it returns false and sets $! to the error message.

If pathname isn't specified, the directory indicated by the $_ variable will be removed.

The directory to be removed must be empty. If you want to remove a directory that still contains files or subdirectories, use the File::Path module's rmtree function.

Example Listing 5.34

```
rmdir "/tmp/olddir" or warn "Cannot remove olddir: $!";
```

> **See Also**
> File::Path module documentation
> unlink and $! in this book

unlink

Usage

```
unlink list
unlink
```

Description

The unlink function removes the directory entries for the files specified in a list. If a list isn't specified, the pathname indicated by $_ is removed instead.

The unlink function returns the number of files successfully deleted. If a failure occurs, Perl will continue with the rest of the list of files. Also, upon failure, the variable $! will be set to the correct error message. If there are multiple failures, only one message is kept for the last file.

The unlink function shouldn't be used to delete directories. If, under Unix, you are the superuser and the -U command-line option is supplied to perl, it is possible but not recommended.

The storage held by the file is not necessarily released immediately. If there are other hard links to the file (Unix) or the file is still open (POSIX), the storage isn't freed until the last reference to the file goes away.

Example Listing 5.35

```
# Remove files named "file*" in the /tmp
#   directory (and below) more than 2 days old.
use File::Find;
```

```
# Hide error messages from find: I'm not interested in them.
#    mostly just permission denied things.
unless (open(SE_COPY, ">&STDERR") &&
    open(STDERR, ">/dev/null") ) {
    print "Failure to redirect STDERR: $!\n";
}
find( sub {
    return if !/^file/;
    return if -M $_ < 2;

    unlink || print SE_COPY "Cannot remove $_: $!\n";

    } , '/tmp' )
```

> **See Also**
> link in this book
> unlink in the C library reference

rename

Usage

```
rename oldname, newname
```

Description

The rename function renames a file from an old to a new name. If the renaming is successful, true is returned; otherwise, undef.

The rename function normally can be used to move a file from one directory to another. The only restriction is that the old and new directories must be on the same filesystem.

Example Listing 5.36

```
# Move a logfile out of the way, renaming it with
#    today's date.
unless ( rename('/tmp/logfile', '/tmp/logfile'
    . (localtime)[3]) ) {
    warn "Could not rename logfile: $!";
}
```

> **See Also**
> rename in the C library reference

mkdir

Usage

```
mkdir pathname, permissions
mkdir pathname
```

Description

The mkdir function creates a new directory at pathname. Under Unix, the permissions are used against the user's umask to set initial permissions for the directory. If permissions aren't specified, the bitmask 0777 will be used. The permissions are ignored under other architectures.

If the directory creation is successful, mkdir returns true. Otherwise it returns false and sets $! to the error message.

The parent directory for pathname must exist already. The mkdir function cannot be used to create a chain of directories. For that, use the standard File::Path module's mkpath function.

Example Listing 5.37

```
mkdir "/tmp/jpegs"
    or warn "Cannot create /tmp/jpegs: $!";
```

> **See Also**
> File::Path module documentation
> umask in this book

symlink

Usage

```
symlink existingpath, newpath
```

Description

The symlink function creates a symbolic link at *newpath* that refers to the filesystem entry at *existingpath* (contrast this with link). The function returns true if successful and false otherwise. The function will fail if *newpath* exists and is a file or there is insufficient permission; $! will be set to the error message.

This function is only available on Unix-like operating systems and will generate a runtime error if it isn't implemented.

After the symlink, *newpath* will now refer to the file at *existingpath* for most purposes. Most Perl (and C) functions cannot distinguish between a symbolic link and a normal file; those that can are lstat (the file test -l by association), readlink, rename, and unlink—they operate on the symbolic link, not the file the link refers to.

The symlink function has many uses under Unix and shares some similarities with directory entries created with link. However, if the original file is removed, the symlink will no longer work correctly (and the data is gone). Unlike link, symlinks can refer to files on other filesystems. Use caution with symlinks: it is possible to create loops of links, or simply extremely long chains, that will cause I/O calls to fail with ELOOP. ("Too many symbolic links encountered.")

Example Listing 5.38

```
# Creates a "shadow directory tree".  Given two
#   pathnames, it takes the first and creates a second
#   full of directories and symlinks -- but no real files.

use File::Find;
my($source, $dest)=(shift, shift);
die "$source is not an absolute directory"
    unless (-d $source and $source=~m#^/#);
die "$dest exists or was not a full pathname"
    if (-e $dest and $dest=~m#^/#);

sub create {
    my($path,$target)=$File::Find::name;
    return if ($path =~ /^\.*$/);
    ($target=$path)=~s/$source/$dest/;
    if (-d $path) {
        mkdir $target or warn "Cannot mkdir $target: $!";
    } else {
```

```
            symlink $path, $target or warn "Cannot symlink $path: $!";
        }
    }
    find(\&create, $source);
```

> **See Also**
> link, unlink, $!, and readlink in this book
> symlink in the C library reference

readlink

Usage

```
readlink linkpathname
readlink
```

Description

The readlink function returns the target pathname referred to by the symbolic link at linkpathname. If linkpathname isn't specified, $_ is used instead. If the linkpathname doesn't refer to a symbolic link, or the operating system doesn't support symlinks, undef is returned and $! is set to the error message.

This function is only available on Unix-like systems.

For example, if a long directory listing shows

```
lrwxrwxrwx    1 clintp    15 Oct 25 19:32 lsample.txt -> ../tmp/sample.txt
```

performing a readlink on lsample.txt would return the string ../tmp/sample.txt.

Example Listing 5.39

```
readlink("/tmp/lsample.txt") or
    warn "readlink failed: $!";
```

> **See Also**
> symlink and lstat in this book
> readlink in the C library reference

`link`

Usage

`link existingpath, newpath`

Description

The `link` function creates a hard link between two directory entries in the filesystem (contrast this with `symlink` and `unlink`). The function returns true if successful and false otherwise. The function will fail if *newpath* exists, if there is insufficient permission, or if *existingpath* doesn't exist; `$!` will be set to the error message.

This function is available only under Unix.

After the `link`, the two directory entries are indistinguishable. Altering one file makes the other file change. In fact, both directory entries actually refer to the same on-disk storage. Neither file is marked as the original or the link—they are peers. Removing (unlinking) one file will leave the other intact.

Unix filesystems will only allow a hard link to occur between two directory entries on the same filesystem. To create a cross-filesystem link or to link directories, see `symlink`.

Example Listing 5.40

```
warn "Cannot link: $!" unless
    link "/tmp/sample.txt", "/tmp/newest.txt";
```

> **See Also**
> `unlink` and `symlink` in this book
> `link` in the C library reference

`chmod`

Usage

`chmod mode, list`

Description

The `chmod` function sets the `permissions` for a list of filenames under Unix. If successful, the `chmod` function returns the number of files from the list whose permissions were changed. Upon failure, it returns false and sets $! to the error message.

The *mode* is simply the lower three bytes of the st_mode portion of the inode structure. Normally, these are represented in Unix documentation in octal (that is, 644) or in symbolic notation (ugo=r,o+w). The chmod function in Perl doesn't use these representations; it just sets the bits according to what you pass in.

If you want to represent the mode as an octal figure, use the literal octal representation (leading 0 without quotes):

```
chmod 0644, $file or warn "Couldn't adjust permissions: $!";
```

Or use the File::chmod module from CPAN for the symbolic notation.

You can use the constants (as you would in C) from the Fcntl module as well. For example, to set the file's permissions to the equivalent of 0755:

```
use Fcntl qw(:mode);

chmod S_IRWXU|S_IRGRP|S_IXGRP|S_IROTH|S_IXOTH, $file or warn "chmod: $!";
```

See the Fcntl module or your system's chmod manpage for a list of constants available.

Example Listing 5.41

```
# Change permissions of files in current directory
#     to add read permission.

foreach( glob '*') {
    next unless -f $_;
    ($mode)=(stat($_))[2];
    $mode=($mode & 0777) | 0444;

    chmod $mode, $_ or warn "Cannot chmod $_: $!\n";
}
```

See Also
Fcntl module documentation

bit operators and numeric literals in this book

chmod in the C library reference

utime

Usage

```
utime atime, mtime, LIST
```

Description

Sets the access and modification timestamps on the files listed in LIST. The times are expressed as the number of seconds since the unix epoch.

The utime function returns the number of files modified.

Example Listing 5.42

```
# "Touches" the file to the current
# time if it can.
$now=time;
utime $now, $now, "utime.txt";
```

Example Listing 5.43

```
# Updates the access time, but not
# the modification time
$file="utime.txt";
$mtime=(stat($file))[9];
unless ( utime time, $mtime, $file ) {
    warn "Couldn't change mtime of $file: $!";
}
```

> **See Also**
> time and stat in this book

chown

Usage

```
chown uid, gid, files
```

Description

The chown function, under Unix, changes the owner and group information for a list of files. If successful, the chown function returns the number of files successfully changed. If there was an error, $! will be set to the error message of the last error that occurred.

The uid and gid are the numeric user and group ID that you want the file changed to. Under some flavors of Unix, using a uid or gid of -1 will leave the file's permission for that component as is.

The chown command can fail for a variety of reasons. For example, under POSIX you might not be allowed to change the ownership of the file unless you are the superuser. You might not be allowed to change the group of the file unless you're the superuser or the process owns the file (and the file's group is the effective group ID of the process or one of the process' supplementary group IDs).

Example Listing 5.44

```
# Accepts three arguments, a user, a group and a pathname.
#   and changes the files (and directories) under that pathname
#   to be owned by that user and group.

use File::Find;

$uid=getpwnam(shift);
$gid=getpwnam(shift);
die "Invalid arguments" if ( !$uid or !$gid or ! defined $ARGV[2]);

sub change {
    chown $uid, $gid, $File::Find::name or
        warn "Cannot change $File::Find::name: $!\n";
}
find(\&change, $ARGV[0]);
```

> **See Also**
> getpwnam and $! in this book
> chown in the C library reference

Directory Handles

opendir

Usage

```
opendir dirhandle, pathname
```

Description

The opendir function connects a directory handle to a directory. This handle can then be used by readdir, closedir, telldir, seekdir, and rewinddir. If successful, it returns true; it returns false if there was an error and sets $! to the error message.

The dirhandle can be an identifier, or it can be a scalar variable that refers to a directory handle object. This is similar to the open function's treatment of a filehandle. The dirhandle will have a separate namespace from any filehandles, however.

Directory handles aren't interchangeable with filehandles. Attempting to read a directory handle as though it were a filehandle will generate the following warning:

```
    readline() on closed filehandle main::dirhandle at line 9.
(Are you trying to call readline() on dirhandle main::dirhandle?)
```

The *pathname* is the name of the directory whose contents you want to read.

Example Listing 5.45

```
# Emulates the Unix utility 'ps' by generating
#    a process listing using features of the
#    Linux 2.x /proc filesystem

print "Pid  Parent PID   Command Line\n";
opendir(PIDS, "/proc") || die "proc: $!";

# each process has a numeric directory in /proc
while($pid=readdir PIDS) {
    next unless ($pid=~/^\d+$/);
    open(PROC, "/proc/$pid/status") || die "Cannot stat pid: $!";
    %e=map { /(\w+):\s+(\S+)/ } <PROC>;
    printf("%8d %8d %20s\n",  @e{Pid,PPid,Name});
}
closedir(PIDS);
```

> **See Also**
>
> `readdir`, `closedir`, `rewinddir`, `seekdir`, `telldir`, and `open` in this book
>
> `opendir` in the C library reference

rewinddir, seekdir, telldir

Usage

```
rewinddir dirhandle
telldir dirhandle
seekdir dirhandle, position
```

Description

The `rewinddir`, `telldir`, and `seekdir` functions are used to alter the order that `readdir` returns directory entries. Each function takes an open `dirhandle` as an argument. Upon error, each will set `$!` to the error message.

The `rewinddir` function will reset the list so that `readdir` will read from the beginning of the directory.

The `telldir` function returns the current position that describes where the read pointer is located in the open `dirhandle`.

The `position` from `telldir` can be given to `seekdir` to allow the program to skip back to the given `position` in the directory list.

It's possible that one (or any) of these functions might not be implemented on an operating system. In addition, the operating system might reorganize the directory as it's being read; thus seeking and telling on an active directory might skip (or duplicate) some entries by `readdir`.

Example Listing 5.46

```perl
# Watch for new files to appear in this directory
#

opendir(HERE, ".") || die "Cannot open .: $!";
%files=map { ($_, 1) } readdir HERE;
do {
    sleep 3;
    rewinddir HERE;
```

```
    while($f=readdir HERE) {
        unless (exists $files{$f}) {
            print "$f is new\n";
                $files{$f}=1;
        }
    }
} while(1);
closedir(HERE);
```

closedir

Usage

```
closedir dirhandle
```

Description

The closedir function closes a directory handle opened with opendir. The dirhandle can be an identifier, or it can be a scalar variable that refers to an open directory handle as described in the opendir entry.

If successful, closedir returns true; otherwise it returns false and sets $! to the error message. Re-opening a directory handle will effectively close it, and then re-open it.

Example Listing 5.47

```
# Simple opening, and closing
opendir(ETC, "/etc") || die "opendir /etc: $!";
@files=readdir ETC;
closedir(ETC);
```

> **See Also**
> opendir in this book

readdir

Usage

```
readdir dirhandle
```

Description

The `readdir` function reads the directory names from the directory referred to by the open `dirhandle`. In a scalar context, the first `readdir` on the handle will return one directory entry, and a subsequent `readdir` will return the next entry until the list is exhausted and `undef` is returned.

In a list context, the entire list of directories will be returned.

The `readdir` function returns all entries as they appear in the directory. Files and directories are both returned, as well as special entries such as the . and .. directories. The names returned by `readdir` don't have the pathname prefixed to them: You will have to do that yourself if you plan on opening or processing the file.

Example Listing 5.48

```
# Given a directory as an argument, sum the sizes of
#     the files in that directory.

my $dir=shift;

opendir(DH, $dir) || die "Cannot open $dir: $!";
while(my $file=readdir DH) {
    next unless (-f "$dir/$file");
    $size+=-s _;
}
closedir(DH);
print "Total size: $size\n";
```

> **See Also**
> `opendir`, `closedir`, `seekdir`, `telldir`, and `rewinddir` in this book

Miscellaneous

`dbmopen`, `dbmclose`

Usage

```
dbmopen hash, database_name, mode
dbmclose hash
```

Description

The `dbmopen` function creates a relationship between a hash and a dbm database file on disk. A dbm database is a key-value type of database with its origins in Berkeley Unix. (But it has been ported almost everywhere—including DOS/Windows). If the `dbmopen` is successful, it returns true; otherwise it returns false and sets `$!` to the error message.

The database will be opened at the pathname specified by `database_name`, and if it doesn't already exist it will be created and have the permissions designated by `mode` (under Unix). If you specify a `mode` of `undef`, `dbmopen` will fail if the database doesn't already exist.

After the `dbmopen`, modifications to the hash will cause the DBM file (or files) to change. The data is saved after the `perl` script exits so that other `perl` scripts (or the same one later) can use the data again. It is possible to `dbmopen` a DBM file that you aren't allowed to write to—in that case, you can read the hash but not modify it. The `exists` and `defined` functions are interchangeable on DBM-tied hashes, but all other hash functions operate normally (`keys`, `each`, `values`, slices, and so on).

The `dbmclose` function disconnects the hash from the DBM file on disk.

Concurrent read/write access to a DBM file might cause data corruption and there is no internal locking to DBM. If you need to have concurrent access, use a locking mechanism similar to the ones described in the `flock` and `bind` entries.

The `dbmopen` function is a holdover from earlier versions of Perl. Underneath, what actually happens is that `dbmopen` ends up calling Perl's more generic `tie` interface. The `dbmclose` function is actually just `untie` in disguise. (For details, see the `tie` entry.) For example, the `dbmopen` call of

```
dbmopen %stuff, "stuffdb", 0666 or die;
# Make changes
dbmclose %stuff;
```

actually runs something along the lines of the following:

```
use AnyDBM_File;
use POSIX;
tie %stuff, 'AnyDBM_File', "stuffdb", O_CREAT|O_RDWR, 0666 or die;
# Make changes
untie %stuff;
```

The `dbmopen` interface to the `tie` mechanism will select from a list of possible DBM databases until one is found and works for your architecture. It does this by attempting to `eval` a `tie` statement for each DBM in the list until one works.

Because the hash is now tied to an on-disk database, the database itself might place some restrictions on your hash. For example, the length of keys and values in the tied hash might be limited. The limits will depend on the kind of database used and the particular build of the database. When sharing a DBM file with applications written in C (such as Netscape, sendmail, or jpilot) the database keys or values might be null-terminated. You will have to preserve the nulls yourself.

Example Listing 5.49

```
# Pre-load a database with some holidays
#

dbmopen(%h, "/tmp/holidays", 0644) || die "dbmopen: $!";
$h{halloween}='Oct 31';
$h{christmas}='Dec 25';
$h{independence}='Jul 4';
$h{groundhog}='Feb 1';
dbmclose(%h);
```

Example Listing 5.50

```
# Dump the holiday database composed above
#

dbmopen %h, "/tmp/holidays", undef or die "dbmopen: $!";
while(($day, $date)=each(%h)) {
    print "\u$day falls on $date\n";
}
dbmclose %h;
```

> **See Also**
> AnyDBM_File module documentation
> tie and dbmclose in this book

umask

Usage

```
umask bitmask
umask
```

Description

The `umask` function is particular to Unix filesystems. The function sets which bits won't be set by default when files or directories are created. The `bitmask` is usually expressed as an octal number:

```
umask 022;
mkdir "/tmp/foo", 0777 or die "Cannot create foo: $!";
```

The directory created would have the permissions of `0777` masked (bitwise anded) with `022`, so the final permissions will be `0755` (`rwxr-xr-x`). File permissions always can be changed later with `chmod`.

The `umask` function returns the value of the old mask. This can be useful if you simply want to modify the existing mask instead of imposing a new one.

This function affects the permissions put on files created with `open`, `sysopen`, `mkdir`, and other functions that will create new files and directories.

Example Listing 5.51

```
# Turn off mask for owner
umask(umask() & 077 );
open(F, ">/tmp/myfile") || die "Cannot open myfile: $!";
```

> **See Also**
> `sysopen`, `mkdir`, `chmod`, and `umask` in the C library reference

glob

Usage

glob pattern

Description

The `glob` function, as of 5.6, only provides a wrapper for the `glob` function from the standard module `File::Glob`.

Prior to 5.6, `glob` was an internal function that emulated the Unix C Shell's file globbing behavior. The functionality is still provided but only through a module. Calling `glob` directly invokes the module implicitly.

See the `File::Glob` documentation for details on `glob`'s functionality.

Example Listing 5.52

```
@headers=glob '{*.h,*/*.h}';
```

> **See Also**
> File::Glob in this book

File Test Operators

Usage

```
-filetestop
-filetestop filehandle
-filetestop pathname
-filetestop _
```

Description

The file test operators are used to test various attributes of files and filehandles on the system. As a general rule, if a pathname is specified, it is tested. A filehandle (an open identifier) is expected otherwise. If no filehandle and no pathname is specified, the pathname in $_ is tested (unless -t is used).

The various tests return true (1) if the test is true, and false ("") otherwise. If an error occurs while performing the test, undef is returned and $! can be set to an error message.

Most of the discussions that follow look at permission bits and other Unix-centric terms. However, where applicable, these tests work under other operating systems as well.

All the file test operators are single-character letters. Beware of using the unary minus neary//, s///, and m//—a minus followed by a single letter is always interpreted as a file test. Use parenthesis where it might be ambiguous.

The first few file operators are used to test the permissions on files, and work only under Unix:

File Test Operator	Meaning
-r	The file is readable by the effective user/group ID.
-R	The file is readable by the real user/group ID.
-w	The file is writable by the effective user/group ID.

File Test Operator	Meaning
-w	The file is writable by the real user/group ID.
-x	The file is executable by the effective user/group ID.
-X	The file is executable by the real user/group ID.
-o	The file is owned by the effective user ID.
-O	The file is owned by the real user ID.

Whether the file is readable, writable, or executable is determined by examining the mode bits on the file, the owner, and group and comparing it with the current perl process. Whether you can actually read, write, or execute the file might depend on other factors such as Access Control Lists. For root, these tests always return true.

The bulk of the file test operators are used to test the mode bits on the file to determine various attributes of the file. Some of these are specific to Unix (symbolic links and FIFOs), but most apply to any operating system.

File Test Operator	Meaning
-e	File exists.
-f	True if the file is a regular file (and not a directory, FIFO, socket, and so on).
-d	File is a directory.
-l	File is a symbolic link.
-p	File is a FIFO (a named pipe).
-S	File is a socket.
-b	File is a block special file (disk, tape or other mass storage device).
-c	File is a character special file (terminal, null, printer).
-t	Filehandle is a terminal (for example, STDIN normally is).
-z	True if the file has a zero size.
-u	File has the set-user-id bit set (S_IFUID).
-g	File has the set-group-id bit set (S_IFGID).
-k	File has the sticky bit set (S_ISVTX).

A few of the operators return values other than true or false. These are listed in the table shown later.

The -T and -B operators determine whether the file is text or binary. They work by reading the first 512 bytes of the file (or the current stdio buffer of the filehandle) and then perform the following tests:

- If the file is empty, both -T and -B return true.

- If any null characters are seen (ASCII 0), the file is binary.

Anything less than ASCII 32 (other than carriage returns, backspaces, escape characters, formfeeds, tabs) is considered an odd (unusual) character. On EBCDIC and Unicode systems, things other than printable characters and spaces are considered odd. If more than 1/3 of the characters are odd, the file is considered binary.

You should probably avoid calling -T or -B on files that are actually devices. Because Perl attempts to read the device and then put the bytes back into the stdio stream, unexpected things can happen on the device (missed tape marks, terminal-control nonsense, and so on).

File Test Operator	Meaning
-s	Returns the size of the file in bytes
-T	Returns true if the file is a text file
-B	Returns true if the file is a binary file
-A	Last access time of the file (see following) at the time the script was started
-M	Last modified time of the file at the time the script was started
-C	Time of the last inode change (unix) or creation time (Windows) at the time the script was started

The special filehandle _ is used as follows: the file test operators (and the stat and lstat functions) use the same buffer to read the stat structure internally. The _ filehandle causes perl to reuse that stat structure again and not re-examine the file on disk. This can make repeated file tests much quicker. The lstat function and the -l operator perform an lstat, but use the same buffer; so the results of testing the _ filehandle will report on the link, not the file that it points to.

The -A, -M, and -C operators each return the number of days (as a fractional number) before the script started of the last modification/change/access time. For example, if the file "logfile" was last modified on November 30th at noon, and this snippet were run at 11:37 p.m. on November 30, the following:

```
$mod=-M "logfile";
```

would return approximately .4856—about half a day earlier. If the file had been modified since the script was run, the number returned would be negative.

Example Listing 5.53

```
# Sum up the kinds of files under /etc and /dev
#

use File::Find;

my %types;
sub accumulate {
    $types{files}++ if -f $File::Find::name;
    $types{dirs}++  if -d _;
    $types{block}++ if -b _;
    $types{character}++ if -c _;
    $types{text}++ if -f _ and -T _;
    $types{binary}++ if -f _ and -B _;
    $types{links}++ if -l $File::Find::name;
}
find \&accumulate, "/etc", "/dev";

for my $type (sort keys %types) {
    print "There were $types{$type} of $type.\n";
}
```

See Also

stat, lstat, and $^T in this book

CHAPTER 6

Processes, Interprocess Communication, and Threads

System Interaction

This section describes those functions and operators used to interact with the operating system.

Description

Specifically, the functions grouped here are used to interact with external services, OS timers, retrieve information about the users and services offered by the OS, manipulate processes, and communicate between processes.

Operating System Information

This section contains an entire class of functions that are designed to retrieve information about the current operating environment. Although they're all derived from Unix commands, many of them map nicely into other environments such as Microsoft Windows.

Most of these functions begin with get. The gethost* family of functions retrieve host information based on name, address, or all available information about the current host. The getserv* and getproto* functions allow you to determine which services and protocols are available on your system—this is needed in order to set up for networking, described in the following section. These functions work on a variety of operating systems.

The `getgr*` and `getpw*` classes of functions are quite Unix specific because they deal with the password and group files used in the standard Unix security scheme.

External Services

The system function and the `qx` operator are in the first category. These allow you to run commands, normally run from an OS prompt, from within Perl.

Perl was originally designed as a Unix tool to replace and compliment awk and shell. The shell language is essentially a few built-in functions (loops, branch, and variable manipulation) that use external programs to do most of the work. Hence, Unix shell programming is mostly the stringing together of small, external utilities.

From this heritage, Perl retains the capability to seamlessly run external commands and manipulate their output for its own needs. The system command simply runs an external command. The `qx` (and `backtick`) operators allow you to run commands and capture their output.

Because Perl is a portable framework, you can continue to program in a very shell-like way under other operating systems.

More elaborate methods of capturing command output are offered by the `open` function; with `open` you actually can create pipelines to and from external commands.

Services that are available in the C API, which are specific to the hardware/OS platform `perl` is running on, can be accessed through the `syscall` mechanism.

Processes

First and foremost, you must understand that Perl's notions of process control come directly from its Unix roots. When possible, these concepts have been brought into the nonUnix environments where Perl is run. For example, `fork()` works under Windows as of Perl 5.6. It is unlikely that `setpgrp()` will ever work in Windows because there are no equivalent concepts in the Windows API. And Windows doesn't support Perl's notion of signals—almost.

A *process* is a container for a running program in Unix. It contains the environment, group and user IDs, open file descriptors, code pointers, attached memory segments, current directory, file creation masks, and many other attributes.

All running processes in Unix (with the exception of `init`) are created with the `fork()` system call. This takes an existing process and creates a nearly exact copy of it. The copy then usually invokes the `exec()` system call that completely changes the underlying program within the process but keeps many of the process's characteristics.

Through `fork` and `exec`, every process on a Unix system is created. A typical network login session, for example, starts when

- `init` forks and execs `inetd` (to listen for connections).

- `inetd` forks and execs `telnetd` (upon `telnet` connection).

- `telnetd` forks and execs `logind` (to handle the login).

- `logind` then execs (upon successful authentication, without a `fork`) a shell to provide the user a prompt to work from.

In this way, a chain of processes can trace their heritage back to `init`. Processes that die will remain as a zombie (defunct) process until their parent process performs a `wait()` to get the exit status. Processes whose parent has died will be inherited by `init`, which will reap them when they die.

Perl provides functions for this entire life cycle. You can create, destroy, and reap processes. There are functions to change attributes of the processes, signal processes, and catch signals. Most of these are presented in this section. Some attributes of processes (the environment, for example) are covered in other sections of this book.

Signals

Signals are, quite simply, software interrupts. They are a mechanism for contacting a process with a small bit of information. Under Unix, signals can come from many sources: terminal drivers, the operating system, other processes, and so on. Some signals on a typical Unix system might be

Signal	Meaning
SIGINT	Interrupt key pressed
SIGKILL	Exit immediately
SIGHUP	Terminal has hung up
SIGSEGV	Illegal memory reference
SIGALRM	An alarm has gone off

On a fairly modern system, there can be more than two dozen potential signals. Some signals are user defined—you can use them for your own purposes. Each signal has a default action. In some cases, the action is to ignore the signal. In other cases, the process will terminate upon receipt of the signal.

Perl allows you to specify behaviors that should take place when the signals are received. These are called *signal handlers*. Using %SIG allows simple signal trapping in Perl.

One process can signal another process using the kill function. The kill function allows simple interprocess communication to take place.

Process Information

The Perl API allows you to gather quite a bit of information about processes that are running, and set that information. For example, getppid can be used to determine which process is the parent—useful for detecting if the parent has died, and the process has become an orphan.

Some attributes of processes also can be set, such as the process group and the priority. The process group determines which processes should be sent the signal for certain sets of signals (SIGHUP, for example).

The priority determines the scheduling priority of the process—how much CPU should be dedicated to running this process, relative to the other processes on the system. A process might want to give up CPU as a selfless act if it really isn't needed. For example, talking to a slow device such as a printer doesn't require much CPU, whereas another process might try to increase its priority.

Basics of Interprocess Communication

Traditionally, in Unix, there are five kinds of IPC: System V IPC, sockets, pipes, signals, and named pipes. Pipes are discussed in the file I/O section of this book because they're very closely related to doing File I/O. Signals are discussed above in the process section because they're very deeply intertwined with Unix notions of how processes are handled—and most of the interesting signals are Unix based.

A full treatment of Interprocess Communication under Unix and Socket programming cannot possibly be given in this text and do them justice. For a good introduction on both topics, see *Advanced Programming in the Unix Environment* and *Unix Network Programming* by W. Richard Stevens.

System V Interprocess Communications

System V Interprocess Communications—henceforth called SysV IPC—offers a variety of mechanisms for passing information between processes: semaphores, message queues, and shared memory. It is one of the older IPC mechanisms and was developed in the mid-1970s, long before sockets existed.

The three types of SysV IPC have advantages and disadvantages as compared to other kinds of IPC:

Advantage—SysV IPC structures (queues, semaphores, and shared memory) are system-wide resources. After a process goes away, information can be left behind for other processes to pick up much later.

Disadvantage—SysV IPC structures are system-wide resources. Thus, if a set of processes die and do not remove the IPC structures they have created, they have to be cleaned up through other means.

Advantage—SysV IPC structures are very flexible; data structures don't have to be mutated into a byte-stream to be passed along.

Disadvantage—SysV IPC structures aren't available under every operating system. Specifically, they're only available under Unix and only those Unix variants that support SysV IPC. For example, Linux and BSD support SysV IPC but only as an option. However, they have their uses.

This leads to the last disadvantage: unfamiliarity. Because many programmers aren't familiar with SysV IPC, they don't use SysV IPC—which leads to fewer programmers being exposed to them, and so on.

Typically shared memory has been used to pass large, complex structures between processes. Shared memory doesn't require that the structures be serialized or that any kind of formal protocol for encoding and decoding the structures be developed.

However, shared memory has problems with concurrency—multiple applications are free to access the same segment of memory at the same time for reading and writing. This causes the memory to become corrupted unless a locking mechanism can be worked out.

Semaphores are one method of implementing locks. Incrementing and decrementing a semaphore are both atomic operations. Typically a semaphore is set to 0 to indicate that a resource is busy and nonzero to indicate that it is free. To decrement the semaphore means that the semaphore must already be nonzero—otherwise the decrement will wait until the value is positive again. When a resource has been freed, the semaphore is incremented. In this way, a lock is established.

Message queues can be used to queue up work. Typically, there are readers and writers to a message queue. A *writer* puts work to be done on the queue, and one or more *readers* pull the work off and do it.

Sockets

Far more common than SysV IPC are *sockets* (sometimes called *Berkeley Sockets* because they derived from BSD Unix).

With the popularity of the Internet and the spread of the TCP/IP protocol, sockets are probably the most widespread form of communications between systems on earth.

The essentials of Berkeley Sockets are this: there are basically two kinds of sockets, connection and connectionless sockets; and there are two kinds of systems in a socket relationship, a client and a server.

The simplest situation to describe is a connection-oriented socket. With a connection-oriented socket, a system that waits for a connection is called a *server*. The system that initiates the connection is called a *client*. Typically, a connection-oriented socket uses the TCP/IP protocol, containing features which ensure that data transmitted will arrive in the correct order.

The server prepares for the connection by first creating a socket. In Perl, a socket is a filehandle-like device used for reading and writing to the network connection once it is established. Next the socket is bound to a port with bind.

A port, together with an IP address, provides a connection point on a system. Binding to a particular port by the server gives the client a well-known target to send information to. In this way, a server can host many different kinds of services, each one bound to a particular port. For example: Port 80 on a server typically has a Web server, and port 25 typically has a mail server.

After the port has been bound by the server, a call to listen is made. This prepares the bound port to accept connections. Finally the accept function is called. The accept function will wait on the bound port for a client to connect to it. When this is done, the server can read and write to the client over the socket created earlier.

The client in a connection-oriented socket first calls socket in much the same way the server does. This will generate a socket that can be used to read and write to the server. Then the client simply has to call connect to actually connect the socket to the bound port on the server. At this point, the socket can now be read and written to by the client.

On the other hand, a connectionless socket typically uses a protocol such as UDP/IP. The UDP protocol doesn't guarantee delivery of data, nor does it guarantee the order in which the data will arrive at its destination. The up side is that it's less of a bandwidth hog than TCP, and in some cases having the data arrive out-of-order or missing a few packets of information is fine.

To set up a connectionless server, the server must still call `socket` and `bind`. However, it's not necessary to call `listen` or `accept`. Instead, a call to `recv` will begin waiting for data to be sent.

To set up a connectionless client, the client also calls `socket` and `bind`. The client then can immediately begin sending data with `send`.

Signal Handling

Signal Handlers

Description

Signal handlers are the subroutines that you want executed when a `signal` is delivered to your process. The list of signal handlers in effect for your process are contained in the `%SIG` special variable.

The key to writing good signal handlers is to do as little as possible within the handler because most operating system's libraries are not re-entrant. This means that if a signal is delivered while `perl` is allocating memory or performing I/O, the state of the system becomes unknown and `perl` might later crash with a segmentation fault. Performing I/O or allocating a new variable in a signal handler will irritate this condition.

The safest thing to do is take an existing global variable and change its value.

To create a handler that's local to a particular block of code, simply make the entry in the `%SIG` hash local within a block:

```
# Don't HANGUP in here!
$hup=0;   # "Safe" variable for handler to change
{
    local $SIG{HUP}=sub {
            $hup=1;
        }
    # Critical code...
}
die "Hangup requested" if ($hup);
```

After a signal handler is called, the handler for that signal is no longer in effect under some Unix architectures, and it should be re-installed within the handler itself. This can be done more easily if the handler is a real named subroutine and not an anonymous subroutine as shown in the previous example. The previous example doesn't need to re-install HUP's handler because it's unlikely that a natural "hangup" will occur twice to a process.

Example Listing 6.1

```
# reaper for child processes
sub reaper {
    $dead_child=wait;
    $SIG{CHLD}=\&reaper;  # Re-install handler
}
$SIG{CHLD}=\&reaper;
```

> **See Also**
> perlsub in the perl documentation
> %SIG, local, wait, and anonymous subroutines in this book

%SIG

Usage

```
$SIG{signal}='IGNORE';
$SIG{signal}='DEFAULT';
$SIG{signal}=handler_ref;
```

Description

The %SIG hash is a container for the handler list for signals. The %SIG hash uses a signal name as a key, and the action to be performed when that signal is triggered as the value.

The signal can be one of two different kinds of values. The signal can be the name of a real signal available to your operating system (INT, TERM, KILL, ALRM, CHLD) or can be a pseudo-signal used by only by Perl (__WARN__, __DIE__).

Signals can be generated by hardware events (PWR, HUP, TSTP) and drivers. Some are the result of memory faults and kernel traps (ILL, BUS, SEGV) and some are delivered with the kill system call by another process (USR1, WINCH). By default, every signal received by a process has a default action. Some signals will cause termination of the process (INT, TERM) with possible core dumps (QUIT), and some will cause nothing to happen. Perl allows you to have signals take their default action, to ignore signals, or to handle them with code when they arrive.

To have a signal take its default action, set the appropriate entry in the hash to the literal string `"DEFAULT"`.

```
# Catching SEGV in Perl is almost
# silly.  Default action is to terminate
# the process.
$SIG{SEGV}='DEFAULT';
```

To have a signal be ignored, set the appropriate entry in the hash to the literal string `"IGNORE"`. Some signals cannot be ignored (or caught): KILL and STOP. Another special case is CHLD. A parent process that is ignoring the CHLD signal under Unix will cause child processes not to become zombies when they die.

To set a handler, assign a code reference, or the name of the subroutine you want executed, to the appropriate entry in the %SIG hash. If you assign the name of the subroutine to the %SIG hash, the subroutine is assumed to be in main::.

```
$SIG{TERM}=\&shutdown;
$SIG{TERM}=sub {
        # subroutine code here.
      };
$SIG{TERM}="shutdown";  # &main::shutdown
```

For information on how to write a signal handler, see signal handlers.

Example Listing 6.2

```
# Catch when the interrupt key
# is pressed (^C usually)
$int=0;
sub break {
    $int=1;
}
$SIG{INT}=\&break;
```

> **See Also**
>
> perlipc in the perl documentation
>
> fork, wait, kill, and signal handlers in this book
>
> signal and perlsub in the C library reference

__DIE__

Usage

$SIG{__DIE__}=*handler_ref*

Description

$SIG{__DIE__} indicates a handler for a special signal that can be caught when the Perl interpreter is about to throw a fatal error. The handler is similar to any other signal handler, and the first argument passed to the handler is the error message that the interpreter would have die()'d with if the handler had not caught it.

$SIG{__DIE__} handlers aren't nested; the handler is disabled while a $SIG{__DIE__} handler is in effect. This allows you to die() from within a __DIE__ handler and not have the handler itself called again.

After termination of the handler, Perl will continue processing the error normally.

Example Listing 6.3

```
$SIG{__DIE__}=sub {
      print "Caught the error: $_[0]\n";
      exit;
   };
$t=0;
print 1/$t;  # Causes a "divide by zero"
```

> **See Also**
> die, %SIG, signal handlers, and anonymous subroutines in this book

__WARN__

Usage

$SIG{__WARN__}=*handler_ref*

Description

The *handler_ref* indicated by the __WARN__ entry in %SIG indicates a routine to be run when the next warning message is about to be printed. The handler is similar to any other signal handler, and the first argument passed to the handler is the message that would have printed to STDERR if the handler had not caught it.

Example Listing 6.4

```
# Catch any warnings in here
# and pretty them up.
{
    local $^W=1;  # Turn on warnings here.  "use warnings;" in 5.6
    local $SIG{__WARN__}=sub {
            print "There seems to be a problem, Dave.\n";
        };
    #
    $r=undef;
    print $r;   # Will (intentionally) throw a run-time warning.
}
```

> **See Also**
> __DIE__, warn, %SIG, signal handlers, and anonymous subroutines in this book

kill

Usage

```
kill signal, list
```

Description

The kill() function sends a signal to a list of processes. The signal is a valid signal for that architecture. A valid list of signals can be obtained using the kill -l command at a Unix shell prompt.

Signal Name	Signal Number	Normal Purpose
HUP	1	Hangup
INT	2	Interrupt
KILL	9	Kill, not cacheable
ALRM	14	Alarm, triggered when an alarm() timer expires
TERM	15	Terminate

The `kill()` function returns the number of processes successfully signaled. If a signal wasn't sent, `$!` will be set to the error message. The `kill()` function can fail if the signal was invalid, the process you were trying to signal didn't exist, or you don't have sufficient privilege to signal a process.

The signal can be a signal number, or it can be a signal name—the signal name should be enclosed in quotes. A negative signal number will cause all the processes in a process group to be signaled. Under Unix, a signal number of `0` is special and will not actually affect the process named but will simply verify whether that process exists and can be signaled.

Example Listing 6.5

```
# Signal my process group with a hangup
kill 'HUP', -$$;
```

Example Listing 6.6

```
# See if the process in $child is still
# running.  $child has the child's PID
if (kill 0, $child) {
    print "Child process is still alive!";
} else {
    die "Child $child has died.";
}
```

> **See Also**
> alarm and %SIG in this book
>
> kill in the C library reference

sleep

Usage

```
sleep duration
sleep
```

Description

The `sleep` function causes the script to pause for `duration` seconds. If no `duration` is given, sleep will pause forever. The `sleep` function returns the number of seconds actually slept.

Under Unix, if the process is sent a SIGALRM signal, sleep will terminate early. Internally, sleep can be implemented using SIGALRM, so calls to sleep and alarm shouldn't be intermixed.

The actual length of time slept might seem longer because the system might not begin execution of the process immediately. For finer grained timers, the select function, the Timer::HiRes module, or the syscall function setitimer should be used.

Example Listing 6.7

```
print "Hello, world!\n";
sleep 5;
print "Same world, just 5 seconds older now!\n";
```

> **See Also**
> alarm and signal handlers in this book
> sleep in the C library reference

alarm

Usage

alarm *delay*
alarm

Description

The alarm function allows you to set a timer that will expire at a future time. This timer will deliver a SIGALRM signal to your program at that time. The SIGALARM must be caught or otherwise dealt with, or the perl script will be terminated. This function only is implemented under Unix, and under other architectures, it will result in a "function unimplemented" error from Perl.

The *delay* indicates the number of seconds to wait. If it isn't specified, $_ is used instead. Note that the signal delivery time is not precise: Vaguarities in operating system scheduling could delay the signal handler you have set up; however POSIX guarantees that the signal won't be delivered early. A *delay* of 0 will turn off an existing alarm timer.

Timers are often used to set a limit on how long a particular set of steps should take and interrupt them if things go on too long. Because system calls might restart on signal delivery, the safest way to do this is to wrap the questionable code in an `eval {}` and use `die` to exit when the alarm is delivered.

Only one of these timers is available to your process. Subsequent calls to `alarm` will disable the previous timer, and `alarm` will return the time that was left on the previous timer. An `alarm` call with `0` as an argument simply disables the previously set timer.

For finer grained timers, the `select` function, `Timer::HiRes` module, or the `syscall` function `setitimer` should be used.

On some architectures, the `sleep` system call is implemented internally using calls to `alarm`. Mixing `sleep` and `alarm` calls should therefore be avoided.

Example Listing 6.8

```
# Timing out an operation
$timeout=3;  # How long to wait...
eval {
    local $SIG{ALRM}=sub { die "timeout"; };
    print "Respond y/n in $timeout seconds: ";
    alarm $timeout;
    $a=<>;  # Wait for slow user...
    alarm 0;
};
if ($@) {
    die unless ($@ =~ /timeout/);
    print "Using default of Yes\n";
    $a="Yes";
}
```

See Also

`Timer::HiRes` module documentation

`sleep`, `syscall`, `select`, signal handlers, and `%SIG` in this book

`alarm` in the C library reference

---

wait

Usage

```
wait
```

Description

The `wait()` function causes the current `perl` process to stop and `reap` the exit code from a child process that has died, or if a child hasn't yet died, it will wait until one does to reap the exit code.

The `wait()` function returns the process ID of the deceased process. The exit status of the process is placed in the `$?` variable along with a set of flag bits indicating whether a core was dumped, a signal was received, and so on. The status is in the lower 8 bits.

The value `-1` is returned if there are no child processes to reap. If `$SIG{CHLD}` is set to `IGNORE`, children might automatically be reaped by the OS and `wait()` will always return `-1`.

Example Listing 6.9

```
$pid=fork();
die "Cannot fork: $!" if (! defined $pid);
if ($pid) { # Parent
    $reaped_pid=wait;   # Wait for the child to die
    print "Exit status: ", ($? >> 8);
} else {    # Child!
    print "I am the child.";
    exit(5);
}
```

> **See Also**
> `perlipc` module documentation
>
> `wait` in the `perl` documentation
>
> `$?`, `waitpid`, `%SIG`, and `fork` in this book
>
> `wait` in the C library reference

waitpid

Usage

```
waitpid pid, flags
```

Description

The `waitpid` function is similar to the `wait` function—it causes the process to stop and reap a deceased child process. The `pid` is the process ID you want to wait for, and `flags` describe how you want to wait. If a `pid` of `-1` is specified, `waitpid` will wait for any child of the current process to exit.

The `waitpid` function returns the process ID of the process reaped. The exit status of the process reaped is in `$?`. If no process was successfully reaped, `-1` is returned. On some systems, `waitpid` can return `0` indicating that processes are still running.

A `flag` of `0` causes `waitpid` to wait forever for a child to exit if the `process` is still running.

If your system has a `waitpid` or `wait4` system call, `waitpid` will accept flags that will allow you to do a `non-blocking` wait. This is done by importing the `sys_wait_h` symbols from the `POSIX` module.

Other flags will allow you to determine whether a process was killed with a signal (`WIFSIGNALED`), which signal was used (`WTERMSIG`), whether the child exited normally (`WIFEXITED`), and others. For details, see your system's `wait(2)` manual page. These flags should by bitwise or'd together to combine effects.

```
use POSIX ":sys_wait_h";

if (waitpid($pid, &WNOHANG | &WIFEXITED)) {
    # Child exited normally...
}
```

Note that if `$SIG{CHLD}` is set to `IGNORE`, waiting for a child might return `-1`.

Example Listing 6.10

```
$child=waitpid($pid, &WNOHANG);
if ($child == -1) {
    print "Child $pid is still processing\n";
}
```

See Also
POSIX module documentation
perlipc in the perl documentation
wait, |, and %SIG in this book
wait(2) in the C library reference

Threads

`new Thread`

Usage

`new Thread` *`coderef, list`*

Description

The `new` method in the `Thread` module returns a new `Thread` object upon success and returns false upon failure. If called with too few arguments, it will throw an exception. You must already have performed a `use Thread` or the equivalent.

coderef is a reference to a subroutine, or any other code reference, that will be executed in the new thread. The optional list is the arguments that you want passed to the subroutine.

Upon execution of `new Thread` (or `Thread->new`), the `perl` program will resume execution in two different threads. One thread will execute the statement following the `new Thread`. The other thread will begin execution at the subroutine *coderef* with the arguments from *list*.

Example Listing 6.11

```
use Thread;
sub saybye {
    print( qw(adios sayonara ciao later)[rand 4] . "\n");
}

foreach(0..9) {
    $a[$_]=Thread->new(\&saybye);
}
foreach(@a) { $_->join; }
```

See Also
async in this book

Thread Conditions

Usage

```
cond_wait variable
cond_signal variable
cond_broadcast variable
```

Description

The `cond_wait`, `cond_signal`, and `cond_broadcast` functions allow you to synchronize actions across threads. They act in a similar capacity to locks, but provide the capability to signal other processes using the variable without unlocking it.

The `cond_wait` takes a variable that has already been locked, unlocks it, and waits for another thread to do a `cond_signal` or `cond_broadcast` for the same variable. The variable is then relocked. If multiple threads are `cond_waiting` on the same variable, only one will be allowed to continue processing with the lock. The other threads will block until the lock can be re-acquired.

The `cond_signal` function allows one thread that's blocked in a `cond_wait` state on the variable and lets it continue processing. If multiple threads are in a `cond_wait` state, only one is unblocked.

The `cond_broadcast` function works similar to `cond_signal` except that all threads which are blocking in a `cond_wait` state are allowed to run.

Thread Class Methods

Usage

```
Thread->self
Thread->list
Thread->new
```

Description

The `self` class method returns a `thread` object referring to the thread instance that called it. This is useful if you want to distinguish your thread from others.

To get a `list` of threads use the `list` class method. Both running threads and unjoined-but-finished threads are returned. Threads that are detached aren't returned by `list`. Beware that when you create a thread, the process that creates the thread is itself a thread—and you can't join yourself.

The `new` method is detailed in the `new Thread` entry.

Example Listing 6.12

```
use Thread;

# Create a bunch of threads that do nothing
#
for(0..10) {
    Thread->new( sub { print "$_" } );
}

# Now reap all of the threads except for myself
#
foreach my $t (Thread->list) {
    unless (Thread->self->equal($t)) {
        $t->join;
    }
}
```

> **See Also**
> new Thread and async in this book

Thread Object Methods

Usage

```
thread->join
thread->eval
thread->equal(throbj2)
throbj->tid
throbj->detach
```

Description

The join method takes a thread (that hasn't been detached) and waits for its completion. You aren't allowed to join on your own thread, only other threads in the process. You don't have to join threads that you've created; you can join threads that were created elsewhere (in the same process). If you can obtain a thread object (through a class method), you can join that thread.

When a thread completes, it remains in existence in order to pass its return value to the thread that performs a join on it. (Detached threads are joined automatically by Perl when they return). Failure to join a thread simply wastes its return value.

The `join` method returns the return value of the thread that is being joined. If an exception was raised in the thread being joined, the exception will be thrown at the time of the `join` and must be caught with `eval {}` if you want to catch it at all.

```
eval { $thr->join() };
warn $@ if ($@);
```

An alternative way of joining a thread is with the `eval` method (not to be confused with the `eval` function). The `eval` method effectively does a `join`, but traps exceptions that result so that the `join` doesn't need to be wrapped by an `eval` block. Sometimes it's easier to deal with scoping issues this way, and it simplifies nested error traps. The variable `$@` is still set if any errors occur as with a normal `eval {}`. With the `eval` method, the previous example would be written as

```
$thr->eval();
warn $@ if ($@);
```

The `detach` method marks threads so that they don't have to be joined when they terminate. Normally, after a thread returns, another thread must reap it with `join`—a necessary step to get the return value also. The `detach` method causes `perl` to automatically reap the thread when it terminates.

Detached threads cannot return a value—there's no opportunity to `join` or `eval` the thread object because you cannot `join` a thread that's been detached. Exceptions are not caught; they're simply ignored. If you need to catch exceptions, you'll need to do it within the detached thread.

```
$thr->detach();
```

Detached threads, however, are still part of the current process. If the overall process attempts to exit when a detached thread is still active, the process will wait until that thread (actually all threads) has completed.

The `tid` method returns a unique thread ID for a particular thread. This can be used to distinguish which thread is doing which task, which thread needs to be joined (based on some outside indicator), or whatever is needed.

```
# Is $thread1 and this thread the same?
if ( Thread->self->tid() == $thread1->tid() ) {
    # They are
}
```

To compare two threads, use the `equal` method (or use the thread IDs). The `equal` method takes a `thread` object as an argument. If the two threads are the same thread, the equal method returns true and false otherwise. This is most useful when processing a Thread->list to determine whether the thread examining the list is the thread being processed. The example in the Thread class methods entry uses this so that it doesn't join on its own thread.

```
# Or, you can use this way
if ( $thread1->equal(Thread->self) ) {
    # They're the same
}
```

Example Listing 6.13

```
use Thread qw(async);

$|=1;
sub do_verylittle {
    Thread->self->detach();
    my $self=Thread->self;
    print "Waiting for ", $self->tid, " seconds\n";
    sleep($self->tid);
    print $self->tid, " all done\n";
}
for(0..5) {
    async { &do_verylittle };
}
```

> **See Also**
> Thread class methods in this book

yield

Usage

yield

Description

The yield function is a function in the Thread module used for yielding the processor to other threads. The function isn't exported by the Thread module; you have to ask for it by name.

The `yield` function's intent is to allow one thread to surrender the CPU to another thread. Unfortunately, exactly how this happens is highly dependent on your operating system. Some operating systems don't bother to yield unless a blocking system call is called, some operating systems task-switch among the threads automatically, some operating systems internally support a POSIX yield function, `sched_yield`, which handles this. Your mileage will vary.

See Also
`sched_yield` in the C library reference

---

async

Usage

`async` *block*

Description

The `async` function provides a shortcut for creating threads. In short, the `async` function

```
$obj=async { foo(); };
```

is almost exactly equivalent to the following:

```
$obj=new Thread(\&foo);
```

except it's a bit more concise. Additionally, the `async` function doesn't accept arguments as the `Thread->new()` method does. Therefore, if you want to pass anything into a block being executed by `async`, it must be a lexical variable in scope when the thread is created.

See the closure entry and consider that the `async` block will be treated in much the same way that an anonymous subroutine will be treated.

To use the `async` function, you must have already performed a use `Thread` or the equivalent. Also, the `async` function isn't exported by default: You will have to ask for it by name during the use, or call it with `Thread::async`.

Example Listing 6.14

```perl
# Factor a number in one thread, while keeping the
#   the user distracted with shiny dots in the other.

use Thread qw(async yield);

my $f=0;
my $number=410;    # Takes 4 seconds to factor.  Change to suit.
my $r=async {
    my $comp=0;

    # This is a very DUMB way to factor a number
    # but it eats CPU cycles, which is the purpose here.
    for($i=0; $i<$number; $i++) {
        for($j=0; $j<$number; $j++) {
            $comp=1 if ($i*$j==$number);
            yield;
        }
    }
    lock $f;
    $f=1;
    return $comp;
};

$|=1;
LOOP: while(1) {
    {
        lock $f;
        last LOOP if $f;
    }
    select(undef, undef, undef, 0.5);
    print ".";    # The distraction!
}
if ($r->join) {
    print "\rThe number is composite.\n";
}
```

> **See Also**
> lock and new Thread in this book

lock

Usage

```
lock variable
lock subroutine
sub subname : locked block;
```

Description

The `lock` function provides a locking mechanism on variables between threads. The only argument is a single variable that is to be locked. The `lock` call is a blocking call and will wait until the resource is unlocked.

The `lock` function creates an advisory lock on a variable in much the same way that `flock` creates an advisory lock on a file. The lock doesn't prevent you (or any other thread) from using the variable; it simply prevents other locks from taking place.

Locks also can be placed on a subroutine, which will prevent more than one thread instance from executing code in the subroutine at a time. Other threads will block waiting for the thread with the lock to exit the subroutine. Subroutine locks are mandatory and are enforced by the interpreter.

To place a lock on a subroutine at runtime, simply use the `lock` function with a subroutine name:

```
lock &critical;
```

To set a lock on a subroutine at compile time, use the `locked` attribute on the subroutine when it's defined. The `locked` keyword follows the subname and a colon. This allows only one thread at a time to enter the subroutine and is enforced by the `perl` interpreter. It also is faster than a runtime lock because the interpreter doesn't have to check for the lock at runtime.

```
sub critical : locked {
    # Body of subroutine
}
```

Locks should be used anywhere that a single resource could be affected by multiple concurrent threads. Erecting a lock around that resource will help prevent data corruption.

You can lock any kind of variable:

```
lock $name;
lock @addresses;
lock %fields;
```

You also can lock individual components of aggregate variables (hashes and arrays):

```
lock $addresses[50];
lock $fields{key};
lock @fields{'thing1', 'thing2'};
```

But locking a member of an aggregate doesn't lock the entire aggregate. And the reverse is true: Locking an element doesn't lock the whole. Locking a reference causes the thing being referenced to be locked. Perl will do the dereference for you. This way, you can lock an object instead of locking the reference itself.

There is no facility for unlocking a resource. The `lock` function's actions are dynamically scoped; when Perl exits the block, `eval`, or file in which the lock was created, the resource will be unlocked.

The `lock` function name is treated specially by the Perl interpreter. If a subroutine named `lock` is declared prior to the `lock` function being used, the user's lock subroutine is used (for backward compatibility). On non-threaded versions of Perl or if `use Threads` isn't in effect, `lock` is a no-op. If you have a user-defined `lock` function and need to use the built-in variable locking version of `lock`, calling `&CORE::lock` will always get the internal version.

Example Listing 6.15

```
# Example of locking
#   This example always prints 1,000,000
#   However, removing the lock will cause the
#   value to vary, more or less depending on your
#   architecture's threading support.

use Thread qw(yield async);
my $count=0;
for(1..1000) {
    push @t, async {
        for(1..1000) {
            lock $count;
            $k=$count;
            $k++;
```

```
            yield;
            $count=$k;
        }
    };
}
for(@t) { $_->join; }
print "Counted to $count\n";
```

Example Listing 6.16

```
# Same as above, except with a locked
#    subroutine, will always yield 1000000

use Thread qw(yield async);
my $count=0;
sub addone : locked {
    $k=$count;
    $k++;
    yield;
    $count=$k;
}
for(1..1000) {
    push @t, async {
        for(1..1000) {
            &addone;
        }
    };
}
for(@t) { $_->join; }
print "Counted to $count\n";
```

> **See Also**
> flock and new Thread in this book

Sockets

socket

Usage

```
socket socket, family, type, protocol
```

Description

The socket function opens a socket for the appropriate address/protocol family, of the correct type for the specified protocol. This is the first step in establishing a network connection for both a client and a server. The function returns true if the socket is created successfully.

The Socket module contains the correct constants for the values family and type. Programs that attempt to set these constants directly will not run portably on supported architectures. The Socket module also contains easy-to-use wrappers for most of the network-related functions.

Usual values for family are AF_UNIX, AF_INET, PF_UNIX, and PF_INET; these indicate what kind of connection will be established—whether it is expected to be local on this Unix system or transmitted over a network (even if it is localized to this machine). Most of the examples in this book use AF_INET.

The type is usually one of SOCK_STREAM, SOCK_DGRAM, or SOCK_RAW. These determine whether a connection will be a stream protocol, datagram protocol, or a raw connection.

The combination of family and type determine what valid protocol can be used. In the AF_INET family, SOCK_STREAM indicates a TCP protocol should be used, SOCK_DGRAM indicates UDP, and SOCK_RAW indicates IP. Values for protocol are retrieved with getprotobyname.

The socket call will fail if the protocol combination is invalid for this system, you don't have permission to create the socket, or there is insufficient memory to set up the socket. The error code will be stored in $! if socket returns false. The socket will be closed when an exec happens on systems with a close on exec flag for file descriptors. This can be avoided by manipulating the $^F variable.

Example Listing 6.17

```
# Retrieves / from the webserver on localhost
# (The Hard Way.  The LWP module should really be used.)
use Socket;
socket(WEBSERVER, AF_INET, SOCK_STREAM, getprotobyname("tcp"))
    or die "Socket could not be created: $!";
$address=inet_aton("127.0.0.1")
    or die "Address didn't convert: $!";
$remote_port=sockaddr_in(scalar getservbyname("www", "tcp"), $address);
unless (connect(WEBSERVER, $remote_port)) {
    die "Server is down\n";
}
```

```
$_=select(WEBSERVER); $|=1;
select(STDOUT);
print WEBSERVER "GET / 1.0\n\n";

print <WEBSERVER>;
```

See Also
Socket module documentation

getprotobyname and $! in this book

socket in the C library reference

bind

Usage

```
bind socket, bindaddress
```

Description

The bind function attaches an existing socket to a port and address on the local host. The function returns true if the port was successfully bound, or false otherwise.

The bindaddress consists of a port and an IP address on the local machine packed with sockaddr_in from the Socket module.

Each address/port combination on a server can be bound to only by a single process. This is necessary to provide a well-known address if the socket will be used by a server and connected to by a client. Also if a client wants to use a connectionless protocol (UDP), the bind will provide a place for UDP replies to be transmitted. The special address INADDR_ANY binds to every interface on the local machine.

```
socket(SOCK, AF_INET, SOCK_STREAM, getprotobyname("tcp")) || die;
# bind to all interfaces on the local machine
$sockaddr=sockaddr_in($port, INADDR_ANY);
bind(SOCK, $sockaddr) || die;
```

The bind can fail if (under Unix) you aren't the superuser and you bind to a port less than 1024, if the port is already bound, if the socket hasn't been created, or for other reasons. The reason for failure is stored in $!.

Example Listing 6.18

```
use Socket;

# Provides an atomic locking and unlocking function
# even on systems which don't support flock().
# my_lock returns true or false if the lock was set or not.
#    If there was an error, undef is returned.
$lock_port=9999;   # Should be unique to each kind of lock you
           # want to set
sub my_lock {
    socket(SOCK, AF_INET, SOCK_STREAM, getprotobyname('tcp'))
        or die "Cannot create socket: $!";
    return(1) if
        bind(SOCK, sockaddr_in($lock_port, inet_aton("localhost")));
    if ($! !~ /already/i) {
        return;
    }
    0;
}
sub my_unlock {
    close(SOCK);
}
```

See Also

Socket module documentation

`socket`, `getprotobyname`, and `flock` in this book

`bind` in the C library reference

`connect`

Usage

```
connect socket, servaddr
```

Description

The connect function is the second step in establishing a network connection to a server. A socket is created with the socket command, and the connect function completes the connection of the socket to the other end of the virtual circuit with the server. If the connection succeeds, connect returns true.

The connection function isn't needed when connecting to a connectionless service (UDP).

servaddr is a packed representation of the remote server's address and port number. This can be constructed using the sockaddr_in and inet_aton functions from the Socket module:

```
$servaddr=sockaddr_in($portnum, inet_aton($servername));
```

The connection function can fail if the connection was refused, timed out, denied for insufficient permissions, or if the socket wasn't created completely. The error code is stored in $! if connect fails.

Example Listing 6.19

```
# Find the user-id of the person running this program.
# Assumes that an identd server is running on this system.
use Socket;
use IO::Handle;  # For autoflush

socket(SOCK, AF_INET, SOCK_STREAM, getprotobyname('tcp'))
    or die "Cannot create socket: $!";
$remoteport=getservbyname("auth", "tcp");
connect(SOCK, sockaddr_in($remoteport, inet_aton("localhost")))
    or die "Cannot connect to server: $!";

# Find my half of the connection
$myaddr=(getsockname(SOCK))[0];
SOCK->autoflush(1);

print SOCK +(unpack_sockaddr_in($myaddr))[0],",$remoteport\n";
print scalar(<SOCK>);
```

> **See Also**
> Socket module documentation
> socket and $! in this book

listen

Usage

```
listen socket, backlog
```

Description

The listen function informs the operating system that this socket is willing to receive connections on a connection-oriented socket (SOCK_STREAM). This is the third step in setting up a server to accept socket connections. This is normally done just prior to an accept. The listen function returns true if it succeeded.

The *backlog* indicates how many connections should queue up waiting to be handled by an accept. The maximum size of the backlog is SOMAXCONN defined in the Socket module, although some systems might silently lower this value.

If the listen fails, $! will be set to the error message.

Example Listing 6.20

```
# A simple echo server.  Connect to it at port 1099
# (with telnet if you like) and type 1 line.  It will
# be echo'd back to you.
use Socket;
socket(SOCK, AF_INET, SOCK_STREAM, getprotobyname('tcp'))
    || die "socket: $!";
bind(SOCK, sockaddr_in(1099, INADDR_ANY)) || die "bind: $!";
listen(SOCK, SOMAXCONN) || die "listen: $!";
# Connections can now queue up and be accepted.
if ( accept(NEWSOCK, SOCK)) {
    $a=<NEWSOCK>;
    print NEWSOCK $a;
} else { die "Accept failed: $!"; }
```

> **See Also**
> Socket module documentation
> accept, socket, and bind in this book
> listen in the C library reference

accept

Usage

```
accept newsock, oldsock
```

Description

The accept function takes one socket request from those that have been queued up on a bound port and connects it to *newsock*. The *oldsock* is the socket that was created with socket, bound to a port with bind and given to the listen function. The oldsock remains unaltered by the accept call: It is merely there to create a clone (newsock). The accept function will wait (block) if no pending client connections are in the queue.

If successful, newsock will be connected to the client's socket and accept will return the packed address of the client (IP address and port). This address can be unpacked with unpack_sockaddr_in from the Socket module.

If the accept fails, it will return false. A non-blocking accept can be created by using fcntl to set the O_NONBLOCK option on the socket before the accept.

Example Listing 6.21

```
# A _very_ insecure file server.  Accepts connections
#    on port 1100 and 1 line of input (telnet can be used
#    to test).  Given a filename will print the contents of the
#    file back to the client.
# Demonstrates forking a child to process a request while
#    the parent waits for more connections -- the basis of most
#    internet services under Unix.

use Socket;

socket(SOCK, AF_INET, SOCK_STREAM, getprotobyname('tcp')) || die;
bind(SOCK, sockaddr_in(1100, INADDR_ANY)) || die "$!";
listen(SOCK, SOMAXCONN) || die "Listen failed: $!";

# Connections can now queue up and be accepted.
while ( accept(NEWSOCK, SOCK) )  {
    $pid=fork();
    die unless (defined $pid);

    # Parent loops up to get another connection..
    next if $pid;

    # ... while the child processes the request
    $a=<NEWSOCK>;
    push(@ARGV, $a);
```

```
        print NEWSOCK <>;
        exit;
}
```

See Also
Socket module documentation
`socket`, `bind`, `listen`, and `fcntl` in this book
`accept` in the C library reference

---

shutdown

Usage

shutdown *socket*, *how*

Description

Sockets are (normally) full duplex communication channels. The `shutdown` function allows one side of a socket to close it's reading or writing channel. Contrast this to `close`, which will close the socket entirely.

To close the reading side of this socket, set *how* to 0. To close the writing side, set *how* to 1. To close both sides, set *how* to 2. The `shutdown` function will return false if it fails and set `$!`.

Beware that `shutdown` (unlike `close`) affects open copies of this socket in forked children as well as the current process under Unix.

Example Listing 6.22

```
# A simple logging daemon.  Connect, and send 1 line
# which will be stored.
# Uses the locking functions from bind() example #2
use Socket;

$logfile="/tmp/a_logfile";
$port=1101;
socket(SOCK, AF_INET, SOCK_STREAM, getprotobyname('tcp')) || die;
bind(SOCK, sockaddr_in($port, INADDR_ANY)) || die "$!";
listen(SOCK, SOMAXCONN) || die "Listen failed: $!";
```

```
while ( accept(NEWSOCK, SOCK) )  {
    shutdown(NEWSOCK, 1);  # No writing needs to be done.
    $message=<NEWSOCK>;
    my_lock();
    open(LOGFILE, ">>$logfile") || die;
    print LOGFILE $message;
    close(LOGFILE);
    my_unlock();
    close(NEWSOCK);
}
```

See Also
Socket module documentation

bind, socket, listen, close, and accept in this book

shutdown in the C library reference

---

socketpair

Usage

```
socketpair socket1, socket2, family, type, protocol
```

Description

The socketpair function creates two sockets connected to each other using the specified family, type, and protocol. See the socket entry for details on those parameters.

The socketpair function returns true on success and false otherwise. If the function fails, the error code will be stored in $!.

This function is typically used before a fork to create a communications channel between two processes, similar to the pipe function but less messy. After the fork, the child closes one socket, and the parent closes the other. The remaining socket in each child and parent can be used for reading or writing to the other.

Example Listing 6.23

```
use Socket;
die "Socketpair: $!" unless
    (socketpair(PARENT, CHILD, AF_UNIX, SOCK_STREAM, PF_UNSPEC));
```

```
$pid=fork();
die "Fork failed?  $!" unless (defined $pid);
if ($pid) {      # I am the parent
    close(PARENT);
    print CHILD "Hello, my child!\n";
    exit;
} else {
    close(CHILD);
    print scalar <PARENT>;
    exit;
}
```

See Also
Socket module documentation

pipe, fork, and socket in this book

socketpair in the C library reference

---

getsockname

Usage

getsockname *socket*

Description

The getsockname function returns the packed address for this side of a connected socket (the local end). This is useful for determining which IP address a socket uses for connecting.

The address returned is in a packed format, and can be unpacked with the sockaddr_in function from the Socket module.

If an error occurs, getsockname returns undef and sets $! to the error message.

Example Listing 6.24

```
# Solves a recurring question: How do I find
# my own IP address?  It does this by establishing
# a foreign connection and then noticing what
# interface was used.  This isn't foolproof and having
# multiple interfaces is one way to fool this.
```

```perl
use Socket;

# Where we connect to is not important...as long as it's
# not *here*.
socket(SOCK, AF_INET, SOCK_STREAM, getprotobyname('tcp'))
    or die "Cannot create socket: $!";
$remoteport=getservbyname("www", "tcp");

# Won't work if you actually run this at Yahoo. Change as necessary.
connect(SOCK, sockaddr_in($remoteport, inet_aton("www.yahoo.com")))
    or die "Cannot connect to server: $!";

# Find my half of the connection
$myaddr=(getsockname(SOCK))[0];

($address)=(sockaddr_in($myaddr))[1];
print "My local IP address is ", inet_ntoa($address);
```

See Also
Socket module documentation

socket and connect in this book

getsockname in the C library reference

getsockopt

Usage

```
getsockopt socket, level, option
```

Description

The getsockopt function retrieves the value for the given socket specified by level and option. The level and option values are explained in the setsockopt entry.

If the option cannot be retrieved, getsockopt returns undef and sets $! to the error message.

Example Listing 6.25

```perl
# Simple program to retrieve 1 option from a
# socket.  This is the Receive Buffer queue size.
```

```
use Socket;

socket(SOCK, AF_INET, SOCK_STREAM, getprotobyname('tcp'))
    or die "Cannot create socket: $!";
$remoteport=getservbyname("www", "tcp");
connect(SOCK, sockaddr_in($remoteport, inet_aton("www.yahoo.com")))
    or die "Cannot connect to server: $!";

# The buffer size is a native integer
print "Receive buffer size is: ",
    unpack("I", getsockopt(SOCK, SOL_SOCKET, SO_RCVBUF));
```

> **See Also**
> Socket module documentation
>
> unpack, socket, and setsockopt in this book
>
> getsockopt in the C library reference

setsockopt

Usage

setsockopt socket, level, option, value

Description

The setsockopt function adjusts the options for the socket. This allows you to control features such as whether the socket blocks (waits for I/O), adjusts timeouts, adjusts buffer sizes, and other options. These options are specific to your operating system, and your OS documentation should be consulted. Some options are more portable than others.

The level parameter specifies what part of the socket's stack you want to manipulate from very low level (IPPROTO_IP) up to the general socket layer (SOL_SOCKET). The options also vary depending on what layer you're trying to manipulate.

The value depends on the option, of course. For some options, this is simply a boolean, and for other options, this is an integer value.

The function returns true if successful; otherwise undef is returned and $! has the error message.

Example Listing 6.26

```
# Normally if a process is bound to a port and dies, it
# can't immediately re-bind to the port.  This is normally
# a feature.  You can circumvent this by setting the SO_REUSEADDR
# option on the socket.

# (Not a self-contained program, it doesn't do anything with the
#   socket it's created...)
use Socket;

$port=1101;
socket(SOCK, AF_INET, SOCK_STREAM, getprotobyname('tcp')) || die;
bind(SOCK, sockaddr_in($port, INADDR_ANY)) || die "$!";

setsockopt(SOCK, SOL_SOCKET, SO_REUSEADDR, 1) || die "sockopt: $!";
listen(SOCK, SOMAXCONN) || die "Listen failed: $!";

while ( $address=accept(NEWSOCK, SOCK) )  {
    #  Processing in here....
}
```

> **See Also**
> Socket module documentation
>
> bind in this book
>
> setsockopt in the C library reference

getpeername

Usage

getpeername *socket*

Description

The getpeername function returns a packed network address representing the other end of the socket. This can be used to see what machine has connected to you (if you're a server) or what port and machine you've connected to if you weren't specific (if you're a client).

The address can be unpacked into a proper IP address and port using the `sockaddr_in` function from the Socket module.

If there is a problem, `getpeername` returns `undef` and sets `$!` to the error message.

Example Listing 6.27

```
# A simple server to echo the IP address of where
# you're connecting from.
use Socket;

socket(SOCK, AF_INET, SOCK_STREAM, getprotobyname('tcp')) || die;
bind(SOCK, sockaddr_in(1100, INADDR_ANY)) || die "$!";
listen(SOCK, SOMAXCONN) || die "Listen failed: $!";
$address=accept(NEWSOCK, SOCK);
die "Cannot accept: $!" unless $address;

# The address returned by getpeername is exactly the same
# as the one you would get from accept on the socket
$otheraddr=getpeername(NEWSOCK);
($port,$addr)=sockaddr_in($otheraddr);
print NEWSOCK "Connected from $port at ",
    scalar gethostbyaddr($addr, AF_INET);
```

> **See Also**
> Socket module documentation
> `socket` and `bind` in this book
> `getpeername` in the C library reference

recv

Usage

```
recv socket, scalar, maxlen, flags
```

Description

The `recv` function receives data on a socket. The data is received and placed in the scalar variable `scalar`. At most `maxlen` bytes are received at a time. The scalar variable will grow or shrink as appropriate to hold the data received.

The recv function returns the sender's socket address if successful. This then can be unpacked into a port and address with sockaddr_in. Otherwise recv returns undef, and sets $! to the error message.

Example Listing 6.28

```
# A small (connectionless!) server.
# Simply binds a socket to a port and waits for
#   messages to arrive and prints them.
# The client is in the send() entry's example.

use Socket;
$|=1;  # auto-flush STDOUT

$port=7001;
socket(SOCK, AF_INET, SOCK_DGRAM, getprotobyname("udp"))
    || die "socket: $!";
bind(SOCK, sockaddr_in($port, INADDR_ANY))
    || die "bind: $!";

# Maximum message size of 256 is arbitrary here.
while(defined (recv(SOCK, $message, 256, 0))) {
    print "Received the message $message\n";
}
```

See Also
Socket module documentation

send, socket, and bind in this book

recvfrom in the C library reference

---

send

Usage

```
send socket, message, flags, dest
send socket, message, flags
```

Description

The `send` function sends a `message` on a socket. This is an alternative to actually using the standard I/O mechanisms (`print`, `<>`) on sockets and might work more reliably on some architectures that don't fully support sockets as standard I/O (MS Windows).

The function works similar to the system's built-in `send` function. The `message` is the data you want to be sent. If the socket is a connectionless socket (`UDP`/`datagram`), `dest` specifies the port and address of the target machine to send the `message` to.

The `flags` parameter allows you to control how the message is sent, and constants are available from the Socket module. For example, `MSG_DONTWAIT` performs a send and doesn't block (on connected sockets). If the socket cannot be sent to, a failure results immediately. For more flags, see your OS's documentation on `send`.

The `send` function returns the number of bytes sent. If the function fails, `undef` is returned and `$!` is set to the error message.

Example Listing 6.29

```
# A small UDP (connectionless!) client.
# Simply drops a message to a waiting UDP server.
# Returns no errors if the server isn't there.
#   (That's what UDP is all about!)
# The server is in the recv() entry's example

use Socket;

$port=7001;          # The port the server is bound to
$server="127.0.0.1";# The server's IP address

socket(SOCK, AF_INET, SOCK_DGRAM, getprotobyname('udp'))
    || die "socket: $!";
$servaddr=sockaddr_in($port, inet_aton($server));
if (! defined send(SOCK, "Hello World!", 0, $servaddr)) {
    print "Error $!";
}
```

> **See Also**
> Socket module documentation
> `recv` and `socket` in this book
> `send` and `sendto` in the C library reference

gethostbyaddr

Usage

```
gethostbyaddr address, addresstype
```

Description

The gethostbyaddr function translates Internet addresses into names. Given an address that is a packed binary representation of the numeric address, it will produce the common hostname that corresponds to that address.

The gethostbyaddr function returns a five-element list consisting of

Position	Name	Type
0	name	"official" name of host.
1	aliases	Alias list, other names for the host. Space separated.
2	addrtype	Usually AF_INET, from the Socket module.
3	length	Length of an Internet address, always 4.
4	@addresses	List of addresses, packed binary.

Many of these fields aren't used currently, or are under used. In a scalar context, gethostbyaddr returns only the name portion.

Packing and unpacking of the addresses in the return value, the address in the argument, and discovering the value for addresstype is not particularly easy. The Socket module contains routines for doing this easily.

To construct address, use the Socket module's inet_aton() function passing it a string that represents the Internet address as a dotted-quad (for example, 127.0.0.1). The addresstype is always AF_INET (Socket will substitute the correct value for this constant.)

To unpack the array of addresses (there is usually just one), use the inet_ntoa function provided by the Socket module.

The address to name lookup is performed using your system's name resolution mechanisms. For example, during the course of a gethostbyaddr /etc/hosts, DNS, NIS, LDAP, or other OS-provided directory services can be consulted.

Example Listing 6.30

```
# Get a host name for an IP address
#   (assumes the IP address points to a valid host)
use Socket;

$ip=inet_aton("192.168.1.2");
$hostname=gethostbyaddr($ip, AF_INET);
print "The host is $hostname\n";
```

Example Listing 6.31

```
# Get alias names for an IP address
#   (assumes the IP address points to a valid host)
use Socket;

$ip2=inet_aton("192.168.1.5");
($hostname,$aliases,$addrtype,
    $length, @addresses)=gethostbyaddr($ip2, AF_INET);
print "Alias for the second machine are: $aliases\n";
print "Addresses are: ",
    join("\n\t", map inet_ntoa($_), @addresses);
```

See Also

Net::hostent and Socket module documentation

gethostbyname in this book

gethostbyaddr in the C library reference

---

gethostbyname

Usage

gethostbyname *hostname*

Description

The gethostbyname function translates hostnames into addresses, and other names for that host. Given a hostname, in a list context, gethostbyname will retrieve a structure outlined in the gethostbyaddr entry consisting of name, aliases, addrtype, length, and addresses.

In a scalar context, `gethostbyname` will retrieve just the address.

The address returned is packed in binary and will need to be unpacked to display properly. The Socket module contains the `inet_ntoa()` function for doing this, or you can use unpack:

```
($first, $second, $third, $fourth)=unpack('C4', $address[0]);.
```

The name to address lookup will be performed using your operating system's normal name lookup mechanisms (DNS, NIS, /etc/hosts). An alternative interface to name and address lookups is provided by the `Net::hostent` module.

Example Listing 6.32

```
use Socket;

($name, $aliases, $addrtype, $length, @addresses)=
    gethostbyname("www.perl.org");
print "The IP Address is: ", inet_ntoa($addresses[0]);
```

> **See Also**
> `Net::hostent` and Socket module documentation
>
> `gethostbyaddr` in this book
>
> `gethostbyname` in the C library reference

getservent

Usage

```
getservent
setservent stayopen
endservent
getservbyname name, protocol
getservbyport port, protocol
```

Description

The family of functions represented by `getservent` are used to read the database that maps Internet services to `port` numbers. Under Unix, this database is typically /etc/services. Under Windows 9X, it's found in c:\Windows\Services, and the database can be supplemented by other network services such as NIS. In a list context, the getservent, getservbyport, and getservbyname functions return a listing of name, aliases, port number, and protocol name. If no matching entries are found or the list is exhausted with getservent, an empty list is returned.

In a scalar context getservent and getservbyport return just the service name; getservbyname returns the port number. If no matching entries are found, undef is returned.

The getservent function returns one entry from the services database, and successive calls will return the next entry until no entries are left. At this point, getservent returns false. The list can be reset to the beginning with setservent, and the database closed with endservent.

The getservbyname function returns the matching entry for the given name and protocol (which is typically the string literal "tcp" or "udp"). The getservbyproto function returns the matching entry for the given port and protocol.

The getservent function isn't implemented under Windows, although getservbyport and getservbyname work just fine.

Example Listing 6.33

```
# See which privileged ports are listening
#   on this system.  A rudimentary security tool.
# Requires the external program "netstat"
#   available on Windows and Unix.  The output format
#   may vary slightly.  Adjust the regular expression
#   accordingly
@ns=`netstat -an`;
foreach(@ns) {
    next unless (($proto, $port)=/(tcp|udp).*?  # Protocol
        (?:[\d.]+):(\d+)                        # Address and Port
        .*LISTEN/ix);                           # and that it's listening
    next unless ($port<1024);
    $name=getservbyport($port, $proto);
    $name="Unknown" unless ($name);
    print "Service $name is open on $port\n";
}
```

> **See Also**
> Net::servent module documentation
> getservent, getservbyname, and getservbyport in the C library reference

gethostent

Usage

gethostent

Description

The gethostent function reads the /etc/hosts file and returns entries from it. The list retrieved is outlined in the gethostbyaddr entry consisting of name, aliases, addrtype, length, and addresses.

The addresses returned are packed in binary and will need to be unpacked to display properly. The Socket module contains the inet_ntoa() function for doing this, or you can use unpack with a 'C4' template.

Successive calls to gethostent will return the next entry until there are no entries left and gethostent will return false. To reset the list to the beginning, call sethostent. To close the /etc/hosts file, call endhostent.

This function is available only under Unix. In fact, because your operating system might have other mechanisms to retrieve host and address information (for example, DNS), it shouldn't be used on systems with name services, and might not even be implemented on such systems.

Example Listing 6.34

```
# Re-write hosts file in sorted (by name) order
use Socket;
%hosts=();
while(  ($name, $ip)=(gethostent)[0,4] ) {
    $hosts{$name}=$ip;
}
foreach my $host (sort keys %hosts) {
    print inet_ntoa($hosts{$host}), " $host\n";
}
```

> **See Also**
> Net::hostent module documentation
>
> gethostbyaddr in this book
>
> gethostent in the C library reference

getprotoent

Usage

```
getprotoent
setprotoent stayopen
endprotoent
getprotobyname name
getprotobynumber protocolnumber
```

Description

The family of functions represented by getprotoent are used to read the database that maps Internet protocols (IP, TCP, UDP) to protocol numbers. These numbers are used exclusively in creating a socket for network communications. Under Unix, this database is typically /etc/protocols. Under Windows 9X, it's found in c:\Windows\Protocols. In a list context, the getprotoent, getprotobynumber, and getprotobyname functions return a listing of name, aliases, and protocol number. If no matching entries are found or the list is exhausted with getprotoent, an empty list is returned.

In a scalar context, getprotoent and getprotobynumber return just the protocol name; getprotobyname returns the protocol number. If no matching entries are found, undef is returned.

The getprotoent function returns one entry from the services database, and successive calls will return the next entry until no entries are left. At this point, getprotoent returns false. The list can be reset to the beginning with setprotoent, and the database closed with endprotoent.

The getprotobyname function returns the matching entry for the given name. The getprotobynumber function returns the matching entry for the given protocolnumber.

The getprotoent function isn't implemented under Windows, although getprotobynumber and getprotobyname work just fine.

Example Listing 6.35

```
# Test to see if the www interface is
# running on this machine
use Socket;  # For constants and functions
socket(WEBSERVER, AF_INET, SOCK_STREAM, getprotobyname("tcp"))
    or die "Socket could not be created: $!";
$address=inet_aton("127.0.0.1")
    or die "Address didn't convert: $!";
```

```
$remote_port=sockaddr_in(scalar getservbyname("www", "tcp"), $address);

unless (connect(WEBSERVER, $remote_port)) {
    die "Server is down\n";
} else {
    print "Server is OK\n";
}
```

> **See Also**
> Net::proto module documentation
> getprotoent, getprotobyname, and getprotobynumber in the C library reference

Process Creation/Modification

pipe

Usage

```
pipe reader, writer
```

Description

The pipe function creates a pair of connected filehandles. One is designated as a filehandle to be read, the other to be written. If the pipe cannot be set up, the pipe function returns undef.

Indirect filehandle names are allowed (as in open). Also, because the standard I/O library is used, buffering is (by default) enabled for the filehandles. The writer might want to turn on auto-flushing for the filehandle to help prevent starvation by the reader.

This function is usually called just before a fork is performed to connect two processes. After the fork, the child should close one of the filehandles, and the parent should close the other. The remaining filehandles can be read (if the reader remains open) or written (if the writer remains open). It is necessary to close the unused ends of the filehandles to allow an EOF to be sent when the writer is finished writing.

It is inadvisable to set up a pair of pipes for bi-directional communication because there is a danger of deadlock.

On some systems, the native C system call `pipe(2)` allows bi-directional communication along the pipes. Perl's `pipe` function doesn't, and it complies with POSIX by allowing traffic to flow only one way.

Example Listing 6.36

```
# Simple communication between a parent and child
#

use IO::Handle;
pipe(READ, WRITE) || die "Cannot build pipe: $!";
WRITE->autoflush(1);

if (! defined($pid=fork())) {
    die "Cannot fork: $!";
}

if (! $pid) {
    close(READ);
    print WRITE "Hello, World\n";
} else {
    close(WRITE);
    $a=<READ>;
    print "Child saw $a\n";
}
```

See Also

IO::Handle module documentation

perlipc in the perl documentation

open, close, and fork in this book

pipe in the C library reference

---

qx

Usage

qx{command}

Description

The qx operator, also known as the *command input* operator, is used to run an external command and return the results of that command. It's function is similar to that of encasing a command in backticks.

First the command is scanned for variables to interpolate, and those are replaced. The result is passed to the operating system and run. Pipes, redirection, and any other command-line features will be used by your operating system as normal.

The output is captured and put in place of the qx expression. In a scalar context, a single string consisting of all the output (including end-of-line characters) is returned. In a list context, the output is returned as a list with each list element being one line of output.

The {} in the usage can be replaced with any other delimiters of your choice. The acceptable values for delimiters are any values that aren't alphanumeric or whitespace. Using a single quote as a delimiter will cause Perl not to do variable interpolation on your command, however.

Choose bracketing delimiters with qx, which makes your code readable.

The exit status from the command is preserved in the variable $?. Internally qx{} and backticks are implemented using fork, exec, and reading a pipe. For particulars and side effects of this implementation, see those sections in this manual.

Example Listing 6.37

```
# Get a listing of files in /tmp
# Note the different delimiters
@files=qx!ls -1 /tmp!;
print "Tempfiles are: ", join(',', @files);
```

Example Listing 6.38

```
# This uses Perl's idea of $HOME.
$HOME="/home/httpd";
@http_files=qx{ls -1 $HOME};

# This uses the shell's idea of $HOME
@home_files=qx{ls -1 \$HOME};
```

See Also
quote operators, $?, fork, exec, pipe, and system in the C library reference

system

Usage

```
system list
system progname list
```

Description

The system function runs an external command on behalf of the Perl program. The return value of the function is the exit status of the external command. The output of the command is sent wherever it normally would go.

To capture the external command's output, use backticks or qx{} instead of system. The Perl program will wait for the external command to be finished before returning control to the rest of the program. If you want to spawn a program asynchronously, you will need to have the operating system's shell start the program in the background, or use fork to create a daemon.

```
# Run the backup, but don't wait.
system("tar cvf /dev/rmt0 /usr &");
```

The return value for system is the same as the wait function. The actual exit status is stored in the lower 8 bits. The wait function entry in this book contains examples for parsing that return value. Note that this normally results in the system returning false when the external command succeeds and true when it fails.

Argument handling is performed exactly as with the exec function; a single argument is scanned for metacharacters and passed to a shell, and a list is passed directly to the underlying exec call. See the exec entry for details.

While the external command is running, SIGINT and SIGQUIT are trapped by Perl. This is done so that pressing Ctrl+C (or however your interrupt key is programmed) will only interrupt that program and not the Perl script.

Example Listing 6.39

```
# Edit the hosts file
system "notepad.exe c:\Windows\hosts";
```

Example Listing 6.40

```
# Run the vi editor in its read-only mode
$realname="/usr/bin/vi";
```

```
unless ( system $realname "view", "myfile" ) {
    print "File edited";
} else {
    print "Editing with vi failed.";
}
```

> **See Also**
> exec, wait, fork, qx{}, and signal handlers in this book

exec

Usage

```
exec list
exec progname list
```

Description

The exec() function overlays the current running process image with a new image. In other words, the code and data associated with the current process are replaced with a new program. The process slot is re-used and any open file descriptors are kept open in the new process image.

The exec() function doesn't normally return—there is no return value to be had. If the exec() fails, $! is set to the error message and your Perl program continues running at the statement following the exec(). (This is how you will know if it fails.) If warnings are enabled, the only legal Perl statements that can follow an exec() are exit, die or warn.

Normally exec() only fails if the program you're trying to exec() isn't a runnable program, you don't have permission to run it, or the OS cannot load the object file (no memory, text file busy, or the argument list is too long). The exec() function can fail; you should always have code in place to catch that condition.

Terminating your program with exec() won't call your END blocks; nor are any DESTROY methods for your objects called.

In its first form, exec() takes a list of arguments to be passed to a command shell. If there's only one argument, exec() will scan that argument for shell metacharacters (pipes, ampersands, and so on). If there are any metacharacters, the argument is passed to the shell for processing and execution. Under Unix, this is handled with

`/bin/sh -c`. If there are no shell metacharacters, it is split into words and then processed as though there were multiple arguments to `exec()`.

```
# Processed with /bin/sh.  $HOME is a shell variable
exec 'du -sk $HOME';
```

If `exec()` is given a list of arguments, they are passed to the `execvp()` system call in Unix.

```
# Processed directly with execvp()
exec 'telnet', 'world.std.com', '25';
```

With multiple arguments, no shell processing is done. This is a faster and safer way to run `exec()` when available.

In some cases, it's necessary to run a program with `exec()` and have that program's name be something other than its execution pathname. (Some programs change behavior depending on the name by which they were called.) To do this, use the second form of `exec()`, which takes a program name and a list to run, as well as a list. The program name is the actual executable file you want to run. The first element in the list is what the program's name will be.

```
# Run a shell, -sh makes it think its
# a login shell
$realname='/bin/sh';
exec $realname '-sh';
```

Note that there's no comma between the `'/bin/sh'` and the `'-sh'` in this form of `exec()`. This is to distinguish it from the exec `list` form.

Example Listing 6.41

```
# Print a message, run netscape

# Turn off buffering, exec() doesn't flush
select(STDOUT); $|=1;
print "Loading netscape...";

exec '/usr/bin/netscape',
    '-remote',
    'openURL("http://www.perl.com")';
die "Netscape did not load: $!";
```

fork

Usage

fork()

Description

The fork() function causes a new process to be created that is a nearly exact copy of the current process. The process that forked (now called the *parent*) and the process that was forked (now called the *child*) continue executing at the instruction immediately following the fork().

The return value is present in both the parent and the child. In the parent, the return value of fork() is the process ID of the child. In the child, the return value is 0. If the fork fails, fork() will return undef and $! will be set to the error message. Typically, fork() will fail if the number of processes for the user has been exceeded, or if there is insufficient system memory to create a new process.

Memory, permissions, environment and all other attributes of the parent process are copied into the child. File descriptors are shared between the parent and the child.

Writing or reading shared file descriptors after a fork() can cause unintended behavior. Any unneeded file descriptors in the parent (or child) should be closed after the fork(). Unflushed data in those file descriptors will be flushed in 5.6 prior to the fork() being executed.

In prior versions of Perl, you must manually flush data from the buffers using the autoflush variable with the file descriptor set (see $|) or use the autoflush() method of IO::Handle before the fork to prevent buffered data in both the parent and the child from being written.

If the child dies, a CHLD signal will be delivered to the parent. The parent process must reap the child using the wait function, or zombie processes will occur. (You can ignore the CHLD signal using %SIG; in which case, you don't have to wait.) If the parent dies, the child might die or it might be inherited by the parent's parent. A child that doesn't have a direct ancestor capable of inheriting the child is an orphaned child and is inherited by the special `init` process under Unix. This is part of the technique for creating a `daemon` process in Unix.

The `fork()` function is available under the Windows architecture since version 5.6 of Perl. On that system, `fork()` is emulated by using threads. To create a daemon process under Windows, you will need to use the `Win32::Process::create` module.

Example Listing 6.42

```perl
my $pid=fork();
die "Cannot fork: $!" if (! defined $pid);
if ($pid) {
    print "I'm the parent, process ID $$.",
        " My child is $pid\n";
} else {
    print "I'm the child.  My PID is $$.\n";
}
```

Example Listing 6.43

```perl
# create a daemon process under Unix
# The recipe for this comes from Advanced Programming
#   in the Unix Environment by Richard Stevens

# POSIX is to set session ID.
use POSIX qw(setsid);

# Change to / so as not to interfere with
# umount
chdir("/") || warn;

# Re-open standard file descriptors to
# something other than the terminal
open(STDIN, "/dev/null") || die "STDIN: $!";
open(STDOUT, ">/dev/null") || die "STDIN: $!";
open(STDERR, ">/tmp/logfile") || die "STDIN: $!";

# Make this process a session leader
die "$!" if (POSIX::setsid() == -1);

$pid=fork();
die "Cannot fork: $!" if (! defined $pid);
```

```
exit if $pid;
# The child at this point is a daemon.
# the parent has exited...
```

> **See Also**
>
> IO::Handle, Win32::Process::create, and POSIX module documentation
>
> perlipc and perlfaq8 in the perl documentation
>
> $|, exec, $$, $!, autoflush, wait, waitpid, and %SIG in this book

times

Usage

```
times
```

Description

In a list context, the times function returns a four-element list containing the user's CPU time, the system CPU time, the user CPU time of terminated children, and the system CPU time of terminated children in seconds. The seconds will be fractional, and the resolution is to the precision of clock ticks per second for your Unix system.

In a scalar context, times returns only the user's CPU usage for the current process.

Example Listing 6.44

```
($user, $system, $cuser, $csystem)=times;
print "You have used ", $user+$system, " seconds of CPU.\n";
```

> **See Also**
>
> times in the C library reference

chdir

Usage

```
chdir pathname
chdir
```

Description

The chdir function is used to set the current working directory of the current perl
process to the pathname. If the pathname isn't specified, perl will attempt to set the
directory to the environment variables HOME, LOGDIR, and SYS$LOGIN (VMS) if set. If
none are available, chdir does nothing without a pathname.

If the directory change was successful, chdir returns true. Otherwise, it returns false
and sets $! to the error message.

Contrast chdir with the Cwd module, which will return your current working directory.

Example Listing 6.45

```
# Change into the system temp directory
$tmp="/tmp";
if ($ENV{TEMP}) { $tmp=$ENV{TEMP}; }
if ($ENV{TMP}) { $tmp=$ENV{TMP};   }
chdir $tmp
    or warn "Cannot chdir to $tmp: $!";
```

> **See Also**
> Cwd module documentation
>
> chdir in the C library reference

chroot

Usage

```
chroot pathname
chroot
```

Description

The chroot function changes the pathname that represents the root directory under
Unix. For example,

```
chroot "/tmp" || die "Cannot chroot: $!";
```

would change any other pathnames used by this process, and child processes so that
they are relative to /tmp. If the pathname /etc/passwd were accessed after the chroot,
the pathname searched would be /tmp/etc/passwd. The old filesystem tree is
inaccessible, and there is no un-doing a chroot.

The chroot function is used for security purposes to put a process into a sandbox. This sandbox is inescapable by the child process and any other processes it creates from then on. Be aware that some common system resources become unavailable because they now lie outside of the chrooted tree.

The chroot function is available only under Unix, and is accessible only by the root user. It will fail if the pathname isn't valid or the caller's effective user ID isn't root. If a pathname isn't specified, $_ is used instead.

Example Listing 6.46

```
# Start a child in a /tmp, uid nobody sandbox
# Must be run as root
$pid=fork();
die unless (defined $pid);
if (! $pid) {
    # Child does this...
    chroot("/tmp") || die "Cannot chroot: $!";
    $<=$>=getpwnam("nobody");
    exec("unsecure_program");
}
```

> **See Also**
> Intro Processes in this book
> chroot in the C library reference

System Information

getnetent

Usage

```
getnetent
setnetent stayopen
endnetent
getnetbyname name
getnetbyaddr address, addresstype
```

Description

The getnetent function represents a family of functions designed to gather information from the /etc/networks file. This file is used to identify networks (not hosts) by name. Because networks aren't typically named these days, the usefulness of this class of functions is suspect.

The getnetent function retrieves one entry from /etc/networks in the manner that gethostent retrieves a line from /etc/hosts. When there are no more entries, getnetent returns false. The list can be reset with setnetent. The flag stayopen indicates whether the /etc/networks file should remain open after each call to getnetbyaddr and getnetbyname. The /etc/networks file is closed with endnetent.

In a scalar context the network name is returned. In a list context the network name, aliases, address type, and network are returned.

The getnetbyname returns an entry corresponding to the name. The getnetbyaddr function returns an entry corresponding to address for the specified addresstype (which is always AF_INET from the Socket module). The getnetbyname function returns an entry corresponding to name.

Example Listing 6.47

```
use Socket;
print "Your local network is known by ",
    scalar getnetbyaddr(127, AF_INET), "\n";
```

> **See Also**
> getnetent, getnetbyname, and getnetbyaddr in the C library reference

getgrent

Usage

getgrent

Description

The getgrent function returns an entry from your /etc/group file. In a list context, the entry returned is a four-element list consisting of the group name, password, group ID, and the members of the group. The members return value is space separated if there are multiple members.

In a scalar context, only the group name is returned.

Successive calls to getgrent will return the next entry until no entries are left, and getgrent will return false. To reset the list to the beginning, call setgrent. To close the /etc/group file, call endgrent.

This is a Unix-only function.

Example Listing 6.48

```
print "Current groups (non-system): ";
while(($group, $pw, $groupid)=getgrent) {
    next if ($groupid < 100);
    print "$group ";
}
```

> **See Also**
> User::grent module documentation
>
> getgrnam and getgrgid in this book
>
> setgrent and endgrent in the C library reference

getgrgid

Usage

getgrgid *groupid*

Description

The gregrgid function retrieves the appropriate entry from the /etc/group file for the given groupid. In a list context, it returns the group name, password, group ID, and members of the group (space separated).

In a scalar context, getgrid returns just the group name for the matching entry. If the groupid isn't valid, undef (or an empty list) is returned.

This function is available only under Unix.

Example Listing 6.49

```
$group=(stat('.'))[5];
$groupname=getgrgid($group) || "Invalid Group";
print "The current directory belongs to group $groupname\n";
```

See Also
User::getgrent module documentation

getgrent in this book

getgrgid in the C library reference

getgrnam

Usage

getgrnam *groupname*

Description

The gregrnam function retrieves the appropriate entry from the /etc/group file for the given *groupname*. In a list context, it returns the group name, password, group ID, and members of the group (space separated).

In a scalar context, getgrnam returns just the numeric group ID for the matching entry. If the *groupname* isn't valid, undef (or an empty list) is returned.

This function is available only under Unix.

Example Listing 6.50

```
print "Group name?";
chomp($group=<STDIN>);
unless (defined($_=getgrnam($group))) {
    print "$group is not valid\n";
} else {
    print "$group is # $_\n";
}
```

See Also
User::getgrent module documentation

getgrent in this book

getgrnam in the C library reference

getlogin

Usage

getlogin

Description

The getlogin function returns the login name of the owner of the process. This is simply an entry point into the native C library routines, and implementation details vary. For example, under Unix, the utmp file is searched for the login. Under Windows this calls GetUserName() in the Windows API.

If unsuccessful, getlogin returns false. If this happens, getpwuid possibly can be used instead.

Example Listing 6.51

```
$user=getlogin || (getpwuid($<))[0];
die "Unknown login" unless $user;
print "Greetings $user.\nHow about a nice game of chess?"
```

> **See Also**
> getpwuid in this book
> getlogin in the C library reference

getpgrp

Usage

getpgrp process_id

Description

The getpgrp function returns the process group ID of the specified *process_id*. If *process_id* is zero or omitted, the process ID of the current process is used.

If your architecture doesn't support the getpgrp(2) system call, an exception will be raised by Perl.

If the process group ID returned is the same as the calling process' PID, that process is considered the process group leader. Process groups can be treated as a single process for signal purposes. In some cases, the process group is signaled, causing all processes within that group to be signaled. See `kill` for details on signaling a process group.

Example Listing 6.52

```
$pgrp=getpgrp(0);
if ($pgrp != $$) {
    print "I am not group-leader.";
    setpgrp(0,0) || die "Cannot setpgrp: $!";
    print "I have become a process group leader.";
}
```

> **See Also**
> `kill`, `setpgrp`, and `setpgrp` in this book
>
> `getpgrp(2)` in the C library reference

getppid

Usage

`getppid`

Description

The `getppid` function retrieves the process ID of the parent process. If 1 is returned, the process likely has been orphaned and inherited by the `init` process (PID 1).

This function is only available under Unix.

Example Listing 6.53

```
if (getppid==1) {
    print "Parent has died!\n";
}
```

> **See Also**
> `fork` in this book
>
> `getppid` in the C library reference

getpriority

Usage

getpriority *which, who*

Description

The getpriority function returns the scheduling priority of the process, process group, or user as indicated by which and who. The value which is one of the following:

Symbolic C Header Name	Meaning	Value
PRIO_PROCESS	Process	0
PRIO_PRGRP	Process group	1
PRIO_USER	User	2

The value of who is a process ID, process group ID, or a user ID. A who of 0 means to use the current process ID, process group, or user ID.

The value returned is between -20 and 20. The default is a priority of 0. A lower number indicates a higher scheduling priority. This function will cause Perl to throw an exception if the underlying architecture doesn't support getpriority(2).

Example Listing 6.54

```
$prior=getpriority(0,0);
print "Your scheduling priority is $prior\n";
if ( $prior < 0) {
    print "This is better than normal.";
} elsif ( $prior > 0) {
    print "This is worse than normal.";
}
```

See Also
setpriority, getpriority(2), and /usr/include/sys/resource.h in the C library reference

getpwent

Usage

```
getpwent
setpwent
endpwent
getpwnam name
getpwuid userid
```

Description

The family of functions represented by getpwent are used to read the /etc/passwd file under Unix. In list context, the getpwent, getpwname, and getpwuid functions return a list consisting of name, password, user ID, group ID, quota, comment, gcos (description), home directory, and login shell. If no matching entries are found, an empty list is returned.

In a scalar context, getpwent and getpwuid return just the user name; getpwname returns just the user ID. If no matching entries are found, undef is returned.

The getpwent function returns one entry from the /etc/passwd file. Each successive call returns the next entry until no entries are left. At this point, getpwent returns false (or an empty list). The list can be reset to the beginning with setpwent, or the password file can be closed with endpwent.

The getpwnam function returns the matching entry for name. The getpwuid returns the matching entry for the given userid.

Depending on your system configuration, the data returned might contain password entries from sources other than /etc/passwd such as NIS or NIS+.

Example Listing 6.55

```
@me=getpwuid($>);
printf("Welcome %s.\nI see you are %s" .
            " (and have %s's permissions)\n",
            @me[6,0], getpwuid($<));
print "Other people in your group are:";
while(($gid,$gcos)=(getpwent)[3,6]) {
    print "\t$gcos\n" if ($gid == $me[3]);
}
```

See Also

`User::pwent` module documentation

`getpwent, getpwname, getpwuid,` and `passwd` in the C library reference

---

setpgrp

Usage

setpgrp *pid*, *pgid*;

Description

The `setpgrp()` function sets the process group ID of the process specified by *pid* to the group specified by *pgid*. If *pid* is 0, the process ID of the current process is used. If *pgid* is 0, the process ID of the current process is used.

This command will raise an exception in Perl if the architecture doesn't support the `setpgrp(2)` system call.

The `setpgrp()` function is necessary to create new process groups. This is useful when a process wants to differentiate itself from the current group; most commonly when trying to daemonize itself.

On POSIX-compliant systems, the `setpgrp(2)` doesn't accept arguments, and only `setpgrp(0,0)` will work in that case.

Example Listing 6.56

```
# Completely separate myself from
# other processes.  Will avoid having
# HUP sent if they hangup the line.
setpgrp(0,0) || die "Cannot set pgrp: $!";
$pid=fork();
die "Cannot fork: $!" if (!defined $pid);
exit if ($pid);
```

See Also

`fork` and `getpgrp` in this book

`getpgrp(2)` in the C library reference

---

setpriority

Usage

setpriority *which, who, priority*

Description

setpriority sets the scheduling priority for the current process, process group, or user to the priority specified.

For an explanation of which and who, see the getpriority entry.

Priorities are specified from -20 to 20. Only the superuser can raise the priority of a process (make its priority value lower).

The value returned from setpriority() is the new priority. To see if setpriority() worked, $! must be cleared and then checked after setpriority() is called. If it's set, an error occurred.

If setpriority isn't implemented on your architecture, Perl will raise an exception.

Example Listing 6.57

```
# Lower my own priority (be nice!)
$!=0;
$prior=setpriority(0, 0, 10);
warn "Did not work: $!" if ($! != 0);
```

> **See Also**
> $! and getpriority in this book
> setpriority in the C library reference

System V Interprocess Communication

semget

Usage

semget *key, nsems, flags*

Description

This function creates a System V semaphore. The C `semid_ds` structure is initialized and the semaphore created if the flag `IPC_CREAT` is specified. A semaphore ID is returned, and this should be used by `semop` and `semget` for manipulating the semaphore.

The `IPC::SysV` module contains the flag constants, which control how the segment is allocated. The symbols aren't exported from the module, so you have to ask for them by name.

The flag `IPC_CREAT` will create the segment if it doesn't exist; `IPC_EXCL` won't create the segment if there is already a segment by that *key*. The *flags* can be bitwise-`OR`'d together to combine them.

If the system were unable to return the semaphore ID, `undef` is returned and `$!` is set to the error message.

This function is available only on those systems that support SysV IPC.

Example Listing 6.58

```
use IPC::SysV qw(IPC_CREAT);
# Create a semaphore set
$semid=semget(65, 1, IPC_CREAT | 0644 );
if (!defined $semid) {
    die "Cannot create semaphore: $!";
}
```

> **See Also**
> `semget` in the C library reference

`semctl`

Usage

`semctl sem_id, semnum, command, argument`

Description

The `semctl` function allows you to fetch or set options associated with the semaphore, destroy the semaphore, or fetch and set various members of the C `semid_ds` structure.

The function will return true if the operation was successful, and undef otherwise. If the command is GETALL, IPC_STAT, or GETVAL, the variable in the argument position should be large enough to hold the results. If semctl returns 0, the special value 0 but true is returned instead. This value has some special considerations, explained in the fcntl entry.

This function is available only on those systems that support System V IPC.

Example Listing 6.59

```
use IPC::SysV qw(IPC_CREAT IPC_RMID);
# Create a semaphore set
$semid=semget(66, 1, IPC_CREAT | 0644 );
if (!defined $semid) {
    die "Cannot create semaphore: $!";
}

# Now destroy it, this removes the whole semaphore
# set, not just a member.  Hence the 0.
semctl($semid, 0, IPC_RMID, 0) ||
    die "Cannot remove semaphore: $!";
```

> **See Also**
>
> IPC::SysV and IPC::Semaphore module documentation
>
> semget in this book
>
> semctl in the C library reference

semop

Usage

semop *sem_id*, *operation*

Description

The semop function provides control over individual semaphores within a semaphore set. It returns true if successful, returns undef otherwise, and sets $! to the error message.

The *operation* string consists of three packed (native) short integers that represent the semaphore number (within the set), the operation you want to perform (either incrementing or decrementing the semaphore), and any flags needed. Multiple operations on semaphores within a set can be performed by concatenating them onto a single operation string, three shorts per semaphore.

This function is available only on those systems that support System V IPC.

Example Listing 6.60

```
use IPC::SysV qw(IPC_CREAT IPC_STAT IPC_NOWAIT);
# Create a semaphore set
$semid=semget(66, 1, IPC_CREAT | 0644 );
if (!defined $semid) {
    die "Cannot create semaphore: $!";
}

# wait on semaphore 0 in the semaphore set $semid
$operation=pack("sss", 0, 1, 0);
semop($semid,  $operation) ||
    die "Cannot get semaphore: $!";
```

> **See Also**
>
> IPC::Semaphore and IPC::SysV module documentation
>
> semctl and semget in this book
>
> semop in the C library reference

shmget

Usage

shmget *key, size, flags*

Description

The shmget function allocates a shared memory segment identified by *key* of *size* bytes. The function returns a shared memory ID that can be used with other SysV IPC functions. The *key* is a numeric ID used to uniquely identify the segment. If multiple processes want to attach to the same segment, they should each use the same key when calling shmget.

The IPC::SysV module contains the flag constants, which control how the segment is allocated. The symbols aren't exported from the module, so you have to ask for them by name.

The flag `IPC_CREAT` will create the segment if it doesn't exist; `IPC_EXCL` won't create the segment if there is already a segment by that key. The flags can be bitwise-`OR`'d together to combine them.

Included in the *flags* are the permissions for the segment. The permissions work similar to the filesystem permissions. For example, `0644` would give write permission to the owner and read-only permission to others and the group.

This function is supported only on Unix systems that have System V IPC.

Example Listing 6.61

```
# Simply create and destroy a segment

use IPC::SysV qw(IPC_CREAT IPC_RMID);

$handle=shmget(52, 1024, IPC_CREAT | 0644 );
die "No shared segment: $!" unless ($handle);

if (! shmctl($handle, IPC_RMID, 0) ) {
    die "Cannot destroy: $!";
}
```

> **See Also**
> `IPC::SysV` module documentation
> `shmctl` in this book
> `shmget` in the C library reference

shmctl

Usage

shmctl *shm_id, command, argument*

Description

The `shmctl` function allows you to control a shared memory segment created with `shmget`. The shared memory ID is specified as *shm_id* and the command you want performed is *command*. The *argument* parameter might or might not be needed depending on the *command*, but it must be present.

The `IPC::SysV` module contains constants for manipulating the segment. If *command* is `IPC_RMID`, the segment is removed after the last process detaches from it. The command `IPC_STAT` and `IPC_SET` can be used to examine the properties of the segment. If these are specified, `argument` must be a variable large enough to hold the C `shmid_ds` structure returned.

If the `shmctl` function fails, `undef` will be returned.

This function is supported only on Unix systems that have System V IPC.

Example Listing 6.62

```
# Prints various usage information about the segment
# See the native shmctl man page to determine the
#   makeup of the structure returned by IPC_STAT
use IPC::SysV qw(IPC_CREAT IPC_STAT);

$handle=shmget(1066, 1024, IPC_CREAT | 0666);
die "No shared segment: $!" unless ($handle);

$struct=""x100;  # $struct has to be large enough
if (! defined shmctl($handle, IPC_STAT, $struct)) {
    die "Cannot stat the segment: $!";
}


# This structure was valid for Linux kernel 2.2
# Your mileage will vary.
printf("Key:%d  Owner:%d  Group:%d  Creator:%d  Group:%d
    Mode: %o  Seq: %d Size: %d
    Last attach (sec): %d  Detach: %d  Change: %d
    Pid: %d  Oper: %d  Attaches: %d
    Pages: %d  %d\n", unpack("LSSSSSSiLLLSSssl", $struct));
```

See Also

`IPC::SysV` module documentation

`shmget` in this book

`chmctl` in the C library reference

shmread, shmwrite

Usage

```
shmread shm_id, var, start, size
shmwrite shm_id, string, start, size
```

Description

The shmread and shmwrite functions are used to place data into (and remove it from) a shared memory segment. Unlike C, in Perl you simply cannot attach to a shared memory segment and have it map to a variable (or structure). It must be read and written similar to a socket or a filehandle.

The shmread function attaches to the shared memory segment shm_id and reads size bytes starting at position start. The data is then copied into the variable var (which must be large enough to hold the data).

The shmwrite function attaches to the shared memory segment shm_id and writes size bytes starting at start bytes from the beginning of the segment from string. If the string is too short, nulls will be used to pad the write out to size.

Each function returns true if successful, false otherwise and sets $! to the error message.

Concurrent access to the shared memory segment might cause data corruption, and a locking mechanism should be used to control access.

These functions are only available on Unix systems that support System V IPC.

Example Listing 6.63

```perl
# Simple example of a reader and writer as
# different processes.
use IPC::SysV qw(IPC_CREAT);

$handle=shmget(1066, 1024, IPC_CREAT | 0666);
die "No shared segment: $!" unless ($handle);

$pid=fork();
die unless (defined $pid);
if ($pid) {
    if (! shmwrite($handle, "Hello, World", 0, 1024)) {
        warn "Could not write segment: $!";
    }
```

```
    wait;  # Hang around for child
} else {
    # No locks here, so sleep a while to "guarantee"
    # that we don't overlap with the write.
    sleep 2;
    $c=" " x 1024;
    if (! shmread($handle, $c, 0, 1024)) {
        warn "Could not read segment: $!";
    }
    print $c;
}
```

> **See Also**
> IPC::SysV module documentation
> shmget in this book
> shmattach in the C library reference

msgget

Usage

msgget *key*, *flags*

Description

The msgget function allows you to connect to a System V message queue (possibly creating it). The function returns a message queue ID, which can be used with msgsnd and msgrecv to send and receive messages on the queue. The key is a numeric ID used to uniquely identify the queue. If multiple processes want to attach to the same queue, they should each use the same key when calling msgget. The msgget function returns undef if the queue cannot be created and sets $! to the error message.

The IPC::SysV module contains the flag constants, which control how the queue is allocated. The symbols aren't exported from the module, so you have to ask for them by name.

The flag IPC_CREAT will create the queue if it doesn't exist, and IPC_EXCL won't create the queue if there is already a segment by that key. The flags can be bitwise-OR'd together to combine them.

Included in the flags are the permissions for the segment. The permissions work similar to the filesystem permissions. For example, `0644` would give write permission to the owner and read-only permission to others and the group.

This function is supported only on Unix systems that have System V IPC.

Example Listing 6.64

```
use IPC::SysV qw(IPC_CREAT IPC_EXCL);

# Create a queue, fail if it's already there
# The queue is #52.
$msgq_id=msgget(52, IPC_CREAT | IPC_EXCL | 0644);
if ( not defined $msgq_id) {
    die "Could not create the queue: $!";
}

# Now, get rid of it.
if (not defined msgctl($msgq_id, IPC_RMID, 0)) {
    die "Could not get rid of queue: $!";
}
```

> **See Also**
>
> `IPC::SysV` module documentation
>
> `msgctl` in this book
>
> `msgget` in the C library reference

msgctl

Usage

msgctl *msgq_id*, *command*, *argument*

Description

The `msgctl` function allows you to query and set attributes on a message queue created with `msgget`. The queue is specified as *msgq_id* and the command you want performed as *command*. The *argument* parameter might or might not be needed, depending on the *command*, but it must be present.

The `IPC::SysV` module contains constants for manipulating the queue. If *command* is `IPC_RMID`, the queue is removed after the last process detaches from it. The commands `IPC_STAT` and `IPC_SET` can be used to examine the properties of the queue. If these are specified, the argument must be a variable large enough to hold the C `msqid_ds` structure returned.

If the `msgctl` function fails, undef is returned and `$!` is set to the error message. If the `msgctl` function returns 0, the special value 0 but true is returned. That value has some special considerations, explained in the `fcntl` entry.

This function is supported only on Unix systems that have System V IPC.

Example Listing 6.65

```
# The unpack uses the msqid_ds structure (which
# in turn uses ipc_perm).  This structure may vary
# on your system.  Check your local documentation.
use IPC::SysV qw(IPC_CREAT IPC_STAT);

# Create a queue.  Use it if it's already there.
$msgq_id=msgget(52, IPC_CREAT | 0644);
if ( not defined $msgq_id) {
    die "Could not create the queue: $!";
}
$struct=""x100;  # $struct has to be large enough
if (! defined msgctl($msgq_id, IPC_STAT, $struct)) {
    die "Cannot stat the segment: $!";
}

# What are the permissions on the segment?
# should be 0644 if the msgget was done right.  :)
printf("Permissions: %04o\n", (unpack("LSSSSSS", $struct))[5]);
```

> **See Also**
>
> `IPC::SysV` module documentation
>
> `msgget` and `unpack` in this book
>
> `msgctl` in the C library reference

`msgsnd, msgrcv`

Usage

```
msgsnd msgq_id, message, flags
msgrcv msgq_id, var, size, type, flags
```

Description

The `msgsnd` and `msgrcv` functions are used to send and receive messages on a SysV message queue. Messages on a queue are identified by the queue itself, and each message has an identifying message type.

The `msgsnd` function takes a message and puts it on the queue identified by *msgq_id*. The message itself must contain a type and the message itself. The type is a (native) long word. This is one way to create a message:

```
$text="Hello, world!";
$type=44;     # Some arbitrary number.
$message=pack("La*", $type, $text);
```

The `msgrcv` function removes a message from the queue and places it in *var*, which will contain both the type and the message text (which then must be unpacked to be usable). The *size* parameter specifies how large of a message should be received. The type of the message is specified by *type*. The possible values for type are:

Value	Meaning
`type == 0`	Retrieves the first message on the queue, regardless of type.
`type > 0`	Retrieves the first message on the queue whose message type matches the type specified.
`type < 0`	The first message on the queue whose type is less than or equal to the (absolute value) of the type specified.

Each function returns true if successful, false otherwise, and sets `$!` to the error message.

These functions are only available on Unix systems that support System V IPC.

Example Listing 6.66

```
# Generic functions to enqueue and dequeue messages
#   on a SysV message queue.
```

```perl
use IPC::SysV qw(IPC_CREAT IPC_STAT IPC_NOWAIT);

# Create a queue.  Use it if it's already there.
#
$queue=52;
$msgq_id=msgget($queue, IPC_CREAT | 0644);
if ( not defined $msgq_id) {
    die "Could not create the queue: $!";
}
sub enq {
    my($type, $text)=@_;
    msgsnd($msgq_id, pack("La*", $type, $text), 0) or
        die "Cannot send message: $!";
}
sub deq {
    my $type=shift;
    my $v=" " x 100;
    return unless
        msgrcv($msgq_id, $v, 1024, $type, IPC_NOWAIT);
    ($text)=(unpack("La*", $v))[1];
    return $text;
}
enq(101, "hacker ");
enq(101, "! ");
enq(99, "another ");
enq(97, "just ");
enq(99, "perl ");
# Note that by retrieving them with a -103, they'll come
# back in numeric order, even though that's not how they went in.
while($msg=deq(-103)) {
    print $msg;
}
```

See Also

IPC::SysV module documentation

msgget in this book

msgsnd and msgrcv in the C library reference

CHAPTER 7
Standard Module Library

Introduction to Standard Module Library

Description

The Perl distribution is bundled with many useful modules already in place. In this section are brief introductions to those modules.

This isn't a comprehensive list of modules that is included with the standard `perl` distribution. Some modules have very limited usefulness, others are documented elsewhere in this book because they are pragmatic modules (`integer`, `strict`, `locale`), and still others are useful only if you're poking around inside `perl` itself.

The module documentation isn't complete. The basic functionality of the module is described with an example. This should be enough to determine whether the module is of use to you and, if so, should get you started.

The intent is that after you've decided that the module is appropriate, you'll consult the module's documentation that was included with the Perl distribution.

B Backend Modules

Description

The B backend modules that come with the `perl` distribution are used to examine the internal workings of the Perl interpreter and compiler.

Some of them act as code generators and will produce code; others simply analyze the `perl` program and produce useful bits such as parse trees.

To use a Backend module, don't use it in the traditional sense. Instead, on the command line, use the `-MO` option and indicate the backend you want to run. So to produce a bytecode dump of a `perl` program:

```
perl -MO=Bytecode,-foo.pbd foo.pl
```

Backend	Description
Bytecode	Generates Perl bytecode. This can be used to run a `perl` script without compiling it first. Example Listing 7.1 gives a demonstration of the `Bytecode` backend.
C,CC	These backends take a `perl` program and generate C program source code to run that program. The program is still linked to the `perl` libraries, so this isn't a standalone C program. Some Perl programs survive translation well, but some not at all. The bugs section of the documentation simply says: "Plenty." Your mileage will vary. The `C` backend produces a C program, the `CC` backend produces a C program which has been optimized and arranged differently.
Lint	Checks your source code for questionable practices (similar to the way that `strict` does). There are very few checks implemented now. These include checks for implicit use of an array in scalar context, using the `$'`, `$&` and `$`` variables, implicit use of `$_`, calling subroutines that don't exist, and using variables that begin with `_`.
Terse	The `Terse` module compiles your program and then walks the syntax tree giving information about the program compiled. If you're trying to figure out what `perl` is doing (for example, if it's implicitly using `$_` or something has been optimized out), looking

Backend	Description

at the output from `Terse` might help. For example, an (annotated) dump of the simple program:

```
while(<>) { print } shows:
LOOP (0x) enterloop
UNOP (0x) null
    LOGOP (0x) and          # So long as the loop-value
    UNOP (0x) defined        #   is defined and not-null
        UNOP (0x) null
        UNOP (0x) null [15]
            SVOP (0x) gvsv  GV (0x) *_    # into $_
        UNOP (0x) readline [1]        # readline from
            SVOP (0x) gv  GV (0x) *ARGV  #    @ARGV
    LISTOP (0x) lineseq
        COP (0x) nextstate
        LISTOP (0x) print                # print
        OP (0x) pushmark
        UNOP (0x) null [15]
            SVOP (0x) gvsv  GV (0x) *_  # Here's the $_
        OP (0x) unstack

    COP (0x) nextstate
```

The implicit use of `$_` is explicitly spelled out (as `*_`), the implied defined and null test in the `while` loop is shown, the implicit use of `@ARGV` is mentioned, and the use of `$_` in `print` is shown.

Deparse   The `Deparse` module will take your `perl` program, compile it, and then re-generate `perl` source code based on the compiled program. Perl throws out comments, whitespace, and anything that isn't necessary to run the program. Additional options cause `Deparse` to insert parenthesis to show precedence, expand double-quoted strings, and so on.

Xref   The `Xref` module will examine your program and create a list of referenced variables, functions, and so on, as well as when they were first used, where they were called, whether they were package or lexical variables, and so on. Running `Xref` against the example from the subroutines entry shows (edited for brevity and clarity):

```
Subroutine (definitions)
  Package main
    &minmax        s19    # Two subs in main
    &sortsub       s7
```

Backend	Description

```
Subroutine (main)
  Package (lexical)
    @list            i20, 21 # not a lexical, won't
                     # pass strict vars...
  Package main
    &minmax          &21
Subroutine minmax
  Package (lexical)        # my()'d variables
    $aref          i9, 11
    $max           i10, 15, 16, 16, 18
    $min           i10, 13, 14, 14, 18
    @$aref         11
  Package main          # global (package) vars
    $_             13, 14, 16
    $a             i12, 13
    $b             i12, 13, 15
    &sortsub       &14, &16
    @_             9
Subroutine sortsub
  Package main
    $a             7   # $a and $b as package
    $b             7   #  variables are seen in sorts...
```

Backend	Description
Debug	Similar to Terse, except that additional debugging information is printed.
Disassemble	Used by the disassemble program (included with the perl source only) to take bytecode and produce a (somewhat) readable op tree.
Showlex	Dumps the pad addresses of the lexical variables in the program.

Some of the backends work better than others; most are marked "experimental." Almost all are probably useful in one way or another.

Example Listing 7.1

```
# Create a byte-code-only perl program

# Create a short perl program to compile
cat << EOF > /tmp/hello.pl
#!/usr/bin/perl -w
```

```
print "Hello, world";
EOF

# Now translate into bytecodes.  These are
#   platform-independant, and not quite source code.
perl -MO=Bytecode,-o,/tmp/hello.plb /tmp/hello.pl

# Create a third file which has a normal preamble,
#   uses ByteLoader, and then has the bytecode
#   appended to the end.
echo "#!/usr/bin/perl" >/tmp/hello_compiled.pl
echo "use ByteLoader;" >>/tmp/hello_compiled.pl
cat /tmp/hello.plb       >>/tmp/hello_compiled.pl

# Now run it!
chmod 755 /tmp/hello_compiled.pl
/tmp/hello_compiled.pl    #  prints "Hello, world"
```

Example Listing 7.2

```
# Generating a C program from a perl script

cc_harness="/usr/local/lib/perl5/5.6.0/B/cc_harness"
perl -MO=CC,-o/tmp/hello.c /tmp/hello.pl
perl $cc_harness -o hello hello.c
```

> **See Also**
> `B::Bytecode, B::C, B::CC, B::Lint, B::Deparse, B::Debug,` and `B::Disassemble` module documentation

Benchmark

Usage

```
use Benchmark;
timethese(count, {
        name => code,
        name2 => code2,
})
```

Description

The `Benchmark` module is used for testing code performance. The primary function for doing this is `timethese`.

The first argument to `timethese` is *count*, which is how many times the test will be repeated. The more often the test is repeated, the more accurate the results (because the cost of starting up the test engine itself is minimized). Using a *count* that causes the tests to run in under one second will generate a warning.

The tests themselves are passed in as part of an anonymous hash. The *name* indicates the name that the test will run under (and display on the report). The *code* parameter can be either

- A code reference, such as a subroutine reference or an anonymous sub.

- A string that contains `perl` code to be eval'd and run.

The `Benchmark` module is demonstrated in the integer, `eval`, and `qr` entries. A sample report is in the integer entry.

See Also
`Benchmark` module documentation

CGI

Usage

```
use CGI qw(:standard);

$q=new CGI;
print $q->header();
```

Description

The `CGI` (Common Gateway Interface) module provides an interface to many of the features needed for writing Web applications. It is, by far, the most popular and heavily used module for doing Web work in Perl. With it and its associated modules, you can

- Generate standard HTTP header elements (Modified, Expires, Content-Type, Redirection, and so on)

- Manage cookies and other session information

- Generate HTML elements

- Generate HTML form elements with default values and "sticky" values

- Process form submissions (GET and POST) to CGI programs

- Handle file uploads to CGI programs

In addition, you can implement many other CGI-related functions.

The CGI module provides both an object-oriented interface and a functional interface. A similar CGI program for both interfaces is demonstrated in Example Listing 7.3. Here is something to remember with the CGI module: Although it provides interfaces to HTML, form logic, and so on, you don't have to use them all. Use your judgement for what works and what doesn't.

Entire books have been written on the subject of CGI programming and the CGI module's use in Web programming. An introduction can be found in *Teach Yourself Perl in 24 Hours*. A thorough course in developing CGI applications can be found in *Writing CGI Applications with Perl*.

Example Listing 7.3

```
# A short CGI program with a form.  This is how
#   the program might look using the OO interface to CGI.


use CGI;
my $q=new CGI;
print $q->header(-type => 'text/html',
        -expires => '+3d');
print $q->start_html("Sample program");
if ($q->param) {
    if ($q->param('answer') ne 'sure') {
        print "Well go then!";
    } else {
        print "Stay a while!";
    }
} else {
    print $q->h1("Welcome to my homepage"),
    "Do you like my site?<BR>",
    $q->start_form,
    $q->radio_group(-name => 'answer',
            -values => ['sure', 'no, it sucks'],
            -default => 'sure'),
```

```
        $q->submit,
        $q->end_form;
}
$q->end_html;
```

Example Listing 7.4

```
# Same program as above, without using the OO interface. The
#    primary differences being:  1. no query object ($q) and
#    2. the use CGI line needs to import functions

use CGI qw(:standard :html :forms);
print header(-type => 'text/html',
             -expires => '+3d');

print start_html("Sample program");
if (param) {
    if (param('answer') ne 'sure') {
        print "Well go then!";
    } else {
        print "Stay a while!";
    }
} else {
        print h1("Welcome to my homepage"),
        "Do you like my site?<BR>",
        start_form,
        radio_group(-name => 'answer',
                -values => ['sure', 'no, it sucks'],
                -default => 'sure'),
        submit,
        end_form;
}
end_html;
```

See Also
CGI module documentation

CPAN

Usage

```
perl -MCPAN -e shell
```

Description

The CPAN module provides both an interactive and batch interface to the CPAN. *CPAN (Comprehensive Perl Archive Network)* is a collection of contributed modules, scripts, and documentation for Perl. The CPAN is, quite frankly, huge. At the time of writing, there were 1,847 modules in the CPAN. CPAN modules also can be downloaded and installed manually, of course, by finding a CPAN mirror near you, downloading a bundle, decompressing it, and following the included instructions. But the CPAN module makes this task far less tedious.

The CPAN module can be used interactively by starting perl with

```
perl -MCPAN -e shell
```

If this is the first time you've used the CPAN module, you will be asked questions about your configuration, where you want the modules built, where you are geographically, and so on. From there, to install a new module (Image::Size in this example):

```
cpan shell -- CPAN exploration and modules installation (v1.57)
ReadLine support enabled

cpan> install Image::Size
CPAN: LWP::UserAgent loaded ok
Fetching with LWP:
[loading of CPAN data from the network]
Fetching with LWP:
ftp://..../perl/CPAN/authors/id/R/RJ/RJRAY/Image-Size-2.92.tar.gz
ok
Image-Size-2.92/
[other package data]
Image-Size-2.92/Size.pm
Image-Size-2.92/MANIFEST
Image-Size-2.92/ChangeLog
Image-Size-2.92/Makefile.PL
Image-Size-2.92/imgsize
Image-Size-2.92/README
Image-Size-2.92/README.Win32
```

```
CPAN.pm: Going to build R/RJ/RJRAY/Image-Size-2.92.tar.gz

Checking if your kit is complete...
Looks good
Writing Makefile for Image::Size
mkdir blib
mkdir blib/lib
mkdir blib/lib/Image
[other build information]
Running make test
Test::Harness qw(&runtests $verbose); $verbose=0; runtests @ARGV;' t/*.t
t/all..............ok
All tests successful.
  /usr/bin/make test -- OK
Running make install
Installing /usr/local/lib/perl5/site_perl/5.6.0/auto/Image/Size/gifsize.al
[other installs]

cpan>
```

Some of the build was omitted for brevity. After the `install` command has finished, the module is installed and ready to use. Other commands are available in interactive mode for searching, uninstalling, and fetching modules without installing.

The CPAN module can be used non-interactively (in batch mode). Example Listing 7.5 contains a script to install a handful of modules. The API for the CPAN module is small but relies on knowledge of how the CPAN is put together. The module's documentation should be consulted for a more thorough grounding in it.

Example Listing 7.5

```
# Install a couple of game modules onto the system

use CPAN;
@games=('Games::Cards', 'Games::Worms');

for $package (@games) {
 my $mod = CPAN::Shell->expand('Module',$package);
 $mod->install;
}
```

> **See Also**
> CPAN module documentation

Carp

Usage

```
use Carp;
```

Description

The Carp module provides an alternative exception and warning mechanism to die and warn. It's used in modules where instead of wanting to report the file and line number where an error occurred, you want to report the caller's file and line number. Using the module provides four functions to control how exceptions are handled.

The carp function works similar to warn, except that the caller's file and line number are reported. The croak function works similarly to die. Example Listing 7.6 demonstrates carp.

The cluck and confess functions work similar to carp and croak, except that in addition to just printing the caller's file and line number, they perform an entire stack trace back to the main body of the application. The cluck and confess functions aren't exported from Carp by default—you have to ask for them when you use the module.

Example Listing 7.6

```
# A short demo for Carp.  The warning (thrown with carp)
#  will be reported at the line FOO::myfunc() is on, not
#  where the carp actually occurred (inside of myfunc).

package FOO;
use Carp qw(:DEFAULT);
sub myfunc {
    print "Okay, I'm here!";
    carp "Danger Will Robinson!"
}

package main;
FOO::myfunc();
```

> **See Also**
> Carp module documentation

Config

Usage

```
use Config;
```

Description

The Config module contains the configuration values available to perl when it was originally compiled for your system. These include OS values, C library constants, locations of various files, perl's installation information, version numbers, shell commands, and a lot more.

The author's installation has over 760 items in the configuration information.

The configuration information is available in the %Config hash that is exported into the current package. Additionally, the myconfig function returns perl's version information. The printf example displays all the configuration options in a nicely formatted output.

> **See Also**
> Config module documentation

Cwd

Usage

```
use Cwd;

cwd
getcwd
chdir dirname
```

Description

The Cwd module is used to determine what your current working directory is. The cwd function uses `pwd`, or whatever your architecture's normal mechanism is for finding the current directory, and returns it. The getcwd re-implements the getcwd(3) C library call to determine your current working directory.

If imported the chdir function overrides the built-in chdir function. The added benefit is that after changing directories successfully, the environment variable in $ENV{PWD} is updated with the new directory.

Example Listing 7.7

```
use Cwd;

$here=cwd;
```

> **See Also**
> Cwd module documentation
>
> cwd in the C library reference

Data::Dumper

Usage

```
use Data::Dumper;
Dumper ref
```

Description

The Data::Dumper module takes a list of references and produces a serialized version of those reference structures. The output is suitable for printing or for eval.

Options are available to control the format of the output ($Data::Dumper::Indent), whether self-referential structures are properly serialized ($Data::Dumper::Purity), how keys are quoted ($Data::Dumper::Useqq), and many others.

Examples of Data::Dumper are in the Calling Subroutines, new, -a, Version special variables entries, and in Example Listing 7.8.

Example Listing 7.8

```
# Example of Dumping an arbitrarily deep structure.

use Data::Dumper;
```

```
my $r;
# Use auto-vivification to create a deep structure
#   hash-of-arrays-of-hashes in this case.
$r->{new}->[0]->{key}="First";
$r->{new}->[1]->{key}="Second";

print Dumper $r;

# Produces output like this:
#$VAR1 = {
#        'new' => [
#                 {
#                    'key' => 'First'
#                 },
#                 {
#                    'key' => 'Second'
#                 }
#               ]
#      };
```

> **See Also**
> Data::Dumper module documentation

English

Usage

```
use English;
```

Description

The English module provides aliases for common built-in variables as full names instead of punctuation names. For example, $_ becomes $ARG, $@ becomes $EVAL_ERROR, and $! becomes $ERRNO. The original names are still available after aliasing.

This module, although making your programs more COBOL-esque, will impose a performance penalty on your programs. The full list of synonyms is in the perlvar manual page.

Example Listing 7.9

```
# Demo of use English for some of the variables

use English;
use strict;
use warnings;
{
    local $INPUT_RECORD_SEPARATOR;

    open(FILE, "/tmp/bigfile.txt")
        || die "Cannot open: $ERRNO";
    while(<FILE>) {
        chomp;
        next unless $ARG;
    }
}
```

> **See Also**
> English module documentation
> perlvar in the perl documentation

Env

Usage

```
use Env;
```

Description

The Env module takes environment variables from %ENV and ties them to scalar variable names (with the same name) in the current package.

By default, all variables in %ENV are tied. If you want to specify particular variables, import just those names:

```
use Env qw(PATH HOME);
```

You can specify the type of the variable as a scalar or an array by prefixing the name with $ or @. Array variables are created by splitting the environment variable's value on $Config::Config{path_sep}.

To remove a tied variable, use the `undef` operator.

Example Listing 7.10

```
use Env;

chdir $HOME or warn "Can't go home: $!";
```

> **See Also**
> `Env` module documentation

Errno

Usage

```
use Errno;
```

Description

The `Errno` module exports constants into the callers package. These constants come from the `errno.h` C Standard I/O header file, and are generally only seen when I/O operations fail.

By default, all constants are exported. You can import selected constant names or `:POSIX` to get all the `POSIX`-defined constants.

An example of `Errno` is in the Error Special Variables entry.

> **See Also**
> `Errno` module documentation

Fatal

Usage

```
use Fatal;
```

Description

The `Fatal` module causes functions to raise an exception when they return false. Calling the `import` routine with the name of the function will cause `Fatal` to place a wrapper around the function, which raises an exception if it returns false.

```
use Fatal qw(open);
open(FOO, "/tmp/not_here_file");   # Will now raise an exception
```

For built-in functions, only those functions that can be overridden can be wrapped with `Fatal`. Calling `Fatal` with a function that cannot be overridden causes an exception.

To wrap a `Fatal` wrapper around your own subroutine, include the `Fatal` module and later call its `import` method directly after the subroutine has been declared:

```
use Fatal;

sub nervous { "Yup!"; }
Fatal->import("nervous");
```

Now, returning false from `nervous` will cause an exception to be raised.

If the symbol `:void` is imported, using a wrapped function in a void context will throw an exception. However, using it in any other context will assume that the program calling the function will handle the error.

> **See Also**
> `Fatal` module documentation
> `context` in this book

Fcntl

Usage

```
use Fcntl qw(:flock);
use Fcntl qw(:seek);
use Fcntl;
```

Description

The `Fcntl` module exports various constants from the C standard I/O library `fcntl.h` header file.

By default, all the `F_*` and `O_*` constants are imported. The `:flock` import group imports the `LOCK_*` constants. The `:seek` import group imports the `SEEK_*` constants and the `S_I*` constants.

The `Fcntl` module is demonstrated in the chmod, do (block), fcntl, flock, seek, select, sysopen, syswrite, sysseek, tell, truncate, and use entries.

See Also
`Fcntl` module documentation

File::Basename

Usage

```
use File::Basename
dirname(path)
basename(path)
```

Description

The `File::Basename` module is used to extract information from a pathname. It is aware of the various pathname oddities for operating systems and can cope with / under Unix, \ under MS-DOS, : under MacOS, and so on.

The routines most commonly used are `basename` and `dirname`. The basename function returns just the filename from a given path. The `dirname` function returns just the directory name from a path.

Example Listing 7.11

```
# Given a pathname, extract out the good bits.
use File::Basename;

# My system is Unix.  So / is the separator...
$path="/home/clintp/tmp/working.pl";
print basename($path);  # prints "working.pl"
print dirname($path);   # prints "/home/clintp/tmp";

# But I can emulate another system if need be.
fileparse_set_fstype("MSDOS");
$path='C:\Windows\Program Files\Mozilla\Mozilla.exe';
```

```perl
print basename($path);   # prints "Mozilla.exe "
print dirname($path);    # prints "C:\Windows\Program Files\Mozilla";
```

> **See Also**
> File::Basename module documentation

`File::Compare`

Usage

```perl
use File::Compare;
compare(file1, file2);
compare_text(file1, file2, coderef);
```

Description

The `File::Compare` module has two functions, `compare` and `compare_text`, that are used to determine whether two files are identical in content.

The files passed in can either be open filehandles or actual file names. If the files compare equally, the `compare` and `compare_text` functions return `0`. If they are unequal, `1` is returned, and `-1` if there was an error.

The `compare_text` function takes an optional third argument that is a subroutine reference. This subroutine will be called and passed each line in `@_`. It should return true if two lines of text are equivalent. This can be used to ignore whitespace, have comparisons that aren't case sensitive, or use computed comparisons (on fields that might be different in a data file).

The `compare_text` function isn't exported by default.

Example Listing 7.12

```perl
# A subroutine to compare two directories.  Notices if there's
#   files in one, but not the other and then compares files that
#   are in both.
# No return value (you can change this) just prints messages as
#   to whether or not they're the same.

use File::Compare qw(compare_text compare);
use strict;
```

```perl
sub dircomp {
    local(*D1);
    my @f;

    # Build two hash structures with the directories in each
    #   (only the files though)
    for my $num (0..1) {
        my $dir=$_[$num];
        opendir(D1, $dir) or die "Can't open $dir: $!";
        $f[$num]={ map { $_, "$dir/$_" } grep { -f "$dir/$_" } readdir D1};
    }
    closedir D1;

    # Now compare the hashes against each other and see what's
    #   missing from each.  Delete extra elements.
    for(0..1) {
        for my $file (keys %{$f[$_]}) {
            if( not exists ${$f[$_?0:1]}{$file}) {
                warn "$file exists in $_[$_] but not the other\n";
                delete $f[$_]{$file};
            }
        }
    }

    # Now that the hashes are the same, compare each file in each
    #   hash.
    foreach my $file (keys %{$f[0]}) {
        if ( compare($f[0]->{$file}, $f[1]->{$file})) {
            print "$file is not the same\n";
        }
    }
}
dircomp("/tmp/backup", "/tmp/original");
```

See Also
File::Compare module documentation

File::Copy

Usage

```
use File::Copy;
copy(source, dest);
move(source, dest);
```

Description

The File::Copy module exports two functions, move and copy. The copy function will copy a file from one location (or name) to another. The *dest* argument of copy can be a filehandle opened for writing; in which case, the contents of the file are copied to it.

The move function allows you to move a file from one directory tree to another, or simply rename a file within a tree. When possible, move uses the rename system call to accomplish its work. If the move involves different filesystems or otherwise can't just be renamed into its new spot, it is copied and the original removed.

Example Listing 7.13

```perl
# A recursive directory copy.
# Bugs: takes a lot of defaults in regards to permissions
#    on files and directories.

use File::Find;
use File::Copy;
use File::Path;
use strict;

sub reccopy {
    my($source, $target)=@_;

    die "reccopy(): No source directory" if (! -d $source);
    my $copysub=sub {
        my($path)=$File::Find::name;
        $path=~s/$source//g;
        if (-d "$source$path") {
            unless ( -d "$target$path" or
                mkpath("$target$path")) {
                die "Creating $target$path: $!";
            }
        } else {
```

```
            unless ( copy("$source$path",
                    "$target$path") ) {
                die "Copying file $source$path: $!";
            }
        }
    };
    find( $copysub, $source);
}

# Sample usage
reccopy("/tmp/backup/today", "/tmp/backup/yesterday");
```

> **See Also**
> File::Copy module documentation

File::DosGlob

Usage

```
use File::DosGlob 'glob';
glob pattern
```

Description

The File::DosGlob module overrides the built-in glob function, and implements DOS-style globbing (wildcard expansion). However, it will do directory globbing, unlike the DOS command interpreter.

Example Listing 7.14

```
use File::DosGlob 'glob';
@progs=glob('c:/Program\ Files/*');
```

> **See Also**
> File::DosGlob module documentation

```
File::Find
```

Usage

```
use File::Find;
find(coderef, dir...);
```

Description

The `File::Find` module exports the `find` function that recursively descends into a directory structure. The *coderef* is a reference to a subroutine (or an anonymous subroutine) that will be run for every file and directory found by `find`.

Multiple directories can be searched with one `find` call. The following package variables will be set for each subroutine call:

Variable	Contents
`$_`	The current filename being processed
`$File::Find::name`	The current full filename (or directory name) being processed
`$File::Find::dir`	The current directory

A `chdir` will be performed so that the subroutine is running in the directory currently recursed into. Options are available to control the search as depth first, breadth first, pruned to a particular depth, and so on.

Examples of `File::Find` can be found in the `chown`, file test operators, `File::Copy`, `push`, `strict`, `symlink`, `unlink`, and `quotemeta` entries.

See Also
`File::Find` module documentation

```
File::Glob
```

Usage

```
use File::Glob;
```

Description

The `File::Glob` module provides access to the BSD file globbing routines, similar to the ones used for the `glob` function in Perl. In Perl 5.6.0, this module is actually used to give functionality to the core `glob` function.

The `glob` function in the `File::Glob` module has some additional features:

- Tilde expansion can take place with the `GLOB_TILDE` option:

```
use File::Glob qw(:glob);
$dir=File::Glob::glob('~clintp', GLOB_TILDE);
    # Returns "/home/clintp" here.
```

- Bracket (option) expansion can be used as with c-shell semantics:

```
use File::Glob qw(csh_glob);
@headers=csh_glob("*.{doc,txt,xml,html}");
```

See Also
`File::Glob` module documentation

`File::Path`

Usage

```
use File::Path;
mkpath(paths, verbose, mode)
rmpath(paths, verbose, skip)
```

Description

The `File::Path` module provides two functions, `mkpath` and `rmpath`, used for creating and removing directory trees recursively.

The `mkpath` function takes a pathname (or an array reference to a list of pathnames) and creates those recursively if necessary. If an element of the path is created, it's given the permissions of `mode` (or `0777` if mode is omitted). The `verbose` flag indicates whether `mkpath` will print the directory names as they're created; omitting it causes `mkpath` to default to no.

The `rmpath` function will remove a directory tree from a path or a list of paths (if an array reference is used). The `verbose` flag causes a message to print after each file or directory is removed. If the `skip` flag is set, files that you don't have delete or write access to will be skipped (even though directory permissions might allow you to remove them).

Example Listing 7.15

```
# Create a fairly deep directory tree, put
#   a file down there, and then remove it all.

use File::Path;

@paths=( '/tmp/testpath1/can/be/very/deep',
     '/tmp/something/shorter');
mkpath(\@paths, 1);

open(NEW, ">$paths[1]/newfile") || die "can't create: $!";
close(NEW);

rmtree(\@paths, 1, 0);
```

> **See Also**
> `File::Path` module documentation

`File::Spec`

Usage

```
use File::Spec;
catfile(component,component)
catdir(component,component)
splitdir(path)
canonpath(path)
```

Description

The `File::Spec` module contains routines for manipulating pathnames under various architectures. For example, the `catfile` method connects various components into a pathname (assuming that the last is a filename):

```
use File::Spec;
$tmp=File::Spec->catfile("usr", "tmp");  # /usr/tmp under Unix
```

The `catdir` function will concatenate pathname components using the correct pathname separator for your architecture. The `splitdir` function takes a directory and splits it into component pieces (suitable for re-assembly with `catdir`).

The `canonpath` function takes a pathname such as the Unix path `/foo/../bar//bax/ foo.c` and re-writes it without the redundant and unnecessary parts as `/foo/bar/bax/ foo.c`.

The `File::Spec` module will use the defaults for the architecture it is running under. Alternate versions exist for other architectures so that you can construct pathnames for the architectures you're not running. At the moment, that list is Mac, OS/2, Unix, VMS, and Windows/DOS.

> **See Also**
> `File::Spec`, `File::Spec::Unix`, `File::Spec::Win32`, `File::Spec::VMS`, `File::Spec::Mac`, and `File::Spec::OS2` module documentation

File::stat

Usage

```
use File::stat;
$statobj=stat(path)
```

Description

The `File::stat` module overrides the built-in `stat` and `lstat` functions, instead giving you versions that return a `File::stat` object. You then can use accessor methods on the components of the object to query the various parts of the `stat` structure by name.

The accessors available are `dev`, `ino`, `mode`, `nlink`, `uid`, `gid`, `rdev`, `size`, `atime`, `mtime`, `ctime`, `blksize`, and `blocks`.

Example Listing 7.16

```
use File::stat;
use strict;
use warnings;

my $statobj=stat($0);
```

```
die "No file? $!" unless $statobj;
print "This program ($0) is owned by ",
    scalar(getpwuid($statobj->uid)),
      "\nand was last changed on ",
    scalar(localtime($statobj->mtime)),"\n";
```

See Also
File:stat module documentation

FileHandle

Usage

```
use FileHandle;
$fh=new FileHandle;
```

Description

The FileHandle module is actually just a front end for the modules IO::File, IO::Seekable, and IO::Handle, re-exporting most of the symbols from those classes necessary to manipulate files. The symbols from Fcntl are imported as well.

See Also
FileHandle, IO::Handle, IO::Seekable, and IO::File module documentation

---

FindBin

Usage

```
use FindBin;
```

Description

The FindBin module imports variables that contain the location of the currently executing perl script. These can be used to manipulate @INC (or other paths) to be relative to where the script was installed.

By default, no variables are exported. The variables that can be used are

- `$FindBin::Bin`—Directory where the script was started
- `$FindBin::Script`—The script name that `perl` was invoked as
- `$FindBin::RealBin`—Same as `$Bin`, with the symbolic links resolved
- `$FindBin::RealScript`—Same as `$Script`, with the symbolic links resolved

Example Listing 7.17

```
# Add the "current directory"/lib to the @INC path
#    so that perl can find locally-installed modules.

use FindBin;
use lib "$FindBin::Bin/lib";
```

> **See Also**
> `FindBin` module documentation

Getopt::Long

Usage

```
use Getopt::Long;
```

Description

The `Getopt::Long` module is similar to the `Getopt::Std` module; it allows you to process command-line arguments to your script. The difference is that `Getopt::Long` allows you to specify long arguments in the POSIX style.

Normal arguments have a single dash:

```
myscript.pl -f -tl -e 'whoa'
```

POSIX (and GNU) style arguments can be either the previous traditional arguments, or using a `--`, they can be long wordy options:

```
myscript.pl --targetdir=/home/clintp --command='whoa'
```

To process these, use the `GetOptions` function. `GetOptions` takes an array of allowable option names and references to scalar variables. If the option is set, the variable will hold the value. Example Listing 7.18 processes a handful of options.

The `Getopt::Long` module also provides mechanisms for processing combinations of options (that is, option A is allowed only if option B is present) and options that can take multiple arguments (`--foo bar --foo morebar`).

Example Listing 7.18

```
# A snippet that allows this script to take three options:
#    --tempdir dir    #  The argument is required
#    --speed num      #  The argument must be an integer
#    --verbose        #  No arguments, just a flag

use Getopt::Long;

($speed, $name, $temp)=("","","/tmp");    # defaults
GetOptions('tmpdir=s' => \$temp,
      'speed=i'  => \$speed,
      verbose    => \$verbose);
print "$speed, $name, $temp";
```

> **See Also**
> `Getopt::Std` and `Getopt::Long` module documentation

`Getopt::Std`

Usage

```
use Getopt::Std;
getopts(option string, hashref);
```

Description

The `Getopt::Std` module allows a `perl` script to process command-line arguments conveniently. Given an option string that consists of the one-character options allowed (followed by a colon if the option takes an argument), the `Getopt::Std` module will populate the hash with the options and their arguments (or 1 if the option was specified but didn't need an argument).

Without a hashref, getopts (and the other function in Getopt::Std, getopt) will create variables called $opt_*optionletter* for each option specified.

Example Listing 7.19

```
# Snippet of a script that uses options.  Takes the options:
#  -v and -e    no argument required
#  -s and -t    arguments required
# You are allowed to bunch group them, all of these are valid
#    $0   -ves foo -t bar
#    $0   -v -t bar -es foo
#    $0   -ve

use Getopt::Std;

my %opts;
getopts('ves:t:', \%opts);
if ($opts{v}) {
    print "Verbose is ON!\n";
}
```

> **See Also**
> Getopt::Std and Getopt::Long module documentation

IO::Dir

Usage

```
use IO::Dir;
$dir=new IO::Dir "/tmp";
```

Description

The IO::Dir module provides an object-oriented interface to perl's directory routines. The new constructor takes a directory name and creates an IO::Dir object. If none is used, a directory can be opened later with the open method.

The methods provided to the object are

```
open(dirname)
close
seek(offset)
```

```
tell
rewind
read
```

These correspond the routines `opendir`, `closedir`, `seekdir`, `telldir`, `rewinddir`, and `readdir` described elsewhere in this book.

You also can tie a hash to the `IO::Dir` class. Creating hash element creates empty files, and deleting hash elements `unlinks` files from the directory. See the module's documentation for more usage information and caveats.

Example Listing 7.20

```
# Simple opening and reading of a directory.

use IO::Dir;
$dir=new IO::Dir "/tmp";
die "Cannot open $dir: $!" unless $dir;

while($entry=$dir->read) {
    print "$entry\n";
}
```

See Also
`IO::Dir` module documentation

IO::File

Usage

```
use IO::File;
$fh=new IO::File ">newfile";
```

Description

The `IO::File` class continues the work of `IO::Handle` by providing object methods for filehandles. In addition to all the methods provided by `IO::Handle`, `IO::File` allows you to open new files either with the constructor or the `open` method.

The constructor (`new`) takes arguments just as the `open` function does, opens a file, creates an `IO::File` object, and associates the file with it.

The IO::File class also contains an explicit open method to open files. Its arguments are identical to the open function.

Example Listing 7.21

```
use IO::File;

my $f=new IO::File "/tmp/bigfile.txt";
die "$!" unless $f;
()=$f->getlines();
print $f->input_line_number();
```

> **See Also**
> IO::File and IO::Handle module documentation

IO::Handle

Usage

```
use IO::Handle;
```

Description

The IO::Handle class serves two purposes: First, all filehandles in Perl are automatically blessed into IO::Handle, and it provides an object interface to filehandles. Second, IO::Handle can be used to generate lexically scoped filehandles (usually with the help of IO::File) that can be operated on by perl's normal filehandle operators and functions. An IO::Handle-derived object is valid anywhere a filehandle is.

The IO::Handle class makes the following methods available:

Method	Brief Description
new	Creates an IO::Handle object.
new_from_fd(*file descriptor*, *mode*)	Creates an IO::Handle object using the existing file descriptor and a mode (>, <, and so on, as with open).
fdopen(*file descriptor*, *mode*)	See new_from_fd.
opened	Returns true if IO::Handle is open and valid.

Method	Brief Description
close	Functions the same as the close function.
eof	Functions the same as eof.
fileno	Functions the same as fileno.
getc	Functions the same as getc.
ungetc(*ordinal*)	Pushes the character with the value of chr(*ordinal*) back onto the I/O stream. Can only be done once per filehandle.
read(*buf*, *len*, *offset*)	Functions the same as read.
write(*buf*, *len*, *offset*)	Functions the same as the C library's write function.
truncate(*length*)	Functions the same as truncate.
sysread(*buf*, *len*, *offset*)	Functions the same as sysread getline. Works like <>, except that it's always in scalar context (returns 1 line).
getlines	Works similar to <> in list context (returns multiple lines). If called in any other context, it throws an exception.
syswrite(*buf*, *len*, *offset*)	Functions the same as syswrite.
print(*list*)	Functions the same as print.
printf(*format*, *list*)	Functions the same as printf.
stat	Functions the same as the stat function.
error	Returns true if the last filehandle operation resulted in an error.
clearerr	Clears any errors on the filehandle.
sync	Takes data waiting in I/O buffers and writes them to disk. Note: This happens at the OS level and not from

Method	Brief Description
	perl. Forcing a write of perl's data out to the OS requires a flush.
flush	Takes pending writes in perl's I/O buffers and writes them to disk. Note: This just releases the data from perl, but doesn't necessarily write it to disk.
blocking(*flag*)	If called with a true *flag*, blocking I/O on the handle is enabled; otherwise it will be disabled. If called with no flag, the current state of blocking I/O for the handle is returned.

Additionally, various attributes of the filehandle can be set with methods that normally can be set only with special global variables ($|, $.). Some attributes are still global, and these are indicated as follows:

Method	Corresponds to
autoflush(*flag*)	The $| variable, for flush-after-writing. Can be set per filehandle.
input_line_number(*num*)	The $. variable. Can be set per filehandle.
IO::Handle->output_record_separator(*string*)	The $\ variable, and is set for all filehandles.
IO::Handle->output_field_separator(*string*)	The $, variable, and is set for all filehandles.
IO::Handle->input_record_separator(*string*)	The $/ variable, and is set for all filehandles.

You will notice that there is no open method. To open a new filehandle as an IO::Handle object, you'll actually have to create an IO::File object—which inherits from IO::Handle but provides methods for opening files.

Example Listing 7.22

```
# Taking over an existing filehandle and using method
#   calls against it.

use IO::Handle;
STDOUT->autoflush(1);
STDOUT->print("Hello, world!");
```

> **See Also**
> IO::Handle and IO::File module documentation

IO::Pipe

Usage

```
use IO::Pipe;
$pipe=new IO::Pipe;
```

Description

The IO::Pipe module creates an object that can be used similar to the file descriptors generated by the pipe function.

The new constructor simply returns the pipe object. To use it, typically you would have your process fork; then one branch of the fork would call the reader method on the IO::Pipe object, and the other would call writer. These will re-bless the object into an IO::Handle class suitable for reading or writing.

For more information on pipes, see the pipe function.

Example Listing 7.23

```
# Simple reader/writer, much like pipe's example
#   but object-based.

use IO::Pipe;
$pipe = new IO::Pipe;

if(fork()) { # Parent process
    $pipe->reader();
    while(<$pipe>) {
        print;
    }
```

```
    } else {
        $pipe->writer();
        print $pipe "Hello, world";
    }
```

See Also
IO::Pipe and IO::Handle module documentation

pipe in this book

IO::Select

Usage

```
use IO::Select;
$pool=IO::Select->new();
$pool->add(filehandle)
```

Description

The IO::Select module provides an object-oriented interface to the four-argument select function.

After creating a select pool with the constructor, use the add method to register filehandles into the pool. When you need to see what's available for reading or writing, call the can_read or can_write methods on the pool.

The can_read and can_write methods return an array of filehandles ready to be read or written.

See Also
IO::Select module documentation

IO::Socket

Usage

```
use IO::Socket;
$sock=new IO::Socket::INET(options);
$sock=new IO::Socket::UNIX(options);
```

Description

The IO::Socket module uses the IO::Socket::INET and IO::Socket::UNIX modules to give you easy access to creating Berkeley and Unix Domain sockets.

The constructors (new) both return a filehandle that can be used in any of perl's functions that accept a filehandle.

The IO::Socket module inherits from IO::Handle, so those methods are available to use on the socket. Additionally, the socket-specific methods of accept, send, recv, peername, socket, socketpair, bind, listen, sockname, and shutdown are provided. They are similar to the functions by the same name mentioned elsewhere in this book, but their arguments differ.

Example Listing 7.24

```
# A simple client (fetches a web page)

use IO::Socket;
use strict;
use warnings;

my $sock=new IO::Socket::INET( PeerAddr => 'www.yapc.org',
        PeerPort => 80,
        Proto => 'tcp',
        Type    => SOCK_STREAM);
print $sock "GET http://www.yapc.org 1.0\n\n";
while(<$sock>) {
    print;
}
```

Example Listing 7.25

```
# A simple server, provides the time to those that
#   connect to port 1066.

use IO::Socket;
use strict;
use warnings;

my $server=new IO::Socket::INET( LocalPort => 1066,
        Type    => SOCK_STREAM,
        Listen  => 10,
        ReUse   => 1);
```

```
die "Unable to bind to port: $!";
while(my $client=$server->accept()) {
    print $client "The time is ", scalar localtime, "\n";
}
```

See Also

IO::Socket, IO::Socket::INET, and IO::Socket::Unix module documentation

IPC::Open2, IPC::Open3

Usage

```
use IPC::Open2;
open2(read filehandle, write filehandle, cmd);

use IPC::Open3;
open3(write filehandle, read filehandle, err filehandle,
cmd);
```

Description

The IPC::Open2 and IPC::Open3 modules allow you to open filehandles connected to a process for both input and output. For example, this syntax isn't allowed:

```
open(FH, "| cmd |"); WRONG
```

The open2 function allows you to capture both the input and output filehandles to a function. The read filehandle and write filehandle can either be a typeglob reference, or a variable initialized to undef. They will be opened as filehandles connected to cmd's output and input, respectively.

The open3 function is identical, except that an additional argument is specified for an error filehandle. (Note also that the arguments are in a different order than open2.)

If the cmd is specified as a single string, a shell is started and the command executed by that shell. If the command is a list, execvp is used to start the command. This is similar to the functionality of open. Both functions return the process ID of the shell or the command started.

Opening a pipe to and from a command is a harrowing experience. Dealing with buffering and deadlocks can age you prematurely (Caveat integrator).

> **See Also**
> IPC::Open2 and IPC::Open3 module documentation
>
> open in this book

Net::Ping

Usage

```
use Net::Ping;
$obj=new Net::Ping;
$obj->ping($host);
```

Description

The Net::Ping module allows you to determine whether a remote host is up on a
network. To ping a host, first create a Net::Ping object, and then call the ping method
on the object.

```
use Net::Ping;
$obj=new Net::Ping;
if ($obj->ping("www.geeksalad.org")) {
    print "It's there!\n";
}
```

During creation of the Net::Ping object, you are allowed to specify the protocol (tcp,
udp, or icmp), a timeout, and the number of bytes to be used in the ping. The ping
method also will allow you to specify a timeout for each individual ping call.

> **See Also**
> Net::Ping module documentation

Net::hostent, Net::netent, Net::protoent, Net::servent

Description

The Net::*ent family of modules override perl's built-in versions of some functions
to provide an easy-to-use object interface. The functions overridden are listed as
follows:

Module	Overrides
Net::hostent	gethostbyaddr and gethostbyname (also provides gethost)
Net::netent	getnetbyname and getnetbyaddr (also provides getnet)
Net::protoent	getprotoent, getprotobyname, and getprotobynumber
Net::servent	getservent, getservbyname, and getservbyport

Calls to the native functions (getservbyname) will return an object of the appropriate type (Net::servent). Accessors are provided to get to the various descriptive parts of the structure.

Example Listing 7.26

```
# Sample of the Net::*ent modules

use Net::servent;
$s = getservbyname('www') || die "no service";
print "Port number for www is ", $s->port(), "\n";
```

See Also
Net::hostent, Net::netent, Net::protoent, and Net::servent module documentation

POD Translators and Utilities

Usage

```
pod2html
pod2text
pod2man
```

Description

The POD Translators are a class of modules and programs that use them to convert POD documentation into various formats. The translators installed with perl (and the modules that are needed by them) are

Translator	Notes
pod2html	Uses the Pod::Html module to accomplish most of its work. The module exports one function, pod2html, which takes a variety of arguments to control the formatting of links (where they're relative to) and formatting of the HTML page.

Translator	Notes
pod2text	Uses the Pod::Text module to convert POD into plain text. If supported, it uses the Pod::Text::Termcap library to highlight text (links, headers, and so on). The function pod2text is exported and does the actual POD conversion. Using the Pod::Text::Color module directly, you can convert POD documents into highlighted text using ANSI escape sequences.
pod2latex	Produces a LaTeX version of the POD documentation.
pod2man	Use Pod::Man to produce a roff document, which is usable by the Unix man command (troff and other utilities).

Additionally, utilities are available for helping you to parse POD within your own programs.

The Pod::Parser module allows you to register a series of callback functions, and as it processes a POD document, it will call your functions where you can then cook the text appropriately. Some of the callback methods used are command (to process = directives), verbatim (called on indented paragraphs), interior_sequence (called within a paragraph), and others. This is a large, complex module, and you will need to consult the module's documentation to understand it fully.

The Pod::Find module has a simple job: Search all the standard paths (or those given as an option) for documents containing valid PODs and return them as a hash.

The Pod::Checker module exports the podchecker function that takes a series of input and output pathnames and a set of options. The POD in the input pathname will be checked for validity (against the given options) and will return the number of errors (or -1 if the document was clean).

Example Listing 7.27

```
# A CGI program to provide a gateway to the POD documentation.
# It first prints a list of all of the available POD (this takes
#   a while the first time) that you can pick from.
# After selecting a POD document, it's converted to HMTL and
#   displayed

use Pod::Find qw(pod_find);
use Pod::Html;
use CGI qw(:standard :forms);
use CGI::Carp;
```

```perl
use strict;

$|=1;
print header, start_html("HTML/POD Gateway");

# Getting the POD takes a while.  So cache it in a
#    dbm file.
dbmopen(my %pods, "/tmp/podcache", 0666)||die "$!";
unless (each %pods) {
    my %foo=pod_find({-inc => 1});
    %pods=%foo;
}
unless (param("POD")) {
    print start_form,
        radio_group(-name => 'POD',
          -linebreak => 'true',
          -values => [ 'none', sort values %pods ],
          -default => 'none'),
        submit,
} else {
    my $file={ reverse %pods }->{param("POD")};
    die "No such pod" unless ($file);
    pod2html($file);

}
print end_html;
```

> **See Also**
> Pod::Text, Pod::Man, Pod::Html, Pod::Parser, Pod::Checker, and Pod::Find module documentation

POSIX

Usage

```perl
use POSIX;
```

Description

The POSIX module gives perl programs access to the *POSIX (Portable Operating Systems Interface)* routines available on your system (or a reasonable facsimile if available).

Far too many POSIX routines exist to list individually; you will need to consult a book on the POSIX API and the POSIX module's documentation for a full list. Some of the items included are

- C functions not available in perl: _exit, abort, atan, asin, creat, ctime, getpid, isspace, ispunct, pow, ceil, floor, setlocale, uname, and so on. (Although the functions specific to C, such as atof, atoi, atol, calloc, and POSIX, are omitted thread support is not included.)

- Predefined OS values available to C through the header files and the compiler: INT_MAX, LONG_MAX, ARG_MAX, and so on.

- Values provided by header files for I/O functions: O_NONBLOCK, F_GETFL, O_RDWR, BUFSZ, and so on.

In general, nothing is exported from the POSIX module. If you want a value or function, you'll need to ask for it by name (or group) during the use directive.

Example Listing 7.28

```
# Demonstration of some POSIX behavior.  SigSet allows you
#    to build a signal set structure and then sigprocmask can
#    block those signals for a while.  SIG_IGN for example would
#    just ignore the signal instead.
# The signal handler _will_ be called, but only after the
#    signal mas has been reset.
use POSIX qw(:signal_h);

$sigset=POSIX::SigSet->new(SIGINT);
$oldsig=POSIX::SigSet->new;

warn "Cannot block INT"
    if (! defined sigprocmask(SIG_BLOCK, $sigset, $oldsig));
$SIG{INT}=sub { print "Caught one!"; };


#
# Do your critical operations here.
sleep(10);  # Demo.
#


warn "Cannot unblock INT"
    if (! defined sigprocmask(SIG_UNBLOCK, $oldsig));
```

> **See Also**
> POSIX module documentation

Shell

Usage

```
use Shell;
shell command(arguments)
```

Description

The Shell module is more of a curiosity than anything else. It exports an AUTOLOAD into the current namespace. And functions called that haven't been defined will trigger the AUTOLOAD.

The AUTOLOAD will then run a shell command with that function's name and the arguments. The output of the command will be the return value of the function.

Example Listing 7.29

```
use Shell;

$tmpfiles=ls("/tmp");
$lines=wc("-l", "/tmp/bigfile.txt");
```

> **See Also**
> Shell module documentation
> AUTOLOAD in this book

Sys::Hostname

Usage

```
use Sys::Hostname;
$host=hostname
```

Description

The Sys::Hostname exports the hostname function, which uses several (sometimes architecture specific) methods to determine the system's hostname.

Some methods tried are the `gethostname` library call, `gethostbyname('localhost')`, `$Config{aphostname}`, `uname`, `syscall(SYS_gethostname)`, `hostname`, `uname -n`, `/com/host`, and various environment variables under VMS (`ARPANET_HOST_NAME`, `INTERNET_HOST_NAME`, and so on) until a match is found.

If a hostname cannot be found, `hostname` croaks.

Example Listing 7.30

```
use Sys::Hostname;

print "This machine is called ", hostname(), ".\n";
```

See Also
`Sys::Hostname` module documentation

```
Term::ANSIColor;
```

Usage

```
use Term::ANSIColor;
color(attributes)
```

Description

The `Term::ANSIColor` module allows you to print escape sequences to control the color output on ANSI-compliant terminals. Some ANSI-terminals are MS-DOS consoles, gnome-terminal, aterm, and many terminal emulator programs.

An entire line can be wrapped with ANSI control codes using the `colored` function:

```
use Term::ANSIColor;
print colored ("White on blue\n", 'white on_blue');
```

Or you can emit the codes directly (when you want) with the `color` function, as demonstrated in Example Listing 7.31.

The necessary constants (color names, reset codes, `bold`, `normal`, and so on) are listed in the module's documentation.

Example Listing 7.31

```
# Display a document with the misspelled words
#   obnoxiously highlighted.
# Relies on the Unix utility spell to find misspellings!!

use Term::ANSIColor;

$doc="/tmp/short.txt";
$words=join('|', grep { chomp } `spell < $doc`);
$badwords=qr/($words)/;

open(DOC, $doc) || die "can't open $doc: $!";
$/="";
while(<DOC>) {
    s/$badwords/color('blink yellow') . $1 . color('reset')/ge;
    print;
}
close(DOC);
```

Term::Cap

Usage

```
use Term::Cap;
$terminal = Tgetent Term::Cap;
$terminal->Tgoto(address)
$terminal->Tputs(attribute)
etc...
```

Description

The Term::Cap module provides a low-level interface to the *termcap (terminal capabilities)* database on a Unix system. They allow you to manipulate things such as cursor position, bold type, and terminal speed.

Consult your operating system's termcap manual pages for information on what capabilities are available, and what they do.

Example Listing 7.32

```
# Small demo of a termcap ability.

use Term::Cap;

$term=Tgetent Term::Cap { OSPEED => 9600 };
print "Hey, buddy.  Wanna see soemthing ",
    $term->Tputs("so"),      # Begin Standout
    "really",
    $term->Tputs("se"),      # End Standout
    " scary?";
```

> **See Also**
> `Term::Cap` module documentation

`Term::Complete`

Usage

```
use Term::Complete;

$result=Complete(prompt, optionlist);
```

Description

The `Term::Complete` module prompts the user with the *prompt* string. It then will accept an answer from the terminal. If the user presses the tab key and the partial answer appears as a prefix in *optionlist*, the rest of the option will be filled out.

Pressing the end-of-file key (Ctrl+D in Unix, Ctrl+Z in DOS) will print the list of options.

Example Listing 7.33

```
# Gives the user a rather indecisive yes/no prompt.
# Filling out the first letter is enough to complete the choice.

use Term::Complete;

@options=qw(Yes yes no No maybe Maybe);
$input=Complete("Are you sure? (Y/N/Maybe) ", \@options);
```

See Also
Term::Complete module documentation

```
Text::ParseWords
```

Usage

```
use Text::ParseWords;

@words=quotewords(delimiter, keep, @lines);
@words=parse_line(delimiter, keep, text);
```

Description

The `Text::ParseWords` is used to extract words from a set of lines, grouping together those words that occur inside of properly nested quotes. For example, the following string:

```
I said, "What are you doing?"  She didn't reply.
```

could be broken up as `I`, `said`, `She`, `didn't`, `reply`, and `"What are you doing?"`.

The `delimiter` argument indicates what will be used to split the line. The `keep` flag indicates whether the quotes themselves will be kept. Other options and variations on `quotewords` and `parse_words` are described in the manual.

Example Listing 7.34

```
use strict;
use Text::ParseWords;

my $t=q{I said "What are you doing?"  She didn\'t reply.};
my @words=quotewords('\s+', 0, $t);

# Results in I,said,What are you doing?,She,didn't,reply.
print join(',', @words);
```

See Also
Text::ParseWords module documentation

`Text::Soundex`

Usage

```
use Text::Soundex;
code=soundex string
codes=soundex array
```

Description

The soundex function will return a soundex code for each word. Soundex codes are hashes based on the algorithm by Donald Knuth in the *Art Of Computer Programming*. Each string given to soundex will be hashed to a four-character code. If an array is given to soundex, each word in the array will return its own soundex code.

Similar sounding words should hash to the same values—in theory. Use your own judgement for how good the matching is. Words that don't have a soundex code will return undef by default.

The wantarray entry contains an example using `Text::Soundex`.

See Also
`Text::Soundex` module documentation

`Text::Tabs;`

Usage

```
use Text::Tabs;
expand(tabbed lines);
unexpand(un-tabbed lines);
```

Description

The `Text::Tabs` module exports the expand and unexpand functions. The expand function will take an array of lines containing tabs and return a new array with the tab characters replaced by an appropriate number of spaces.

The unexpand function does the reverse—takes lines containing spaces and changes them to tabs where possible.

The variable $tabstop also is exported and determines how wide a normal tab stop is. It defaults to 8.

Example Listing 7.35

```
# Change the file on STDIN to have spaces instead of
#   hard tabs.
use Text::Tabs;

@with_tabs=<>;
$tabstop=4;
@no_tabs=unexpand(@with_tabs);
```

> **See Also**
> Text::Tabs module documentation

```
Text::Wrap;
```

Usage

```
use Text::Wrap;
wrap(firstline,subsequent,text array);
```

Description

The Text::Wrap module exports the wrap function that is used to format text into paragraphs.

The first argument will be prepended to the first line, the second argument to the second, and all subsequent lines accordingly. The *text array* contains the text that will be joined together and wrapped at the specified column width.

The width of the paragraph is set with $Text::Wrap::columns and defaults to 76.

Example Listing 7.36

```
# Take the opening stanza of this Gilbert & Sullivan
#   tune and word-wrap it appropriately for a
#   Commodore-64! (40-column screen)

use Text::Wrap;

$text=<<EOS;
I am the very model of a modern Major-General,
I've information vegetable, animal, and mineral,
I know the kings of England, and I quote the fights historical,
```

```
From Marathon to Waterloo, in order categorical;
I'm very well acquainted too with matters mathematical,
I understand equations, both the simple and quadratical,
About binomial theorem I'm teeming with a lot o' news---
With many cheerful facts about the square of the hypotenuse.
EOS

$Text::Wrap::columns=40;
print wrap("\t", " ", split("\n", $text));
```

> **See Also**
> `Text::Wrap` module documentation

Tie::RefHash

Usage

```
use TieRefHash;
tie hash, 'Tie::RefHash';
```

Description

The `Tie::RefHash` module allows you to tie a hash to the class, and then store references in the hash keys. The references will not be stringified and can still be used for reference later.

Otherwise, `Tie::RefHash` is used the same as any other tied hash, and the `Tied Hashes` entry should be consulted for details.

Example Listing 7.37

```
# Trying this with a regular hash will cause ref()
#   to return false for all of these.

use Tie::RefHash;
tie %h, 'Tie::RefHash';

$arr=[];
$hash={};
$glob=\*main;
$scalar=\"";
```

```
%h=( $arr    => 'the',
     $hash   => 'data',
     $glob   => 'doesn\'t',
     $scalar=> 'matter', );

$h{sub { "whoa" }}="at all!";

for my $key ( keys %h ) {
    print ref($key), "\n";
}
```

> **See Also**
> Tie::RefHash module documentation
> Tied Hashes in this book

Tie::SubstrHash

Usage

```
use Tie::SubstrHash;
tie hash, 'Tie::SubstrHash', keylen, valuelen, size;
```

Description

The Tie::SubstrHash module creates a fixed-size hash table. The length of the keys are limited to *keylen*, the values to *valuelen*. The size of the hash table is also fixed at *size*.

The purpose of this is to create a hash table that occupies less space (memory) than perl's hashing tables, which have no limits to the size of keys, values, and the size of the hash itself.

Example Listing 7.38

```
# Running this against a 16,188-line file with a key fixed
#   at 5 and a data-length of 77 used 712K fewer bytes of memory
#   than using a conventional hash.
# This is despite the 417K of padding that needed to be added for
#   padding the short lines out to 77 characters
```

```
use Tie::SubstrHash;
tie %h, 'Tie::SubstrHash', 5, 77, 16189;
open(BIG, "bigfile.txt") || die;
$i=0;
while(<BIG>){
    chomp;
    $_.=" " x (77-(length $_));   # Pad to fit
    $h{sprintf("%05d", $i++)}=$_;
}
close(BIG);
```

> **See Also**
> `Tie::SubstrHash` module documentation
>
> `Tied Hashes` in this book

Tie Base Classes

Usage

```
use Tie::Array;
use Tie::Hash;
use Tie::Handle;
use Tie::Scalar;
```

Description

These modules serve as base classes for tying variables and filehandles. They provide subroutines to provide the base functionality for each of the types, or a stub when the base functionality can't be guessed (or provided by the implementation).

A description of what's offered in these classes is covered in the individual sections on tying variables.

> **See Also**
> `Tie::Array`, `Tie::Hash`, `Tie::Scalar`, and `Tie::Handle` module documentation
>
> Tied Arrays, Tied Hashes, Tied Scalars, and Tied Filehandles in this book

`Time::Local`

Usage

```
use Time::Local;
timelocal( sec, min, hour, mday,
        mon, year, yday,);
timegm( sec, min, hour, mday,
mon, year, yday,);
```

Description

The `timelocal` and `timegm` functions do the opposite of the `localtime` and `gmtime` functions; they take an array of values describing the current time and return the number of seconds since the epoch.

The arguments are nearly the same as those returned by `localtime` and `gmtime` so that

```
use Time::Local;
timelocal((localtime)[0..5,7])
```

is a no-op.

The year as passed in should be the offset since 1900. However, Perl will make an effort to accept a four-digit year, or determine whether a two-digit year really means what you think it means. This behavior is complex and documented in the module.

See Also
`Time::Local` module documentation

Symbols

W

X-Y-Z